D0711164

GUIDE TO WISCONSIN *Outdoors*

GUIDE TO WISCONSIN *Outdoors*

JIM UMHOEFER

FROM THE NORTHWORD
NATURE GUIDE COLLECTION

The author is most grateful to his wife, Margy, and the Wisconsin Department of Natural Resources for assistance in the preparation of this guide.

Copyright 1982 Jim Umhoefer
Copyright © 1990 Jim Umhoefer
All rights reserved

Published By:

NorthWord Press, Inc.
P.O. Box 1360
Minocqua, WI 54548

ISBN 1-55971-009-8

Designed by Moonlit Ink, Madison, WI

Printed in Singapore

Guide to Wisconsin Outdoors

Symbol Key

swimming

boating

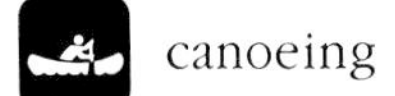
canoeing

fishing

nature trails

hiking trails

biking trails

horseback trails

cross country ski trails

snowmobile trails

picnic area

overlook and vista

historical significance

camping

camping with electrical outlets

boat ramp

handicapped camping, picnic area and restrooms

handicapped picnic area and restrooms

flora & fauna

natural area

wildlife refuge

TABLE OF CONTENTS

INTRODUCTION

"Oh, that glorious Wisconsin wilderness!" wrote the young John Muir in *The Story of My Boyhood and Youth.* "Everything new and pure . . . Young hearts, young leaves, flowers, animals, the wind and the streams and the sparkling lakes, all rejoicing together."

John Muir would feel at home in Wisconsin's state and national park lands. Over six million acres of his home state are publicly owned or controlled. The state park system, along with the national forests, parks, trails and refuges, preserves the best of Wisconsin's scenic landscape for recreational enjoyment.

Wisconsin has a long and impressive record of identifying and preserving its natural beauty. The state park system consists of 51 parks, nine forests and 12 trails (other projects are being developed). National recreation lands include a lakeshore park, a scenic riverway, an Ice Age trail and reserve, a portion of a seven-state hiking trail, two forests and four refuges. Wisconsin boasts 14,900 lakes with about 9,000 of them unnamed (over 20 acres in size). The state has 1,000 miles of Mississippi River, Lake Michigan and Lake Superior shoreline; 9,200 miles of trout streams; 3,400 miles of canoe trails, 2,000 miles of major hiking trails and 10,000 miles of mapped bicycle routes (along Wisconsin roads).

Wisconsin lacks the grandeur of the West and the notoriety of the East, but it is loaded with variety and surprises that few states can match. Just when you get used to the closeness of the forest, the road winds up a hill and you can see for 30 miles. If you catch your limit of trout in a cold stream, you can try for a fighting muskie in a northern lake or charter a boat for some Great Lakes sportfishing. Gaze down on the mighty Mississippi from a blufftop or pedal through the hills-and-hollows country that gives birth to its boisterous tributaries. Hike on ridges deposited by mammoth glaciers, then turn around to see a land

(opposite page)

Wisconsin's parks and trails preserve the best features of the state for all to enjoy.

the ice never touched. Wisconsin is flatlands, hills and water; forests, field and fun.

State Park System

The first land to be called a state park consisted of 50,000 acres (78 square miles) of forest set aside in 1878 in Iron and Vilas counties. Parts of this original park are now in the Northern Highland–American Legion State Forest. The modern park system began in 1900, when Wisconsin and Minnesota cooperated to form Interstate State Park, spanning the St. Croix River.

(opposite page)

Interstate became the first state park when the modern state park system was established in 1900.

Since then, the state park system has grown in response to recreational needs and has become a model for the nation. The creation of the Elroy-Sparta State Trail, for example, marked the first time that an abandoned railroad right-of-way was converted into a state recreation corridor. To remain responsive to changing recreational demands, the DNR has developed a plan to guide the system to the year 2000. The plan was designed to consider the DNR's traditional goals of outdoor education, resource protection and outdoor recreation.

Outdoor education will be expanded in the park system by using more naturalists and publishing more materials about park geology, history, and plant and animal life. Resource protection involves adding more "special" areas to the system. These areas must have scenic, ecological, historical, recreational, cultural, geologic or archaeological value. A full 90% of the land will be left undeveloped, with plenty of places designated for quiet and solitude. Recreation improvements will include more campsites, better fishing, more year-round parks and easier access to park facilities for visitors with disabilities.

Wisconsin's park system is accessible to all people. Barrier-free campsites and picnic areas have been installed at nearly every state park. Many parks also feature trails, overlooks, beaches and piers that are fully accessible. Resident senior citizens (65 years and older) may buy a lifetime Natural Resources Senior Citizen Recreation Card for a one-time fee. The

NATURALIST
KIDS! PARENTS!
EXPLORE TOGETHER
EVENING PROGRAMS

card allows free admission to state parks and forests and also gives the holder lifetime privileges of small game hunting and fishing.

Volunteers are playing a bigger role in the park system. They choose to work in areas of personal interest, such as naturalist programs, trail patrols, work projects, historical research, habitat improvements, etc. The most visible volunteers may be the Campground Hosts. Occupying a site for about a month, Hosts help campers, share information and do some campground maintenance. Many state parks enjoy the support and assistance of Friends Groups. These groups are nonprofit corporations organized to help a state park with its programs and facilities. For details about volunteering and Friends Groups, contact the DNR or any park office.

The park system sponsors an open house day each year, usually in mid-June. The public is welcome in all parks, forests, recreation areas and trails free of charge. Many parks offer special events for the open house day. Some parks hold other free days throughout the year that often correspond to special anniversaries, dedications or local festivals. The open house day is usually scheduled on the same day as Free Fishing Day (when you can fish without buying a fishing license). Several state parks feature free fishing clinics to promote fishing in Wisconsin.

Certain state parks and recreation areas offer facilities for hot air ballooning, trail motorcycling, target range shooting, golfing, speed skating, indoor group camping, dog training and many other unusual forms of outdoor recreation. Contact the DNR (address is in the INFORMATION section) for details.

The park system contains a number of "undiscovered gems," parks that are less crowded because they are off the beaten track. Each of these less-visited parks has unique attractions, and they all offer camping, nature trails and fishing. They can be a refreshing alternative to the six most popular parks that attract half of all state park users. The DNR publishes a brochure entitled "Undiscovered Gems" that highlights parks such as Wildcat Mountain, Big Bay, Merrick and other units that feature peacefulness with a view. You might also want to visit the parks in spring, autumn or winter. An off-season or mid-week adventure in even the busiest parks can be a relatively private experience.

National Parks, Forests, Trails and Refuges

Perhaps less well known than the state park system, Wisconsin's national recreation lands offer more elbow room and wild country than the typical state park. Some of these national lands are managed cooperatively with the Wisconsin DNR (i.e., Ice Age Reserve, Ice Age Trail, North Country Trail, and St. Croix Riverway). You'll find lakes, wetlands, forests, campgrounds, beaches, boat landings, rivers, islands and hiking trails among the attractions in these areas.

Much of Wisconsin's national recreation lands, especially the Chequamegon and Nicolet national forests, are open to public hunting. The DNR also manages hundreds of thousands of acres of state-owned public hunting grounds. Funds for purchase of hunting areas, game habitat development and protection of endangered species partially comes from excise taxes on sporting arms, ammunition and archery hunting equipment. The excise tax was set up over 50 years ago (in 1937) by the Pittman-Robertson Federal Aid in Wildlife Restoration Act. Over $41,000,000 in Pittman-Robertson funds have been spent in Wisconsin.

Senior citizens and disabled visitors are eligible for discounts in Wisconsin's national recreation lands. Depending on whether they visit a unit administered by the National Park Service or the National Forest Service, they can obtain Golden Eagle, Golden Age or Golden Access (for disabled visitors) Passports. Check with individual unit offices for details (addresses are listed in the back of this book).

Jim Umhoefer
Sauk Centre, Minnesota

P.S. Although Wisconsin's state and national park system can satisfy the recreational needs of the city-soft as well as the wilderness-experienced, it can't offer guarantees on the weather. It's easy to appreciate Wisconsin's scenic lakes, woods and trails when the sun is warm, but the trick is to keep your perspective when the rain soaks your tent and the wind is so cold that you wonder why you bothered to pack a swimsuit. To top it off, the mosquitoes seem to know your blood type and the raccoons admire your taste in food. Don't forget your sense of humor. If you don't like the weather in Wisconsin, the saying goes, wait until tomorrow.

HOW TO USE THIS BOOK

This is a comprehensive guide to Wisconsin's state and national recreation lands. A graphic commentary describes what you can see and do in the parks, forests, recreation areas, trails and major wildlife refuges of the Badger State. Historical and geological information is woven through the text to give a more complete picture of each unit. Maps and photographs offer a glimpse of what's waiting for you outdoors in Wisconsin.

The book is designed for both on-the-road reference and armchair vacation planning. Maybe you'd like to canoe, camp or hike in the Indian Head Country of northwestern Wisconsin. Before your trip, read through that section of the book to get a feel for the parks, forests and trails in that region. Why is the Brule River State Forest a favorite destination for canoeists and trout anglers? Which of the islands in the Apostle Islands National Lakeshore have hiking trails and campsites? What will a bicycle trip on the Red Cedar State Trail be like? Then, when you leave on your vacation, take the guide with you as a fingertip source of information about side trips and other parks that you might wish to visit.

A key explaining the use of symbols in this book can be found on page VI.

Most of the parks described in this guide include a state highway map index number to help you locate the unit. This will be useful to you only if you have an official Wisconsin State Highway Map. You can get a free copy by contacting the Wisconsin Division of Tourism (address and phone number are listed in the INFORMATION section).

Wisconsin's recreation lands are constantly changing: a trail is enlarged, a new visitor center is constructed or an interpretive program is expanded. A campground that didn't have showers last year may have them this year. Camping and vehicle permit fees may have gone up since your last visit. So, to keep abreast of year-to-year changes, you may wish to check with an individual park office before you leave home. You'll find the addresses and phone numbers for all state and national recreation lands listed in the back of this book.

You can also use this book in conjunction with the "Visitor's Guide," a free brochure about the state park, forest and trail system published by the Wisconsin Department of Natural Resources. The brochure lists details about fees, recreational opportunities, campsite reservations, regulations and facilities (i.e., number of campsites, trail mileage, etc.). To get your copy of the Visitor's Guide, ask at any park office or refer to the DNR and Tourism phone numbers and addresses listed in the INFORMATION section of this book.

Just slip the Visitor's Guide inside the front cover of this book and you'll be ready to go. Turn to the commentary about the state park, forest or trail that you want to visit to get a sense of its character and why it's worth a trip. Then refer to the brochure for specific details. If your copy of *Guide to Wisconsin Outdoors* comes back from a trip smudged with dirt and smelling of campfire smoke, it will have served its purpose.

PLANNING YOUR VACATIONS

The bumper sticker says "Escape to Wisconsin," but as with all successful escapes, you need a plan first. It's easy to get information about traveling in Wisconsin before you pack your tent and camera. Although this book focuses on state and national parks, forests and trails, you can use the following information to request other tourism materials or to ask questions about a Wisconsin vacation.

Toll-Free Numbers

1-800-ESCAPES (in Wisconsin and neighboring states). This is the number of the Wisconsin Division of Tourism Development. When you call, you'll be asked if you just want to receive the seasonal vacation packet or if you'd like to talk to a travel consultant. The vacation packet includes an events calendar, an official highway map, an attractions and recreation guide and either the spring & summer or the fall & winter picture guide. The picture guides are handy seasonal references to travel in Wisconsin. They show off the state in color photos and text and also list addresses and phone numbers for those who need further information.

The travel consultants are able to answer general tourism questions about your Wisconsin trip. If necessary, they can refer you to specific chambers of commerce or other agencies that can give you detailed information. The consultants will send, on request, other free publications including the *State Park Visitors Guide, Auto Tour Escapes* and general information about lodging and bed-and-breakfast inns.

Call the ESCAPES number to find out about specific events in Wisconsin. During the autumn color season, you can call to get the current "leaf report." When the snow flies, call to get the latest snow and ski conditions report for cross-country skiers, downhill skiers and snowmobilers.

In short, 1-800-ESCAPES should be your first call before starting out on your Wisconsin adventure. Calls are answered during normal business hours.

1-800-432-TRIP (in the continental United States). Call this number if all you need is a vacation packet. The people who take calls can only get your name and address. They cannot answer your questions about travel in Wisconsin. If you wish to talk to someone about your travel questions, call 1-800-ESCAPES.

Camping Information

STATE PARKS AND FORESTS. To request a free state park visitor guide, a campsite reservation application or a guide for the mobility impaired, contact Wisconsin Department of Natural Resources, Bureau of Parks and Recreation, Box 7921, Madison, WI 53707 (608-266-2181). This is the number to call if you have questions about maps, interpretive programs, camping or other components of the park system. Individual park, forest, recreation area and trail addresses and phone numbers are listed in the back of this book.

NATIONAL FORESTS AND RECREATION AREAS. Most camping is on a first-come, first-served basis. For more information, contact the individual unit (addresses and phone numbers are listed in the back of this book).

WISCONSIN ASSOCIATION OF CAMPGROUND OWNERS (WACO). Privately owned campgrounds provide 75% of the campsites in Wisconsin. WACO represents many of these campgrounds. To get a campground directory (for a small fee), contact WACO, P.O. Box 1770, Eau Claire, WI 54702 (715-839-9226).

WISCONSIN CAMPERS ASSOCIATION (WCA). A statewide organization of camping families working to promote better camping and camping fun. Contact WCA, Box 10214, Milwaukee, WI 53210.

Fishing, Hunting and Boating

For information on laws and licenses for fishing, hunting and boating, contact Wisconsin Department of Natural Resources, Box 7921, Madison, WI 53707 (608-266-2105).

For a booklet of boat launching sites on Wisconsin's inland waters, contact Wisconsin Boat Launching Guide, c/o Milwaukee Sentinel-Public Service Bureau, Box 371, Milwaukee, WI 53201 ($2.75 for booklet).

Road Conditions

For statewide reports of detours, closures, traffic inconveniences or winter road conditions, call: 1-800-ROAD-WIS (in Wisconsin and neighboring states); 608-246-7580 (in Madison); 414-342-2211 (in Milwaukee).

Wisconsin Tourist Information Centers

Official Wisconsin Tourist Centers are located where major highways enter Wisconsin and downtown in Madison and Chicago. You can ask questions and pick up a variety of free information, maps and brochures.

Wisconsin's Tourism Regions

CENTRAL WISCONSIN RIVER COUNTRY, Box 308, Friendship, WI 53934 (608-339-3382).

EAST WISCONSIN WATERS, 1901 S. Oneida St., Box 10596, Green Bay, WI 54307 (414-494-9507).

GREATER MILWAUKEE, Convention and Visitors Bureau, 756 N. Milwaukee St., Milwaukee, WI 53202 (414-273-7222 or 273-3950).

HIDDEN VALLEYS, Riverside Park, Box 2527, La Crosse, WI 54602 (608-782-2467).

INDIAN HEAD COUNTRY, 217 Dallas St., P.O. Box 628, Chetek, WI 54728 (800-472-6654 in Wisconsin; 800-826-6996 or 6967 elsewhere in U.S.).

NORTHWOODS COUNCIL: Contact individual counties for travel and accommodations information.

SOUTHERN GATEWAY, Box 451, Elm Grove, WI 53122 (414-273-0090).

Miscellaneous Resources

NATURAL RESOURCES FOUNDATION OF WISCONSIN, INC. The foundation is a nonprofit corporation that channels contributions from individuals and organizations toward land acquisition for park, recreation and natural areas; educational programs; research efforts and land management. Write: P.O. Box 129, Madison, WI 53701.

WISCONSIN DEPARTMENT OF DEVELOPMENT. Division of Tourism Development, 123 West Washington Ave., P.O. Box 7606, Madison, WI 53707 (608-266-2161).

WISCONSIN PARK AND RECREATION ASSOCIATION (WPRA). This is an active professional organization that represents those people who devote their time and knowledge to the leisure service profession. WPRA is dedicated to the advancement of recreation in Wisconsin by providing professional and educational opportunities to the state and local park and recreation movement. The Association is affiliated with the National Recreation and Park Association.

If you are interested in leisure services and the positive effect they have on the quality of life in Wisconsin, then you may want to learn more about WPRA. Membership is open to those employed in leisure services on a full-time, part-time, volunteer or student basis. Contact Wisconsin Park and Recreation Association, 7000 Greenway, Suite 201, Greendale, WI 53129 (414-423-1210).

SPECIAL ATTRACTIONS

Outdoor fun in Wisconsin consists of more than state and national recreation lands. Other selected attractions are briefly outlined below.

Bicycle Routes

To some, Wisconsin is as famous for its bicycle routes as it is for its cheese. The state is the national leader in off-road bicycle trail development (based on mileage of converted railroad right-of-ways). These abandoned railroad corridors are easy to pedal (the grade is less than 4%), yet they wander through some of the most beautiful forests, hills, dales and meadows in Wisconsin. Currently, there are 12 state trails, though not all of them are surfaced for bicycles. You'll find details about each of the state trails in this guidebook.

Wisconsin's excellent system of paved secondary roads seems tailor-made for bicycle touring. These roads wind through lush countryside and cool forests, past glacial lakes and historic sites, and through major cities as well as villages not on the highway map.

To help plan a two-wheel adventure in the state, send for a copy of the *Wisconsin Bicycle Escape Guide*. The guide consists of two maps that outline over 10,000 miles of recommended routes throughout the state. You'll find information about facilities and services along the way, mileage, parks and accommodations. Suggestions for tour planning and safety are also given. The maps show the route of the Wisconsin Bikeway (from La Crosse to Kenosha), which became the nation's first designated bikeway in 1964. The La Crosse-to-Bayfield route was added to the Bikeway in 1976. The updated second printing of the *Bicycle Escape Guide* is available for $2.25 from: Wisconsin Division of Tourism, 123 West Washington Ave., P.O. Box 7606, Madison, WI 53707 (1-800-ESCAPES).

Canoe Rivers

Rivers were the first "highways" in Wisconsin, used by Indians, explorers, missionaries, fur traders, settlers and lumbermen. Today they're used mostly for fun, offering scenic paddling for beginners and experts alike. Wisconsin has an enviable record nationwide for protecting its best streams: the Black, Brule and Flambeau flow through state forests; the Pine, Pike and Popple are State Wild and Scenic Rivers; the St. Croix and Namekagon are designated as a National Scenic Riverway (the Wolf River was also designated a National Wild and Scenic River, but is not at present being managed as one); and the Lower Wisconsin is protected as a State Riverway. Twenty-nine Wisconsin rivers are noted for their mixture of quietwater and whitewater canoeing. Contact the Wisconsin Division of Tourism or the DNR for details (addresses and phone numbers are in the INFORMATION section).

Wisconsin has worked hard to protect its wild streams, such as the Wolf River, to provide scenic recreation.

County Parks and Forests

Less well known than their state and national counterparts, county parks and forests are often bypassed. That's too bad, because they usually offer scenic beauty in an uncrowded setting. Locations of county parks and forests are shown on the official state highway map. For camping information, write to the counties you plan to visit.

Great Lakes Circle Tours

Wisconsin's two Great Lakes, Superior and Michigan, are famous for their beauty, beaches and fishing. Adventuresome travelers can experience these lakes on intimate terms by driving around them on designated Circle Tours. If you have the time, take in a fishing or sailing charter, visit a maritime museum or just get some sand between your toes.

Lake Superior, Wisconsin's northern border, is the world's largest freshwater lake. The 1,300-mile Circle Tour of Lake Superior takes you through Wisconsin, Minnesota, Ontario (Canada) and Michigan. For a copy of the *Lake Superior Circle Tour Travel Guide,* send $1.00 to: North of Superior Tourism, 79 North Court Street, Thunder Bay, Ontario P7A 4T7.

The Lake Michigan Circle Tour is a new cooperative effort of Wisconsin, Illinois, Indiana and Michigan. Although a map of the 300-mile route is not available yet, you can follow the distinctive highway signs that are placed about five miles apart. For details on area facilities and attractions, contact the chambers of commerce of the cities located along Lake Michigan.

Great River Road

In a state noted for its scenic drives, the Great River Road should rank near the top of your priority list. The route shadows the 200-mile path of the Mississippi River along the state's western border. You can start your car tour in Prescott, where the St. Croix River merges into the Mississippi River, and end in the southwestern corner of the state near Dubuque, Iowa.

River time moves slower than highway time, so it's a good idea to stop often to savor life along the Mississippi. You'll cross broad river plains and pass through picturesque towns that cling to the stately bluffs lining the river valley. You can also enjoy lofty vistas of the majestic river from some of the overlooks and parks along the way. Camping, fishing, hiking and boating are some of the popular river pastimes. Watch for the river barges that navigate the twisting channels of the Mississippi and the bald eagles and hawks that soar overhead.

For a map of the entire Great River Road (covering the 3,000 miles from Canada to the Gulf), write: Great River Road Commission, Wisconsin Department of Transportation, P.O. Box 7910, Madison, WI 53707 (608-266-1113).

Historic Sites

Wisconsin's past is long and colorful. You can relive the days of Indians, explorers, fur traders, miners, settlers and lumbermen at the State Historical Society Museum in Madison or participate in a slice of the state's story at any of seven "living history" sites.

The historical sites and museum, maintained by the State Historical Society of Wisconsin, remind visitors of the state's rich and diverse cultural roots:

(opposite page)
Old World Wisconsin offers a glimpse of Wisconsin's past at a group of seven historical sites, each reflecting a particular ethnic influence in the development of Wisconsin's diverse culture.

CIRCUS WORLD MUSEUM—Baraboo. "Big Top" circus acts, circus art and memorabilia and the world's largest collection of circus wagons await you at the former winter quarters of the Ringling Bros. Circus. 426 Water St., Baraboo, WI 53913 (608-356-8341).

MADELINE ISLAND HISTORICAL MUSEUM—La Pointe. The museum stands on the site of the old American Fur Company trading post. Madeline Island is the largest of the 22 islands in the Apostle Island archipelago on Lake Superior. La Pointe, WI 54850 (715-747-2415). Board the ferry at Bayfield.

OLD WADE HOUSE—Greenbush. An old stagecoach inn appearing as it did when pioneers settled the area around 1850. Greenbush, WI 53026 (414-526-3271).

OLD WORLD WISCONSIN—Eagle. The only multicultural, multinational outdoor museum in the world, portraying the lifestyles of Wisconsin's pioneers. Rt. 2, Box 18, Hwy. 67, Eagle, WI 53119 (414-594-2116).

PENDARVIS—Mineral Point. A complex of restored Cornish miners' homes, built during the lead mining era of the 1830s. 114 Shake Rag St., Mineral Point, WI 53565 (608-987-2122).

STONEFIELD VILLAGE—Cassville. The estate of Wisconsin's first governor, Nelson Dewey, and the site of a re-created turn-of-the-century village. Cassville, WI 53806 (608-725-5210).

VILLA LOUIS—Prairie du Chien. Preserves the art and literary treasures of Hercules Dousman, Wisconsin's first millionaire who built the mansion in 1872. Box 65, Prairie du Chien, WI 53821 (608-326-2721).

STATE HISTORICAL SOCIETY MUSEUM—Madison. This free museum features changing exhibits, a theater, gift shop and extensive Indian history displays. 30 N. Carroll St., Madison, WI 53703 (608-262-7700).

For details about hours and fees, passports (all-season passes), and membership information, contact The State Historical Society of Wisconsin, 816 State St., Madison, WI 53706 (608-262-9606). Check local chambers of commerce for information about community-operated and private historical sites.

Natural Areas

Wisconsin's landscape has changed dramatically since settlement began about 150 years ago. Little remains of the natural plant and animal communities that formed following the melting of the last glaciers about 12,000 years ago. The scattered remnants that have escaped most, if not all, exploitation are called natural areas.

Wisconsin has designated over 200 natural areas since originating the program in 1951 (the first of its kind in the United States). These small parcels are often the last refuges for rare and endangered plants and animals. Some natural areas also include unique and important geological and archaeological features.

The natural areas serve as outdoor laboratories for research and teaching. Use of the least fragile sites by environmental education and conservation groups is permitted, but they are not intended for intensive recreational uses like picnicking or camping. Though some natural areas are protected from human disturbance, many others are easily accessible to the public (with parking lots, trails, fences and gates). For more information, contact Wisconsin Natural Areas, Bureau of Endangered Resources, DNR, P.O. Box 7921, Madison, WI 53707 (608-266-7012). You might also want to contact the Natural Areas Preservation Council, an advisory group to the Department of Natural Resources (ask the DNR for details).

The Nature Conservancy

While the natural areas program works through the state government to preserve Wisconsin's finest natural forests, prairies, wetlands and aquatic features, the Nature Conservancy labors quietly and effectively toward the same goal through the private sector. The partnership pays off. By the year 2000, at least 290 state natural areas encompassing 55,000 acres should be established, many through the assistance of the Nature Conservancy.

The Nature Conservancy is a national conservation organization that has safeguarded nearly three million acres of land and water in the United States, Canada, the Caribbean and Latin America since its founding in 1951. Its main goal is the preservation of natural diversity. TNC accomplishes its goals by identification, protection and stewardship of critical natural areas.

The Wisconsin Nature Conservancy, founded in 1960, is an active chapter that continually tries to preserve unique natural areas. Some of the chapter's most outstanding sites include the Mink River Estuary with its pure water, open marsh and waterfowl; the Baraboo Hills' mix of rolling wildflower meadows, steep bluffs and caves; and Spring Green Reserve, the finest remaining sand prairie in southwestern Wisconsin, filled with stately prairie grasses, cacti and spectacular wildflowers.

If you would like to join the Nature Conservancy, make a contribution or just find out more about this private, nonprofit organization, contact Wisconsin Chapter of The Nature Conservancy, 1045 E. Dayton St., Room 209, Madison, WI 53703 (608-251-8140).

Rustic Roads

To some travelers, it's the journey, not the destination, that matters. Wisconsin's Rustic Roads System lets you travel for travel's sake on over 50 scenic, lightly used country roads. The routes may be dirt, gravel or paved, ranging from 1.5 to 26 miles in length. They may also be one-way or two-way. Some have bicycle or hiking paths adjacent to the road, though the traffic pace is slow enough (maximum speed is 45 mph) that you can hike or bike on the road itself.

The rustic roads each feature a special vista of Wisconsin: rugged terrain, native wildlife or vegetation, lakeshore or rolling farmland. If there is a common characteristic among them, it would be the frame of mind of those who seek out these roads. If you're driving, roll down the window, stick your head out and inhale the sweet smell of wildflowers. If you're hiking or bicycling, notice how the sounds of crickets and birds take over your awareness.

However you wander down Wisconsin's rustic roads, you're in for a treat. To get a map and find out more details, contact Rustic Roads Board, Wisconsin Department of Transportation, P.O. Box 7913, Madison, WI 53707 (608-266-0639).

ICE AGE NATIONAL SCIENTIFIC RESERVE AND ICE AGE NATIONAL SCENIC TRAIL

Reserve: Over 40,000 acres divided among nine units that represent unique features of continental glaciation.

Trail: When completed, will stretch for 1,000 miles across the state, tracing the farthest advance of the last glacier.

Ice Age National Scientific Reserve

Imagine a river of ice more than a mile thick. It lifts, grinds and mixes huge boulders and soil in its icy mass as it spreads outward. Beyond the glacier's leading edge is a land untouched by ice: well drained, with naturally eroded hills and valleys. Most of Wisconsin was carved and shaped by the great ice sheets, but the southwestern part of the state, called the Driftless Area, was not.

The Ice Age lasted for more than a million years, with at least four major periods of glacial advances and retreats. The Wisconsinan stage was the most recent, beginning about 70,000 years ago and ending only about 10,000 years ago. In fact, we may still be in the Ice Age, enjoying a warm period between two glacial advances.

As the glaciers retreated, some of Wisconsin's most scenic and fertile landscapes were formed. Conical hills (kames) grew as debris washed through funnel-shaped holes in the ice. Eskers, serpentine ridges of gravel and sand, formed when stream channels beneath stagnant glaciers filled up with debris. Kettles are depressions in the ground that formed as sand and gravel settled over a melting ice block. End moraines are glacial dumps at the end of moving ice. Potholes were worn into rock formations by swirling sand, gravel and stones carried by the powerful current of meltwater rivers. As the ice melted, huge glacial lakes formed, eventually draining into broad, flat lake beds that now are rich agricultural lands.

To preserve Wisconsin's distinctive glacial landforms, the Ice Age National Scientific Reserve was created as a joint venture by the National Park Service and the State of Wisconsin. The dynamo behind the idea was the late Ray Zillmer of Milwaukee. He pictured an 800-mile-long national park to tell the story of how the glaciers shaped Wisconsin's topography and to provide recreational enjoyment. His dream, though altered slightly, was realized when the reserve was established in 1971.

Rather than one long park, the reserve consists of nine separate units spread in an arc across Wisconsin, from Lake Michigan on the east to the St. Croix River

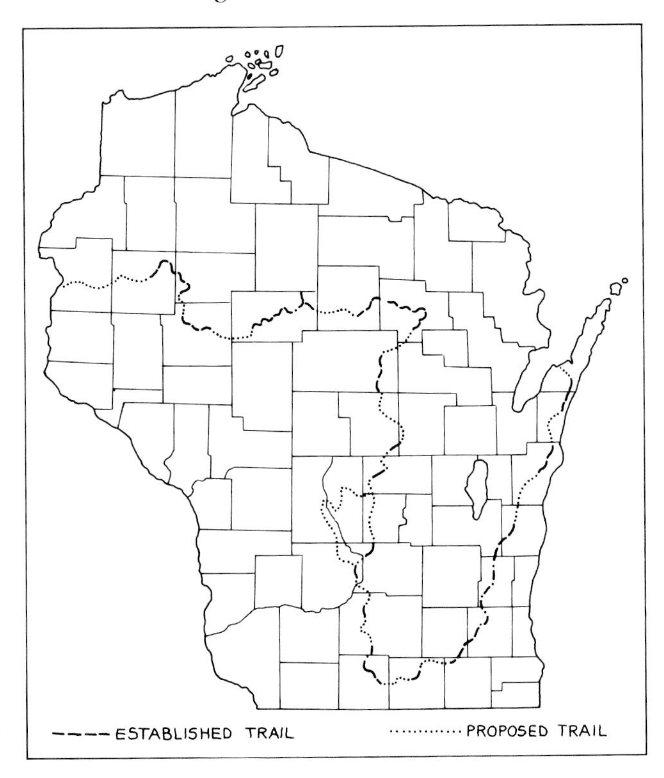

(opposite page)

Wisconsin's fascinating glacial history has been preserved in the topography of parklands such as the North Kettle Moraine State Forest.

on the Wisconsin-Minnesota border. Each unit features present-day evidence of glacial events that happened thousands of years ago. Five of the units are state parks, forests or wildlife areas: Kettle Moraine State Forest, Horicon Marsh Wildlife Area, and Devil's Lake, Mill Bluff and Interstate state parks. The other four units will be open to the public when land acquisition and development are completed.

The Two Creeks Buried Forest Unit (not yet in operation) features an 11,000-year-old buried forest of spruce and hemlock on Lake Michigan. The Kettle Moraine State Forest (northern unit) preserves a collection of kames, eskers, kettles and other glacial features. A cluster of drumlins (elongated, rounded hills) comprises the Campbellsport Drumlins Unit (not yet in operation). Horicon Marsh lies in the bed of an extinct glacial lake. At the Cross Plains Unit (not yet in operation), you can see the contrast between the glaciated land to the northeast and the Driftless Area (free of glacial debris, or "drift") to the southwest.

The Devil's Lake State Park Unit demonstrates the size and power of the ice sheet. The ancient Wisconsin River flowed through the gorge here, but was rerouted nine miles to the east when the glacier plugged both ends of the gap. Meltwater and springs formed the scenic lake, which still rests on hundreds of feet of glacial debris. At Mill Bluff State Park, steep sandstone buttes stand as rocky island reminders of an ancient glacial lake. The Chippewa Moraine Unit (not yet in operation) is a series of wooded hills speckled with kettle lakes, bogs and marshes. The sheer-walled gorge and large potholes at Interstate State Park, the westernmost reserve unit, were carved through lava formations by new drainage systems formed by torrents of glacial meltwater.

Though the Wisconsinan glacial stage covered much of the northern United States from the Atlantic coast to the Rocky Mountains, it was named for the state because that's as far south as the great ice sheet advanced. Nowhere is the evidence of the glaciers better preserved than across Wisconsin. The state's lakes and ponds, forested hills and ridges, marshes and sandy plains, and gently rolling farmlands are reminders of the glaciers that ground through here.

Ice Age National Scenic Trail

Like the seven other National Scenic Trails, the Ice Age Trail grabs the imagination of outdoor enthusiasts in both its scale and its scenery. The Ice Age Trail is a 1,000-mile greenway that meanders across Wisconsin's glacial landscape in a great, sweeping route, tracing the entire length of the moraines that mark the furthest advance of the last glacier in the state.

When Ray Zillmer of Milwaukee first proposed the idea for an Ice Age Glacier National Forest Park in the 1950s, he visualized that an extensive footpath would be the central feature of the park. His original idea has evolved into the Ice Age National Scientific Reserve and the Ice Age National Scenic Trail. The reserve protects prime portions of Wisconsin's glacial terrain while the trail links most of the nine units of the reserve and many national, state and county parks and recreation areas.

Both the reserve and trail have always been community efforts. In 1958, the Ice Age Park and Trail Foundation was formed by a group of Wisconsin citizens to promote the creation of the national glacial park. Volunteers were already at work building the first segments of the future Ice Age Trail in the Kettle Moraine State Forest.

Efforts to construct major segments of the trail mushroomed in 1975, when the Ice Age Trail Council was formed. Through local chapters, the volunteers of the Trail Council worked cooperatively with public agencies and hundreds of private landowners to establish the Ice Age Trail. Existing portions of the trail are maintained by the U.S. Forest Service, the Wisconsin DNR and several county park and forest departments. Many individuals, outing clubs, youth groups and local civic organizations also help the council to maintain and develop the trail.

In the fall of 1980, Congress recognized the national significance of the Ice Age Trail and the grass roots efforts to establish it by designating it a National Scenic Trail. The National Park Service administers the trail as a unit of the National Park System in co-operation with the Wisconsin DNR, the Ice Age Trail Council and the Ice Age Park and Trail Foundation. Since its designation as a national scenic trail, the Ice Age Trail joins the ranks of other eminent foot-paths such as the Appalachian, Pacific Crest and North Country national scenic trails (the North Country Trail cuts through northwestern Wisconsin along part of its 3,200-mile route).

Over 400 miles of completed trail are ready for use by hikers and backpackers. Bicycling, horseback riding, cross-country skiing, snowshoeing and jogging may be permitted on a given segment according to the policies of the managing group or agency. Hunting, fishing and snowmobiling are also permitted on certain portions. Trail users are responsible for obtaining appropriate licenses and for checking with local trail authorities regarding regulations and fees.

Camping facilities, support services and trail conditions can vary from one segment to the next. Interpretive programs and information centers will be further developed as the trail is completed. Currently, two interpretive centers (along the trail in the Northern Unit of the Kettle Moraine State Forest and in Interstate State Park) depict Wisconsin's glacial history and geology.

The Ice Age Trail leads to unique glacial landscapes that are close to urban areas as well as some of the most remote parts of Wisconsin. The trail begins in Potawatomi State Park in Door County and passes through or near Old Wade House, Pike Lake, New Glarus Woods, Devil's Lake, Mirror Lake, Rocky Arbor, Roche-a-Cri, Hartman Creek, Council Grounds, Brunet Island and Interstate state parks. You can hike through the Northern and Southern Kettle Moraine State Forests, through the county forests of Langlade, Marathon and Chippewa counties, and through the Chequamegon National Forest in Taylor County.

The Ice Age Trail wanders through the Blue Hills of Rusk County, the Baraboo Hills of Sauk County and the Harrison Hills of Lincoln County. It follows the Ahnapee, Sugar River and Tuscobia state trails and crosses the Glacial Drumlins and Military Ridge state trails. It crosses the Wisconsin River on the ferry at Merrimac and the power dam at Castle Rock.

The Wisconsin legislature recently designated the Ice Age Trail as the state's first scenic trail. This gives the state more power to help in the development of the route.

The Ice Age National Scientific Reserve and the Ice Age National Scenic Trail provide recreational access to some of the most unusual and exciting landforms in Wisconsin. There were other great glaciers that covered much of North America, but the Wisconsin Glacier was the most recent. That is why its features are not yet completely eroded. When you hike the trail and visit the units of the reserve, you'll see this glacier's imprint impressed on the landscape more starkly than anywhere else in the nation.

For information about the Ice Age Trail and Reserve, contact:

Wisconsin Department of Natural Resources
Box 7921
Madison, WI 53707

Ice Age Trail Council
2302 Lakeland Avenue
Madison, WI 53704

Ice Age Park and Trail Foundation
735 North Water Street
Milwaukee, WI 53202

CENTRAL WISCONSIN RIVER COUNTRY

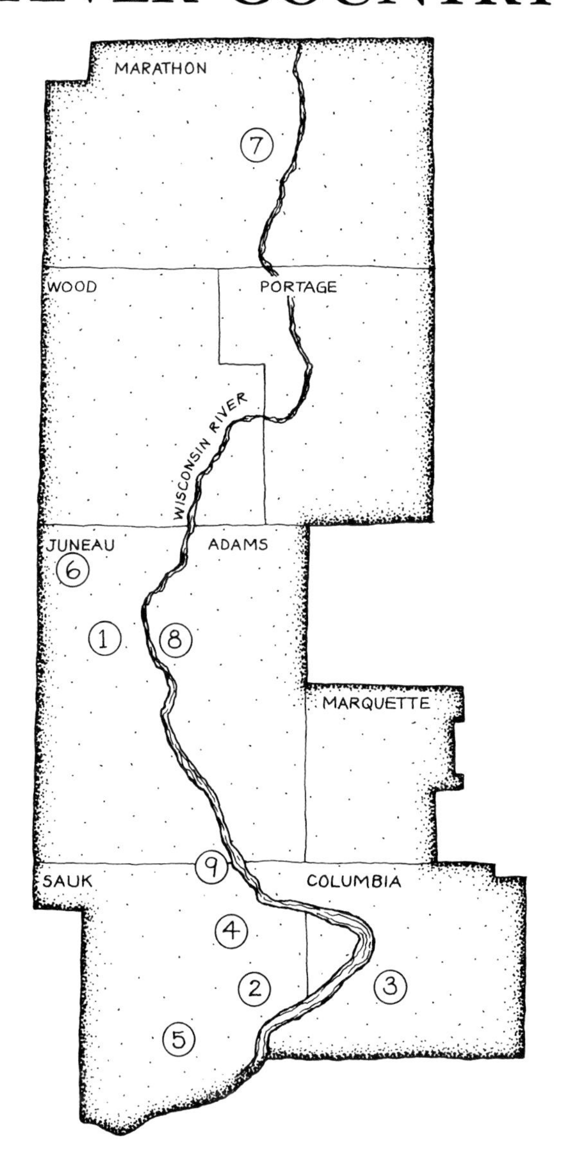

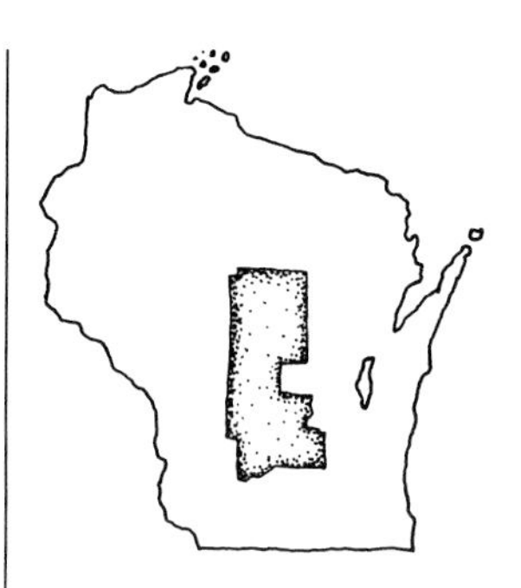

1. Buckhorn State Park
2. Devil's Lake State Park
3. MacKenzie Environmental Education Center and State Game Farm
4. Mirror Lake State Park
5. Natural Bridge State Park
6. Necedah National Wildlife Refuge and Meadow Valley Wildlife Area
7. Rib Mountain State Park
8. Roche-a-Cri State Park
9. Rocky Arbor State Park

(opposite page)

Climbing the hills and bluffs of Central Wisconsin rewards visitors with panoramas of woods, fields and water.

BUCKHORN STATE PARK

Juneau County. About nine miles north of Mauston on County Q, then turn east on County G for about four miles to the park entrance. Highway map index: 8-F.

Main Attraction

For some, the memory that lingers longest about Buckhorn State Park is of a pleasant summer evening spent splashing in the warm lake water and watching the orange sun set from a beach-side picnic table. Others remember Buckhorn as wild country. For them, the 3,500-acre park means hunting, hiking or canoeing in the solitude of the Buckhorn Wildlife Area.

The park, one of Wisconsin's newest, spreads across the southern tip of the Buckhorn Peninsula between the Yellow and Wisconsin rivers on the Castle Rock Flowage. The flowage forms one of the state's largest lakes and is a big reason why people visit the park.

The bays, marshes and forests of Buckhorn have a wild touch that resembles the land as the Winnebago Indians knew it in the early 1800s. They named this wilderness "Necedah," or "land of yellow waters," and camped here on the west shore of the Wisconsin River among the big pines. Later, white men came by boat or stagecoach from Grand Rapids—now Wisconsin Rapids.

Things To Do

The swimming beach (unguarded) and picnic grounds attract the most people. You get a front-row view of the lake if you arrive early enough to claim a beach-side table. Even if you're just there to be a beach bum, the lake frontage is large enough to accommodate lots of daydreamers. From the beach, you can see how popular the lake is among water sports lovers as boats, canoes, windsurfers and sailboats play on the big water. You can rent boats, canoes and other outdoor gear from private outfitters in the area.

Powerboats and fishing boats launch from the park's landing, which has a 40-foot pier. The 13,387-acre flowage offers some of the best freshwater fishing in the state. Largemouth bass, northern and panfish are plentiful in the sloughs, while perch, white bass, northern and walleye frequent the deeper water far-

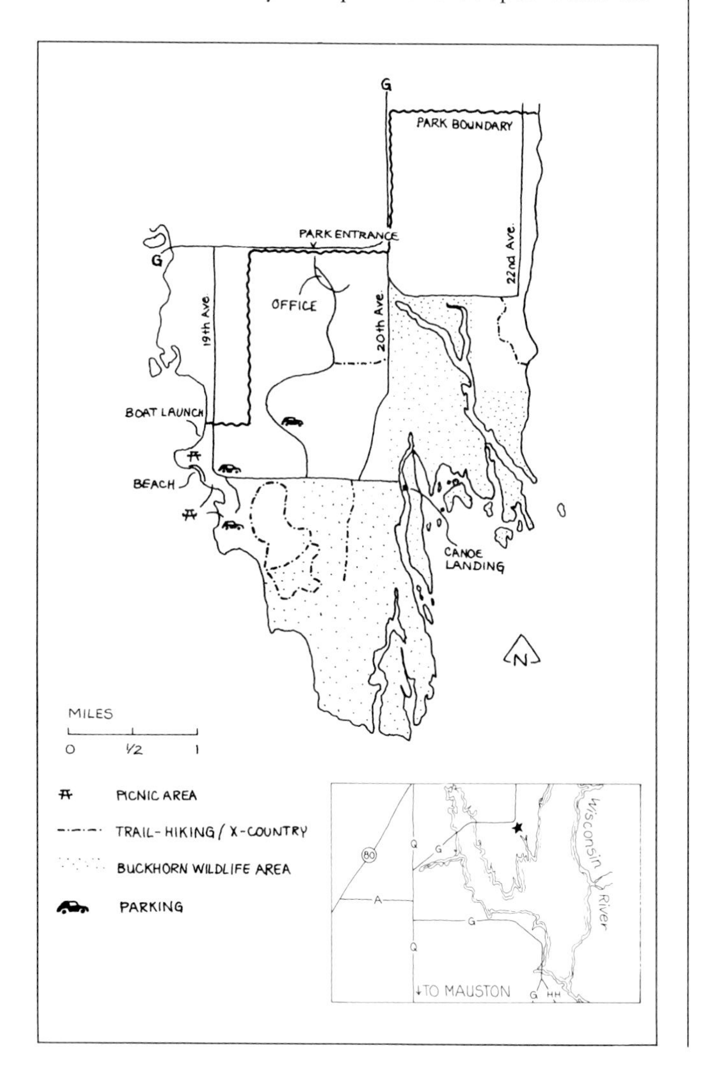

Relaxing at the beach is a favorite pasttime for visitors to Buckhorn State Park. Arrive early for a beachside table.

ther from shore. Small motors or trolling motors will let you poke into some of the shallow water bays and sloughs.

Some of the locally known fishing hot spots include the railroad bridge crossing, the area near the Buckhorn Bridge and the east bank below the dam. Because Castle Rock is a flowage, it naturally becomes more shallow further upriver. The waters also conceal shallows in other unexpected areas, even long distances from shore. Boaters should be cautious. To get maps of the Castle Rock and Petenwell flowages, contact the Wisconsin River Power Company, P.O. Box 50, Wisconsin Rapids, WI 54494 (715-422-3073), or ask at the park office or the Necedah Ranger Station.

The Buckhorn Peninsula is tailor-made for canoeists. The finger-shaped sloughs and small islands on the park's south and east sides hold new sights and sounds around each bend. Canoeists can put in from the landing at the head of a backwater on the east side of the park.

You can hike through part of the woods on 2.5 miles of hiking and nature trails.

The Buckhorn Peninsula has traditionally been a productive hunting area. You can still enjoy hunting in the park and Buckhorn Wildlife Area, but certain restrictions apply. All park and wildlife area lands are open for the early bow season for deer only and are closed during the deer gun season. This means that the number of deer harvested here annually is relatively low and that some survive to reach trophy size. The early bow season generally runs from mid-September to mid-November. Though the park is closed to all other hunting, the wildlife area is open during regular seasons for trapping and small game and waterfowl hunting. Special parking lots are maintained to allow hunting access to more remote areas of the park.

Nearly surrounded by water, this peninsula park invites visitors to fish, boat, canoe, swim or sail on the 13,000-acre Castle Rock Flowage.

Winter at Buckhorn means that you're able to explore parts of the park that aren't accessible during the summer. You can cross-country ski, hike or snowshoe, though the trails aren't groomed. Snowmobiling and ice fishing are the most popular cold weather sports. Keep an eye out for bald eagles that nest along the shore and feed in the open water of the flowage during the winter.

The park's annual open house is usually scheduled for the third Sunday in June and features guided canoe outings on the flowage, interpretive hikes and displays. Other naturalist programs are offered on re-

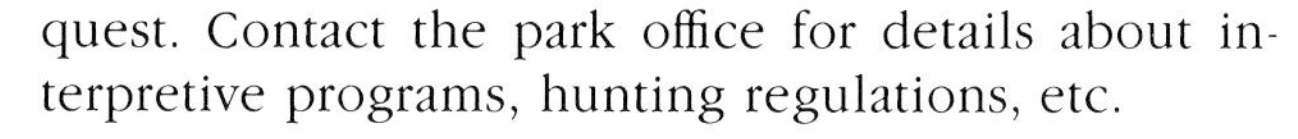
quest. Contact the park office for details about interpretive programs, hunting regulations, etc.

Flora and Fauna

A canoeing adventure is usually filled with the promise of wildlife observation. Canada geese, herons, wood ducks, muskrats and mink all live here.

The forest is mostly oaks and jack pine, but the rough-edged character of the land is still here.

Facilities

Camping is not available yet, but 9 to 12 wilderness campsites and a group campground will be developed in the near future. An 80-unit family campground may also be built, depending on the demand for it. Two nearby county parks do provide camping, though. Juneau County Castle Rock Park is on the west side of the flowage, while Adams County Castle Rock Park is on the east side. There are also private campgrounds near the state park.

Surrounding Area

The park staff can point out nearby sidetrips, including Roche-a-Cri, Mill Bluff and Rocky Arbor state parks and the Necedah National Wildlife Area–Wisconsin Conservation Area.

DEVIL'S LAKE STATE PARK

AND PARFREY'S GLEN NATURAL AREA

Sauk County. Three miles south of Baraboo on Highway 123. Take Interstate 90-94 and exit on either Highway 12 or Highway 33 to Baraboo, then take Highway 123 to the park. Parfrey's Glen is about four miles east of Devil's Lake on County DL. Highway map index: 9-F.

Main Attraction

Devil's Lake State Park is the closest thing to "mountain scenery" in Wisconsin. Sheer rugged bluffs that rise 500 feet above a glacial lake on three sides, plus a wide range of year-round outdoor activities make Wisconsin's largest state park (about 8,000 acres) also one of its most loved.

Devil's Lake State Park is one of nine units in the Ice Age National Scientific Reserve in Wisconsin, which preserves distinctive features of continental glaciation. Devil's Lake was formed when the most recent glacier crushed across this region. The gap between the bluffs, where the lake is now, used to be the channel of the Wisconsin River. The glacier rerouted the river to the east and plugged the open ends of the gap with rock and gravel. You can learn more about the Ice Age Reserve and the park's glacial scenery by participating in the naturalist programs.

Geologists feel that the quartzite rock formations of the park, and of the whole Baraboo Range, were formed about 1.5 billion years ago, making them one of the most ancient outcrops in North America. More than 100 colleges and universities conduct geological field trips to Devil's Lake to study the history of the rocks.

Why is it called Devil's Lake? No one is certain, but

it's possible it was misnamed. The Winnebago Indians, who camped on these shores and fished the lake, called it Spirit Lake. White settlers passed along many myths and legends about the lake. One describes a great meteor that penetrated far into the earth, throwing up rocks on all sides. Heat waves radiated from the hole for several days. Then it rained. When it was safe for people to approach, they found a great gap in the earth and at the bottom a beautiful body of water. Maybe such stories made people think of evil spirits, thus inspiring the name change.

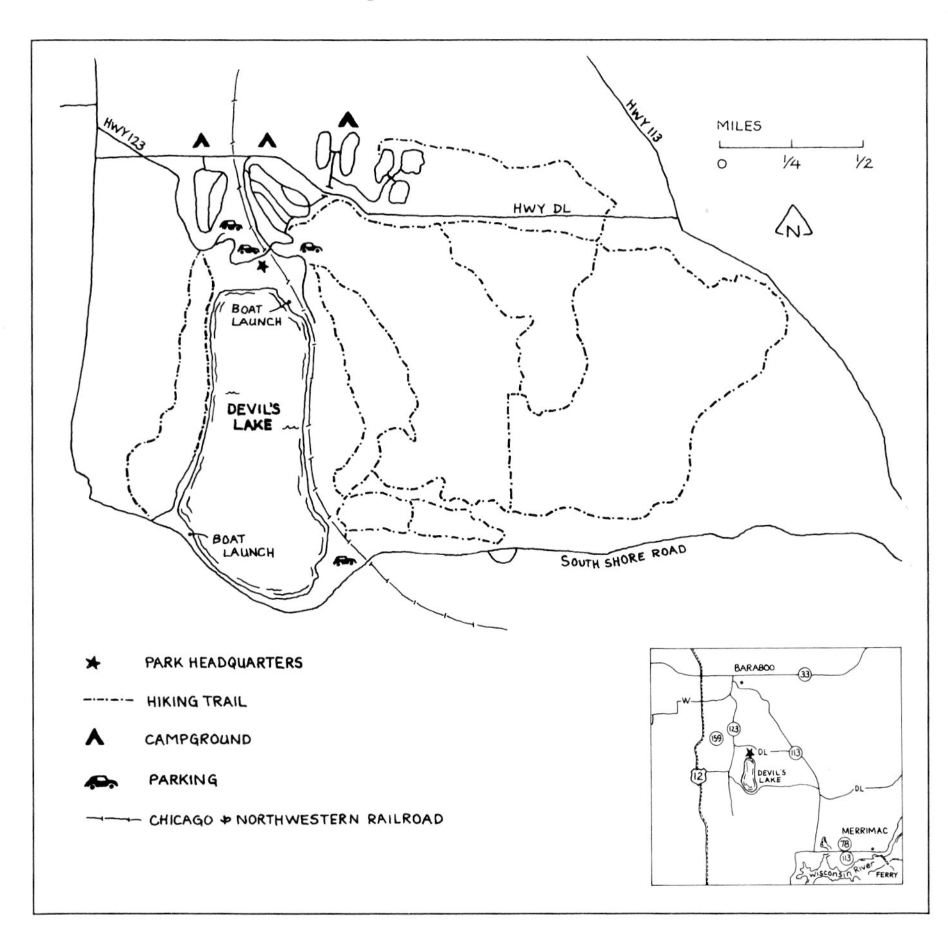

Things To Do

Today, stories about the lake come mostly from visitors discussing last weekend's catch. Fishing is good year-round here for rainbow and brown trout, walleye and northern pike, bass and panfish. Resident and nonresident fishing licenses and trout stamps are available at the park office. Rowboats can be rented at both the north and south concession stands. The concession stands also rent fishing poles, sailboards and snorkeling gear, as well as sell supplies and host teen dances during the summer.

No gasoline motors are allowed on Devil's Lake, so bring your canoe or sailboat instead for a quiet day on the water. If you want to scuba dive, all you need is a "buddy" and the proper equipment. The 360-acre lake is 45 feet deep and clear enough to eyeball the fish while you poke into some of the shallow holes and drop-offs. Launch ramps and supervised beaches with bathhouses are located at each end of the lake.

Devil's Lake has been a state park since 1911, but it's been a popular tourist attraction for over a century. Nine passenger trains stopped here every day in the 1890s, and four grand hotels were built around the lake. To find out where the hotels were located and what the area was like in the "good old days," join a human history hike or browse through the collection of photos and maps in the nature center.

Devil's Lake State Park has an active nature program. A naturalist, on duty year-round, leads guided hikes on such topics as wildflowers, glaciers, human history and the park's Indian burial mounds (some of which are in the shapes of animals). The nature center, at the north end of the park, also sponsors evening programs (usually slide shows) about the area. For details about the hikes, programs and center hours, check the naturalist program schedules posted throughout the park. The nature center, open by appointment in the winter, makes a good first step in the park for orientation and background information.

Sheer, rugged bluffs rise 500 feet above a clear glacial lake—what more could you ask for in a state park?

Take time to hike part of the 16.5-mile hiking trail system. Wear comfortable hiking shoes, and bring a camera for those blufftop vistas of the lake. It's easier to climb the bluffs from the north because the trails are less steep than from the south end. As you climb a winding trail, you can see farther across the forested bluffs of the Baraboo Range. Seen from a tree-lined cliff, sailboats on the lake make good photo compositions. There are many overlooks along the West Bluff Trail from which you can get a bird's-eye view of the lake and the feeling that it's just the wind, the hawks and you up there.

Among the rock formations visible from the trail are the Devil's Doorway and Balanced Rock, both on the rocky and rough East Bluff. For more wilderness-type hiking, try the East Bluff Woods loop or the Ice Age loop, where you can escape the busy lake activity to experience the forest in the fragrance of a patch of wildflowers or listen to the sound of a chipmunk's chatter. The rocky slopes of Devil's Lake are famous among midwestern climbers who like to practice here before trying more challenging climbs out West.

Fresh winter snow beckons cross-country skiers who can tour on about 16 miles of groomed trails with loops for all skill levels. There are uphill climbs and downhill runs, and the snowy ridges lined with silent rock formations overlooking the valley. Through the trees you can see miles of wintry forest and rolling farmland.

You might change your mind about winter after ice fishing, camping, hiking or cross-country skiing at Devil's Lake (no snowmobiling is allowed in the park). Imagine getting up at dawn to photograph the fresh snow patterns in the campground, or taking a trail break on a blufftop with the wind in the trees and the rugged winter landscape below you. Or, glide down the gentle, curving mile-long East Bluff Woods Trail on cross-country skis as the snowy forest swooshes by. If you haven't done it yet, consider a winter exploration trip to Devil's Lake State Park.

(opposite page)

Sailing on the clear waters of Devil's Lake is only one way to enjoy this spectacular park.

Flora and Fauna

Park vegetation varies from prairie remnants to oak woods, red and sugar maples, pine plantations, aspen

and scattered old white pines. A few timber rattlesnakes live in the park, but they are not a problem. About 90 species of birds nest here. Bald eagles often fly over the lake and the bluffs in winter, but aren't seen during the summer. The turkey vulture, with its gliding flight and large size, is easy to spot in the park.

Facilities

Because the park is so popular, the three individual-site campgrounds (427 sites, 125 with electrical hookups, showers) are busy during the peak summer season. Campers may make reservations for these sites, plus the outdoor (175 people) and indoor (40 people) group camps, beginning the first workday after January 1, for the period from May 1 through the last weekend in October. About 70 sites stay open for winter use. The park has three major picnic grounds with shelters, water, tables, grills and fireplaces. Check at the park office for details about renting the south shore shelter. Some groceries and supplies are available at the concession stands and at the Ice Age Campground store.

Surrounding Area

Parfrey's Glen Natural Area, about four miles east of Devil's Lake in the south flank of the Baraboo Range, is a rocky 100-foot gorge. Because the gorge receives minimal sunlight and because cold air settles at the bottom of ravines, the plants in the glen are more typical of northern Wisconsin than of this part of the state. The gorge is a fragile place. Visitors can hike from the parking lot to the upper end of the glen, but must stay on the marked trails to prevent erosion and other damage. Since the purpose of a natural area is conservation, research, education and preservation, other "park" activities (i.e., camping and picnicking) are prohibited.

Besides the park and natural area, there are many things to do and see in the area. One of the last operating river ferryboats is a few miles south of the park at Merrimac, and authentic steam passenger trains still chug through rolling farmland at the Mid-Continent Railway in North Freedom (west of Baraboo). Baraboo is the home of the famous Circus World Museum, birthplace of the Ringling Bros. Circus ("The Greatest Show on Earth"). The circus attraction, owned by the State Historical Society of Wisconsin, features displays, performances and demonstrations designed to bring out the kid in even the most indifferent visitor. Nearby state parks include Natural Bridge, Rocky Arbor and Mirror Lake.

This ladyslipper blossoms in Parfey's Glen, a gorge with a cool, damp environment that supports unique vegetation.

MACKENZIE ENVIRONMENTAL EDUCATION CENTER AND STATE GAME FARM

Columbia County. Two miles northeast of Poynette on County Q. Highway map index: 9-G.

Main Attraction

The MacKenzie Environmental Education Center and State Game Farm has, since 1934, attracted visitors to its outdoor classroom. The Center's original goals of environmental study, recreation and conservation are still met today. Thousands of visitors continue to come here each year as registered day users, tourists or participants in Resident Center programs. They hike the nature trails, view the native bird and animal exhibits and learn about environmental issues.

The State Game Farm specializes in pheasant propagation. New breeder and chick brooding buildings (1983) make the game farm one of the largest and most modern facilities of its kind in the country. The production area is closed to the public for security and disease prevention reasons.

Things To Do

The Center has a series of self-guiding loop trails (each is less than one mile long) at the south end of the property. The trails illustrate different environmental themes: woodland ecology, hardwood forest management, coniferous forest management and wildlife habitat. Hikers can pick up trail guides at the office or in the boxes at the trail heads. Two of the self-guiding trails are accessible to disabled and elderly visitors.

The nature trail at the northern end of the over 500-acre property features a number of interest-catching displays. You can see deer and buffalo from a nearby observation tower. An old log cabin, turned into a logging history museum, shows tools and pictures from the lumberjack era in Wisconsin. Other displays relating to Wisconsin's forest include a model tree nursery, a large pine log and an old sawmill. The Aliens Museum depicts plants and animals not native to the state. Many native trees are identified along this trail.

The wildlife exhibit, next to the deer pen at the northeast corner of the nature trail, is designed for easy observation of wildlife species you may not normally see. Deer, wolves, coyotes, foxes, badgers, otters, hawks, owls, eagles and other animals represent

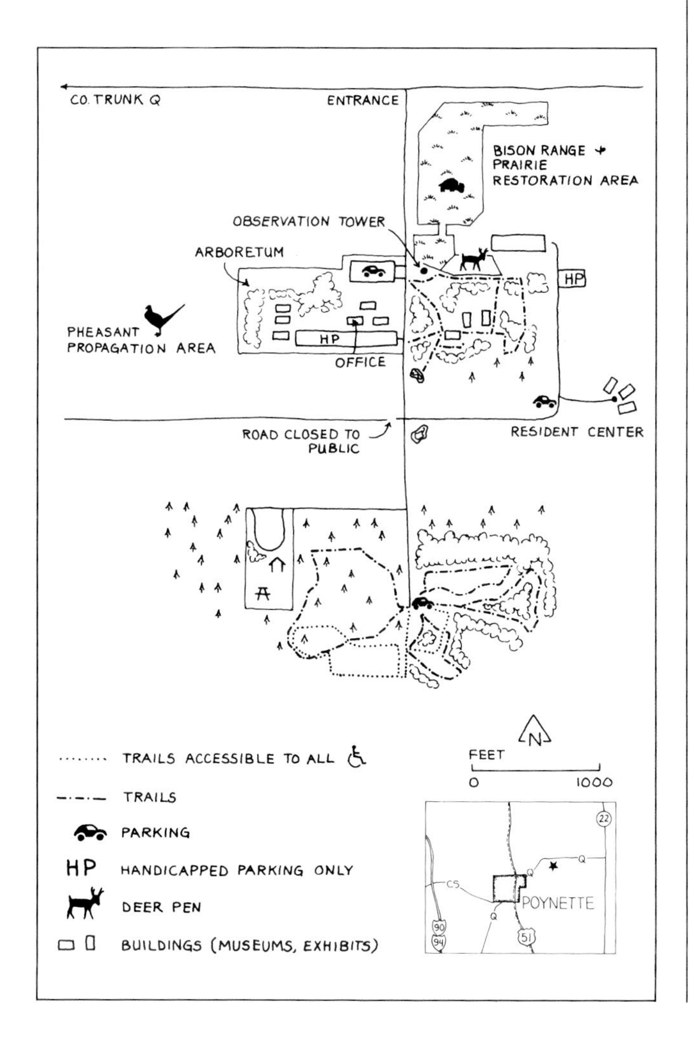

the diversity of Wisconsin's wildlife. Many of these animals have been injured, orphaned, turned in or confiscated from people who tried to make pets of them. Most would not be capable of surviving in the wild.

The wildlife exhibit here will let you see Wisconsin wildlife species that you might never observe in the wild: wolves, coyotes, badgers, otters, buffalo and owls. It's a great first stop for people interested in exploring Wisconsin's wild areas.

Teachers and group leaders are encouraged to make use of the center's facilities to inspire an awareness of the state's natural resources in the young people they work with. Groups must make reservations to avoid crowding. Individuals and families don't have to make reservations to visit the center.

Volunteers play a vital role at MacKenzie. They help conduct adult and student workshops, orient groups and develop museum exhibits. If you'd like to volunteer or just want to get details on programs and reservations, contact the center at the address and phone number listed in the back of this book.

Facilities

The MacKenzie Resident Center provides a live-in facility, staff and field equipment necessary to run environmental education programs in an outdoor setting. Schools, universities and environmental interest groups are invited to use the Resident Center. Facilities include two bunkhouses (40 people each) and a lodge with kitchen, dining room, workshop, lobby, classroom and library. All buildings are winterized and showers are available. The Resident Program Coordinator handles reservations and along with other staff can help plan educational programs for organized groups.

The MacKenzie Environmental Education Center is for day use only. Visitors can picnic in a designated area a short distance from the trails and exhibits. There is space in the picnic area for volleyball, frisbee and softball. No camping is allowed at the center and no motorized vehicles are allowed on the trails. You can camp at a number of private campgrounds in the area, or at Devil's Lake State Park near Baraboo.

Surrounding Area

For a fun side trip, take the Merrimac Ferry across Lake Wisconsin, west of Poynette. The ferry, part of Highway 113, is free for all vehicles. Be prepared to wait your turn, though, because the ferry is popular, especially on weekends. The ride is short (less than ten minutes) but pretty with the lush green lakeside bluffs providing a scenic backdrop. Bring your camera.

The trails and exhibits at the MacKenzie Center are designed to teach visitors about Wisconsin's environment and wildlife.

MIRROR LAKE STATE PARK

Sauk County. South of Lake Delton on Highway 12, about one-half mile beyond Interstate 90-94 (Exit 92). Turn right (west) on Fern Dell Road from Highway 12 and drive about 1.5 miles to the park. Highway map index: 9-F.

Main Attraction

Mirror Lake is fine for canoeing, and the park offers a variety of terrain, flora and fauna that makes it a popular stop for tourists in the Dells-Lake Delton area.

In the midst of the famous Wisconsin Dells–Lake Delton area, the calm reflective waters of Mirror Lake offer respite to weary travelers.

The 2,050-acre state park that encompasses part of the lake is a visitor attraction in itself. Swimming, hiking, picnicking, camping and winter sports attract more than 200,000 people each year.

Mirror Lake was formed by the old mill dam near Lake Delton in 1860. The dam, on Dell Creek, was used for years as part of a flour mill. Today, canoeists set out above the remodeled dam for a peaceful day on the lake.

Things To Do

The small size of Mirror Lake and its narrow gorge are ideally suited for exploration by small boats and canoes. There is not enough space on the lake for water-skiers, and powerboats are limited to 5 mph by local ordinance. Nearby Lake Delton and the Wisconsin River have more elbow room for powerboating and waterskiing. You can rent canoes or boats in the area. Anglers try for panfish, northern and bass from boats or from the boardwalk near the boat landing.

A popular canoe outing on Mirror Lake is to paddle downstream, under the Interstate 90-94 bridge, to visit the dam. After the return trip, you'll probably be ready for a swim or for some lazy time on the spacious

200-foot beach. Picnic grounds and a shelter building are just behind the beach.

Hikers may notice the varied shoreline of beach and sandstone cliffs while walking through pine and

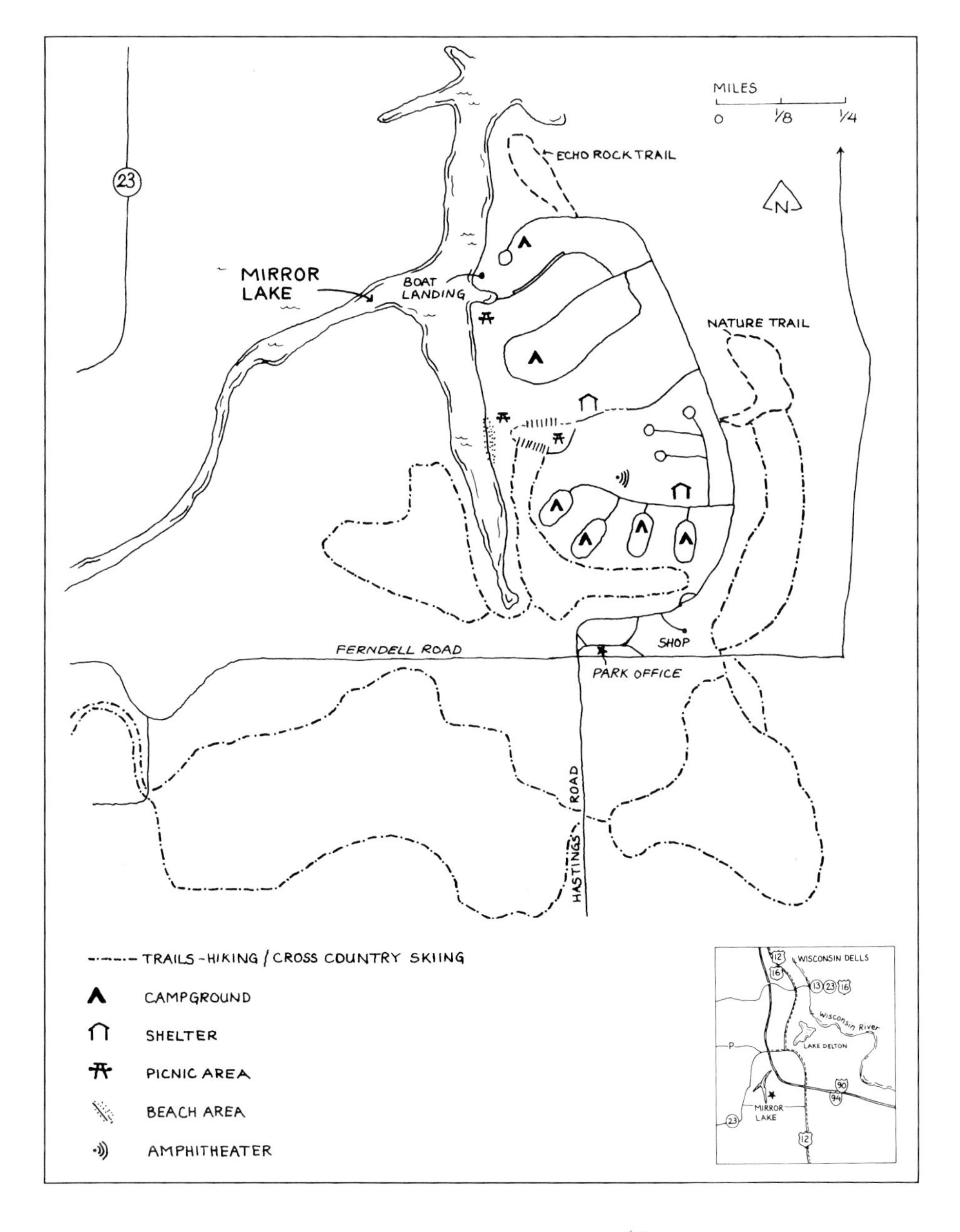

oak woods surrounding the lake. Beyond the trees are sandy prairies and abandoned farm fields, overgrown with wildflowers, shrubs and trees.

Winter is almost as active a season as summer at Mirror Lake State Park. Cross-country skiers tour the woods, open fields and prairies on over 12 miles of marked trails. They're favorites of beginning and intermediate skiers because they twist and roll enough for a bit of a challenge without being too difficult. Ice fishing on Mirror Lake can be good for panfish and occasional catches of northern and bass. Winter camping, hiking and snowshoeing lure increasing numbers of hardy outdoor lovers.

Flora and Fauna

The park is rich in wildlife. Observant hikers may spot deer, beaver, raccoon or red fox while exploring the park on more than 10 miles of hiking trails. For bird-watchers, spring and fall migrations are the best

Mirror Lake is an ideal place for a peaceful paddle enjoying the rock formations and the forested shoreline.

times for peak numbers and greatest variety of species. The park's lofty pines are also home to the pileated woodpecker, rarely seen outside northern forests.

Facilities

Tall trees in the 144-site campground (showers, 25 electrical hookups) impart a feeling of privacy, which can be a welcome change from the constant flow of people in the Dells. The park's 210-person group camp and many of the individual sites may be reserved. Mirror Lake is a convenient destination for visitors to the Dells area, and the campgrounds fill almost every night in the summer, especially on the weekends. The electrical sites are at a premium. There are many private campgrounds around the Dells in addition to Devil's Lake and Rocky Arbor state parks. Camping and picnic supplies are available in Wisconsin Dells or Lake Delton.

Surrounding Area

Besides the tourist attractions of Wisconsin Dells–Lake Delton, visitors to Mirror Lake have other options for side trips. Baraboo, to the south of the park, is home to the Circus World Museum, a State Historical Society of Wisconsin site that is filled with the sights, sounds and smells of the circus. The Baraboo Range, a region of wooded hills and hollows south and west of the park, is a great place to meander back roads for those with a wandering spirit.

The International Crane Foundation is another worthwhile family day trip from the park. The Foundation, between Baraboo and the Dells area, is dedicated to the protection of cranes and their wetland homes all around the world. You can take a guided tour to see the great white cranes, among the largest, rarest and most beautiful birds on earth. You'll also see the sacred cranes of the Orient. Watch new chicks hatch, take in an interpretive program or enjoy a picnic lunch. Trails lead through groves of oak and cherry trees, over rolling fields of prairie flowers and around a wetland left by the glacier. An admission fee is charged.

NATURAL BRIDGE STATE PARK

Sauk County. Take Highway 12 south of Baraboo or west and north of Sauk City to County C. Turn west on County C for 10 miles to the park. Highway map index: 9-F.

Main Attraction

Natural Bridge State Park is named for an impressive natural rock bridge that, according to a park historical marker, is "one of the oldest visible physical features carved in sandstone on the face of the earth."

The countryside around the natural bridge has a wild touch. Deer like to feed in the fields near the park at dawn and dusk, and hikers may observe other wildlife at quiet times.

The impressive natural rock bridge here was spared by the massive glaciers that stopped only 12 miles away. The cave beneath the arch provided shelter for Native Americans some 500 generations ago.

The wind-carved arch is in Wisconsin's Driftless Area, meaning that it was untouched by the massive glaciers. It's the state's largest natural bridge (the opening is 25 feet high by 35 feet wide), and among the most beautiful in North America.

The cave below the bridge provided shelter for Native Americans some 500 generations ago. White settlement dates back six generations. Excavations indicate that Native Americans lived here 11,000 years ago when the Wisconsin glacier, only 12 miles away, was melting along its farthest line of advance. This is one of the oldest authenticated sites of human habitation in the Upper Midwest.

Things To Do

To see the bridge, leave your car and take the marked trail that climbs up a gentle slope through the trees. This is a part of the nature trail with signs explaining in simple text how various Indian cultures used the vegetation in the area for medicine, food, charms and the like. Goldenrod, for example, was used as a cure for kidney ailments, while witch hazel was used as a thirst quencher. Take time to read the signs, to listen to the forest, to see the hills and to smell the woodsy fragrances.

The trail winds around a hill and climbs higher. Then, around another turn, is the sturdy, soft sandstone arch that forms the natural bridge.

You can enjoy a peaceful picnic in a clearing overlooking the dense woods of the Baraboo Range. Nearby is an old log homestead and smokehouse. This scene is most striking when the forest green transforms into the yellow, red and rust of autumn. The natural bridge photographs well in the fall when it's quiet here and the grand arch stands out more in the thinning foliage of the forest. The distinctive

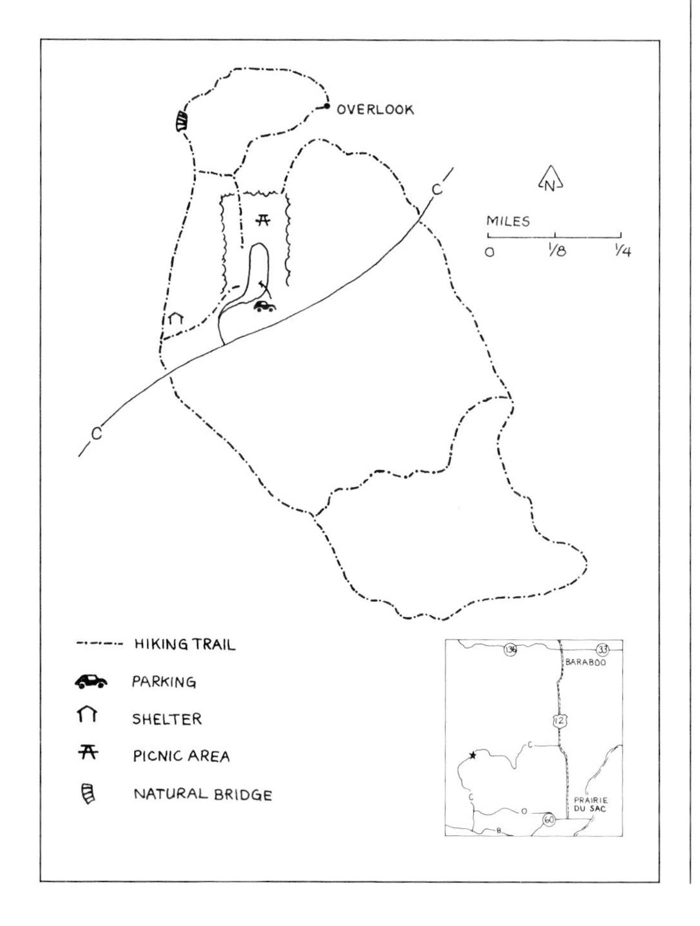

NATURAL BRIDGE

scent of dead leaves brings thoughts of winter and images of Indians preparing their cold-weather shelter in the sandstone cave. Rustle through the fallen leaves on the Indian Moccasin Nature Trail or while hiking the two-mile-long Whitetail Trail through the woods on the other side of the highway. The 530-acre park also features a 60-acre designated state natural area.

Flora and Fauna

The forest is mainly oak, with patches of prairie and open fields. Wildflowers bloom throughout the growing season. Bird-watchers might spot turkey vultures, pileated woodpeckers and, in winter, bald eagles.

Facilities

The park is usually uncrowded, partly because it's a day-use only facility (no camping). During a weekday or off-season visit, you may be the only person standing below the graceful natural bridge, bearing silent witness to its beauty. Camping is available at many local private campgrounds, or at Mirror Lake, Devil's Lake and Rocky Arbor state parks in the Wisconsin Dells–Baraboo area and at Tower Hill State Park near Spring Green.

Surrounding Area

The hilly, forested countryside around the natural bridge is fun to explore by car or bicycle. Sauk County is one of the state's most scenic, and the twisting, tree-lined roads often surprise the traveler with unexpected vistas. One of Wisconsin's rustic roads (R-21) winds down through the Baraboo Bluffs to Natural Bridge State Park.

Visitors also have a chance to ride and photograph a full-size steam train at the Mid-Continent Railway Museum in nearby North Freedom. You can see displays of antique railroad coaches, cabooses and freight cars as well as take a nine-mile trip on an authentic steam train through the Baraboo River Valley. Besides the daily summer season runs, special events like Autumn Color Weekend and Snow Train are favorites of train and photography buffs.

(opposite page)

The graceful natural bridge that gives this park its name is also one of the oldest sites of human habitation in the Midwest.

NECEDAH NATIONAL WILDLIFE REFUGE AND MEADOW VALLEY WILDLIFE AREA

Juneau County. The refuge office is about 5 miles northwest of Necedah off Grand Dike Road. Or, drive west of Necedah for about 3.5 miles on Highway 21 to the entrance road (marked by signs). Turn right on the entrance road for about two miles. Meadow Valley Wildlife Area headquarters is one mile west of Babcock on County X.

Main Attraction

The Necedah National Wildlife Refuge was established in 1939 primarily to give sanctuary and provide food and cover for migratory waterfowl. The 44,000-acre refuge is characterized by ponds and marshes separated by sandy ridges and islands. Administered by the U.S. Fish and Wildlife Service, the unit is part of the chain of refuges of the Mississippi Flyway, extending from Canada to the Gulf of Mexico.

This marshy land was clear-cut and drained for farmland in the 1800s and early 1900s. Now it's being reforested and the wetlands restored as a waterfowl refuge. The spring and fall migrations produce impressive numbers of birds resting here as they use the Mississippi flyway.

Necedah, a Winnebago Indian word meaning "land of yellow waters," lies within the bed of Glacial Lake Wisconsin. When the lake receded, a vast peat bog remained. Sand ridges developed and modified the flat topography of the lake bed. Gradually, islands of timber formed, completing the diverse landscape similar to what we see today—wetlands, openlands and woodlands.

Before the refuge was formed to restore the land to a productive wildlife habitat, settlers tried to make the land productive in other ways through logging, draining and farming. The large white and red pine that dominated the upland forest were clear cut during the late 1800s. After the logging was completed, numerous drainage ditches were dug in an attempt to farm the area in the early part of this century. A short, unpredictable growing season, poor soil and excessive drainage taxes caused most of the farms to be abandoned in the late 1930s. During the Civilian Conservation Corps era, several areas were reforested and drainage ditch plugs were installed to maintain water levels in man-made impoundments.

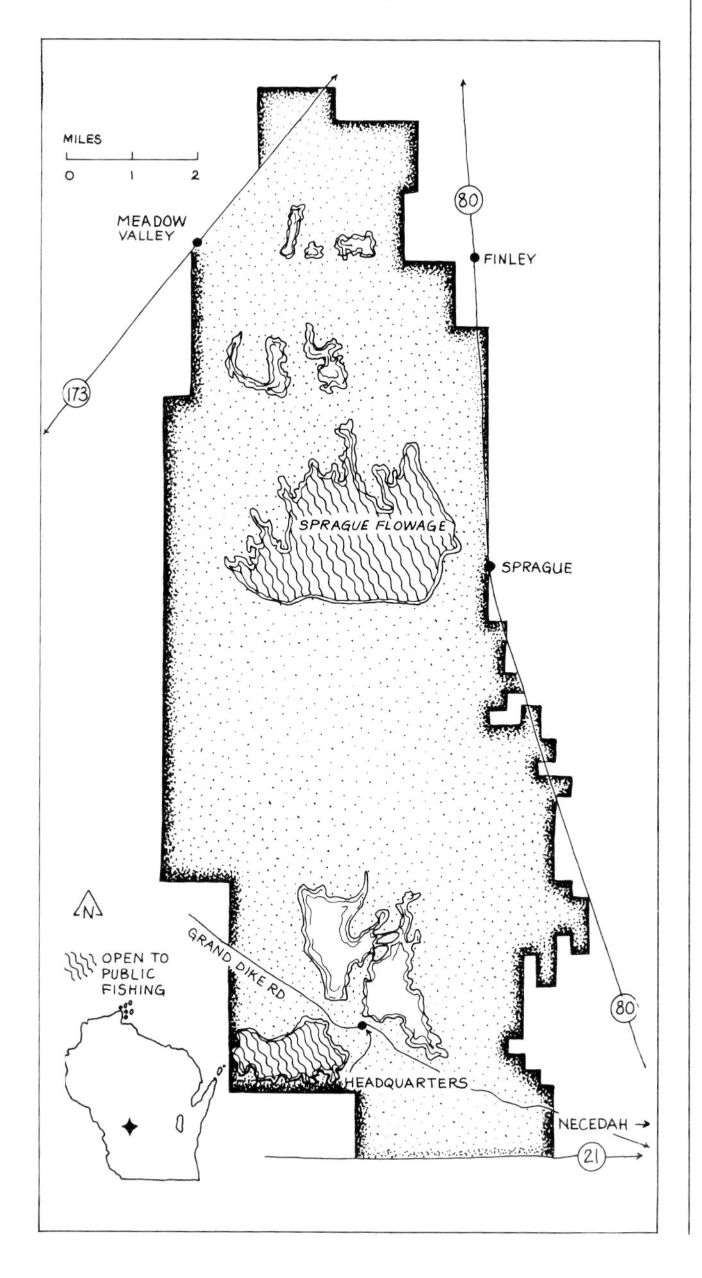

Now, wetland management in the refuge involves manipulation of water levels to benefit waterfowl. About one-fourth of the Necedah habitat is wetland, including the major impoundments and 70 miles of ditches used to move water from one area of the refuge to another.

Although many species of birds nest here, the spring and fall migrations of waterfowl are the most interesting feature of the refuge. The peak populations in fall are usually reached in mid-October, including thousands of Canada geese and some snow geese. In spring, the refuge plays host to the greatest number of birds in late April. A small breeding flock of Canada geese was introduced here in the 1950s. The descendants of these birds return to the area each spring to raise about 100 young.

The refuge openlands are just as important to waterfowl as water is. The prairie provides nesting cover and farm fields provide feeding grounds. Occasional prescribed burning kills undesirable grasses, weeds and oak sprouts, preserving habitat for sharp-tailed grouse and white-tailed deer. Green browse and some grain crops are planted in fields to serve as a fall food source for Canada geese, ducks, sandhill cranes and white-tailed deer.

Things To Do

You can explore the various habitats of the refuge by hiking or cross-country skiing on designated trails or township roads. An auto tour is also mapped out. Hunting for deer and some types of upland game is permitted in certain zones during portions of the state hunting season. The Sprague Mather and Goose pools are open for fishing from December 15 through March 15 and June 1 through September 15. Only canoes and boats without motors may be used in these pools. Stop at the refuge office for details about touring, hunting and fishing at Necedah.

Thousands of sportsmen, bird-watchers, berry pickers, hikers and other outdoor enthusiasts visit Meadow Valley (Central Wisconsin Conservation Area) each year. Hunters and trappers are attracted to the area by its size and abundant wildlife populations. You can also fish, canoe, observe wildlife, cross-country ski and snowmobile (only on marked trails).

Flora and Fauna

The wetlands and adjacent shoreline provide feeding grounds and nesting cover for geese, ducks and cranes. Beaver, muskrat, and mink also live here.

The refuge woodlands consist mostly of jack pine and scrub oak mixtures on the uplands and aspen and scrub willow in the lowlands. Clearing and cutting will help to maintain woodland habitat for deer, skunk, squirrel, opossum, coyote and ruffed grouse.

The Meadow Valley Wildlife Area (west and south of the refuge) is a 98-square-mile tract owned by the U.S. Fish and Wildlife Service but leased to and managed by the state of Wisconsin. The wildlife area has the same geological and human history as the refuge and is also managed for the benefit of forest wildlife and waterfowl.

Facilities

Primitive campsites, open from September 1 through December 31, are spread throughout Meadow Valley. No camping fee is charged, but campers should still self-register.

Surrounding Area

Two other state wildlife areas are north of Meadow Valley and the Necedah Wildlife Refuge. The Wood County Wildlife Area, 35 square miles, is managed for upland wildlife such as white-tailed deer, and sharp-tailed and ruffed grouse.

The Sandhill Wildlife Demonstration Area (9,320 acres) is used for experimental game management practices. A 12-mile, all-weather road runs through the unit. Called the Trumpeter Trail, this self-guiding nature trail stops at points of interest explaining wildlife management and natural history. Two observation towers are accessible from this road. The North Bluff Tower provides a panoramic view of the area and the

(continued)

(overleaf)

The wetlands and shorelines at Necedah provide feeding grounds for wading birds such as these blue herons.

Marsh Tower gives a close-up view of migrating waterfowl and sandhill cranes. Visitors may also view a small buffalo herd in a 280-acre fenced pasture. Sandhill's 20-mile hiking trail has four picnic sites spaced along its route. No camping is allowed in the demonstration area, but you can camp in a 40-unit campground adjacent to the Wood County Wildlife Area.

If you run out of outdoor activities in the central Wisconsin wildlife areas, you won't have to go far to find more fun. Just to the east is the Castle Rock–Petenwell Lakes area. Mill Bluff and Buckhorn state parks are also a short drive away.

RIB MOUNTAIN STATE PARK

Marathon County. Just west of Wausau off Highway 51. Exit Highway 51 at County N and follow the signs to the park. Highway map index: 5-F.

Main Attraction

Rib Mountain is really just a hill, and not even Wisconsin's tallest spot, as once believed. (There are two hills farther north—Pearson Hill and Tim's Hill—that are slightly higher.) Even so, it's the state's most prominent land mass, rising 650 feet above the surrounding flatlands.

Rib Mountain is one of the best downhill ski areas in the state, and Marathon County offers an extensive cross-country ski trail system.

Based on the geological evidence, the quartzite rock formations that form the backbone of the mountain were at one time submerged below a great inland sea. Then, with a tremendous upheaval caused by pressures within the earth, Rib Mountain was formed along with other massive hills in the area. The Indians called these protruding formations "ribs," which in turn has inspired the park's name.

The park was born in 1929 after the Kiwanis Club of Wausau bought the first 160 acres and donated the land to the state. A portion of the existing ski chalet, the stone toilet building, trails, trail shelters and the water system were all built by the Civilian Conservation Corps. The CCC also helped develop the ski slopes on the northern side of the mountain.

Things To Do

The vistas from the 860-acre park are the reason most visitors come here. From the 60-foot observation tower, you'll get long-distance views of Wausau and the surrounding farm and woodland. A camera, a picnic lunch and a little time are all you need for a relaxing visit to Rib Mountain. A rustic gazebo and a new park shelter stand by in case of rain. Picnic and camping supplies are available in Wausau. You can buy soft drinks or browse for souvenirs in the park concession stand.

Over three miles of hiking and nature trails twist back and forth along Rib Mountain. The Mountain Maple Nature Trail is marked with 30 signs that depict the geology, and the plant and animal life of the park. Among other trails that run the length of the park are some that lead to Sunset Point, some to the campground or scenic lookouts. A small hilltop rock formation, featuring the Queen's Chair, is a fun climb and easy to scale for kids of all ages.

The downhill ski area keeps Rib Mountain busy during the winter. The state used to maintain the ski runs, but the property is now leased to a private operator who works in conjunction with a community civic group and the DNR. Chair lifts, new slopes, snow-grooming and snow-making equipment help to make this one of Wisconsin's best downhill ski areas. Nighttime skiing is another attraction of the ski area, which is open from early December through March.

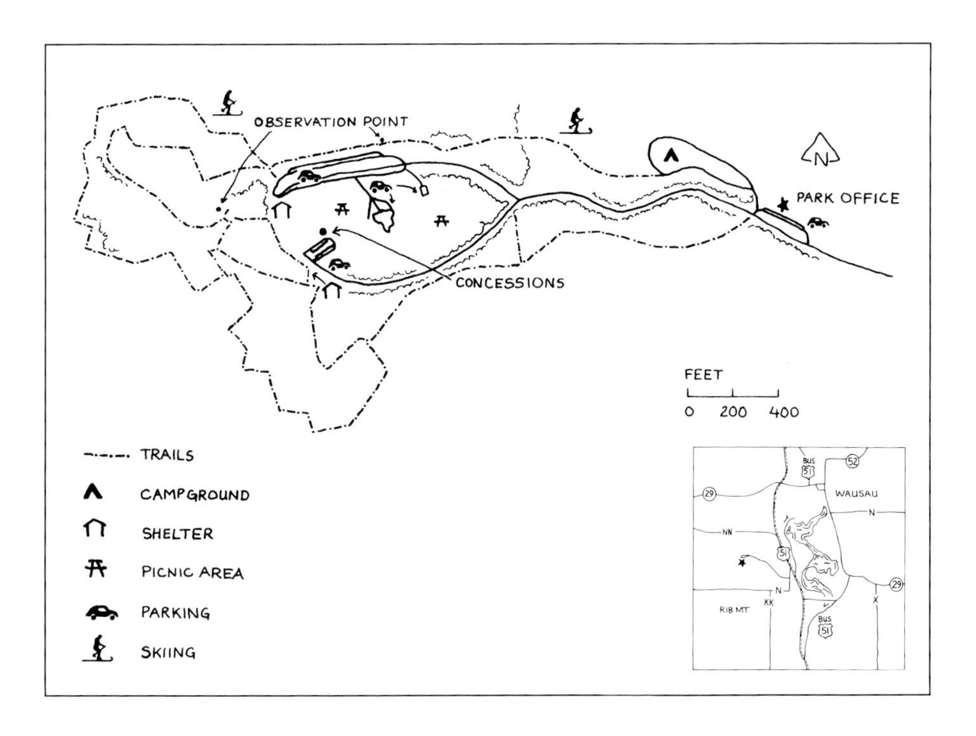

Rib Mountain caters to downhill skiers of all ages and abilities.

To reach the slopes, exit on County NN from Highway 51 and drive west for three quarters of a mile.

Facilities

Rib Mountain State Park's campground is small (30 sites), but shaded and peaceful. Even though the campground currently has no showers or electrical hookups, it attracts a loyal corps of campers who return each season. There is no swimming in the park, but you can find out about local facilities by asking at the contact station.

(continued on next page)

Surrounding Area

Wausau, by rough translation of an Indian word, means "place from which you can see far." The Marathon County countryside that sweeps below Rib Mountain is a national leader in the production of dairy products, especially cheese. The Wausau area is also a major producer of cultivated ginseng (shang), a root highly valued by eastern cultures for its folk medicinal powers. The ginseng, mostly exported to Korea and China, grows on large plots of land covered by mesh or lattices. To get a closer view of ginseng plots, drive west of Rib Mountain on County N.

Other Wausau attractions include the Leigh Yawkey Woodson Art Museum and the Marathon County Historical Museum. The art museum specializes in wildlife art and features a famous collection of bird art.

Cross-country skiers are in luck in Marathon County. Seven major groomed trail systems provide over 52 miles of skiing for all ability levels on county forests, parks and private land. The rolling glaciated terrain of the county makes for scenic touring and a chance to observe deer and other woodland wildlife. Trail information and maps are available from the Marathon County Ski Trail Coordinator, Park Department, Courthouse, Wausau, WI 54401 (715-847-5235). You can also contact the Park Department about county snowmobile trails.

ROCHE-A-CRI STATE PARK

Adams County. One mile north of Adams-Friendship on Highway 13. Highway map index: 7-F.

Main Attraction

The big flat-topped, cliff-sided rock that juts above the surrounding woods gives Roche-a-Cri State Park its name. French explorers and fur trappers called it Roche-a-Cris, or "crevice in the rock," referring to the large cleft in the rock's structure that is visible at some distance. The best view of the 300-foot sandstone bluff is from Czech Road, just south of the park entrance. From here, you can see the proud-looking formation from several angles across a grassy field.

The Roche-a-Cri butte, listed on the National Register of Historic Places, was used as a landmark by Indians, explorers and pioneers. Some tribes fashioned petroglyphs (rock carvings) of crowsfeet, arches and curved and straight lines on the south side of the mound and in a nearby cave. Since an 1851 government survey crew discovered the carvings, so many others have scratched their marks on the massive monolith that the original inscriptions are almost gone in many places. A fence now prevents further mutilation, but you can still see some of the petroglyphs as well as graffiti. One inscription reads: "A.V. Dean, NY 1861." This may have been carved by a soldier from a Union Army troop bivouacked here briefly during the Civil War.

The Roche-a-Cri Butte has been a landmark for Indians, explorers and pioneers. Now the intimate atmosphere here attracts a loyal group of visitors including many bicyclists.

Like many similar formations on Wisconsin's sandy central plain, Roche-a-Cri is composed of Cambrian sandstone about 500,000 years old. The plain is the ancient bed of Glacial Lake Wisconsin, which covered 1,800 square miles of central Wisconsin about 15,000 years ago. Roche-a-Cri, Mill Bluff (in Mill Bluff State Park) and other buttes were islands in the immense lake.

Today, the many faces of Roche-a-Cri are good examples of nature's erosive power. Visitors probably won't notice the changes from season to season, but wind, rain, freezing and thawing continue to work away at the rock.

Things To Do

Of the 3.5 miles of trails in the park, the Snowbird Cross Country Ski and Nature Trail (Trail A) is the longest, looping through the woodlands surrounding the rock. Pause to read the trail signs to find out about the human and natural resource history of the area. The Chickadee Rock Trail (Trail B) leads to small rock formations on the park's northeast corner. The

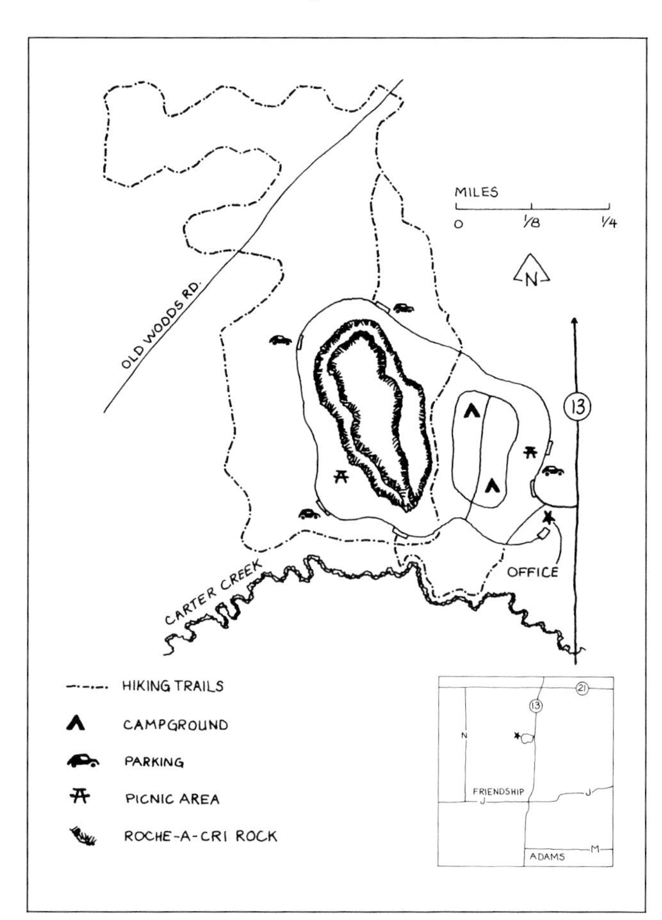

(opposite page)

A hiker pauses to inspect rock carvings in a small cave at Roche-a-Cri State Park.

Kingfisher Trail (Trail C) follows part of Carter Creek near the grass field south of the great rock.

Climbing is allowed on the mound but only with a free permit. To get one, contact the Forest Ranger, DNR Ranger Station, P.O. Box 100, Friendship, WI 53934, and briefly describe how you'll complete the climb, when you plan to go, your climbing experience and the number of other people involved. The forest ranger will send an application back to you that will take about two weeks to process and, if it's approved, he'll send a climbing permit that is valid for a specific day.

Originally a roadside park, Roche-a-Cri's intimate atmosphere still makes it an attractive spot for a picnic lunch or a hike in the shadow of the butte. The park has developed a loyal group of visitors who return each summer, including many bicyclists.

Facilities

The 411-acre semi-wilderness park offers shaded peaceful picnic areas with fresh water. The campground (45 sites) is in a scenic stand of mature white pines and red oaks. Showers and electrical hookups are not provided. All campsites are available on a first-come, first-served basis, and campers will usually find a vacancy except on holiday weekends. You can pick up supplies in nearby Adams and Friendship.

Surrounding Area

Roche-a-Cri is close to other public recreation lands including the Castle Rock–Petenwell Lakes area to the west of the Wisconsin River. Buckhorn, Mill Bluff and Rocky Arbor state parks and the Necedah National Wildlife Area are within easy driving distance of the park.

ROCKY ARBOR STATE PARK

Sauk County. Two miles north of Wisconsin Dells on Highway 12. Highway map index: 8-F.

Main Attraction

Rocky Arbor State Park (225 acres) is a small but pretty park noted for its attractive rock formations. Just down the road is the tourist bustle of Wisconsin Dells–Lake Delton, yet a visit to Rocky Arbor seems distant in comparison.

Try a picnic in the large grove of pines in this small park, then hike the tree-covered rocky ledges for which the park is named.

Complete peace and quiet is not possible here. The park is sandwiched between Highway 12 and Interstate 90-94, yet it's relatively easy to let traffic sounds blend into the background while you enjoy the beauty of the woods and sandstone bluffs.

The sandstone formations were cut when the Wisconsin River flowed through here. The river now winds one and a half miles east of the park. The tiny stream in the gorge at Rocky Arbor actually flows in the opposite direction that the river did when it carved this scenic area. Geologists believe that the rock that forms the gorge is about 500 million years old. The sand grains may have been deposited by rivers draining into shallow seas. When the seas receded, the sand compacted into sandstone.

Things To Do

A special experience in the park is a picnic lunch in a large grove of pine trees. The aroma of the tall pines adds an olfactory spice to the meal that the Dells-area restaurants just can't match.

A leisurely hike along the self-guided nature trail is a good way to get the feel of Rocky Arbor, named for its many tree-covered rocky ledges. Signs posted along the path describe the natural features of the park in simple language. You'll be able to see the difference between the warm- and cool-climate plant communities. Northern plant species inhabit a shaded, moist gorge below the bluffs while a dry oak woods, typical of southern Wisconsin, grows on top.

Try camping at Rocky Arbor for a few nights while on a bicycle touring trip. From the park, you have access to back roads to explore, yet can avoid heavy traffic, and it's an easy ride into Wisconsin Dells.

Facilities

Weekdays are not crowded at Rocky Arbor, and campsites are usually available then in the 89-site wooded campground (showers, 18 electrical hookups). Of

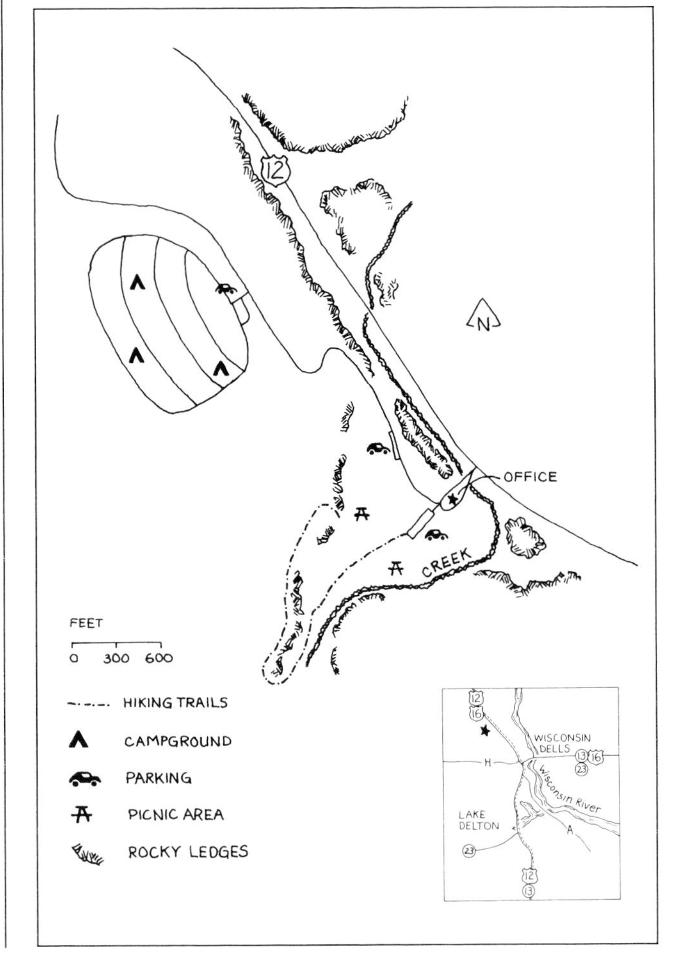

the three state parks in the Wisconsin Dells–Lake Delton area (Rocky Arbor, Devil's Lake and Mirror Lake) it is easiest to get a campsite at Rocky Arbor. The other two are larger, better known and have swimming beaches. Campsites are on a first-come, first-served basis at Rocky Arbor.

The sandstone rock formations cut by the Wisconsin River make this an attractive place for exploring and picnicking.

EAST WISCONSIN WATERS

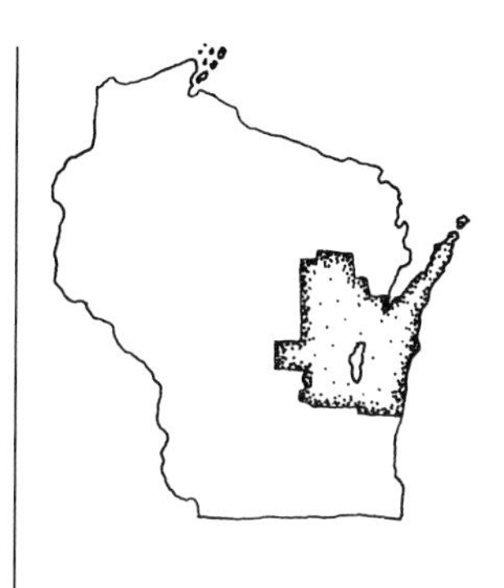

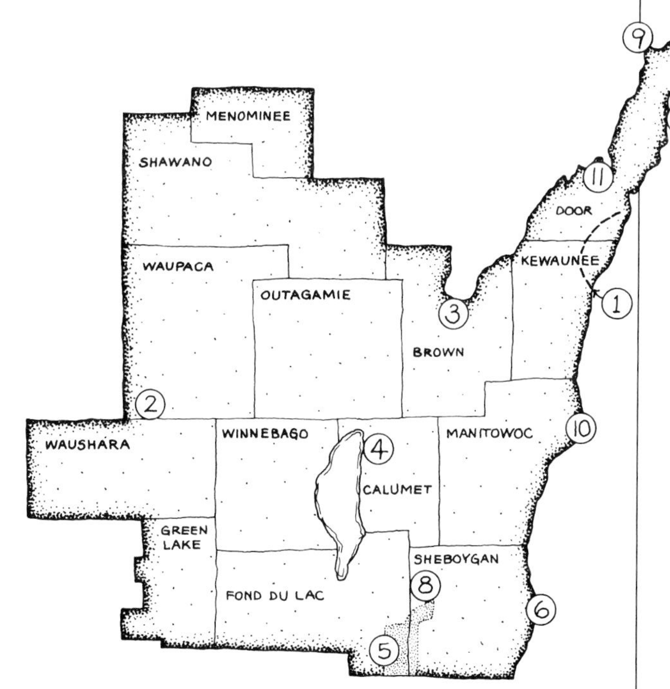

1. Ahnapee State Trail
2. Hartman Creek State Park
3. Heritage Hill State Park
4. High Cliff State Park
5. Kettle Moraine State Forest—Northern Unit
6. Kohler-Andrae State Park
7. Newport State Park
8. Old Wade House State Park
9. Peninsula State Park
10. Point Beach State Forest
11. Potawatomi State Park
12. Rock Island State Park
13. Whitefish Dunes State Park

(opposite page)

The meltwaters of the glaciers left an abundance of lakes in Wisconsin.

AHNAPEE STATE TRAIL

Door and Kewaunee counties. 15.3 miles, between Sturgeon Bay and Algoma. Trail heads: One mile north of Algoma on County M; take Shiloh Road (south) from the State Highway 42/57 bypass around Sturgeon Bay and follow the signs. Highway map index: 6-J.

Things To Do

The Ahnapee State Trail is a former railroad grade that was designated a National Recreation Trail in 1976. It is also part of the 1,000-mile Ice Age Trail, which begins in the nearby Potawatomi State Park.

Hiking, snowmobiling and cross-country skiing are the main trail uses. It currently is not surfaced for bicycles. The trail is named for the Ahnapee River, which parallels the route for about five miles. Hikers will pass through the Ahnapee Wildlife Refuge and walk past the Forestville Millpond. The millpond, a peaceful spot for a lunch break, is especially pretty in the fall. Door and Kewaunee counties are known for their maple trees, and hikers are in for a treat when the leaves light up.

The trail leads hikers through a wildlife refuge and along the Ahnapee River. The Forestville Millpond is especially pretty in the fall when the maples are in full color.

The Ahnapee is mostly a level trail, passing rich farmland, wetlands and a county park just north of Forestville. There's a parking lot at the northern trail head. At the southern end of the trail, a wooden bridge spans the Ahnapee River where waterfowl rest and feed. You can try your luck with the trout and salmon here or scout for some of the deer that frequent the neighboring stands of cedar and pine.

Whatever supplies you need can be picked up at the trail heads in Sturgeon Bay and Algoma, or in the mid-trail towns of Maplewood and Forestville. Camping is not available along the trail, but you can camp at the Potawatomi State Park near Sturgeon Bay or at one of the private campgrounds in the area.

Surrounding Area

For general information about Door County, the famous "thumb" of Wisconsin that sticks out into Lake Michigan, stop at the Door County Chamber of Commerce visitor center in Sturgeon Bay on Highway 42/57.

Sturgeon Bay, the largest community in Door County, is worth a visit after your day on the Ahnapee Trail. The city of 8,000 has been a canoe portage, a fur trading post and a sawmill town. Today it is the

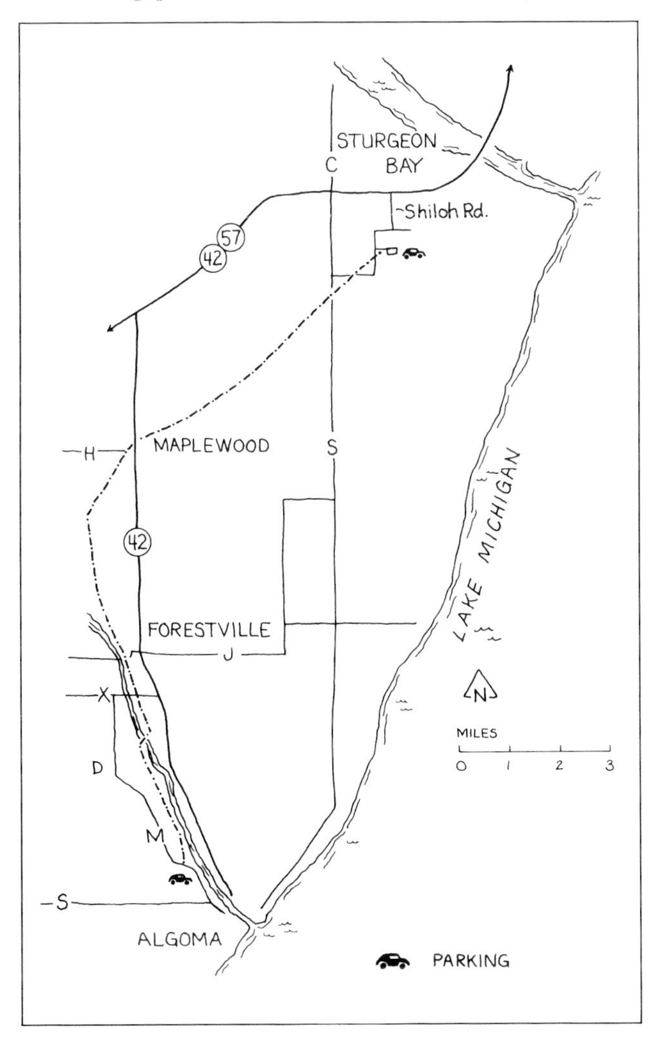

largest inland shipbuilding port on the Great Lakes. There are three major shipyards in Sturgeon Bay that build everything from racing yachts to lake "boats" up to 1,000 feet long. Climb aboard the *Lollipop* excursion boat for tours around the bay, the shipyards and the ship canal. Sturgeon Bay is also a center for fishing charters, sailing charters and boat rentals. Some visitors may be interested in the county historical museum and the maritime museum. At the Lake Michigan end of the ship canal is a Coast Guard station and a picturesque breakwater and lighthouse. When the cutter *Mobile Bay* is in her berth, visitors can sometimes go aboard for a tour.

HARTMAN CREEK STATE PARK

Waupaca County. Six miles west of Waupaca on Highway 54. Highway map index: 7-G.

Main Attraction

Hartman Creek State Park is a year-round recreation area of peaceful woods and spring-fed lakes. If you like to boat, bike and hike, you'll probably want to visit here more than once.

Things To Do

The four lakes provide good fishing action for largemouth bass, northern, perch, bluegills and a few muskies. Though there are no public landings, small boats and canoes may be portaged to Allen, Hartman, Grebe or Middle lakes and launched from the shore. Electric motors (no gas) are allowed on the park lakes. Resident and nonresident fishing licenses are available in the park office. Public access to the 22 connecting spring-fed lakes that form the Waupaca Chain O' Lakes is less than a mile from the park.

Commercial tours of the Chain O' Lakes are available by motor yacht and sternwheeler. Visitors can rent boats, canoes and bicycles at private outlets within a short drive of the park. For more information about the lake excursions, equipment rentals and county recreation (including 240 lakes, 35 trout streams and four good canoeing rivers), contact the Waupaca County Chamber of Commerce, P.O. Box 262, Waupaca, WI 54981 (715-258-7343).

Whether you rent a bicycle or bring your own, Hartman Creek State Park is an excellent place for biking because of four area trails that are easily accessible from the park. The one-mile Coach Road Bicycle Trail is named after the old stagecoach route from Oshkosh to Stevens Point. This is a popular trail for families because it's free from motor vehicle traffic. Pick up the trail in the park just east of the "T" intersection. When you reach the metal gate at the end of the trail, you can either return to the trail head or connect with the Whispering Pines or Rural Excursion bike trail.

The four-mile Rural Excursion Trail passes by a handful of historic homes, each posted with an information name plate (ask at the park office for a brochure about these historic sites). Although this trail is scenic, winding through the Chain O' Lakes, there is motor vehicle traffic on the roads. After you ride over the Indian Crossing Bridge, the trail connects with the Whispering Pines Bike Trail, which will take you back to the park.

The Whispering Pines Bike Trail (seven miles) begins in the park's family campground. You'll pass the park lakes and continue through the Chain O' Lakes before looping back to the entrance. The Allen Creek

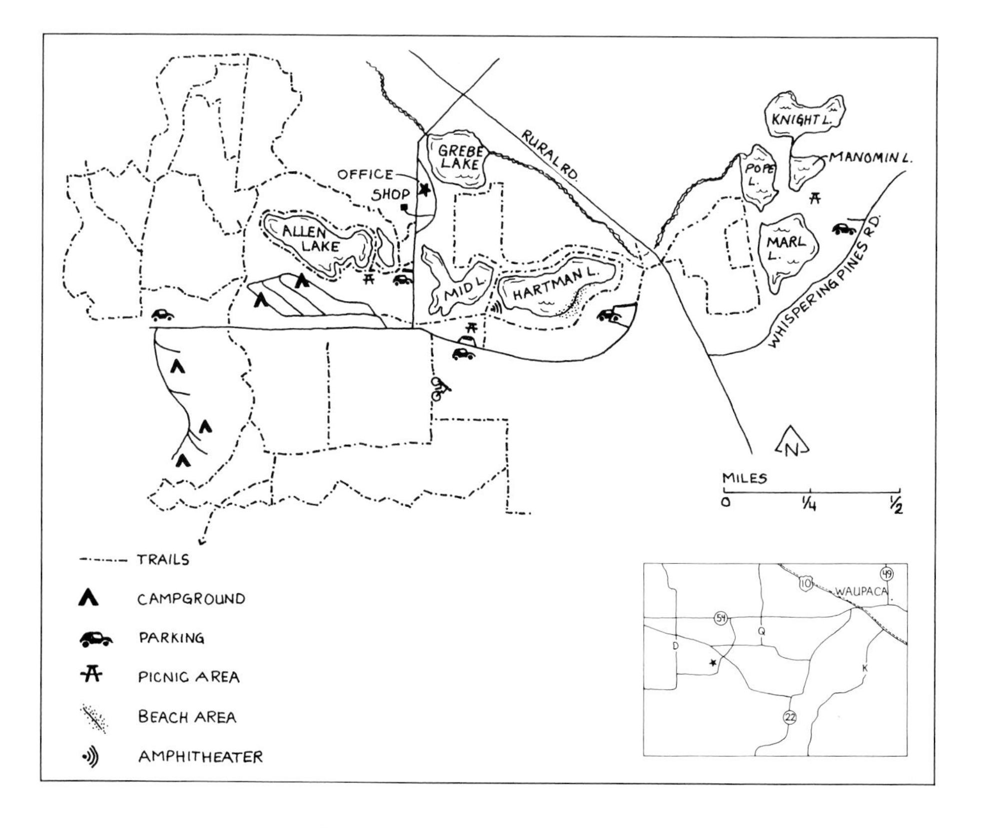

Bike Trail (5.5 miles) also starts in the campground, but loops around the western end of the park on public roads. Before starting out on any of these bicycle adventures, pick up a map and trail descriptions at the park office.

The 14-mile hiking trail system at Hartman Creek is a good one. Paths wind around the lakes, through natural hardwood stands and red pine plantations and across rolling fields. A self-guided nature trail loop begins at the west end of Allen Lake. If you like to look for plants, insects, birds and animals to identify, allow yourself extra time to explore Hartman Creek's trails.

The combination of glacial features, forests and lakes makes Hartman Creek a wonderful place for hiking.

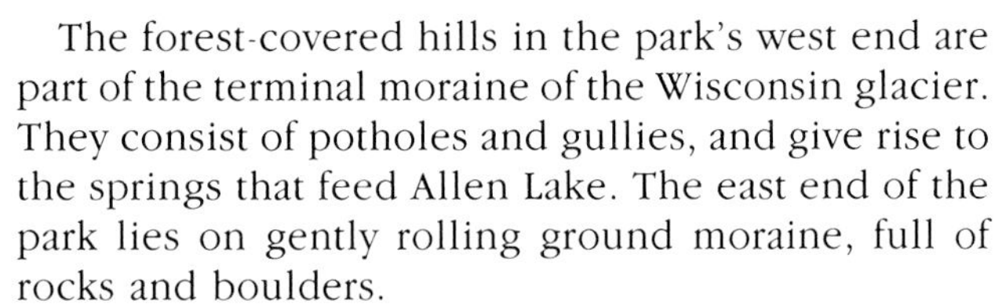

The forest-covered hills in the park's west end are part of the terminal moraine of the Wisconsin glacier. They consist of potholes and gullies, and give rise to the springs that feed Allen Lake. The east end of the park lies on gently rolling ground moraine, full of rocks and boulders.

The four lakes in the park provide good fishing. You'll also be close to another 240 lakes, 35 trout streams and four good canoeing rivers. Add bike trails, biking trails and lake excursions, and you have the basics for a great vacation.

Part of the 1,000-mile Ice Age National Scenic Trail (Wisconsin), which traces the farthest advance of the last glacier, passes through the state park and the Emmons Creek Fishery and Wildlife Area to the south. Look for the yellow blazes on trees and yellow signs that mark the route. The trail and 370 acres of the park are posted open for the deer hunting season only. The rest of the park is a wildlife refuge.

As winter arrives and covers the fields and woods with snow, Hartman Creek State Park becomes a popular winter sports area. Snowmobilers, cross-country skiers and hikers each have their own marked trails that offer scenic views of the lakes, fields and forests. Some prefer the fun of tobogganing or sledding on the park's snowy slopes. Others try their fishing luck on the park's frozen lake. The four miles of snowmobile trails connect to the Waupaca County trail system. Cross-country skiers and other winter visitors are welcome to warm up in the wood-heated shelter. Several campsites are open during the winter, so bring your snow weather toys along and stay for a couple of days.

Flora and Fauna

Hartman Creek's vegetation is in the transition zone where oaks and prairies of the south meet northern hardwoods and pines. The park has many acres of meadows that resemble the prairies and an interesting mixture of plant life common to both northern and southern Wisconsin. Interested visitors can learn more about the park by participating in the weekly summertime naturalist programs and guided hikes. Check the schedule at the park office.

Facilities

While hiking on the 1,300-acre park, take a picnic lunch along for a trail break. Or, you can plan a picnic in one of the four picnic areas in the park. There is a large picnic ground among the hardwoods and pines on a knoll overlooking Allen Lake. The pleasing view makes this a popular relaxation spot. Hartman Lake has picnic tables with a shelter. There are also picnic tables near the swimming beach on Hartman Lake. The picnic area at Whispering Pines, at the east end of the park, is bordered by three of the Chain O' Lakes—Marl, Pope and Manomin—and is a favorite among anglers and canoeists on the lake.

The family campground (100 sites, showers) is on a small bluff among red pine trees and old apple orchards overlooking Allen Lake. There's also a large group camp in the southwest corner of the park. Reservations are accepted for both campgrounds. The park has a Volunteer Campground Host program and, in addition, benefits from other volunteers who present evening naturalist activities or offer their labor for park projects.

HERITAGE HILLS STATE PARK

Brown County. Junction of highways 172 and 57, 2640 S. Webster Avenue, Green Bay. Highway map index: 6-I.

Main Attraction

History lives at Heritage Hills State Park where visitors get hands-on experience in discovering the past of northeastern Wisconsin. Costumed interpreters recreate the life and times of pioneers, fur traders and settlers from when Jean Nicolet set foot in present-day Wisconsin in 1634 to the decline of the Victorian era around the end of the 19th century.

A cooperative effort makes Heritage Hills a success. The park is owned by the Wisconsin Department of Natural Resources and is operated by the Heritage Hill Corporation, a local nonprofit group. Funds for development are raised by the Heritage Hill State Park Foundation. Some of the interpreters you will meet are members of the Heritage Hill Guild, a support group that provides thousands of volunteer hours each year in addition to sponsoring many of the park's special events.

Things To Do

Living history is fun, and you can learn a lot without even trying. When you visit the fur trader, you can barter with him over the price of the fox and beaver pelts "you brought him." Afterward, you can help his wife dip candles or go to the Fort Howard Officers' Mess Hall to see the hard work involved with fireplace cookery. Wherever you go at Heritage Hill, you'll see and have a chance to participate in living history demonstrations. The interpreters, who seem like they just stepped out of a time machine, will happily answer your questions.

The park has four theme areas: Pioneer Heritage,

Military Heritage, Agricultural/Ethnic Heritage and Small Town Heritage. The present structures range from a French missionary bark chapel to restored Fort Howard buildings and small-town homes and businesses. Stop at the Tank Cottage, one of Wisconsin's oldest homes (built in 1776) to chat with Madame Tank while she works at her needlework, music or art. Visit the blacksmith shop, fur trader's cabin or Wisconsin's first courthouse. Your nose may lead you to the turn-of-the-century Belgian Farmstead, where the aroma of freshly baked bread and traditional Belgian dishes fills the summer kitchen.

During the May to mid-December season, nearly a dozen special events are held at Heritage Hill. An

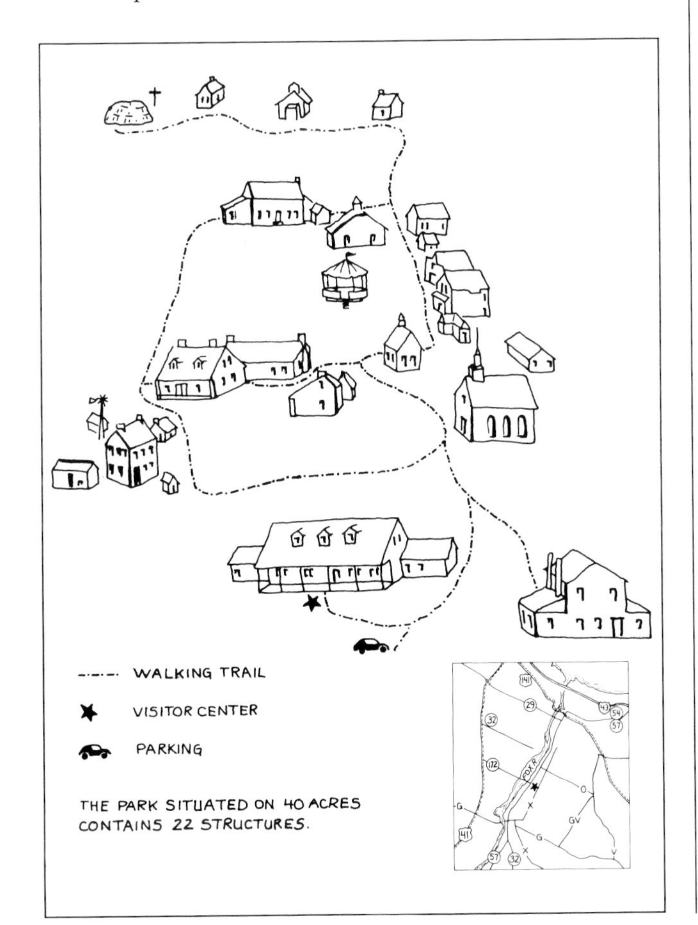

Relive the history of Wisconsin from 1634 to the Victorian Era with the help of costumed interpreters and a detailed setting for each period. Holidays are especially fun.

authentic Civil War reenactment features simulated skirmishes, the Rendezvous relives the spirit of Wisconsin's fur trade, and the old-fashioned Independence Day festivities include an ice cream social and podium-thumping speeches. You can enjoy the "Music on the Green" concerts on the Victorian bandstand at various times during the summer as the Green Bay Summer Symphony and a variety of groups provide the entertainment.

The County Fair in September is full of family activities and games. Craft demonstrations, races and cakewalks are just part of the old-time fun.

You may enjoy the two-week Christmas Festival the most. Called the "Spirit of Christmas Past," the festival is a wonderful mixture of sights, smells and sounds. The houses are decorated beginning the Friday after Thanksgiving according to the ethnic background of the occupants. Decorations vary from practically none at the fur trader's cabin to elaborate Victorian settings in Cotton House. The aromas from kitchen ovens, the tinkle of sleigh bells and the echoes of caroling bring back the tradition of Christmas past in Wisconsin. Check at the visitor's center or call the number listed in the back of this book for dates and times of specific special events.

Allow over two hours to experience Heritage Hill. (Horse-drawn transportation is available on weekends and a shuttle takes visitors to all areas of the park. An admission fee is charged.) With all the seasonal special events, it's hard to say that you've seen the park. That's why many people purchase season passes to return for more fun. Heritage Hill has a friendly ambiance that comes from people who enjoy their roots. You can come here to share this feeling, but be forewarned that it's contagious.

Surrounding Area

Green Bay is the center of arts and entertainment for northeastern Wisconsin. To find out what there is to see and do in the area, get a copy of *Leisure Times*, published twice yearly by the Green Bay Area Visitor and Convention Bureau (P.O. Box 10596, Green Bay, WI 54307-0596; 414-494-9507).

(opposite page)

"Traders" discuss the finer points of fur pelts before settling on a purchase at the general store.

(opposite page)

Old world ways of doing things are preserved and demonstrated at Heritage Hills.

HIGH CLIFF STATE PARK

Calumet County. Northeast shore of Lake Winnebago. Ten miles east of Appleton on highways 10, 114 and 55 (follow the signs). Highway map index: 7-H.

Main Attraction

In winter, frozen Lake Winnebago is covered with shanties as people fish for everything from panfish to 100-pound lake sturgeon. The view from the cliffs is inspiring in any season.

High Cliff State Park borders on Lake Winnebago, one of the largest inland lakes in the United States. The 1,145-acre park gets its name from the limestone cliffs that parallel the eastern shore of the lake through the park lands.

Lake Winnebago, 215 square miles, fills a massive depression gouged out of the earth by the Green Bay lobe of the Wisconsin glacier that covered this area about 25,000 years ago. The limestone cliffs, locally known as the "ledge," rise 223 feet above the lake. The ledge is actually the exposed western edge of the Niagara Escarpment. The dolomite rock layer that forms the escarpment tilts to the southeast with the exposed edge for 900 miles to Niagara Falls via Wisconsin's Door Peninsula, Michigan and Canada.

Things To Do

Most park visitors come to enjoy the lake and the scenery. Boats up to 30 feet long may use the marina near the north park entrance and occupants may stay aboard overnight while moored here. Water-skiers, fishermen and pleasure boaters enter the lake by any of six launching ramps. Fishing on Lake Winnebago usually includes sand pike, walleyed pike, panfish and white bass. Winter visitors have an unusual opportunity to spear lake sturgeon through the ice during special spearing seasons. Sturgeons, Wisconsin's largest fish, can range from 50 to 100 pounds.

The small High Cliff general store near the beach used to be the main building of the Western Lime and Cement Company, which operated a limestone quarry here in the late 19th century. Ruins of the lime kilns and the remains of the quarry are still visible in the park. Today, the old general store serves as the nature center and the park museum where you can find out more about the effigy mound builders, kiln and quarry operations and the Wisconsin glacier. The naturalist program features guided hikes, campfire

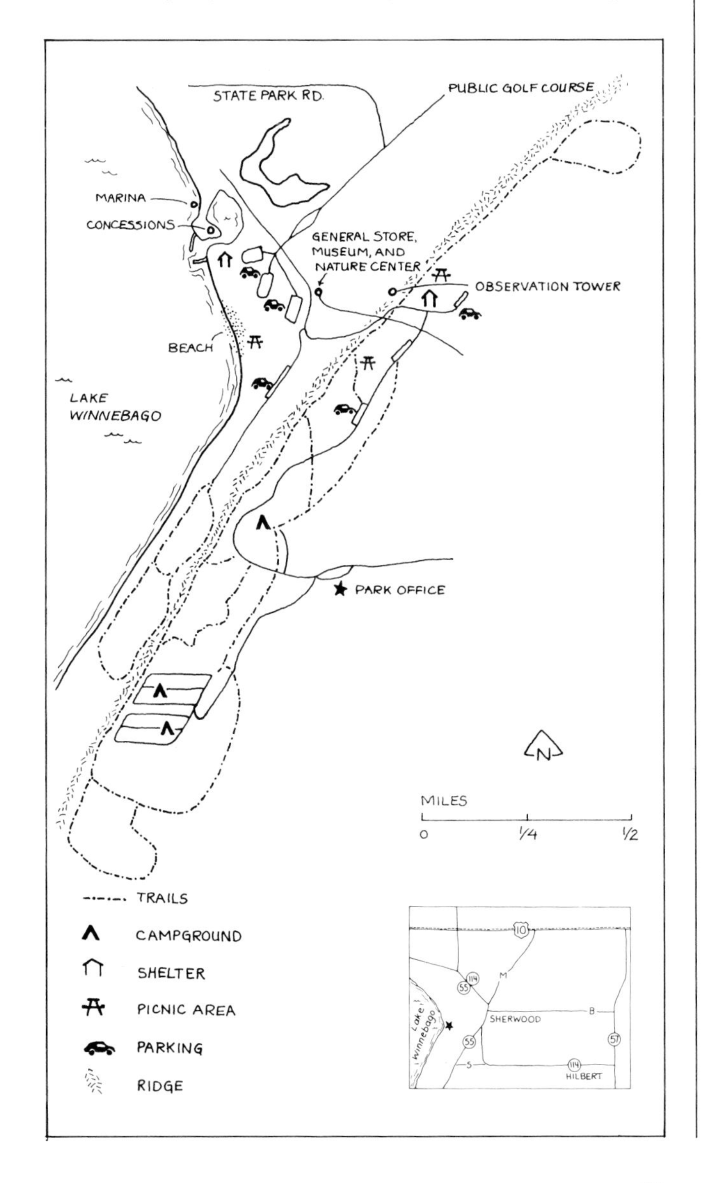

The statue of Chief Red Bird reminds visitors of the native culture that flourished in this area.

(opposite page)

Huge Lake Winnebago has room for all kinds of boats and recreation.

programs and night explorations. Check the park bulletin boards for schedules.

High Cliff State Park has a good variety of hiking trails (7.5 miles). The nature trail makes two loops through a scientific area between the ledge and the lake. The Red Bird Trail meanders along the ridgetop and through woods and rolling meadows. Pause by the 12-foot statue of Chief Red Bird and gaze across the lake as he did in the early 1800s. Described as a peacemaker, Red Bird liked to stand on this cliff with tribal children, telling them of the good life beyond the lake's calm waters. The Winnebago chief called the lake "Wiskooserah"—"water by the flowering banks." On clear days you can see for more than 30 miles from the lookouts along the ridge.

The Indian Mound Trail follows the ridge up from the kiln ruins and through the rugged quarry. The effigy mounds here were constructed about 500 to 1,000 years ago by the nomadic Woodland Indians. They usually made the mounds in the shapes of familiar forest animals or in geometric shapes. Four of the mounds are panthers, one of which is 285 feet long. Another is called Twin Buffaloes. Other mound types are conical (round, and pointed in the middle) and linear (long and narrow). Please respect the effigy mounds for the religious sense in which they were built.

The appealing combination of wooded bluffs, lake scenery and the photographic quarry will make you want to return to High Cliff in other seasons to "rediscover" it.

In winter, the frozen lake looks like a busy shantytown of ice-fishing shacks and pickup trucks. If you want to try winter hiking or snowshoeing, High Cliff is a good place to begin. It's peaceful and there are enough places to explore to keep you active and warm. Please stay off the cross-country ski trails, though. The park's four miles of ski trails are ideal for family skiing because of the level terrain and the many overlooks. Snowmobilers can explore the park on five miles of groomed trails that also connect to the county's extensive trail system.

Flora and Fauna

The uplands of the park are mostly covered by maple, hickory and oak forest where you might spot deer and other woodland wildlife. High Cliff is home to dozens of songbird species, and the lake attracts thousands of waterfowl (including Canada geese) during the spring and fall migrations.

Facilities

In warm weather, High Cliff operates two campgrounds. The 112-site family camping area (showers, electrical outlets at 32 sites) is on the ridgetop near the Indian effigy mounds. The three-foot-high stone fence that runs east from the cliff behind some of the campsites is an old line fence that separated the quarry from a homestead. Groups can camp in the

campground near the south entrance office. Reservations are accepted at both campgrounds. Basic supplies can be purchased at the marina concession and from local merchants near the park. Those campers who also golf might be interested in the public golf course adjacent to the park.

Day visitors have a choice of two shaded picnic areas. One follows along the ridge overlooking Lake Winnebago and has a large shelter (with a concession stand). A big playground, trail heads and a good view of the lake are pleasant extras here. For a bird's-eye panorama of Lake Winnebago and the surrounding countryside, climb the 40-foot observation tower in this picnic area. The other picnic spot is down the hill by the swimming beach with a shelter and bathhouse nearby.

KETTLE MORAINE STATE FOREST—
NORTHERN UNIT

Fond du Lac, Sheboygan and Washington counties. Northern access from Highway 23 at Greenbush halfway between Fond du Lac and Sheboygan. Southern access from Highway 45 at Kewaskum, seven miles north of West Bend.

Main Attraction

At first glance, you can tell that the countryside in the Kettle Moraine State Forest is different. Conical hills (kames), snakelike ridges (eskers) and bowl-shaped depressions (kettles) combine to form a fascinating topography of visual surprises.

Billions of tons of sand, gravel and rock were squeezed between the two lobes of the last glacier 20,000 years ago, and deposited as the glacier slowly receded. Today, an abundance of glacial features are preserved in the 45,000 acres of the northern and southern units of the Kettle Moraine State Forest. The northern unit of the Kettle Moraine (over 27,000 acres) is the largest and most varied of the nine units in the Ice Age National Scientific Reserve in Wisconsin.

Things To Do

The reserve was established in 1971 to protect, preserve and interpret Wisconsin's glacial features. The best way to find out about the forest's scenic, unusual topography and how the Wisconsin glacier created it is by stopping at the Henry S. Reuss Ice Age Visitor Center (½ mile south of Dundee on Highway 67) when you first arrive. Located high on a moraine ridge (which marks the glacier's farthest advance), the attractive center offers film programs, exhibits and a self-guided nature trail briefly describing the Ice Age and its effects on the landscape and mankind.

Naturalists conduct evening programs, hikes and guided auto tours through the forest from late spring through early fall as an aid in exploring the glacial features. If you prefer to explore and learn on your own, try one of the four labeled nature trails at Kettle Moraine. Visitors might also want to ask a naturalist

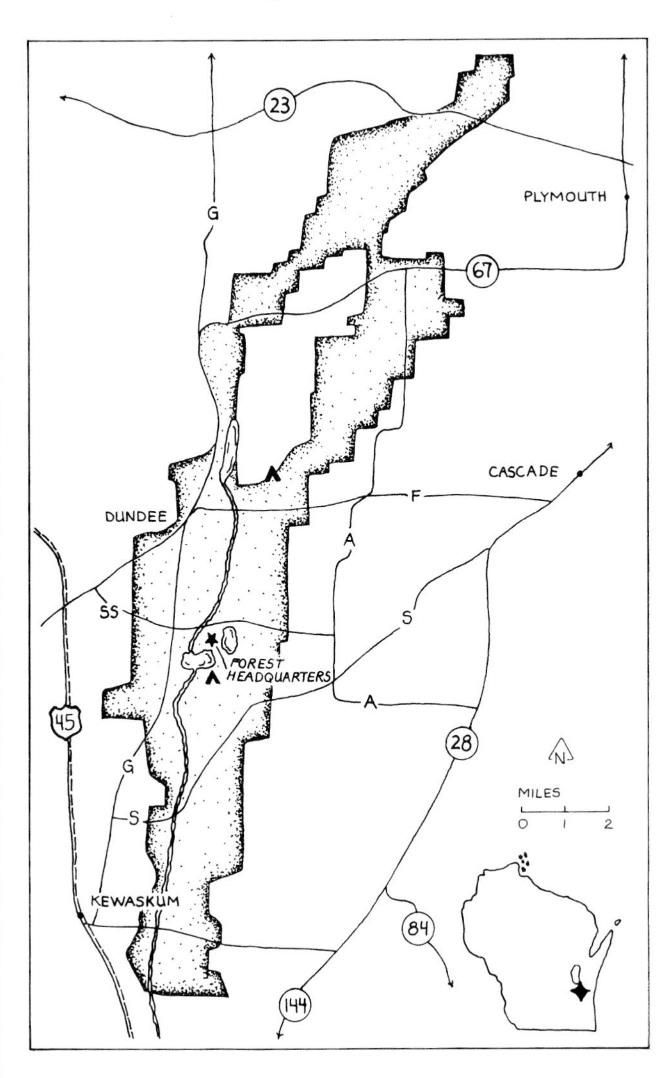

Of all the parks that preserve the features of the glaciers, this offers the most variety. Hills, ridges and bowl-shaped depressions (kettles) are the glacial legacy that makes this a fascinating place to explore.

Bunchberries bloom in the Kettle Moraine State Forest. Park naturalists can help visitors identify the flowers and features that make this park unique.

to point out on a forest map where to find the most vivid examples of kames, eskers, kettles and moraines before striking out on their own. The naturalist activities are based in the Ice Age Center. For a complete listing of the programs offered, check the schedules posted at the center, forest headquarters or the recreation areas.

The Kettle Moraine State Forest is laced with over 73 miles of hiking trails. The longest path, the Glacial Trail, is a 29-mile segment of Wisconsin's Ice Age National Scenic Trail, which traces the farthest advance of the glacier for about 1,000 miles through the state. Backpacking by permit is allowed at five shelters along the Glacial Trail.

The main recreation developments in the northern

unit are at Long Lake, north of Dundee, and at Mauthe Lake, south of New Prospect. Both offer camping, picnic and water activities as well as being the starting and ending points for some of the hiking and riding trails in the forest.

Water sports on the forest lakes and streams attract the most people. There's trout fishing at Butler Lake, Watercress Creek and Lake Fifteen Creek. Both Long and Mauthe lakes contain walleye, northern, largemouth bass and panfish. These two lakes also have guarded swimming beaches during the summer. Fishing licenses are available at the manager's office and at area sport shops.

Many of the dozen or so lakes in the Kettle Moraine have boat launching ramps, but motorboats aren't permitted on Mauthe Lake, Butler Lake or Lake Seven. Rental boats are available in the area.

The Kettle Moraine is large enough to allow horseback riding and hunting in most areas of the forest. Of the variety of game available, deer is hunted most, but be aware that hunting is limited to shotguns with slugs and is not allowed in restricted areas. Check first with the park manager. For horseback riders, the 33-mile Kettle Moraine Bridle Trail runs from County H at the south end of the forest to the village of Greenbush. You can also ride on the Crooked Lake (2.5 miles) and Forest Lake (4 miles) bridle loops. There's a horseman's camp near Mauthe Lake. Horses can be rented from private stables nearby.

Bring your bicycle along when you pack for your trip. The rolling, twisting Kettle Moraine Forest roads make for scenic cycling. Bicycles share these roads with cars, though, so basic bike safety is essential.

Cross-country skiers will find the 33 miles of groomed trails to be some of the best in southeastern Wisconsin. Since the forest is close to the Milwaukee metro area, however, they can be crowded on weekends. Get an early start to avoid the afternoon rush. There are 58 miles of snowmobile trails in the forest.

(continued)

(opposite page)

Over 30 miles of groomed cross country ski trails await winter visitors to the Northern Unit of the Kettle Moraine State Forest.

Flora and Fauna

Common hardwood trees identified from the forest trails include oak, maple and basswood; softwoods include white pine, red pine, white cedar and tamarack. For an above-the-treeline look at the forest, climb the Parnell observation tower off County A, northeast of Parnell.

Facilities

There are 338 individual family campsites available at Mauthe and Long lakes. Both campgrounds have showers, but only Mauthe Lake has electrical hookups (49 sites) and is open during the winter months. Supplies are sold at area merchants and at the Mauthe Lake concession stand. Organized groups can tent at an outdoor site near Greenbush or reserve the 132-person capacity indoor group camp north of New Fane. Forest headquarters and the contact stations have camping reservation details for the family and group camps. Besides campsites, Mauthe and Long lakes have large picnic grounds, or you can stop for a roadside lunch at one of the picnic areas along Kettle Moraine Drive.

Surrounding Area

While visiting the Kettle Moraine, take the time to explore Old Wade House, a small state park in the village of Greenbush. You can tour a restored 19th-century country inn with original period furnishings and see a unique collection of carriages. Other nearby state parks include Kohler-Andrae and Harrington Beach on Lake Michigan, and Pike Lake, southwest of the forest.

KOHLER-ANDRAE STATE PARK

Sheboygan County. Take the County V exit east from I-43 (just south of Sheboygan) to County KK. Turn right (south) on KK to Old Park Road, then turn left (east) to the park entrance. Highway map index: 8-I.

Main Attraction

Shifting wind-blown dunes and nearly two miles of Lake Michigan beach make an irresistible combination at Kohler-Andrae State Park. The park also features a large wooded campground, hiking trails and an attractive nature center overlooking the lake. Inland, the park landscape is an interesting mix of river marsh and pine and hardwood forest.

The park was established in 1927 by a gift of 122 acres of land from the widow of Terry Andrae, the former landowner. Mrs. Andrae donated lakeshore and other acreage as a memorial to her husband. A large addition was made in 1966 when the Kohler Company of Kohler, Wisconsin, gave 280 acres of land to the state as a gift in memory of John Michael Kohler, a local civic-minded businessman. In the years following these land donations, the state purchased an additional 358 acres of property to bring the park to its present size of 760 acres. Although still considered as two parks with adjacent boundaries, the parks are operated as one unit by the state Department of Natural Resources.

Things To Do

Lake Michigan dominates the park's activities. With the long beach, there's plenty of space to sunbathe and swim. Bathhouses are provided but no lifeguards are on duty.

Skin divers like the park area because the water, though cool, is clear. In this area alone, over 50 vessels have sunk, including an 87-foot schooner called *Challenge*. The ship was built in Manitowoc in 1852 and was an historic sailing vessel because it was the first centerboard "clipper"-type schooner. In 1982, a section of this ship's keel washed ashore at the park

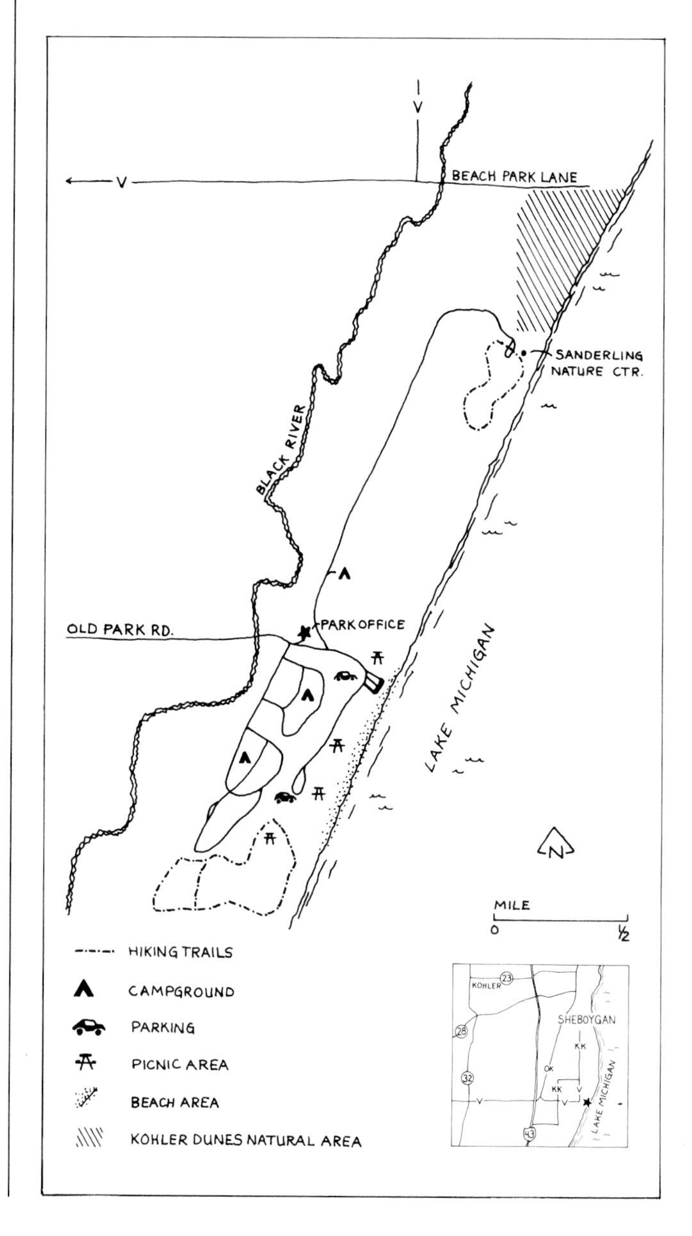

and is now on display outside the Sanderling Nature Center. Recently divers have been searching for the site of a lake vessel that went down just off the park about 60 years ago, although it has not been located.

The lake contains dozens of kinds of fish. Surf fishing for trout and salmon is growing in popularity and quality each year. There are no launching ramps or docks at Kohler-Andrae, but private and public facilities are within a short distance of the park. If you'd like to try the trophy fishing that the deeper water has to offer, contact one of the charter fishing boat services in the Sheboygan area.

A trip to the Sanderling Nature Center in the north section of the park is a great way to have some family fun and learn something, too. The center houses displays of the park's animals, wildflowers and glacial history. You can also find out about how a Frenchman and local Indians started the fur trading era here, as well as how early farming and commercial fishing helped this region to grow. The kids (and probably their parents, too) will enjoy the computer with park and nature trivia games.

The center's auditorium has scheduled slide shows, movies and guest speakers. You can climb to an observation deck on top of the building from an inside stairway for a sweeping view of Lake Michigan. Sanderling is often staffed by local volunteers who donate their time and talent to keep the center open for others to enjoy. Watch the park bulletin boards or ask at the contact station for times and locations of naturalist programs.

Skin divers like to search the clear water here for some of the 50 vessels known to have sunk in this area. Sunbathing and surf fishing for trout and salmon along the two-mile beach are also popular.

The park has two self-guided nature trails. The Creeping Juniper Trail, just south of the nature center, winds through some of the beautiful sand dune areas of the park. The Indian Pipe Trail runs through the forest south of the campground. Pick up a brochure that describes the various trees found along this trail at the nature center and the contact station. Both trails are about a mile long.

If you explore north of the Sanderling Nature Center, you'll be able to see many unique examples of dune vegetation in the Kohler Dunes Natural Area. Though beautiful, these species are fragile. Hikers

are asked to be careful not to damage any vegetation in the natural area. This section of the park is less crowded than the more developed southern part and provides a chance to take a peaceful beach stroll.

Winter at Kohler-Andrae attracts those who enjoy the quiet and solitude of the park in the off-season. You can wander along the ice-encrusted shoreline to photograph the ice sculptures created by the lake waves, or search the inland woods for signs of deer and other wildlife. Cross-country skiers wind through a majestic white pine forest and the heavily wooded south campground area on a 1.5-mile trail. Although the park has no facilities for snowmobilers, there is a short section of trail in the park's northwest corner that connects with other local trails.

(opposite page)

Nearly two miles of Lake Michigan shoreline make Kohler-Andrae State Park a favorite for beachcombing, surf fishing, sunbathing and swimming.

Flora and Fauna

The shore of Lake Michigan is a major flyway for thousands of birds during the spring and fall migrations. Impressive numbers of diving ducks are often seen in rafts of 2,000 to 5,000 birds just offshore from the park. Ask at the contact station for more information about the species of common and endangered birds that nest in the park or fly over it during the migrations. The contact station also has a listing of local parks, festivals and other attractions in the area.

Facilities

The campground has 105 sites with 49 electrical hookups. A group camp can accommodate up to 50 campers with adult leaders. Showers and laundry tubs are available in the camp shelter. The picnic area is close to the campground, extending for half a mile along the lakeshore. Camping and picnic supplies can be purchased at the park concession stand during the summer, or from merchants in Sheboygan. The beach picnic area fills up fast, so get to the park early in the day (especially on weekends) if you want to eat and relax with a lake view. The campground generally fills most days during July and August. Though half of the campsites can be reserved, the rest are on a first-come, first-served basis.

Winter campers can set up in one of the 28 campsites that are kept open during the snow season. Electrical hookups are available at each site. You can get water at the park office. Other winter sports here include hiking, snowshoeing, sledding and tobogganing.

NEWPORT STATE PARK

Door County. Five miles east of Ellison Bay on Highway 42 and Newport Road. Highway map index: 5-J.

Main Attraction

Newport State Park is one of Wisconsin's wild and undeveloped parks. Its 2,200 acres of rugged, scenic beauty stretch along 11 miles of Lake Michigan shoreline. Here you can hike, backpack, swim, snowshoe and cross-country ski in the 90% wooded park.

While hiking, you might find the foundations of some old logging cabins left over from the lumbering days of the 1880s and 1890s. At that time, Newport was a bustling logging town. It was one of the many isolated "pier towns" along Lake Michigan. Great Lakes schooners would dock here to take on cordwood and Christmas trees for larger cities of the Lakes region. After the forests were cutover, Newport deteriorated into a ghost town. You can still see outlines of the store and post office overgrown with lilac bushes and grapevines in the beach and picnic area.

Things To Do

To keep the park's wild atmosphere, no motor vehicles are allowed off the road. There are two parking areas near the beach, but you have to get out of the car to experience Newport. A walk along the beach will help you to sense the feeling of isolation that the forest and lake inspire. The graceful curve of the shoreline is outlined by tall evergreens that are more typical of Canada than of Wisconsin. Gulls glide and swoop over beach and water. If you poke into the cool, low-lying areas of cedar and fir trees just off the beach, you might spot a snowshoe hare.

Winter offers a different kind of solitude. At Newport you can experience the stillness of the snowy forest, or feel the wind's power as it howls through the treetops. You might hear the staccato rhythm of a pileated woodpecker, or spot a deer silently watching you. Lake Michigan in winter is cold and icy, and the wind off it can sting, but winter feels refreshing and peaceful here. Newport State Park is open year-round and all of the trails are open for cross-country skiing and snowshoeing. Campsites are available, but check in with the ranger first. No snowmobiles are allowed in the park.

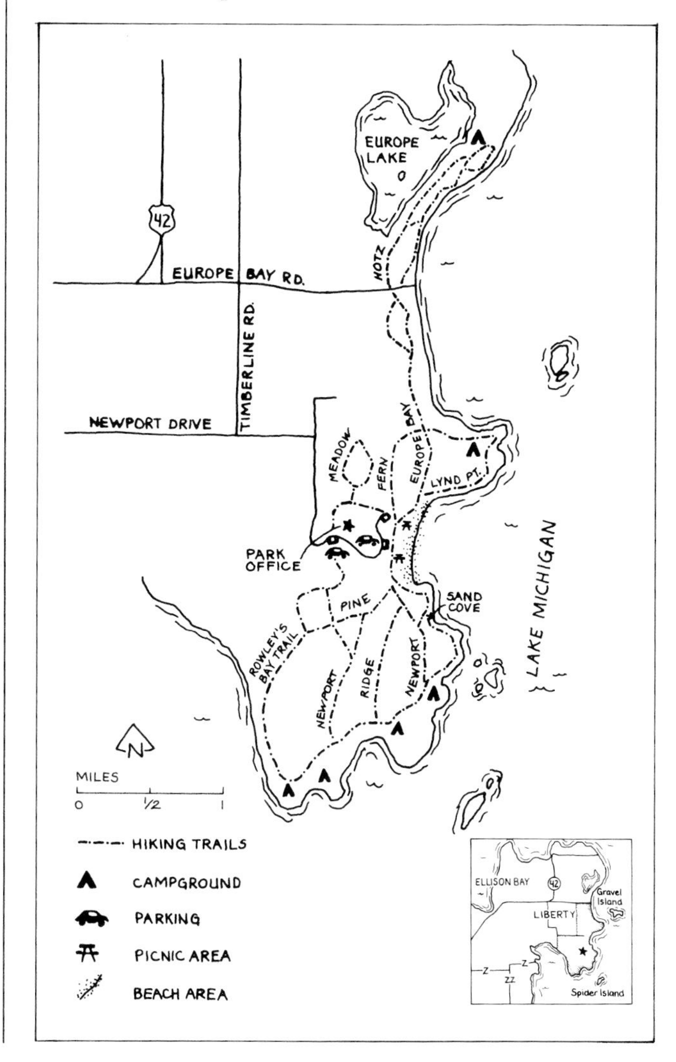

The two-mile Meadow Trail is a self-guided nature loop that shows off a variety of plant and animal communities including open meadow, hardwood forest and cedar swamp. The park also offers a weekly naturalist program of guided hikes and slide shows.

The Europe Bay Trail, the park's longest, follows the path of an old logging road. The seven-mile trail starts near the last parking lot, and passes the site of an old homestead and sawmill just beyond the Lynd Point Trail junction. Farther along, past the Fern Trail junction, are several long ridges running in a north-south direction paralleling the beach. These old sand beaches were formed in prehistoric times when Lake Michigan was enlarged with runoff from Ice Age glaciers. Water is trapped between the ridges, forming small bog communities. Half of the 1.5-mile-long sand beach on Europe Bay belongs to the park. From the beach, you'll get great views of Lake Michigan, Death's Door Passage, Plum Island, Detroit Island and the Pilot Island lighthouse. Maybe you'll see a huge lake freighter crossing the horizon.

The terrain around the Hotz Trail is different from that of the rest of the park. North of Europe Bay Road, the forest changes to red pine, oak and beech. Soon you'll see the inland Europe Lake on your left (over one mile of its shoreline is in the park). As you hike farther north, you can see both Europe Lake and Lake Michigan from the hilly terrain of the narrow isthmus. Notice the sand dunes that line the northern end of Europe Bay beach. The dunes support a variety of unique plants, including beach wormwood, sea rocket and beach pea. Three of Newport's backpack campsites are located on the isthmus.

This rugged, undeveloped park stretches for 11 miles along Lake Michigan. Backpack into a rustic shoreline campsite and enjoy the peaceful seclusion among the evergreens.

The southern park trails have some surprises. Rowley Bay Trail, for example, winds past meadows that were old farmsteads. The forest is slowly reclaiming the former fields. The trail also skirts rock ledges in a quiet, cool cedar woods that offers protection for many songbirds. The Newport Trail and Ridge Trail meander through a scenic mixed forest preserved as the Newport Conifer/Hardwoods Scientific Area. The Newport Trail also is a good vantage point for observing waterfowl. Spider Island (visible from the

The long shoreline at Newport State Park offers privacy and pristine scenery.

Newport Trail) and Gravel Island (visible from Lynd Point and Europe Bay) are national wildlife refuges for nesting gulls and shorebirds.

Flora and Fauna

Newport's 28 miles of hiking trails wind through remnants of boreal forest and virgin white pine, cut across meadows where deer feed at dawn and at dusk, and follow the shoreline. There are protected sand beaches, rocky ledges and abandoned shorelines of ancient Glacial Lake Nipissing, an ancestor of Lake Michigan. Watch for porcupine, fox, coyote, rabbit, deer and other forest dwellers. Ruffed grouse like this area, too, for its protection and food. If you hike here in early summer, look for tasty wild strawberries. Some 175 species of birds frequent Newport State Park. To help satisfy your curiosity about Newport's natural world, the park has compiled bird and plant checklists for hikers.

Facilities

The Newport Trail, five miles long, is the main path in the park's southern peninsula. A number of shorter trails intersect Newport, allowing for shorter hiking loops that connect with the bulk of the park's 16 wilderness campsites. The hiking distance to these sites varies from one to three and a half miles. Allow enough time to hike in and set up camp before dark. All of these sites are wooded with lakeside views except for number 6. The shorelines vary from sand and gravel to rocks and boulders.

Cooking may be done in the grills at each site using downed or dead wood. Pack stoves are preferred. There are no wells in the campsites, so water has to be carried in from the hand pump at the main picnic area. Disposable items should be burned in the fire rings or packed out. If you take in nonburnables, take them out, too. Although Newport is not a huge wilderness, use backcountry common sense. Plan your hikes, be prepared for bad weather, hike with someone else and "take nothing but pictures, leave nothing but footprints."

A picnic area facing Lake Michigan has tables, grills, a well and a shelter. You can soak up the sun or swim along the sandy half-mile-long beach. Changing booths are located by the shelter. No boat launching facilities are provided.

OLD WADE HOUSE STATE PARK

Sheboygan County. On Highway 23 in Greenbush, halfway between Fond du Lac and Sheboygan. Highway map index: 8-I.

Main Attraction

Old Wade House, a restored stagecoach inn, is a mirror of early Wisconsin pioneer days.

In 1845, a plank road was laid from the port of Sheboygan to Fond du Lac along the trail on which Sylvanus Wade and his family had built a log cabin a year earlier. As stagecoach and wagon traffic increased, Wade built a blacksmith shop to service the horses and wagons. In 1851, he built an inn for the travelers and immigrants. The lumber for Wade House was provided by Wade's son-in-law, Charles Robinson, who built a nearby sawmill. Robinson also cut the wood for his own Butternut House, which stands just behind the inn.

The restored stagecoach inn and the surrounding buildings re-create the atmosphere of pioneer life in Wisconsin. Costumed guides demonstrate everyday crafts of the era, but on special occasions lucky visitors may witness a harvest festival or a cotillion dance.

In its heyday, the 28-room Wade House offered welcome respite to weary travelers, and its taproom and ballroom became social centers for the infant community of Greenbush. The town declined after the Civil War because the railroad bypassed it and the plank road waned, leaving both the village and the inn frozen in time.

Both Wade House and Butternut House were meticulously restored under the supervision of Ruth De Young Kohler, and because of her efforts and the financial support of the Kohler Foundation, the park's buildings still look as if they could entice a passing horseman to stop in for a rest. Modern travelers can see some of the original Early American furniture and tableware in the Wade House.

OLD WADE HOUSE STATE PARK

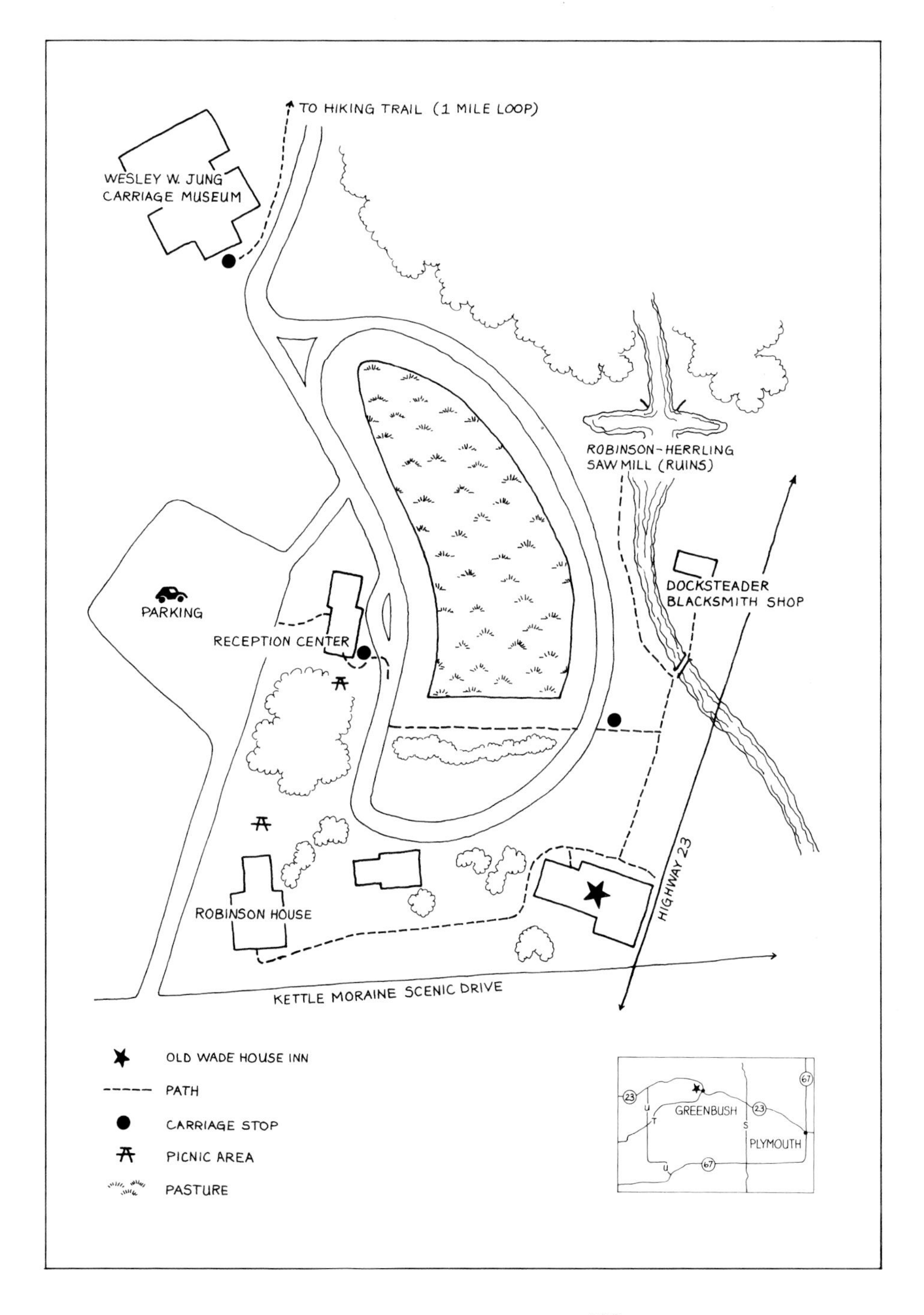

Things To Do

Today's visitors are also invited to observe and participate in the activities, chores and entertainments of the early inn and community. Depending on the day and season, you'll find costumed guides cooking over the fireplace, making soap or candles, spinning and weaving, gardening, blacksmithing or grooming horses. On special occasions, you may come upon a cotillion dance, a patriotic holiday, harvest festival, or Yankee Christmas.

Old Wade House and the Jung Carriage Museum invite people to step back in time to relive horse-and-buggy days.

The Wesley W. Jung Carriage Museum, a short hike from Wade House (or a ride in a horse-drawn buggy), features about 100 restored carriages in one of America's finest collections. Established by the legislature as the state carriage museum, the collection contains a variety of vehicles from 1870 to 1915. Visitors will see rare, like-new carriages and wagons used for firefighting, hauling freight and pleasure. Many of them were manufactured by the Jung Carriage Company, established in 1855 by Jacob Jung.

The 260-acre park grounds also include a blacksmith shop, smokehouse, maple sugaring cabin, gift shop and visitor center. Bring a picnic lunch along, because you could easily spend a day wandering through the restored buildings and museum.

The Old Wade House historical site, though part of the state park system, is owned and operated by the State Historical Society of Wisconsin. For information on seasonal hours and rates, write to Old Wade House, Greenbush, WI 53026.

Surrounding Area

If you're going to be in the area for a while, head south into the Kettle Moraine State Forest (northern unit). There's enough camping, hiking and water sports there to sidetrack you for a few days at least. Both the state forest and Old Wade House are within easy driving distance of the Milwaukee metro area.

PENINSULA STATE PARK

Door County. Between the villages of Fish Creek and Ephraim on Highway 42. Highway map index: 5-J.

Main Attraction

Peninsula State Park is a Door County landmark because of its size (3,763 acres), facilities and eye-catching panoramas of shoreline and water. Bicycling or hiking through rolling, forested parkland with views of islands is fun here, but there's also golf, year-round camping and water sports in the expansive bay. Chances are you'll return next year to try some of the activities you didn't have time for this trip.

Things To Do

Hiking on Peninsula's 17 miles of trails covers a wide range of scenery and walking conditions, allowing a glimpse of Door County before the onslaught of axe, plow, fire and developer. A good trail to start with is the White Cedar Nature Trail. The 30 trail stations on this half-mile guided loop interpret area geology, vegetation, animals and ecology. It begins at the White Cedar Nature Center at the west junction of Shore and Bluff roads. The center also has graphic exhibits on park landforms and wildlife. A naturalist is on duty from mid-June through Labor Day and leads regularly scheduled nature hikes and evening programs.

Another popular summer evening program is the University of Wisconsin–Madison Heritage Ensemble. Centering on regional and national historic themes, the ensemble presents musical productions that re-create history with all its humor, tragedy and intrigue. These family-oriented shows are lively and informative, covering a variety of subjects from the Great Lakes to portraits of famous Americans. An ad-

PENINSULA STATE PARK

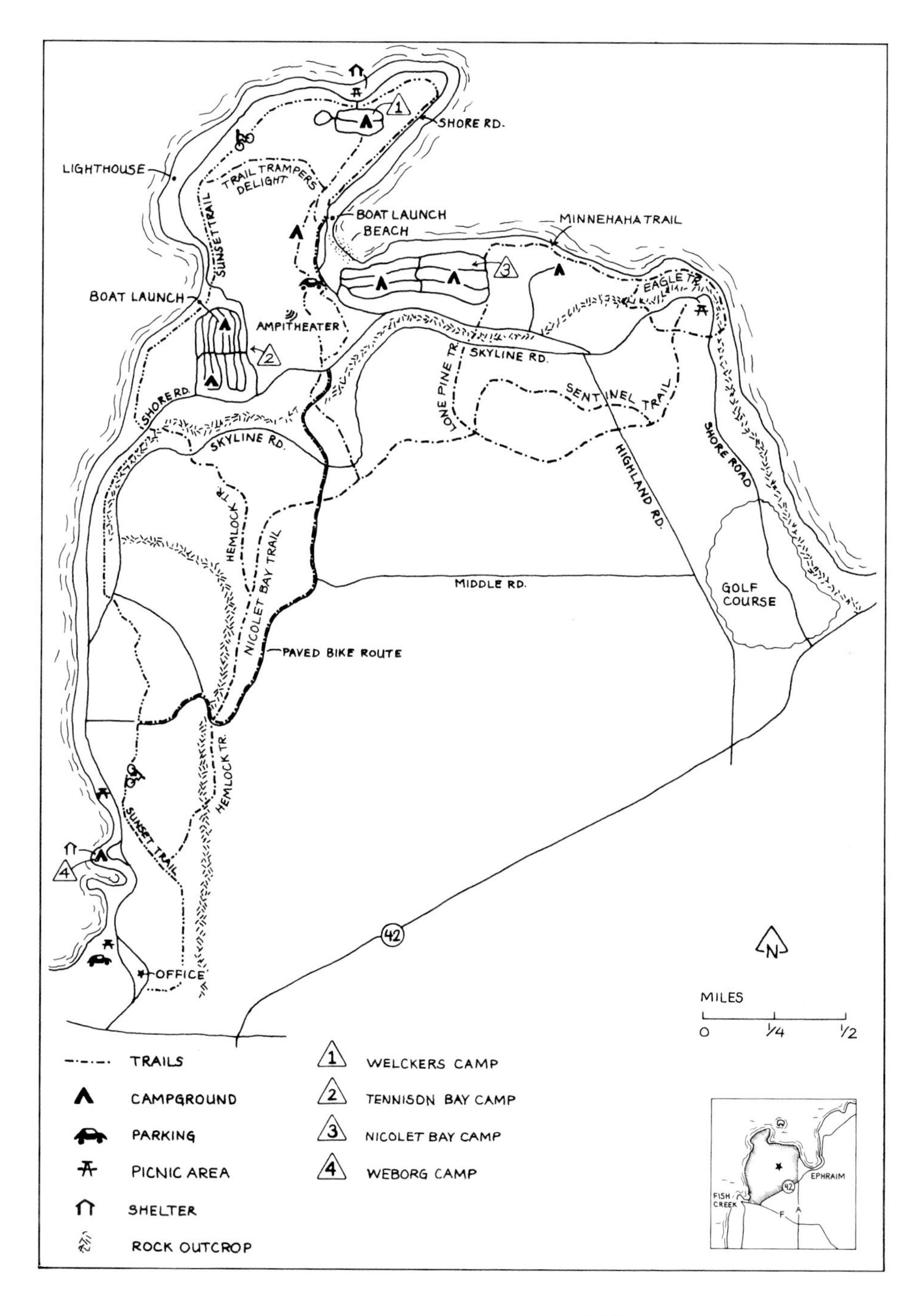

mission is charged for the performances (nightly except Sunday, end of June through Labor Day in the amphitheater). Don't forget your mosquito repellent.

The Sunset Trail is popular among hikers because it traverses a variety of marsh, forest and shoreline. The 5.1-mile trail connects the Fish Creek office and the Nicolet Bay beach. The trail is graveled so hikers, bikers and the disabled in wheelchairs can use it. You can hike the trail in three to four hours or bike it in one, but take your time and bring along a camera to photograph the shoreline and scenic bluffs during the evening's golden light. Sunset Trail also passes by the Eagle Lighthouse (built in 1868). This photogenic landmark, now fully automated, still guides ships on Green Bay. The living quarters have been restored and are open for guided tours during the summer, operated by the Door County Historical Society. A fee is charged.

Hikers and joggers at Peninsula can improve their balance, coordination and conditioning with the Vita Course, a one-mile exercise circuit located in a woods near the three campgrounds at the northern tip of the park. To use the course, jog or walk to each of the exercise stations spaced along the trail and follow the directions at each stop.

You'll find eye-catching panoramas of shoreline and water here, and you'll also find the Heritage Ensemble. The ensemble produces lively, family-oriented musical shows based on local history with all its humor, tragedy and intrigue. It's unique.

A favorite trail is the Eagle Trail, a two-mile loop. It follows along the Green Bay shoreline for more than a mile, then climbs the highest cliffs in Door County. You can start at Eagle Panorama or Eagle Terrace, but either way the trail is steep in several places, and requires some climbing. Sheer 200-foot limestone bluffs can make dramatic photos when combined with fall colors and blue sky. On top of the bluffs is the Eagle Tower observation deck. It gets breezy up here, so grab your jacket and climb up for the best view of the park in any season.

Good views of Horseshoe Island and other islands in Green Bay can be seen from the overlooks along Shore Road. Skyline Road winds over the highest park terrain, providing sweeping views of the park and Green Bay. The long low island to the west is Chambers Island and beyond that is the Wisconsin–Upper Michigan mainland. As you look northeast along

Door County's wooded shore, you can see the forested finger of land by Ellison Bay.

The park roads seem tailor-made for bicycling. They twist and wind through the woods and follow the shoreline with places to stop for a view of gulls over the bay. But best of all is coasting down the other side of the hill you just climbed, with the wind cooling you, trees sweeping by and the derailleur purring in your ears. Beware of traffic and pedestrians before cruising down that inviting hill, though. A helmet, common sense and a sound bicycle are prerequisites to safe biking in the park. Bicycle rentals are available in Fish Creek.

The Door County peninsula offers a sufficient variety of scenery and terrain to delight any cyclist.

Peninsula's roads, though scenic, are often busy. Motorhomes and other vacation vehicles (many with protruding mirrors) are a hazard to bicycles, especially when the drivers want to see the scenery and may not be paying attention to bicyclists. The safest way to enjoy the park on your bicycle is to pedal on the nine-mile designated bikeway, which includes the five-mile Sunset Trail.

Lifeguards are on duty at Nicolet Bay beach from mid-June to late August. The beach is a short walk from the Nicolet Bay camping area and is a favorite haven of sunbathers when the breeze off Green Bay is slight. Swimming is best in late summer, after the water has warmed up to a refreshing temperature. A bathhouse-concession building is next to the beach and picnic area. Boaters can use the launch ramps at Nicolet and Tennison, but overnight tie-ups are prohibited. Weather permitting, rental rowboats, canoes, windsurfers, sailboats and sailing lessons are available from a private concessionaire near the Nicolet Bay beach from the end of June through Labor Day.

If you like to fish, try your luck in the waters of Green Bay. There are coho and chinook salmon; brown, rainbow and lake trout; yellow perch, northern pike and smallmouth bass. Fishing is also popular in Lake Michigan and several nearby inland lakes. Resident and nonresident licenses are available at the park office. Fishing charters, yacht charters and sailboat excursions are available in the area. Pick up a copy of the Door County Vacation Planning Guide for details.

Boaters like to stop at Horseshoe Island near Nicolet Bay. The 38-acre island, part of the state park, has limited hiking and picnic facilities. No overnight camping is allowed, but boaters can use the harbor and dock for refuge.

Adding to an already impressive list of recreational opportunities, Peninsula sports the state park system's only golf course.

Peninsula provides for play, too. Playground equipment is available near the Fish Creek overflow parking area, at Nicolet Bay beach and at the Tennison Bay campground. A tennis court is located off Shore Road between Mengelberg Lane and Skyline Road. From early May through mid-October, golfers can tee off on a beautiful 18-hole golf course overlooking Green Bay. Snacks, rental carts, golf supplies and golf lessons are available in the clubhouse. Tee times may be reserved in person or by mail for a small fee.

To experience Door County's winter beauty, visit Peninsula State Park when it's under a blanket of snow. Door County has relatively moderate winters, due to the mellowing influence of Green Bay and Lake Michigan. Spring, however, is usually delayed because of the "icebox effect" of frozen Green Bay. The park maintains 17 miles of snowmobile trails and 19 miles of cross-country ski trails. The ski trails are fun, with loops for all abilities. Other winter activities include tobogganing and sledding on the golf course, snowshoeing, bird-watching and ice fishing.

Flora and Fauna

The forest in the park is mostly northern hardwood, consisting of sugar maple, birch, oak, beech, white pine, hemlock and balsam fir. Deer, fox, porcupine and other woodland wildlife are common here in any season. Bird-watchers can pick up a bird checklist at the nature center before trying to spot some of the over 100 species of birds that live in or migrate through the park throughout the year. Lucky hikers may observe pileated woodpeckers, ospreys and several varieties of hawks usually found in Canada. Colonies of gulls and cormorants can be seen on the Strawberry Islands off the park's western shore.

(opposite page)

The hiking trails at Peninsula State Park offer glimpses of Green Bay through the autumn trees as hikers follow the shoreline bluffs.

(continued)

Facilities

Campers can pick from 473 individual campsites in the park, divided into four campgrounds. About 100 of these sites have electricity, and four have full hookups (sewer, water, electricity). A tent camp for organized groups is also available. Three of the campgrounds, Nicolet Bay, Welckers Point and Weborg, are generally open from early May through the last weekend in October. Check with park personnel about specific dates. Winter visitors can set up camp at the Tennison Bay campground, which keeps about 12 sites open for winter use. Electricity and water are available.

Peninsula is an extremely popular park, and the campgrounds are busiest from late June through August and on weekends through October. Reservations are suggested. The park receives about 3,000 reservation requests in early January, so even an early application does not guarantee that you'll get the campsite that you want.

Surrounding Area

Special events in the area include cherry and apple blossom time (mid- to late May), cherry harvest (mid-July to mid-August), golf tournaments at Peninsula golf course (first full week in August) and the Sister Bay Fall Festival (second weekend in October). Don't miss one of Door County's famous fish boils: whitefish steaks, potatoes and onions thrown in a pot and boiled over an open fire. The meal is served with plenty of butter and maybe a slab of Door County cherry pie.

A major attraction at Fish Creek is the Theater in a Garden, where the Peninsula Players, America's oldest professional resident summer stock company, present a series of Broadway and off-Broadway plays and musicals each year. The theater is just south of Fish Creek. North of town, at Gibralter High School, the Peninsula Music Festival is held for two weeks each summer, with guest musicians, soloists and conductors from orchestras and conservatories all across the country.

POINT BEACH STATE FOREST

Manitowoc County. To reach the campground entrance road, drive about five miles northeast of Two Rivers on County O (also called Rustic Road 16). Highway map index: 7-I.

Main Attraction

A six-mile sandy Lake Michigan shoreline is the major attraction at Point Beach State Forest. The "point" is Rowley Point, jutting seven miles into Lake Michigan with a Coast Guard lighthouse on it. The lighthouse is one of the largest and brightest on the Great Lakes, and is visible for 19 miles. Before the lighthouse was erected, 26 ships foundered or stranded on the point.

At sundown and dusk the golden, rich colors at day's end quietly fade to pink and blue pastels, the gulls and terns still patrol over the beach, and couples walk slowly in bare feet, not caring if a wave catches their ankles. The Coast Guard Lighthouse starts working one half hour before sunset, but nobody seems to notice it yet. As darkness creeps in from the lake, the light begins to have more of a presence. Finally, when the last shreds of pale sky are absorbed, the two-million-candlepower lamp rules the night. The two beams sweep overhead opposite each other. Every 10 to 12 seconds, a powerful shaft of light reaches out over the lake, reflecting off the water in the inky distance.

It's refreshing to experience solitude on Point Beach at night. The smell and feel of moist air and the lulling sound of the surf soothe the spirit, releasing tensions with the undertow.

Things To Do

The forest remains a wild area, with the developed areas for camping and picnicking grouped along a mile of beach in the northern section. Access to the forest is by 10 miles of hiking trails that begin near the ranger station.

The naturalist program offers guided hikes, a self-guided nature trail and evening programs where you

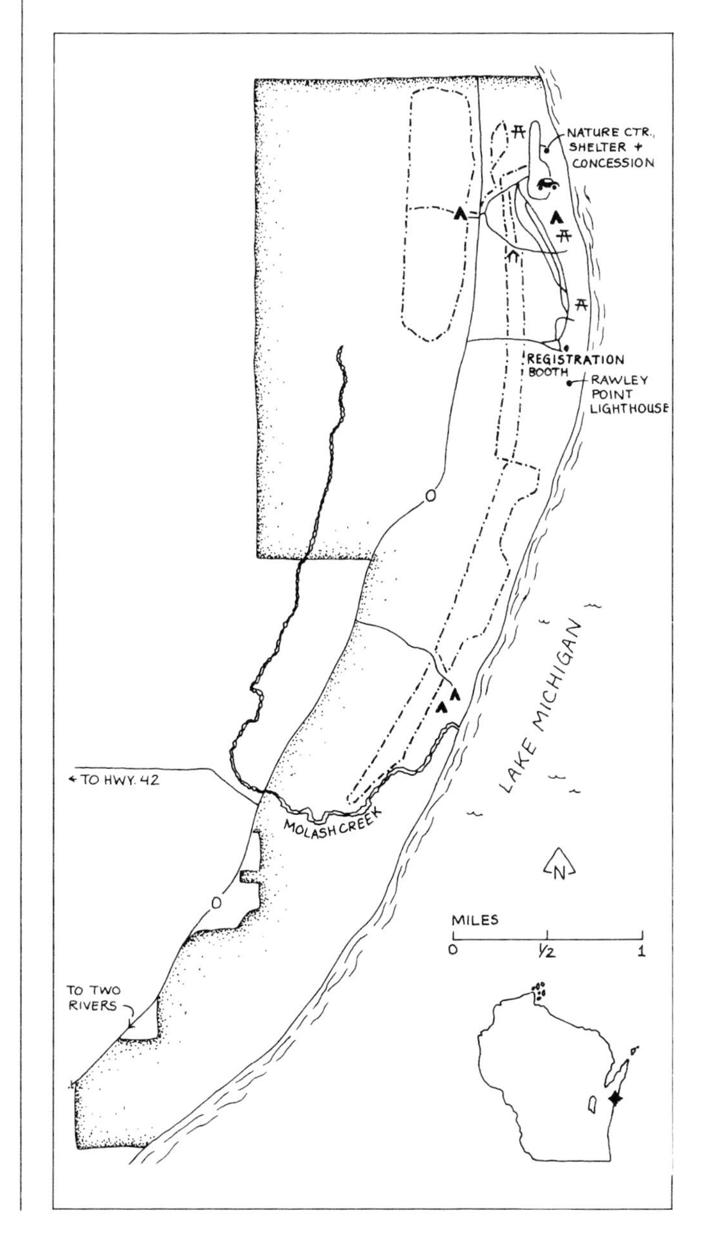

may learn more about the natural history of the area. Check the program posters for times of in-season hikes, lectures and evening movies (shown in the main lodge).

Point Beach's waterfront is a fascinating place for daydreamers and beachcombers. It's fun to look for remnants of some of the wooden ships that broke apart after running aground off the point in bad weather. Several pieces of these old wrecks can still be found along the beach—and the boiler of the steamer *Continental* is still visible just offshore.

Daytime beach activities include swimming, sunning and surf fishing. Swimming is allowed, but there is no designated swimming area or lifeguard on duty, except in the city of Two Rivers. Surf fishing for trout and salmon is popular at Point Beach, or you can try charter boat fishing for lake trout and salmon with private operators in Two Rivers.

Try the beach here at dusk as the lighthouse on Rowley Point starts working. The air is cool and fresh, the sound of the surf is relaxing and the sweep of light across the water punctuates the solitude.

Bicyclists will find that the paved forest roads and Rustic Road 16 (County O) to Two Rivers are good for a scenic ride.

Winter is less crowded at Point Beach, but there is still plenty to do. Some campsites remain open during the winter and cross-country skiers have the run of the forest's 10-mile groomed trail system. There is a through-trail for snowmobilers that connects Two Rivers with the county trail system. Since there are no facilities for off-loading snowmobiles within the forest, many riders park their vehicles and trailers at Port Sandy Bay tavern (2.5 miles south on the entrance road) to gain access to the trail.

Bring your camera on a winter outing at Point Beach State Forest. The lighthouse and icy shoreline make scenic winter photo subjects.

Flora and Fauna

The marshes and swales between the ridges are home to aquatic plants, several types of ferns and wildlife (such as red-backed and blue-spotted salamanders). The 2,870-acre forest is a mixture of northern softwoods and southern hardwoods. The white pine, the mainstay of Wisconsin's early forest industry, towers over the other trees in the forest. Hikers may spot deer in the forest at dawn or dusk, plus a variety of smaller game animals, forest birds and shorebirds. Blue herons are occasionally seen along Molash Creek.

Facilities

The camping and picnic area includes individual campsites, an outdoor group tent site, picnic tables, a shelter lodge and a concession stand. An indoor group camp is on the shoreline, about halfway down the forest's six-mile beachfront. This site has a mess hall and bunkhouse. Ask park personnel for registration and facility details. The family campground has 127 sites, 59 with electrical hookups. Reservations are accepted for all the campgrounds in the forest. You can get some supplies at the park concession stand or from local merchants near the forest or in Two Rivers.

Surrounding Area

The Lake Michigan port cities of Two Rivers and Manitowoc, southwest of Point Beach, are worth a side trip for state forest visitors. Both communities offer services and attractions such as Lake Michigan fishing charters, private campgrounds, parks, museums, etc., but there are at least two attractions deserving special mention. The Manitowoc Maritime Museum provides an eye-catching look at 100 years of maritime and shipbuilding history in this proud port city. The prize exhibit is the full-scale World War II submarine, the *USS Cobia*, which is similar to the submarines built in Manitowoc during the war. The submarine, a National Historic Landmark, is moored next to the museum and is open for tours.

Two Rivers is home to the Rogers Street Fishing Village, a collection of authentic sheds and buildings that tells the story of 150 years of commercial fishing in this area. The village has recently been enrolled in the National Registry of Historic Places. For more information about this area, get a copy of *Enjoy the Scenic Lakeshore Route*, a free guide to the port cities region of Manitowoc and Kewaunee counties. The guide is published by Maritime Promotions, P.O. Box 74, Francis Creek, WI 54214.

(opposite page)

Wandering the shoreline at Point Beach can produce surprises as visitors come upon remnants of wooden ships that broke up in storms as they rounded the point.

POTAWATOMI STATE PARK

Door County. Take Highway 42/57 south of Sturgeon Bay to County S. Turn right (north) on County S; left (west) on County C; then right (north) on Park Road to the entrance. Highway map index: 6-J.

Main Attraction

Potawatomi State Park, like the other state parks in Door County, is famous for its scenic views of big water and forested shorelines. From the overlooks and 75-foot observation tower, you can see the northern entrance to Sturgeon Bay and the waters of Green Bay beyond. On clear days you can see the Wisconsin–Upper Michigan mainland.

The 1,200-acre park, named for a tribe of Indians that once lived here, is mostly flat to gently rolling upland forest terrain, bordered by steep slopes and rugged limestone cliffs along the Sturgeon Bay shoreline. The park lies on the edge of the Niagara Escarpment. The exposed, steep edge of the escarpment forms the backbone of the Door County Peninsula, then arcs for over 900 miles through Michigan and Canada all the way to New York State where it supports the plunging waters of Niagara Falls.

Things To Do

Hiking is the best way to see the limestone bluffs, shoreline and forest at Potawatomi. The park features two hiking trails. The 2.5-mile Hemlock Trail begins at the south picnic area and follows the Sturgeon Bay shoreline. This is a popular spot for anglers. The trail heads west through the woods and borders the campground. Above the campground you'll retrace the ancient shoreline of Lake Algonquin, which existed about 8,500 years ago. The trail loops south and east returning to the picnic area.

The Tower Trail (3.5 miles long) starts at the park-

in the park in one of the south campground sites that are kept open year-round.

Flora and Fauna

Most of the park is covered by a dense mixed forest of hardwoods and softwoods. You can see red oak, maple, beech and a variety of large conifers along the roads and trails. The distinctive aroma of pine trees reminds you of the northwoods. The forest is home to wildflowers, ferns and mosses. There are more than 50 kinds of birds in the woodlands plus many types of shorebirds. It's difficult to ignore the antics of gulls and terns in their competition for food. Common forest residents are deer, fox, raccoon and chipmunk. Beware of the raccoons: they're not ashamed to steal the food from your picnic table.

Potawatomi offers a dense mix of hardwoods and conifers reminiscent of the northwoods.

(continued on next page)

Facilities

Potawatomi's Daisy Field campground is split into two sections with a total of 125 individual sites. Twenty-three sites have electrical outlets. Drinking water is available, but there are no showers. Two campsites are designated for handicapped visitors, one of which is reservable. Half of the campsites may be reserved in the campground, which fills up often in the summer.

Surrounding Area

The Ice Age National Scenic Trail starts in Potawatomi State Park. When completed, the Ice Age Trail will wind for 1,000 miles through Wisconsin's countryside, closely following the extent of the last glaciation. This most recent ice age, called the Wisconsin Glaciation, lasted from about 100,000 to 10,000 years ago.

The eastern end of the Ice Age Trail begins at the observation tower in the park, following the Tower Trail along the Sturgeon Bay shoreline and leaving the southern park boundary off Shore Road. Look for the Ice Age National Scenic Trail symbols that first appear at the tower. The Ahnapee State Trail, just south of Sturgeon Bay, is the next segment of the Ice Age Trail, though a trail link has not been officially established yet. For further information about the Ice Age Trail and the Ice Age National Scientific Reserve, see page 19

For information about Door County, stop at the chamber of commerce information center, just south of Sturgeon Bay on Highway 42/57. They have information about Door County's four other state parks, the Ahnapee State Trail and private attractions.

ROCK ISLAND STATE PARK

Door County. Off the northeast shore of Washington Island in Lake Michigan. Highway map index: 4-J.

Main Attraction

It's easy to forget about time in the 900-acre wilderness of Rock Island. Once you've left it's hard to forget the island's gulls, sand beaches and beauty.

All boats that head toward Washington Island must cross Porte des Morts Strait (Death's Door). The combined effects of wind, current, shoals and rocky shores between the mainland and the island took quite a toll on ships and boats in the days before diesel engines and navigational aids. The "door" in Door County had its origin here. Today's ferryboats make the crossing in safety, but the name remains.

Things To Do

Part of the fun of Rock Island is getting there. Take the Washington Island Ferry from Northport to Washington Island, then drive across the island to Jackson Harbor to catch the Rock Island Ferry. If you feel adventuresome, leave your car on the mainland and take the Northport Ferry or the passenger ferry that leaves from Gills Rock. You can rent bicycles on Washington Island for the pedal trip to Jackson Harbor. Ferry schedule information will be sent on request from the park office on Washington Island.

Private boats can reach Rock Island from the launching ramp at Jackson Harbor or directly from the Door County mainland. Lake Michigan and Green Bay are hazardous, though, because of reefs and fast-forming storms.

Before you get to Rock Island, you have to tear yourself away from the distractions on Washington Island, which is worth a visit in itself. Shops, mu-

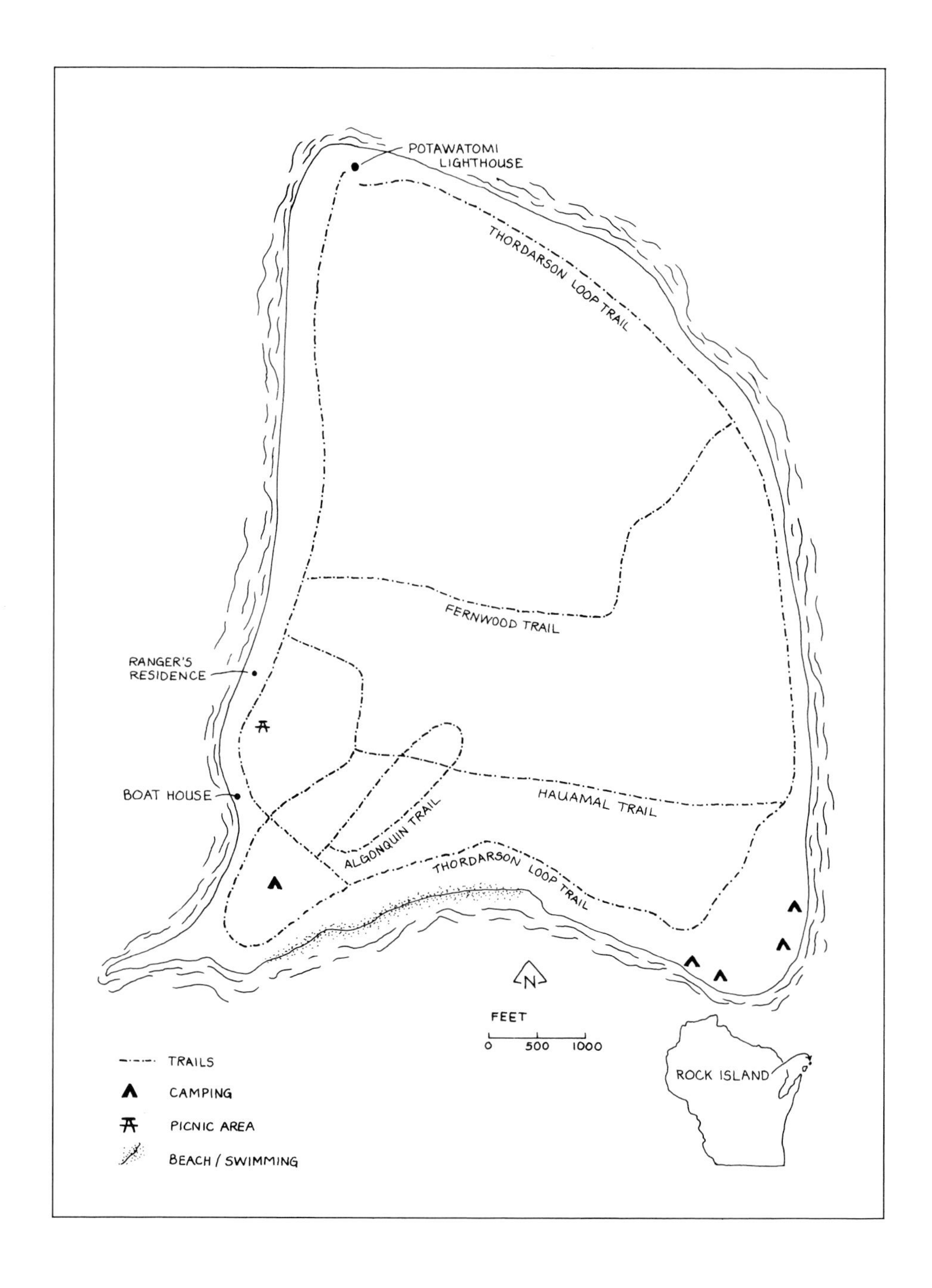
POTAWATOMI LIGHTHOUSE
THORDARSON LOOP TRAIL
FERNWOOD TRAIL
RANGER'S RESIDENCE
BOAT HOUSE
HAUAMAL TRAIL
ALGONQUIN TRAIL
THORDARSON LOOP TRAIL
N
FEET
0 500 1000
ROCK ISLAND
TRAILS
CAMPING
PICNIC AREA
BEACH / SWIMMING

seums, marinas, charter fishing, festivals and island tours are just some of the options for those who choose to linger on this large island. There are limited resort and campground facilities for overnight visitors.

While Washington Island has a distinctive charm with its quiet roads, cottages and lakeside harbors, Rock Island's lure lies in the mysterious attraction that small islands seem to hold for vagabond souls. The island, at various times, has been an Indian settlement, perhaps a French fur trading outpost, a fishing village and a private estate before becoming a primitive park.

Part of the fun of Rock Island is getting there. Two ferry rides are necessary with a stop on Washington Island (a delight in itself).

The half-mile sand beach is a favorite spot on the island. When the waves are right, try some body surfing or take a swim in the cool water. Farther down the beach by the campsites are some cliff carvings. Try the sailing or fishing yourself, or even scuba diving. The waters around Door County are the resting place for more shipwrecks than anywhere else on the Great Lakes.

From the campground, it's easy to get on the 10.5-mile network of hiking trails (one of which is a self-guided nature trail) that circle the island. One of the trails follows an old road to the Potawatomi Lighthouse on the north shore. This is Wisconsin's oldest lighthouse (built in 1836) and still guides ships through Lake Michigan's waters. Take the steps down from here to the shore where you can look across to St. Martin Island. In the southeastern corner of Rock Island, you can see the foundations of an abandoned fishing village if you look closely. The island also has some old cemeteries.

The beautiful stone Viking Hall boathouse and other island buildings (like the water tower on the east shore) were built by the electrical inventor Chester Thordarson. He bought this island in 1910 with visions of creating his own Icelandic kingdom, similar to the island he had known as a child. Icelanders did the construction work from native stone, the prize of which is the impressive boathouse. Viking Hall houses the park's nature center now, but it once held the largest collection of Icelandic literature in the

world. You can sense the heritage of Iceland here in the high-beamed ceiling and massive fireplace, and in the view across the water. The boathouse with surrounding structures and water tower area have been entered in the National Register of Historic Places.

You can visit the island for a day to hike, be a beach bum, picnic or join in a naturalist program, but a camping trip gives you more time to relax and discover the island. No motor vehicles are allowed on Rock Island, so you have to carry picnic or camping supplies. Bottles, cans and other nonburnables must be packed out.

(opposite page)

The wild beauty of Rock Island draws visitors who enjoy the isolation.

Facilities

The campground has 40 individual sites and two group sites (up to 80 people). Reservations are required for the group sites. Drinking water is near the picnic area by the dock. The campsites have a feeling of privacy, and some have good views of Lake Michigan or the shoreline by the boathouse. It's a good idea to reserve ferry space and campsites ahead of time because Rock Island is a popular destination.

WHITEFISH DUNES STATE PARK

Door County. Between Clark Lake and Lake Michigan. Turn east on Clark Lake Road from Highway 57 just north of Valmy. Highway map index: 5-J.

Main Attraction

Whitefish Dunes is the newest of Door County's six state parks and trails. The young park features the highest sand dunes (90 feet) on the western shore of Lake Michigan. The shifting dunes and moody Lake Michigan form a wild shoreline that imparts a sense of isolation.

As you follow the graceful curve of the beach, take off your shoes and socks and play tag with the chilly waves. Close your eyes and let the lake take over your senses: the sound of gently rolling surf and the coarse cries of gulls, the feel of the cool breeze on your face and wet sand between your toes, and the distinctive smell of sand and large water. Look out across the water and you may see a lake freighter, or down along the beach you may spot a commercial fisherman checking the nets that are marked by poles in the bay.

Things To Do

The park's 849 acres are laced with 11.3 miles of hiking trails divided into four color-coded loops of varying distances. Hikers will notice two distinctive regions in the park. The northeastern portion of the park is relatively flat and rocky, due to thin soils with bedrock at or near the surface. The limestone formations are part of the Niagara Escarpment, the rock layer that supports the Door Peninsula. The shoreline in this part of the park is rugged, with sheer cliffs up to 20 feet above the lake. Wave action is slowly undercutting the rock face into caverns.

Southwest of this area the landform changes from

a rocky surface to sand dunes and sandy soil. The dunes are part of either an active zone or a stabilized zone. In the active zone, little vegetation is growing and the dunes are continually reshaped by wave and wind action. Vegetation prevents the building and erosion of the dunes in the stabilized zone.

The dunes of Whitefish were formed by water and wind. Wave action (often from storms) deposited sand in the Whitefish Bay basin that the last glacier had carved out. As the waves bulldozed the sand inland a large sandbar was formed, which isolated pres-

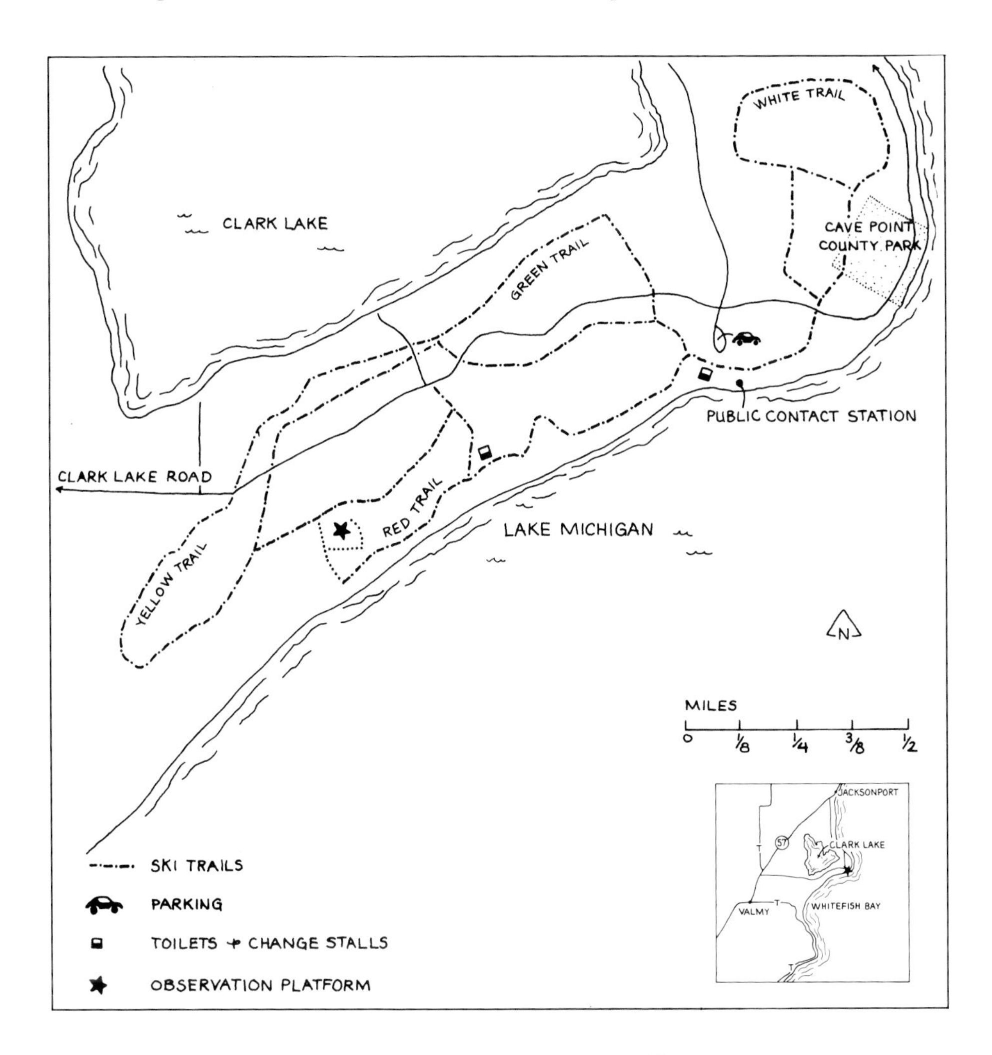

ent-day Clark Lake from Lake Michigan. Much of the state park straddles this old sandbar.

As the seasons progressed, the wind carried sand up the incline of the sandbar, increasing its height. The same winds eroded the lake sides of the dunes, slowly moving them, inch by inch, farther inland where they were stabilized by plant life.

The dunes are fragile to human touch. Tough dune grasses, such as beach pea and a rare quack grass, help to hold the sand, but they are easily uprooted by tramping feet. Farther inland, the sand supports creeping juniper, goldenrod and milkweed. Birch and cedar trees cap the dunes as you hike away from the beach. "Old Baldy" is the only dune that visitors

The rocky shore at Cave Point is most impressive when waves are crashing against the limestone cliffs.

are allowed to climb and has a wooden walkway provided for that purpose. From the top of "Old Baldy," the park's highest dune, you'll get a commanding view of Clark Lake and Lake Michigan.

The sand beach is the most popular part of the park. The water temperature is usually too cool for swimming (no lifeguards on duty), but the beach is often busy with sunbathers. Changing stalls are just off the beach. If you're early enough you might get a lakeside picnic table that gives you a view of the curving shoreline and the blue expanse of Lake Michigan.

People like Whitefish Dunes for its solitude, though the beach can be crowded on warm summer afternoons. If you time your visit for mornings or evenings, brooding days or other seasons, the park becomes a refreshing switch from some of the more people-oriented attractions in Door County. Whitefish Dunes is a great location for photographers. The sweep of the lake and beach provide attractive photo subjects.

Facilities

Whitefish Dunes is a day-use park. There are no campsites here (or at Cave Point—see below), but you can camp at public and private campgrounds in the area. Check with the Door County Chamber of Commerce office in Sturgeon Bay for further details. Winter use of the park is primarily for cross-country skiers. No snowmobiling is allowed.

Surrounding Area

Cave Point County Park, at the north end of Whitefish Dunes, is another special spot for photographers and sightseers. Waves breaking against undercut limestone cliffs cause a "booming" sound that can be heard a quarter mile away. The six-foot waves can be impressive during a storm or when there's a strong east wind. As they pound the shore, the ground at Cave Point trembles with the impact. On calmer days, you can enjoy a picnic lunch in the county park, wander along the shore, or just daydream as the lake takes over your senses.

(continued on next page)

The shifting dunes on this wild Lake Michigan shoreline, the cries of gulls and the sound of the surf make this a wonderful place to wander and contemplate the natural world.

The Lake Michigan side of the Door Peninsula has a wilder personality than the Green Bay side. This is reflected in the less-settled nature of Whitefish, Newport, and Rock Island state parks. Besides the parks, there are other natural areas on the Lake Michigan side as you drive up the shore. The Ridges Sanctuary, near Baileys Harbor, is a 910-acre preserve for rare native plants and wildlife. A series of 16 low ridges (former lake shorelines) gives the preserve its name. Between the ridges are bogs. The diversity in landform results in a range of plant communities from open water to climax forest and is home to 25 kinds of orchids, trailing arbutus, fringed gentians and Arctic primrose. Visitors enjoy self-guided hikes, conducted tours and evening nature programs. Pets, picnics and camping are prohibited. Trails are open in winter on a limited basis for cross-country skiing and snowshoeing. Donations to The Ridges Sanctuary, a nonprofit corporation, are suggested for hikers.

Cana Island Lighthouse, northeast of Baileys Harbor, has guided ships on Lake Michigan since 1869. The tiny island on which it stands is reached by a causeway, under shallow water most of the time (wear shoes with a good tread that you don't mind soaking). The small island and idyllic lighthouse have an almost mystical quality. Times were often hard here. The lighthouse keeper's logs tell stories of anguish and struggle, rescue and survival, and of the pleasures of the simple life. The keeper's house is being restored and maintained by the Door County Maritime Museum, which also operates two other museums: one at Gills Rock commemorating fishing and the other in Sturgeon Bay on a shipbuilding theme. The lighthouse is on the National Register of Historic Places. Visiting hours at the lighthouse are from 10 a.m. to 5 p.m.

The Mud Lake Wildlife Area, two miles north of Baileys Harbor, is a 2,000-acre state-owned tract that is habitat for deer, waterfowl, ruffed grouse and small game. It is open for hunting and is a favorite of cross-country skiers who enjoy seclusion and a chance to observe wildlife around a lake, marsh and wooded lowland.

Toft's Point, on North Bay, is named for the woman who protected more than 300 acres of pine, northern hardwoods and conifer swamp. In 1968 she deeded the land to the Wisconsin Nature Conservancy, which in turn passed it on to the University of Wisconsin–Green Bay as a sanctuary for plants and animals. Toft's Point, along with The Ridges and the Mud Lake Wildlife Area, is a National Natural Landmark.

Another Wisconsin Nature Conservancy project in Door County is the Mink River Estuary in Rowley Bay. The area, currently over 600 acres, is habitat for several rare dune and wetland plants. The estuary supports 12 different plant communities, provides breeding grounds for fish and waterfowl and has a rare "tidal effect" in which lake water flows upstream several times a day.

HIDDEN VALLEYS

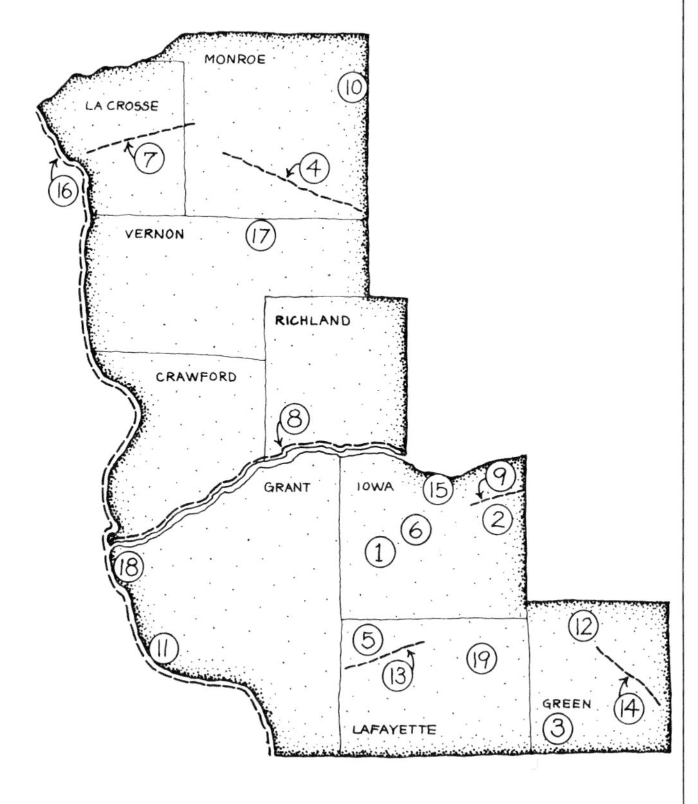

1. Blackhawk Lake Recreation Area
2. Blue Mound State Park
3. Browntown–Cadiz Springs State Recreation Area
4. Elroy-Sparta State Trail
5. First Capitol State Park
6. Governor Dodge State Park
7. La Crosse River State Trail
8. Lower Wisconsin State Riverway
9. Military Ridge State Trail
10. Mill Bluff State Park
11. Nelson Dewey State Park
12. New Glarus Woods State Park
13. Pecatonica State Trail
14. Sugar River State Trail
15. Tower Hill State Park
16. Upper Mississippi River National Wildlife and Fish Refuge (see page 352)
17. Wildcat Mountain State Park
18. Wyalusing State Park
19. Yellowstone Lake State Park

BLACKHAWK LAKE RECREATION AREA

Iowa County. Turn north on Highway 80 in Cobb for 3.5 miles to County BH. Turn east (right) on County BH to the Recreation Area. (Cobb is about halfway between Madison and Prairie du Chien on Highway 18.) Highway map index: 10-E.

Main Attraction

(overleaf)

The bluffs and valleys of the unglaciated southwestern part of the state produce unsurpassed vistas.

Blackhawk Lake Recreation Area is separate from the state park system. Though it is owned by the Wisconsin Department of Natural Resources, it's operated by a local park commission through an easement with Iowa County. The park is a nonprofit operation, supported entirely from admission and camping revenues (no tax support). Its fees, though similar, are unique from those of other state park facilities.

Blackhawk Lake Recreation Area is named for Chief Blackhawk, a southern Wisconsin tribal leader who said, "This was a beautiful country. I loved my towns, my cornfields, and the home of my people. I fought for it. It is now yours. Keep it as we did."

Things To Do

That sentiment has guided the development of the 2,200-acre recreation area. Visitors can gain a similar appreciation of the meadows, wooded bluffs and rock formations by hiking the Red Pine Nature Trail or one of the many other paths that roam the park. Weekend naturalist programs help to interpret the natural and human history of the area by guided hikes, talks and films.

Most people make a beeline for Blackhawk Lake.

This clear, spring-fed lake (formed by two dams) has a supervised beach, bathhouses and a concession stand. Picnic grounds and shelters are at either end of the lake. Boat rentals and moorings are available from late spring to early fall through the concession stand. Fishing enthusiasts can launch from the new

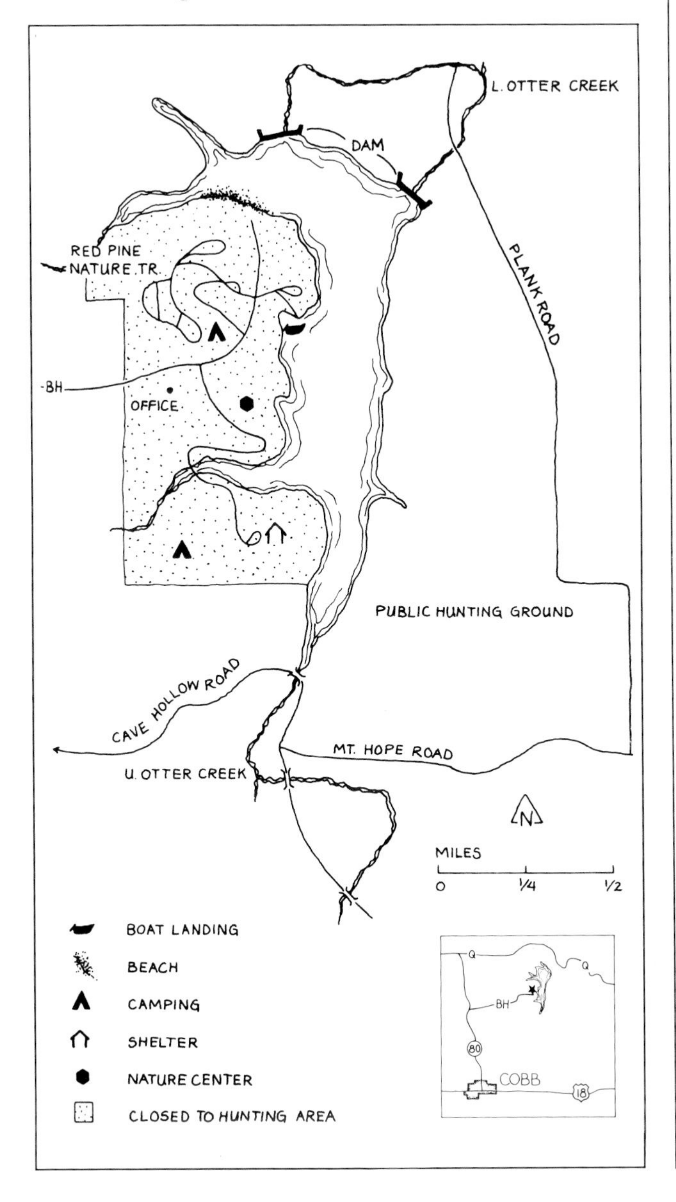

Spring-fed Blackhawk Lake offers fishing enthusiasts trout, walleye, bass and catfish. There's also a bathhouse and a supervised beach.

pier at the boat landing and try their luck with the lake's walleye, bass, trout, catfish and panfish. Both gas and electric motors are allowed on the lake but a 5-mph (no wake) speed limit is enforced. Breezy days lure sailboaters and windsurfers out on the 220-acre lake.

Winter is an active season at Blackhawk Lake. Ice fishing shanties resemble a village on the frozen lake as anglers try for walleyes and panfish. Cross-country ski trails are designed for skiers of all abilities. Ski rental is available through the park office, and cross-country skiing instruction is provided on designated weekends.

Flora and Fauna

The bulk of the recreation area is a 1,500-acre public hunting ground. Waterfowl and shorebirds are best observed during the spring and fall migrations; songbirds may be seen and heard in warmer weather. Hikers and hunters (in season) may also spot deer, wild turkey, ruffed grouse, ring-necked pheasant, beaver and muskrat. Interested hikers can pick up a bird checklist at the office before exploring the recreation area. Hunters should also check at the office for details about use of the public hunting ground.

Facilities

The 125-site campground (showers, 29 electrical hookups) offer both wooded and open sites. Reservations are accepted after January 1 each year. Contact the park office by mail or phone (listed in the back of this book) for information about reservations for either the family campground or the group campground.

Surrounding Area

When you visit Blackhawk Lake, you'll also find a wealth of state parks and trails in the area. If you bring your bicycle, ask at the Blackhawk office for directions for a 20-mile scenic, hilly route to the Military Ridge State Trail near Dodgeville. Governor Dodge, Tower Hill and First Capitol state parks are short drives away. The communities of Mineral Point, Dodgeville and Spring Green are also worth side trips because of local attractions such as Pendarvis and the House on the Rock. Blackhawk Lake Recreation Area personnel can give you more details.

BLUE MOUND STATE PARK

Iowa County. About 25 miles west of Madison on Highway 18-151 to Blue Mounds. Follow signs from Blue Mounds one mile northwest to the park. Highway map index: 10-F.

Main Attraction

Blue Mound, southern Wisconsin's highest point (1,716 feet above sea level), looks blue when seen from a distance. There are really two "Blue Mounds." The east mound is the site of Brigham County Park in Dane County where you can hike through a mature sugar maple forest. The west mound, taller of the two, is Blue Mound State Park. Winnebago Indians called the west mound "Weehaukaja," meaning "a high place with a wonderful view."

Things To Do

The state park takes advantage of its height. For the best vantage point in the 1,100-acre park, climb one of the two 40-foot observation towers at either end of the hilltop picnic area. Each tower has a landmark locator to help you pinpoint various cities and geologic features, some as far away as 25 or 30 miles. On a clear day you can see the State Capitol, the Baraboo and Mississippi River bluffs, and the Belmont and Platteville mounds. For those who are unable to climb the towers, ground level vistas have been cut through the trees on the north side of the picnic area. The view from the towers is inspiring in any season, but is perhaps the most picturesque during autumn or following a winter snowfall.

While you can get the broad picture of the surrounding countryside from the towers, you'll experience the park on a more intimate level by taking the trails. For an easy hike, circle the picnic area on top of the mound, staying close to the edge of the woods. Or you can hike down the East Tower Trail to the open land near the swimming pool. Early morning hikers enjoy this spot as a productive bird-watching location.

For a longer, more rugged hike, try the Pleasure Valley Trail. This two-mile loop begins at the far end of the swimming pool parking lot. The path winds through a variety of plant communities as you descend into the valley, including lowland brush, a sugar maple forest, prairie and dense oak woods. Watch for the state's largest known slippery elm tree along the way. This giant tree stands 88 feet tall, and has a 10-foot circumference.

The Flint Rock Nature Trail helps hikers understand more about the park through 31 trail-side labels. You can start your hike on the wooded trail from the west observation tower, the picnic area shelter

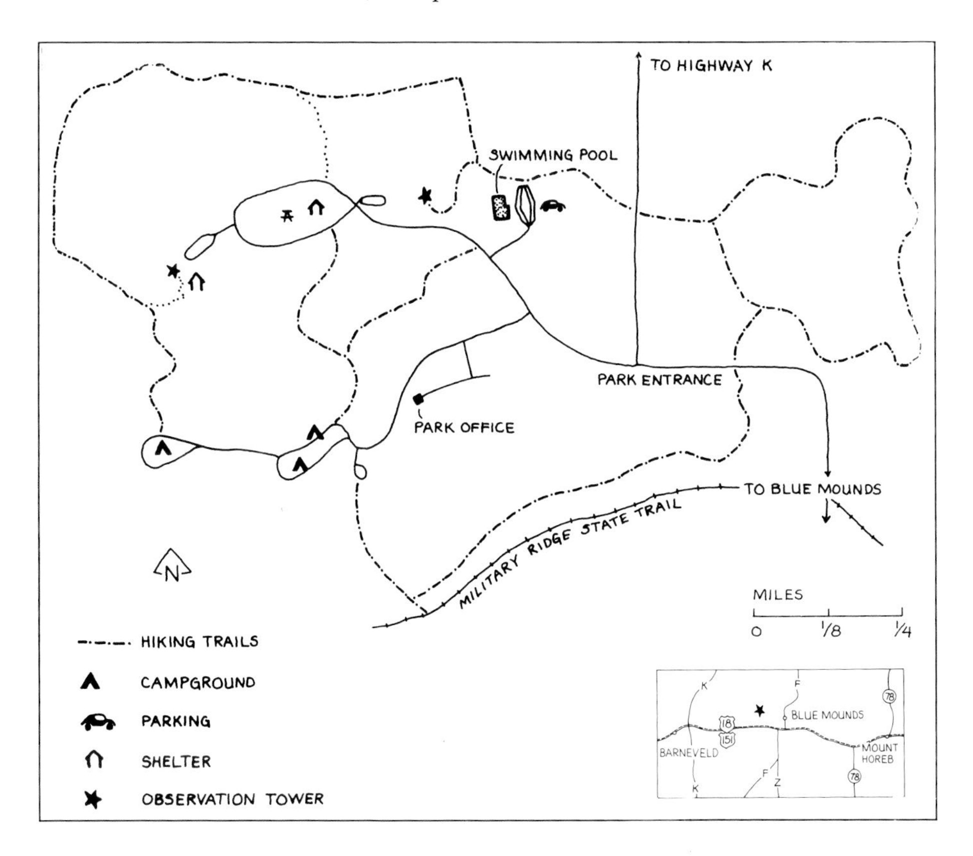

building or the campground. The Flint Rock Trail is a good place for bird-watching (over 100 species have been observed in the park) or for trying to catch a glimpse of a white-tailed deer.

Blue Mound State Park is open for camping during the winter, too. But you don't have to camp to have snow fun here. The park maintains nine miles of groomed cross-country ski trails that roam the forests and fields around the mound. The variety of terrain means that skiers of all abilities can enjoy themselves on the park's trails. If you bring kids along, you may wish to pack a couple of sleds, too.

Facilities

The park's picnic ground covers the entire top of Blue Mound, including a playground, ball field and regulation-size horseshoe links (bring your own horseshoes). Shelters are located at each end of the hilltop. The east shelter has electricity and may be reserved for family or group gatherings. After a picnic you can go swimming in the park's spacious pool, unique in the state park system. A wading pool, diving area and bathhouse are provided.

The campground's 78 sites are all wooded, and half of them can be reserved. Showers are not available in the campground at this time. Some camping and picnic supplies are sold at the concession stand near the pool. You can buy other supplies in nearby Blue Mounds. Campers and daytime visitors are welcome to participate in the guided hikes and evening slide programs presented by the park naturalist throughout the summer months. Stop by the nature center in the picnic area to see the displays on the park's human and natural history.

From the towers, you can see the State Capitol, the Baraboo and Mississippi River bluffs and a vast amount of surrounding countryside. Try it during autumn's peak color.

Surrounding Area

The area around the park has many attractions for visitors who wish to see more of southwestern Wisconsin. Mt. Horeb, east of the park, is a small but scenic town known for its arts and crafts shops. You can tour an underground cave at Cave of the Mounds, near the park (admission fee). This part of the state

The Indian word for the west mound means "a high place with a wonderful view."

is proud of its Norwegian heritage and shows it off to visitors with such attractions as Little Norway (a pioneer homestead) and The Song of Norway, a light romantic musical performed on an outdoor stage at Cave of the Mounds during certain summer weekends. Ask at the park office for more details about times and fees.

The park office can also give you information about other nearby points of interest, including Tower Hill and Governor Dodge state parks. The Military Ridge State Trail (39.6 miles) runs from Madison to Dodgeville, skirting the southern edge of Blue Mounds State Park. Bicyclists who wish to camp at the park can turn off the bike trail to the campground on a short spur trail.

BROWNTOWN–CADIZ SPRINGS
STATE RECREATION AREA

Green County. Seven miles west of Monroe on Highway 11. Highway map index: 11-F.

Main Attraction

Browntown–Cadiz Springs State Recreation Area is in southwestern Wisconsin's Driftless Area of rolling hills and spring-fed streams untouched by glaciers. The damming of one of these streams formed the two lakes in the recreation area.

Things To Do

The lakes, Beckman and Zander's, are the center of many of the recreational activities. Fishing is the most popular with both warm- and cold-water species available. Zander's Lake is stocked yearly with both rainbow and brown trout; Beckman Lake contains northern pike. Both lakes have large populations of smallmouth bass and panfish.

Zander's Lake is stocked yearly with rainbow and brown trout, and both lakes in the recreation area have large populations of smallmouth bass.

Beckman Lake's beach is a favorite spot for sunbathers and swimmers. The lakes are also used for canoeing and sailing, but both are too small (95 acres) to allow motorboats.

If you want to wander a bit, there is a 1.5-mile hiking trail around Beckman Lake and a 30-station interpretive nature trail at Zander's Lake.

Hunting is allowed in the recreation area, but contact the ranger for specific details.

Flora and Fauna

A variety of wildlife lives here, including deer, fox, Hungarian partridge, pheasant, ruffed grouse, ducks and great blue heron. The terrain varies from upland fields and forests to lowland streams and swamps, providing an array of vegetation that will challenge the observation powers of any hiker.

The recreation area includes a 40-acre natural area called the Browntown Oak Forest. The natural area (no trails) preserves a remnant of the once larger red and black oak forest of southwestern Wisconsin.

Facilities

Picnic grounds in the 629-acre recreation area are furnished with shelters, tables, grills and drinking water. All picnic sites have lake views. Because of the

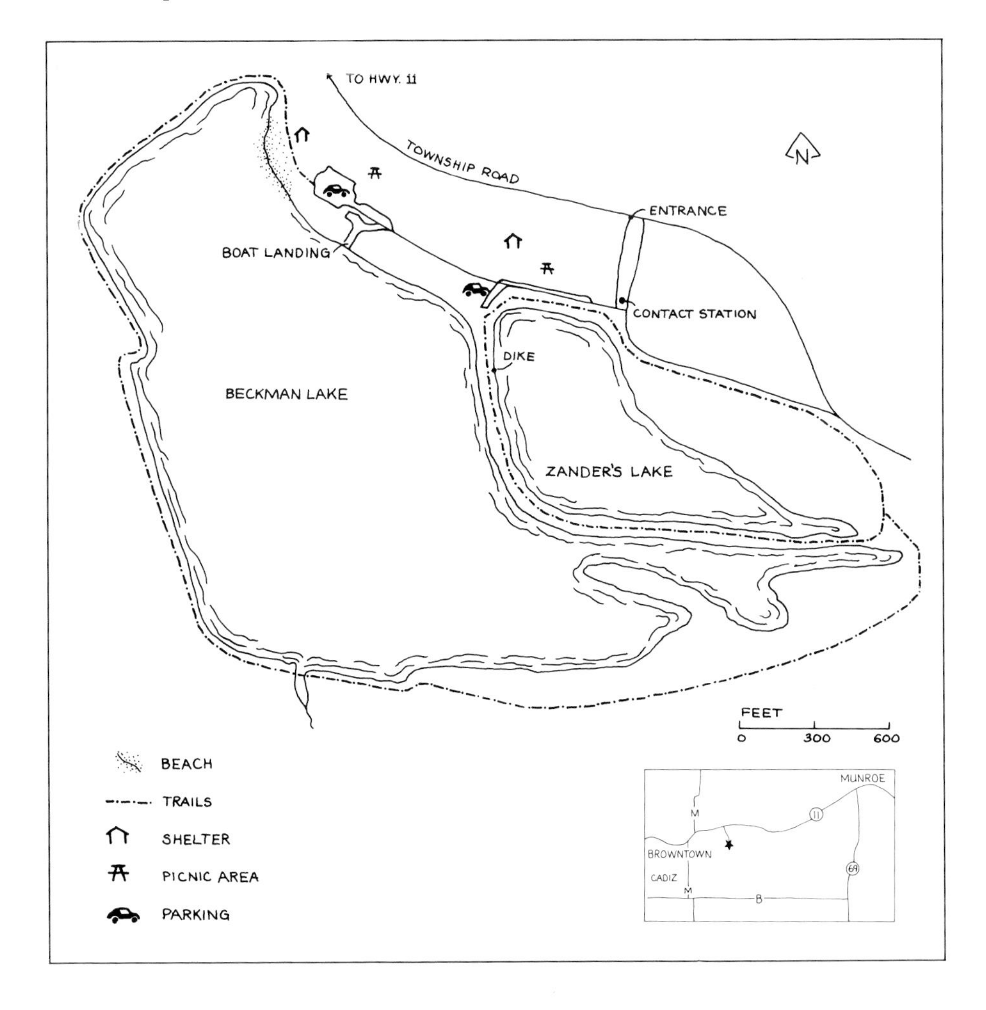

lakes and picnic areas, this is a good place for family visits. There are no camping facilities, though.

Fishing is popular here with a variety of fish awaiting all ages.

Surrounding Area

Other nearby state parks are New Glarus Woods and Yellowstone Lake and the Sugar River State Trail.

ELROY-SPARTA TRAIL

Juneau and Monroe counties. 32 miles, between Sparta and Elroy. Access from Highway 71 at Norwalk, Wilton, Kendall, Elroy and Sparta.

Main Attraction

Even when our eyes adjust to the darkness of tunnel #3 on the Elroy-Sparta Trail, there's still not much to see. You can turn around and look back upon the lush foliage of the countryside that you just pedaled past, feeling the warmth of summer against your face again. But when you begin walking your bicycle through the tunnel, the daylight behind fades and the sliver of light in the inky distance is three quarters of a mile away.

You can hear the echoes of other cyclists long before spotting their shadowy forms against the growing light of the opposite entrance. To add to the eerie atmosphere, water from overhead springs drips down through the rock faults onto the heads of hikers. The tunnel is not lighted, so it's best to walk your bicycle through and to bring a flashlight along. A jacket is a good idea, too, to ward off the cave-like temperatures (around 50 degrees) of the tunnel.

The other two tunnels (each about one third of a mile long) are also cool, dark and damp, sustaining a constant temperature year-round. You'll get dripped on in these tunnels, too, as the natural stone walls and arched ceilings of layered brick in all three tunnels provide drainage for the underground (above the tunnel) springs.

When the Chicago and Northwestern Railroad constructed a line from Chicago to St. Paul in the 1870s, they wanted to maintain a 3% gradient. That's why three tunnels had to be bored through the hills in this area. Tunnel #1 (between Kendall and Wilton) and tunnel #2 (between Wilton and Norwalk) each took about two years to complete. Tunnel #3, west of Norwalk, took nearly three years to build.

The huge double doors at each of the six tunnel entrances were closed by the railroad during the winter. This helped to prevent the weakening of the tunnel entrances caused by freezing and thawing from the cold outside and the warmth inside. Six "tunnel keeps" were hired to open and close the mammoth doors for the daily trains. One of the watchman's shacks still stands at the rest area at the southeast end of tunnel #3. Today, the tunnel doors are still closed for winter (around November 15) and reopened in April. The snowmobile trail is diverted around the three tunnels.

As the railroads declined in importance in the middle of the century, the Chicago and Northwestern discontinued some routes. By 1953, passenger service was halted. Freight service stopped in 1964, and the railroad right of way was sold to the Wisconsin Con-

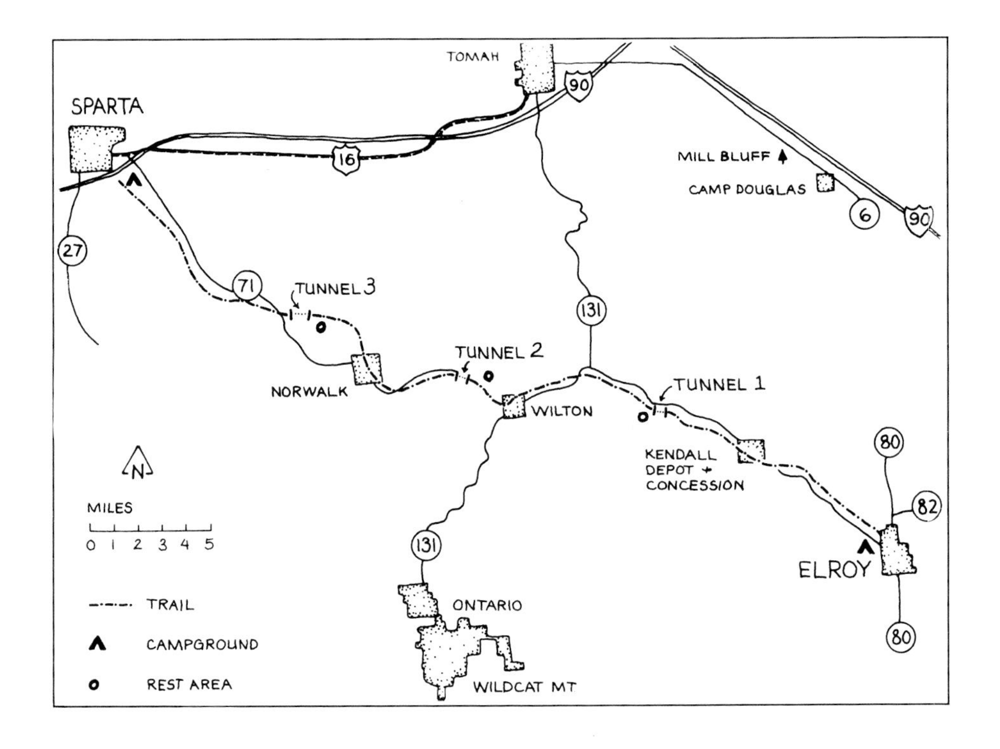

servation Department (now the DNR) for development as a recreation trail.

The southwestern Wisconsin countryside hasn't changed much since the locomotives chugged around the bend and roared through the tunnels. Bicyclists and hikers can enjoy the same vistas of rolling hills, wooded slopes, rocky bluffs and fertile fields that train passengers gazed at from their window seats of a century ago.

Comfortable day rides are easy to plan if you don't wish to cycle the whole trail at once. Besides the five towns, rest stops are spaced along the trail. You can pick up trail maps and information about area services and activities at the trail headquarters in Kendall or at many of the local businesses.

The Elroy-Sparta Trail, one of the first of its kind in the country, has earned a national reputation among bicyclists. Over 50,000 people are lured here each year because of the tunnels, the scenery and the friendly welcome they receive along the way.

Facilities

Each of the trail communities (Elroy, Kendall, Wilton, Norwalk and Sparta) put out the welcome mat for bicyclists and hikers every year. You'll find campgrounds (public and private), rest areas, restaurants, bike rentals, swimming pools (in Elroy, Wilton and Sparta) and other services in the trail towns. The local chambers of commerce can tell you about nearby bed-and-breakfast inns and private campgrounds in the area, some of which sponsor guided bicycle tours of the countryside.

When you start walking your bikes through the tunnels on this trail, the daylight fades behind you, and the sliver of light at the other end can be three-quarters of a mile away.

The trail headquarters and concession is a restored railroad depot in Kendall. The depot, listed on the National Register of Historic Places, houses an interesting collection of historical photos and artifacts that depicts the railroading years in the area. The information service and concession (including bike rental) is operated by the Elroy-Sparta State Trail Association. You can buy the required trail user fee tag

at the depot and at various businesses in the trail towns.

Surrounding Area

Watch for the special events and celebrations during the summer months in the trail communities. The Wilton Lions Club, for example, serves pancake and sausage breakfasts every Sunday morning from Memorial Day through Labor Day for trail users. Each town boasts at least one festival that may tempt you to linger for a day or more before pedaling on.

The Elroy-Sparta State Trail, part of the National Recreation Trail System, will soon be linked to two other state trails. The La Crosse River State Trail, when completed, will stretch for 23 miles from Sparta to the La Crosse area. The Great River State Trail runs for about 22 miles from Onalaska (just north of La Crosse) north to Trempealeau. Besides bicycling, you may wish to visit nearby Mill Bluff State Park and Wildcat Mountain State Park (well-known for leisurely canoeing on the Kickapoo River).

(opposite page)

The tunnels are only part of the fun on the Elroy-Sparta Trail. The scenery and the easy grade make this a popular place for hiking and cycling.

FIRST CAPITOL–BELMONT MOUND STATE PARK

Lafayette County. Three miles north of Belmont on County G. Highway map index: 10-E.

Main Attraction

First Capitol State Park is one of Wisconsin's historical parks. It is the site of the first capital of the Territory of Wisconsin, which included all of present-day Wisconsin, Iowa, Minnesota and parts of both Dakotas. When Madison was chosen as the permanent capital, the town quickly declined. Its final demise came when the railroad passed three miles to the south.

The Council House and the Supreme Court Building are all that remain of the small village of Belmont. A Governor's residence and a boardinghouse for legislators were built in the same style as the other two buildings. Lumber for these four buildings was precut in Pittsburgh and transported down the Ohio River by boat, then overland by oxen through the wilderness. The village also had a blacksmith shop, tavern, grocery store, variety store and a few residences.

Belmont was originally chosen as the capital because it was centrally located between the lead mining centers of Platteville and Mineral Point. At that time, this region was the territorial population center.

But not everyone was satisfied with Belmont as the capital. By the time the territorial legislature first met with Governor Henry Dodge in the autumn of 1836, an assortment of lobbyists were already promoting other sites for the capital. Among them was James Duane Doty, who was to become the second Territorial Governor. He was successful in promoting

Madison even though it existed only as a "paper" town on the maps of the day.

As Old Belmont faded, the Supreme Court building was moved across the road and used for a time as a home and later as a barn. The Capitol was also moved across the road and converted into a barn.

Efforts to preserve the rapidly deteriorating first Capitol began in 1907. Since then, through the commitment of the Wisconsin Federation of Women's Clubs and appropriations by the legislature, the buildings have been restored and moved back to their former sites. First Capitol became a park in 1924.

In addition to seeing the carefully restored first capitol, try a trip up the observation tower on Belmont Mound. The view extends over 30 miles to Illinois and Iowa, and to the Blue Mounds to the northeast.

Things To Do

Today's visitors can see the Supreme Court and Council House side by side as planned in the early 1800s. The interior of the Council House has been carefully re-created according to records describing the original furnishings. Exhibits in the Supreme Court building depict lead mining, agriculture and home life in southwestern Wisconsin in 1836. The buildings are open daily, 9 a.m. to 5 p.m., Memorial Day weekend through Labor Day. Appointments for group

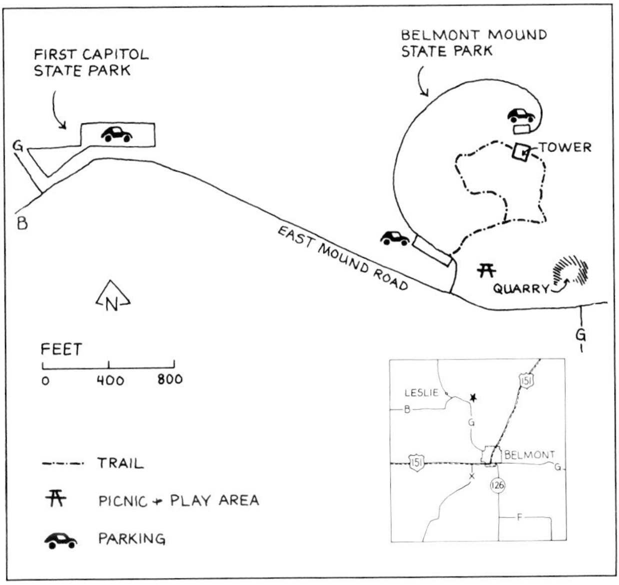

The Supreme Court and Council House buildings have been meticulously restored and house exhibits of early Wisconsin.

tours during May and September can be made by phone through the office at Yellowstone Lake State Park (listed in the back of this book).

After your tour, take the time to enjoy a picnic in the shade of the grove that catches the prairie breezes. This is a restful spot, far removed from that brief time when a tiny frontier town was the hub of a vast territory.

Just down the road is the Belmont Mound picnic and playground area. The French called the 1,400-foot hill "Belle Monte," meaning "beautiful mountain." The Belmont Lions Club operates the 256-acre park that was the site of a limestone quarry and kilns. From the observation tower at the crest of the mound, you can see parts of Iowa and Illinois. You can also see the Blue Mounds, about 33 miles to the northeast. Belmont Mound is mostly covered by oak and walnut woods. Part of this area is designated as the Belmont Mound Woods Natural Area.

Surrounding Area

Southwestern Wisconsin is a region rich in history and beauty. Several other state parks are relatively close to Belmont: Yellowstone Lake, Governor Dodge, and the Mississippi River parks of Wyalusing and Nelson Dewey. These parks have camping and other recreational facilities. The Pecatonica State Trail is just south of First Capitol, stretching between Belmont and Calamine. Of historical interest is the Badger Mine and Museum (offering lead mine tours) in Schullsburg and the Rollo Jamison and Mining Museums (lead mine tour and train ride) in nearby Platteville.

Mineral Point, 11 miles northeast of First Capitol on Highway 151, is a scenic old town (founded in 1827) of hilly, winding streets and stone buildings. Now a popular artist community, Mineral Point began as a lead mining boomtown. Most of the early residents lived in temporary shacks or hillside dugouts, dubbed "badger holes," thus coining Wisconsin's nickname as the Badger State. If you take time to wander the shops and galleries here, you may also wish to visit Pendarvis to catch a glimpse of Mineral Point's early days.

Pendarvis, a group of restored Cornish miners' homes built nearly 150 years ago, recalls the days when southwestern Wisconsin was a rough-and-tumble lead mining region. Pendarvis is one of seven sites operated by the State Historical Society of Wisconsin. For schedule and rate information, write to Pendarvis, 114 Shake Rag Street, Mineral Point, WI 53565, or call 608-987-2122.

GOVERNOR DODGE STATE PARK

Iowa County. About three miles north of Dodgeville on Highway 23. Highway map index: 10-E.

Main Attraction

Governor Dodge State Park's rugged sandstone bluffs, forested ridges and deep green valleys were carved by wind and water over the last 400 million years. Untouched by the great glacier that influenced the topography of most of the state, this corner of Wisconsin is called the Driftless Area, referring to the lack of "drift," or glacial debris.

Governor Dodge is popular with explorers and geology buffs because of the variety of terrain and the sculpted sandstone formations. This land has been a refuge for over 8,000 years, when early Indian people first made winter camps at the base of rock overhangs. Archaeologists have uncovered hundreds of spearpoints and arrowheads at the foot of the park's sandstone bluffs. More recently the Fox, Sauk and Winnebago Indians lived here. European settlement (lead mining and farming) began in the 1820s. Governor Dodge, Wisconsin's second largest state park (Devil's Lake State Park is the largest), is named for Henry Dodge. He was a pioneer resident of the area and the first governor of the Wisconsin Territory.

The ridges in the driftless area once supported a vast treeless prairie with no natural lakes in the well-drained land. But as Governor Dodge State Park evolved, two man-made lakes, Cox Hollow and Twin Valley, were formed with earthen dams.

Things To Do

Today, the busy lakes form the focal point of the large park's (over 5,000 acres) recreational picture. Fishing

GOVERNOR
DODGE
STATE PARK

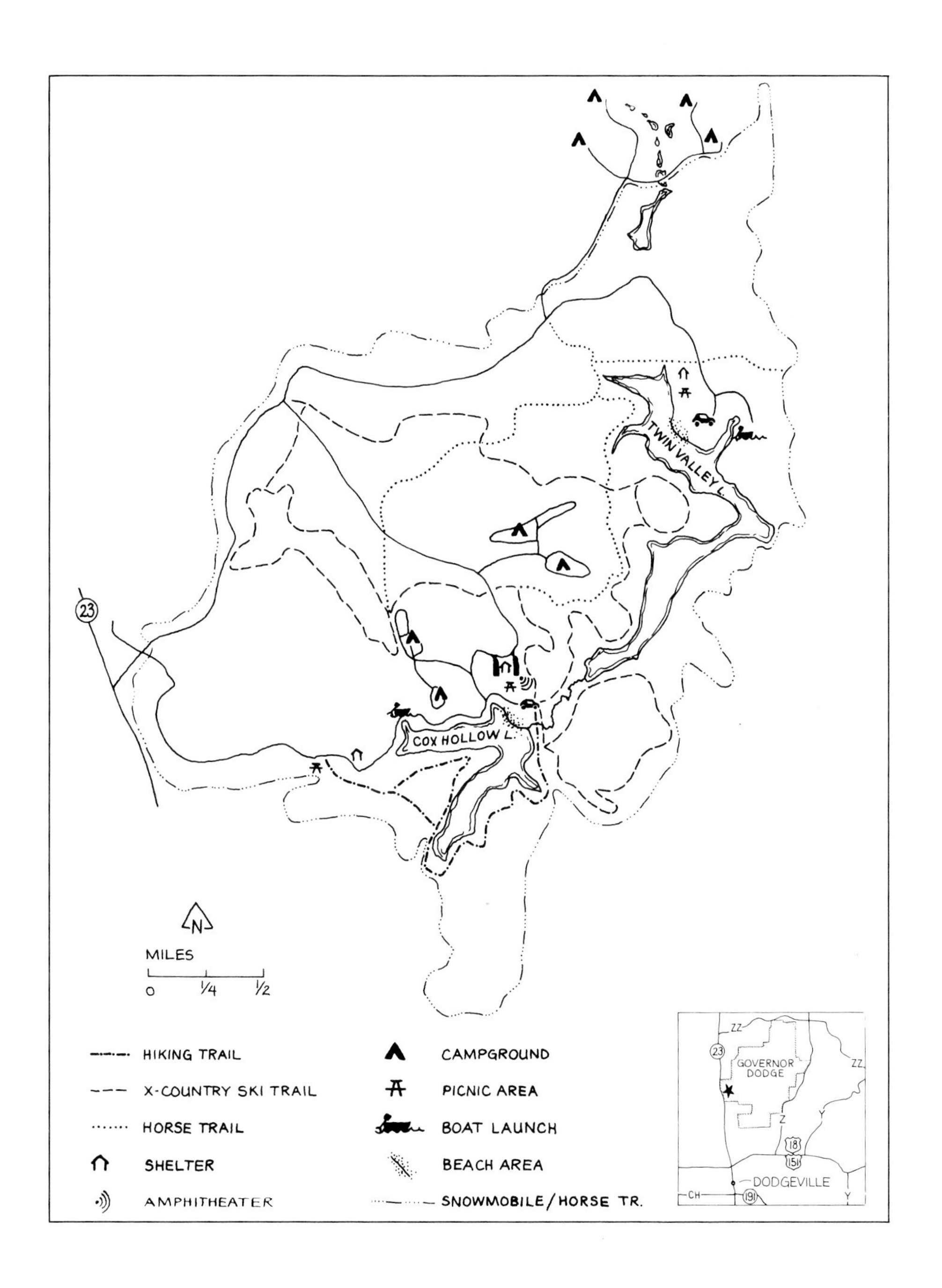

is good here year-round for bass, walleye, muskie and panfish. The countryside around the park has several good trout and smallmouth bass streams. Boats and canoes may be rented at the Cox Hollow beach concession stand from Memorial Day through Labor Day. Rentals are also available on weekends during the spring and fall. You can launch from ramps on both Cox Hollow and Twin Valley lakes. Electric motors only can be used on both lakes. Both lakes have beaches, and lifeguards are on duty at Cox Hollow during the summer.

Though the park's road system is extensive, exploration by car barely scratches the surface of what Governor Dodge has to offer. You'll experience the park on a more intimate level if you head for the trails. Two hiking trails begin at the Enee Point picnic shelter—the self-guided White Pine Nature Trail (two miles) and the White Oak Trail (3.5 miles). You can also hike on over 35 miles of snowmobile and cross-country ski trails during the summer. The trails meander through meadows and oak-hickory woods, climb pine-covered ridges and lead to rocky overlooks.

Horseback riders can enjoy the park's mixture of woods and rolling open country on 22 miles of bridle paths. Bring your own horse or rent one from a nearby stable. No overnight camp is available for horse riders at this time, but a day-use facility is provided.

The naturalist leads scheduled summer hikes of varying lengths designed to grab your curiosity about the park. You'll find out the aromatic skunk cabbage is edible, which wildflowers thrive in the park and what the land was like when the Indians lived here. Other nature hikes include prairie, marsh and early-morning bird hikes. Maybe you'll spot some beavers at work in the lowlands or catch sight of a doe and her spotted fawns. Times and places of naturalist programs are posted, but group hikes should be arranged at least a week in advance.

For some, fall is the favorite hiking season at Governor Dodge. When the temperatures are cool and the daylight wanes, they grab their camping gear and cameras and head for the hills to enjoy the sounds and smells of autumn as they shuffle through the dry

(overleaf)

A field of dandelions heralds the approach of spring at Governor Dodge State Park.

leaves and appreciate the solitude of the forest trails. The fall colorama is best photographed from the ridges and bluffs, where you can breathe deeply of the crisp air and record the park vistas.

Some people visit the park just for winter camping. With the proper gear and plenty of stamina you can find lots of action to keep you warm, such as snowshoeing, tobogganing and sledding. The frozen lakes offer a challenge to optimistic ice fishermen while snowmobilers can zip around on 15 miles of marked trails. The park's trail system connects with the 36-mile Military Ridge State Trail.

Head for the trails here in any season to explore the meadows and oak-hickory woods, or wander the forested ridges to find a rocky overlook for a dramatic view. You can do your exploring here on horseback, too.

The park grooms about 18 miles of cross-country ski trails that are split into three loops of varying degrees of difficulty. Skiers of all abilities will find a loop to fit their tastes. The trails wind through the best of the park's scenery, wandering around lakes, through natural stands of hardwoods and across open fields. The loops are well-marked and usually not crowded, especially if you get a morning start. Pack a lunch and take a snack break near a sandstone ridge or by one of the lakes. Picnic tables and grills are provided at the trail head.

Facilities

Picnickers can choose from eight separate picnic grounds. Picnic shelters are available at Enee Point, the amphitheater and Twin Valley picnic areas. You can buy some picnic supplies at the Cox Hollow beach concession stand or in Dodgeville.

The park's lakes and natural beauty make it a popular destination for campers. The two family campgrounds have a total of 267 sites (showers, 71 sites with electricity). The group camp (tents only) can accommodate up to 1,000 campers. Reservations for the group camp and for a limited number of family campground sites may be made in advance. If you plan on visiting the park during peak summertime use periods, it's a good idea to make camping reservations.

(continued on next page)

Surrounding Area

Dodgeville boasts a variety of historic buildings, including the oldest courthouse in Wisconsin still in use (built in 1859–61). You can buy fresh fruit and vegetables at the farmer's market every Saturday morning during the growing season in the City Hall parking lot.

If you have time, drive west to see First Capitol State Park at Belmont, where the first territorial Capitol was built. Other nearby state recreation lands include Tower Hill, Blue Mound and Yellowstone Lake state parks, Military Ridge State Trail (from Dodgeville to Madison) and the Lower Wisconsin State Riverway. Pendarvis, in Mineral Point, is a complex of restored Cornish miners' homes operated by the State Historical Society of Wisconsin (public tours, admission fee). The famous House on the Rock is on Highway 23 north of Dodgeville.

LA CROSSE RIVER STATE TRAIL

Monroe and La Crosse counties. 23 miles, between Sparta and Medary Junction (several miles east of La Crosse). Highway map index: 8-D.

Main Attraction

The La Crosse River State Trail is one of Wisconsin's recent efforts at converting an abandoned railroad grade into a recreation trail.

The 23-mile trail generally follows the La Crosse River northeast to Sparta. From there, it's a short mile and a half to the popular Elroy-Sparta State Trail (32.5 miles; surfaced for bicyclists; three tunnels). Hikers and snowmobilers are the primary users now, but plans for the La Crosse River State Trail call for bicycle surfacing (by summer 1989) and possibly some camping or rest areas. Private campgrounds are available in West Salem and Medary Junction. The trail passes Neshonoc Lake and crosses four trout streams along the route.

Although the grade is mostly flat, it takes you through coulee country, a region of ridges with steep wooded valleys eroded by water that helped give the La Crosse area its nickname "God's Country." If you like to hike or bike on steeper slopes, get a county map and try some of the local roads that twist and climb through the surrounding hills. Take time to stop and relax, to photograph a valley vista, or just slip off your shoes beside the trail. Smell the hay, listen to the birds or imagine animal shapes in the clouds—trail entertainment can be cheap.

Although the trail is flat, all around are the ridges and steep wooded valleys that give La Crosse the nickname "God's Country."

Surrounding Area

In the La Crosse area, the legendary Mississippi, with its stately bluffs and wildlife areas, lures many a modern-day Huckleberry Finn. The view from Granddad's Bluff sweeps over three states and stretches for miles up and down the Mississippi River valley. Stop at the tourist information center just off the interstate near La Crosse for further details about coulee country and the rest of the state. For more information about the city of La Crosse and its numerous festivals, beautiful parks and visitor attractions (e.g., Mississippi River excursion trips, Riverside USA, etc.), contact the La Crosse Area Convention and Visitor Bureau, P.O. Box 1895, Riverside Park, La Crosse, WI 54601 (608-782-2366).

The La Crosse River Trail is a good addition to this region of recreation-conscious people where joggers are as common as hikers and bikers. When the La Crosse River State Trail is completed, it will form the middle link in a series of three state trails including the Great River (from Onalaska to the Trempealeau National Wildlife Refuge) and the Elroy-Sparta. Bicyclists will then be able to bike from the Trempealeau area to Elroy.

Be sure to include Perrot State Park, a Mississippi River park north of La Crosse, in your travels to God's Country. Other nearby state recreation lands include Mill Bluff and Wildcat Mountain state parks. The Upper Mississippi River and Trempealeau national wildlife refuges are also in the La Crosse area.

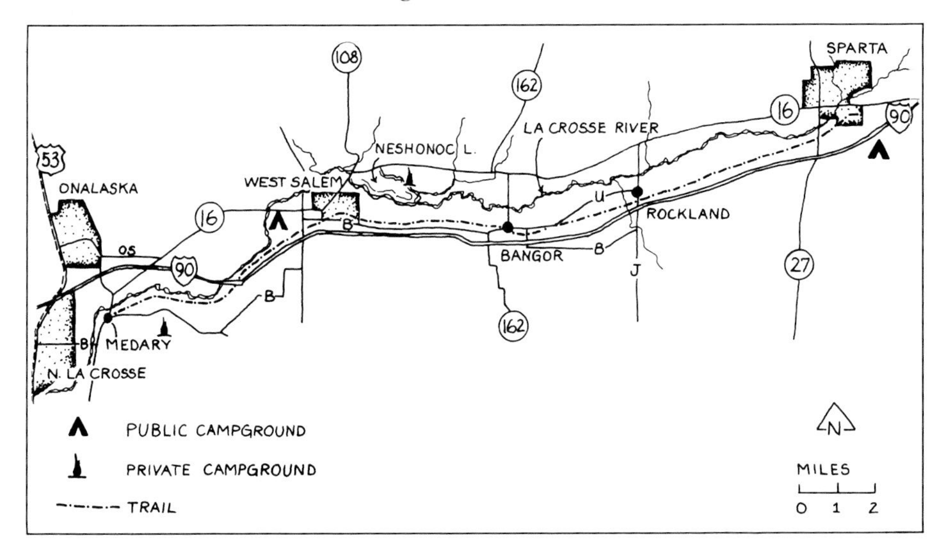

LOWER WISCONSIN STATE RIVERWAY

Sauk, Dane, Richland, Iowa, Crawford and Grant counties. 92 miles, from Prairie du Sac to the Mississippi River.

"He saw that the water continually flowed and flowed and yet it was always there; it was always the same and yet every moment it was new . . . [t]hat the river is everywhere at the same time, at the source and at the mouth, . . . everywhere, and that the present only exists for it, not the shadow of the past, nor the shadow of the future." (From *Siddhartha*, by Hermann Hesse; copyright 1951 by New Directions Publishing Corporation.)

Main Attraction

While you are peacefully paddling down the Lower Wisconsin River, it is the present moment that counts the most—not yesterday's thunderstorm or tomorrow's workday. It's part of the magic of a river that makes time vanish. Yet the shadow of the past and future do have an effect on the Wisconsin River.

The river's past is alive to those who appreciate that the grand bluffs, shifting sandbars and gnarled bottomlands still resemble the broad river valley that other generations knew. Bald eagles and hawks still ride the updrafts near the cliffs above the river. And herons still stand like statues in the brush along the riverbank. The Indians, explorers, fur traders, missionaries, lumbermen and settlers who took their chances on the river would, for the most part, recognize it today.

Though the free-flowing Lower Wisconsin River has retained some of its youth, the signs of man's intrusion and affection are obvious. About 500,000 recreationists enjoy this section of the river and its bluffs each year by boating, canoeing, fishing, swimming, camping, horseback riding, hunting, bicycling and car touring. This section of the river is known for playing hard. (In contrast, the upper 337 miles of the Wisconsin River are belted by 26 hydroelectric power dams and 21 storage reservoirs, giving it the reputation as the "nation's hardest-working river.")

The present moment may be the only thing that counts when canoeing on the river, but the shadow of the future hangs over it when one considers the consequences of increasing user demands. Some river users seek a solitary experience; others prefer a social setting. Likewise, private and public rights are sometimes at odds. Recreationists and landowners do have something in common, though: their enjoyment of the scenic beauty of the Lower Wisconsin River.

With this common thread, and a desire to decide for future generations what will become of the river, the Lower Wisconsin River Citizen Advisory Committee was formed. The DNR, mandated to preserve and enhance natural resources in the state, appointed

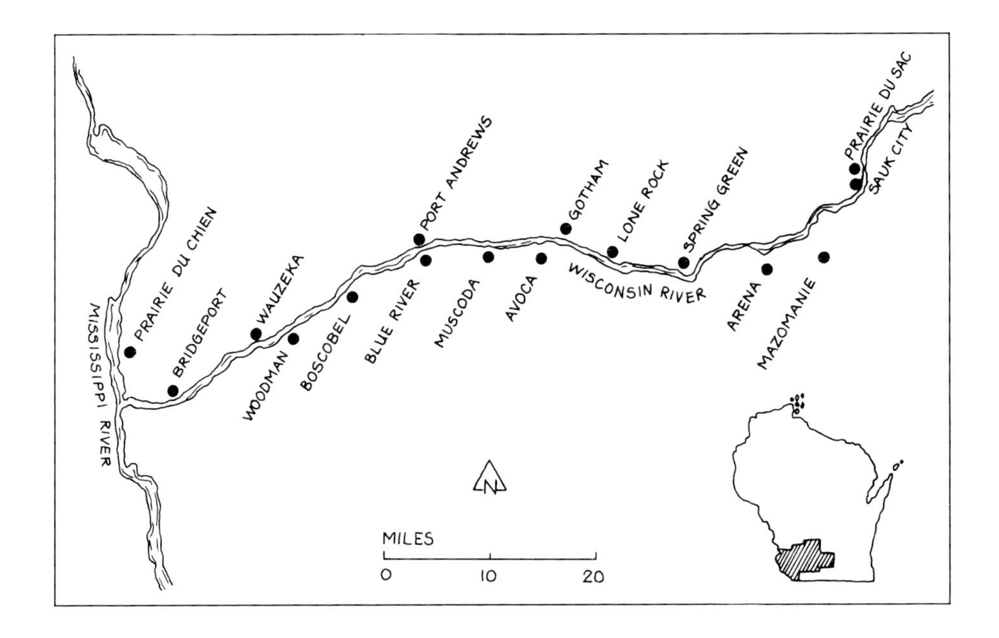

a 30-member committee as diverse as the river itself: farmers, professors, planners, local politicians and merchants, teachers, landowners, recreationists and others. Their job was to form a plan that considered human demands for recreation and livelihood as well as the scenic and ecological integrity of the river corridor.

The Lower Wisconsin State Riverway was born from the joint efforts of the DNR and the Citizen Advisory

Canoes remain a popular way of exploring the sandbars and shores of the Wisconsin River.

Committee. The riverway is the longest remaining undammed stretch of river left in Wisconsin and possibly in the Midwest. The goal of the new designation (the Lower Wisconsin State Riverway is the first state river so named) is to provide a program for recreational use, resource management and scenic preservation of the bluffs and shorelands in the river corridor.

People's ideas of fun vary along the river. Some enjoy picnics and volleyball games on a sandbar with friends while others prefer to spend solitary hours gliding along quiet wooded shores. Patterns of usage vary, also. The upper segment of the riverway, from Prairie du Sac to Spring Green, receives about 68% of the total lower river recreational use. The middle segment, between Spring Green and Boscobel, receives 20% of the use, and the lower section, from Boscobel to the Mississippi River, 12%.

It's part of the magic of a river that makes time vanish.

Recreational development on the upper segment, which sports a beach party atmosphere on peak use days, will be larger and will include more facilities and conveniences than the other segments. This development includes two new canoe/boat landings and upgrading of existing landings. Some campsites will be developed that are accessible only by watercraft or on foot. From four to six reservable island and bankside campgrounds from 1 to 10 sites each are proposed (limited facilities). Sandbar camping may be regulated by permit. It's also possible that a local government or private group may develop a 100-unit family (auto access) campground somewhere in the upper river area.

The middle segment will receive only moderate recreational development. A new canoe/boat launch site and a water access campground (20 to 30 units) near Gotham are planned. Several small, scattered and reservable island or bankside campgrounds (primitive) are also on the drawing board.

The lower segment will remain a lightly used, primitive area with little development. A new boat landing at the Highway 18 bridge in Crawford County is proposed. Camping development will include six to eight small, scattered island campgrounds with one to three sites each.

The riverway experience involves more than river travel. It also includes recreational use of some of the scenic uplands that flank the river corridor. This means new trails for hiking, backpacking, cross-country skiing, snowmobiling and horseback riding. A proposed Riverway Interpretive Center at Tower Hill State Park will depict the natural and human history of the bluffs and the river corridor. Points of historical interest will also be preserved, such as the Black Hawk Indian War battle site downriver from Sauk City. An auto tour trail will follow local roads with four new waysides proposed to make vehicle vagabonding more relaxing.

Endangered and threatened wildlife species will also benefit from the riverway. Protection of bald eagle roosting sites and re-introduction of the peregrine falcon are primary concerns. About 14 new state natural areas and public use natural areas will protect hundreds of rare and endangered plants and animals. One of the new natural areas, between Muscoda and Gotham, will be underwater, highlighting seven rare mussels and a variety of unusual dragonflies and mayflies.

The Lower Wisconsin State Riverway is the first river in Wisconsin to be included in the new state riverway system. Other rivers will also be designated as planning and funding resources permit.

Two state parks are part of the riverway: Tower Hill and Wyalusing. Nearby state recreation lands include Natural Bridge, Blue Mound and Governor Dodge state parks, and the Military Ridge State Trail.

MILITARY RIDGE STATE TRAIL

Iowa and Dane counties. 39.5 miles, between Dodgeville and Fitchburg (near Madison). Access from Highway 18-151 at Dodgeville, Ridgeway, Barneveld, Blue Mounds, Mt. Horeb and Verona.

Main Attraction

Describing his travels on the Old Military Road in March, 1855, Herbert Quick wrote: "Here we went, oxen, cows, mules, horses, coaches, carriages, rags, tatters, silks, satin caps, tall hats, poverty, riches; speculators, missionaries, land-hunters, merchants, gold-seekers, politicians, adventurers . . . a nation on wheels, an empire in the commotion and pangs of birth."

You can be certain that your hiking or bicycling journey on the Military Ridge State Trail will not be nearly as colorful or crowded as Herbert Quick describes. You'll probably see some cows, though. The trail's lure consists of a peaceful bike ride past farms, woods, wetlands, prairies, villages and small towns.

The abandoned rail grade wanders through prairie remnants and past wetlands, farms and villages, providing cyclists with a delightful pastoral ride.

The trail connects Dodgeville and Fitchburg near Madison, following the route of the Old Military Road. The road, built in 1835–36, connected Fort Crawford at Prairie du Chien and Fort Howard at Green Bay, via Fort Winnebago at "the portage" between the Fox and Wisconsin rivers. The soldiers who built the crude road cleared brush two rods (33 feet) wide, plowed two furrows to mark the roadway and placed crosswise logs, called corduroy, over marshy spots.

The ride is much smoother today. Most of the trail follows the former Chicago and Northwestern Railway line, which has a gentle grade of only 2 to 5%. Between Dodgeville and Mt. Horeb, the packed limestone trail follows the crest of the Military Ridge, the divide between the Wisconsin River watershed to the north and the Pecatonica and Rock River watersheds to the south. Between Mt. Horeb and Verona, the trail traverses the Sugar River Valley.

The trail section between Ridgeway and Barneveld (about five miles) is closed until land acquisition is complete. A short section (2.4 miles) on the trail's eastern end is also closed from Fitchburg to east of Verona. But there are long sections of scenic cycling on the rest of the trail: 21 miles from Verona to Barneveld and 9 miles from Dodgeville to County H (about one mile east of Ridgeway). Biking on busy Highway 18-151 is dangerous. To get safely from Ridgeway to Barneveld, the DNR suggests transporting your bicycle by vehicle. Adventuresome bicyclists with good maps and extra time can still bike between the two towns by detouring on county roads.

Flora and Fauna

Along the trail, you may spot wild raspberry and blackcap bushes, wild strawberries, wildflowers and prairie remnants. Some of the wetlands you'll pass provide habitat for ducks, geese, beaver and other wildlife.

Facilities

Trail towns include Dodgeville, Ridgeway, Barneveld, Blue Mounds, Mt. Horeb, Klevenville, Riley and Verona. You can exit in these towns to find food, ac-

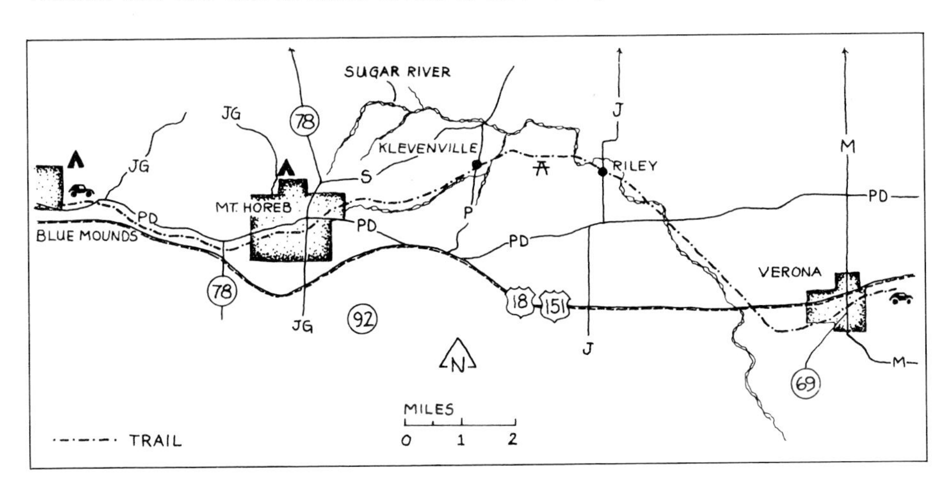

Walking or biking lets you experience Wisconsin's special places up close.

commodations and other services. Vehicle parking lots are at the trail heads: at the junction of Highway 18-151 and County PB east of Verona, and on County YZ, just east of Highway 23 in Dodgeville (across from Pizza Hut).

Future development may include buildings at Verona and Dodgeville; rest facilities at Barneveld, Ridgeway and Mt. Horeb; parking lots at Blue Mounds and Mt. Horeb; an access trail to Governor Dodge State Park; a link with bicycle trails in Madison, Fitchburg and Dane County; bicycle campgrounds at Blue Mound and Governor Dodge state parks; and interpretive displays. County and local governments also have plans for recreational facilities near the trail.

Currently there are no camping facilities on the trail. You can bike into Blue Mounds State Park campground on a trail spur, and until a similar spur is developed in Dodgeville, you have to enter Governor Dodge State Park off Highway 23 and camp in the family campgrounds. Both parks accept reservations.

Bicyclists can also camp in three county parks near the trail: Badger Prairie County Park near Verona, Stewart County Park just north of Mt. Horeb and Brigham County Park just north of Blue Mounds. Several of the trail towns maintain community parks, some of which have campgrounds and swimming areas. To get more details about local public and private campgrounds, swimming, fishing, horseback riding and other local activities and attractions, stop at the visitor information buildings in Mt. Horeb and Dodgeville. State park personnel at Governor Dodge and Blue Mound state parks will also be able to answer questions about what there is to see and do in the area.

Surrounding Area

Trails tidbits: Mt. Horeb boasts many 19th-century buildings and a variety of craft and antique shops; the Dane County Prairie Heritage Trail begins about .4 miles south of the Military Ridge State Trail in Mt. Horeb; Little Norway (an outdoor ethnic museum) and Cave of the Mounds (a commercial cave) are both near the village of Blue Mounds; as you approach Barneveld from the east, you can see the path taken by a tornado that devastated the town in June, 1984 (it left a notch in the skyline of trees north of the trail)—the town was reconstructed in 1985; southwestern Wisconsin was famous as a lead mining region in the mid-1800s, including the area around Dodgeville and Blue Mounds; and bicyclists can buy fresh fruits and vegetables every Saturday morning during the growing season in the City Hall parking lot in Dodgeville.

To learn the most from your bicycling experience

on the Military Ridge State Trail, pick up a copy of the booklet *History and Guide to the Military Ridge State Park Trail* ($1.00) at the Governor Dodge State Park office. Mileposts along the trail show distances from each end. The top number indicates miles traveled and the bottom number indicates miles left to go. Posts with orange numbers mark points of interest that correspond to the numbered descriptions in the booklet.

Trail admission cards are required for bicyclists 18 years of age and older from April through October. The inexpensive cards are available at Governor Dodge and Blue Mound state parks, the DNR district office in Madison and at several private outlets marked along the trail.

MILL BLUFF STATE PARK

Monroe County. Park access is from Highway 12/16, which runs parallel to Interstate 90-94. Exit at Oakdale, five miles northwest of the park, or at Camp Douglas, two miles southeast. Highway map index: 8-E.

Main Attraction

The buttes and mesas of Mill Bluff State Park served as landmarks for westward-bound settlers and are often mentioned in their journals and diaries. The distinctive formations were given picturesque names, such as Ragged Rock and Bee, Bear, Wildcat and Camel bluffs. They rise so suddenly from the surrounding plains that they fire the curiosity of many park visitors.

When the last glacier plugged the Wisconsin River in the Baraboo Hills, it created Glacial Lake Wisconsin. This vast lake covered most of present-day Adams and Juneau counties and parts of adjacent counties. At that time, some of these formations were islands; others were submerged. The mesas and buttes, unique east of the Mississippi River, range in height from 80 to more than 120 feet and are capped by a layer of resistant sandstone. Large bluffs (such as Mill Bluff) are called mesas; the smaller abrupt bluffs (such as Bee Bluff) are called buttes; and the slender abrupt bluffs (such as Devil's Needle) are pinnacles.

The buttes and mesas here rise up suddenly from the surrounding plain—former islands of a vast glacial lake. They are unique east of the Mississippi River.

Erosion of the sides of the rock forms was hastened by wave action on the mammoth lake. Since the formations are striking examples of glaciation, Mill Bluff State Park was designated as one of nine units in Wisconsin's Ice Age National Scientific Reserve. An historical marker in the east picnic area describes the features in the 1,220-acre park.

(continued on next page)

Things To Do

You can get a lofty view of the park's bluffs and the surrounding forest from the crest of Mill Bluff. The bluff, named for a sawmill that operated near here years ago, can be climbed by a stone stairway built

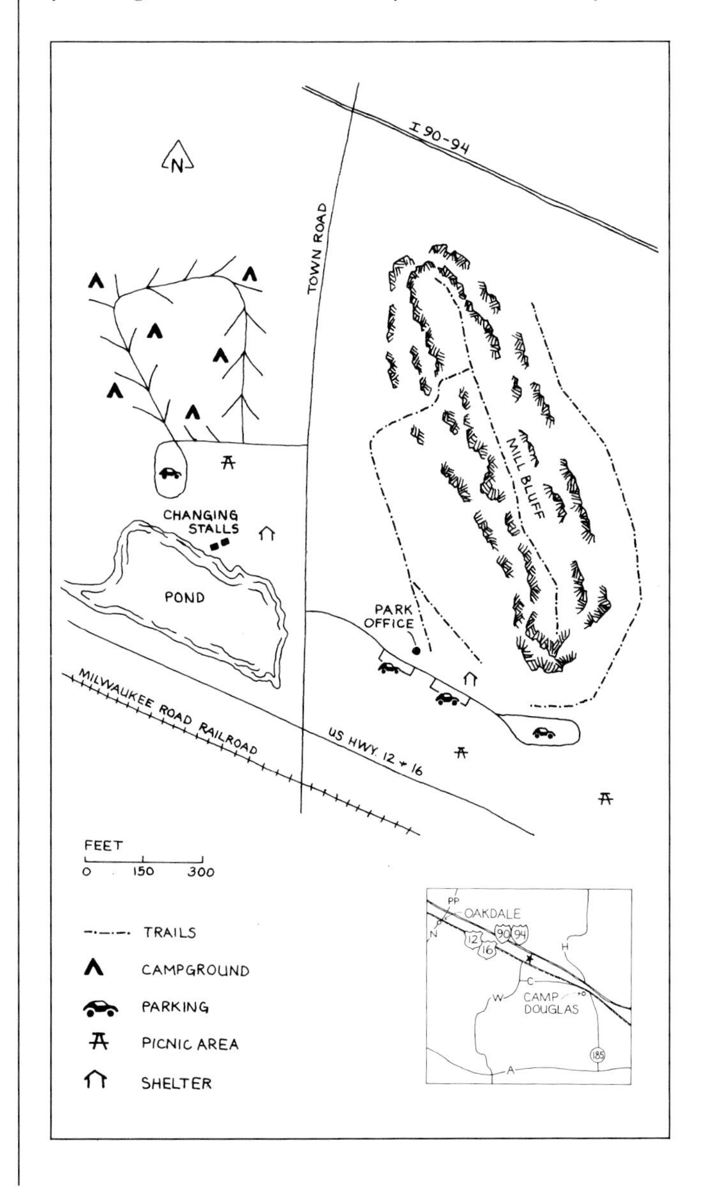

by the Civilian Conservation Corps (CCC) in the mid-1930s.

Once you've invested the time and effort to climb the 175 steps, hike the length of the bluff on the marked trail and enjoy the view. Bring along your camera and some sandwiches in a day pack, and you could easily spend a lazy afternoon on Mill Bluff. Most of the park's rock formations are visible from the observation deck at the north end of Mill Bluff.

Even the park office adds to the rustic scenery at Mill Bluff.

Although you may be the only person on the deck, the solitude is broken by the steady stream of traffic below you on Interstate 90-94.

Petroglyphs (rock carvings) have been found on some bluff faces. Shaped like bird tracks about 6 to 12 inches long, the carvings are believed to date back to the Upper Mississippi Indian culture.

Facilities

Most of the 21 campsites (no showers or electricity) are in or near the woods and all are issued on a first-come, first-served basis. A small sandy beach on a 2.5-acre groundwater pond near the campground provides a chance for some sunbathing or a cool swim. There's plenty of space for picnics with two shelters and many tables by the camping area and below the bluff. Being so close to the interstate highway, Mill Bluff State Park is a convenient roadside rest area that also has the scenery and facilities to tempt you into staying longer. The park is open Memorial Day weekend through Labor Day weekend.

Surrounding Area

The park is in the center of a popular recreation region that includes the Black River State Forest and the Necedah National Wildlife Refuge to the north, the Elroy-Sparta State Trail and Wildcat Mountain State Park to the south and Buckhorn State Park to the east. A camping trip to Mill Bluff puts you in easy range of these other areas.

NELSON DEWEY STATE PARK

Grant County. Two miles west of Cassville on County VV. Highway map index: 10-D.

Main Attraction

Nelson Dewey State Park, overlooking the Mississippi River, has a rich past and a lot to offer, whether you're a history buff or merely want to enjoy the Mississippi River scenery. Stonefield, settled among the bluffs in the park, was the home of Nelson Dewey, Wisconsin's first governor. The governor's first home was a large brick Gothic mansion. It was gutted by fire in 1873 and the more modest Greek Revival structure that you can see today was built on the old foundation.

Things To Do

From the blufftops you can see a rural town of the 1890s, Stonefield Village, built on the flatland along the river where Dewey's outbuildings were located. In the village you can wander along the boardwalks as you visit shops, a school, the railroad station, and other buildings. Stop to watch the blacksmith at his forge or the printer setting type. Chat with the butcher, buy some ice cream at the confectionery or hop on the horse-drawn wagon for a ride around the town (over 30 buildings).

The Mississippi River blufftops overlook a re-creation of an 1890s rural village built on the flatland along the river. You can wander either the ridges or the village boardwalk.

The State Farm Museum, a short walk north of Stonefield Village, depicts the story of Wisconsin agriculture from frontier days to the beginning of mechanized farming. Dewey's 2,000-acre plantation was one of the state's first large-scale farming operations, so it's fitting that the stone foundations of what was once his cow barn now support the State Farm Museum's walls. Stonefield Village and the Farm Museum are operated by the State Historical Society of Wisconsin. For rate and schedule information, write to Stonefield, Cassville, WI 53806 (608-725-5210).

(opposite page)

Stonefield Village nestles close to the Mississippi River, providing visitors with a chance to experience turn-of-the-century life in a rural town.

Combine a visit to Stonefield with the outdoor activities of the park. There are boat launching ramps in Cassville and along the river. You can rent boats from private sources near the park. The backwaters of the Mississippi offer excellent sportfishing for bass, walleye, northern pike and panfish. Exploring the sloughs is a good way to see waterfowl and aquatic plants. There are sand beaches on the river, but the park has no designated beach and no lifeguards are on duty. The public swimming pool in Cassville does have lifeguards. Check at the park office for pool hours.

There are many lookouts with spectacular views for those who choose to hike the forested bluffs along the river. About three miles of hiking trails, including a half-mile nature loop, cover the upland and lowland

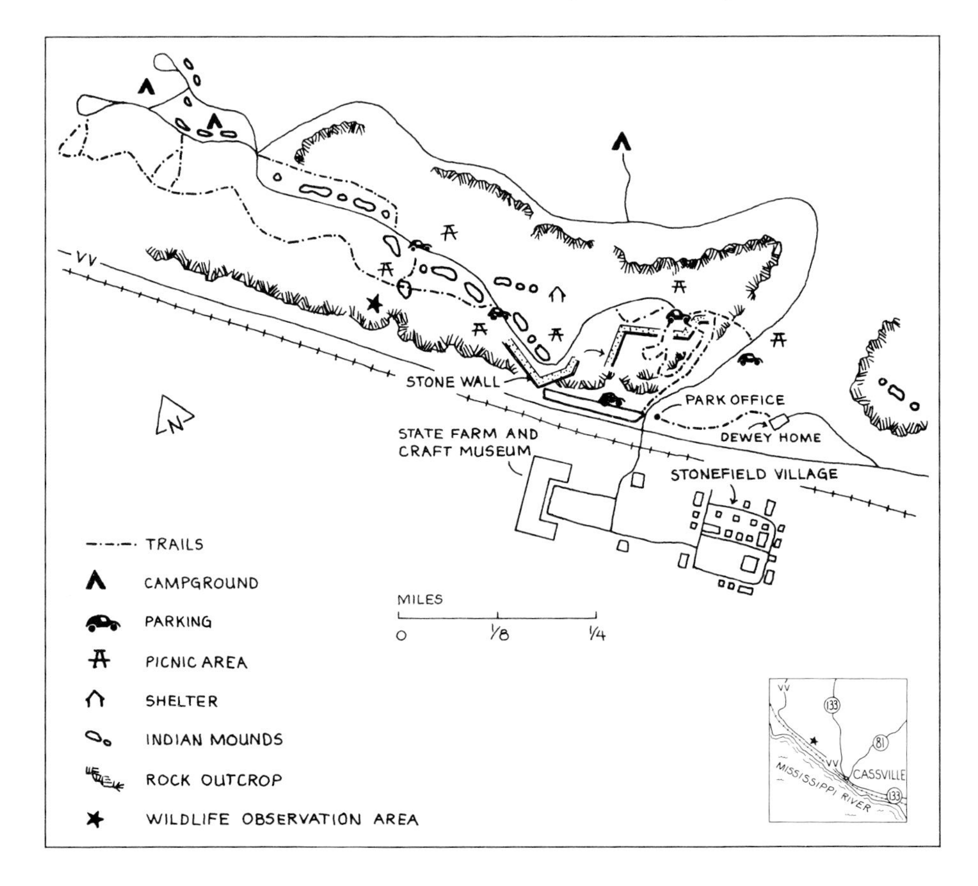

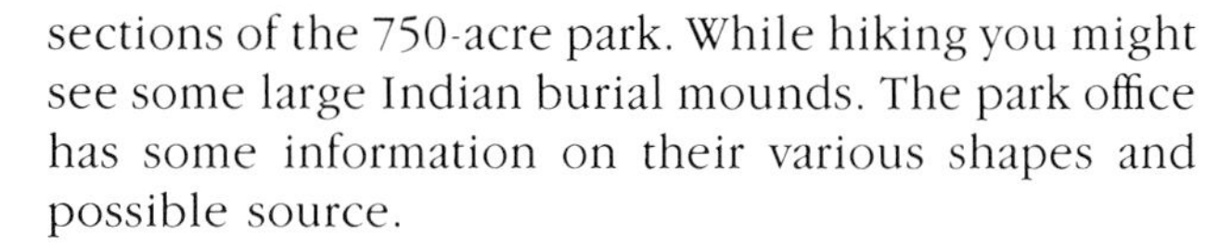

sections of the 750-acre park. While hiking you might see some large Indian burial mounds. The park office has some information on their various shapes and possible source.

Flora and Fauna

If you stop at the wildlife observation post you'll have a chance to see a great blue heron rookery, or, in spring and fall, migrating songbirds. At night, you can hear nighthawks and whippoorwills. The winter months are a good time to see and photograph the bald eagles that swoop down to fish in the open waters of the Mississippi.

Facilities

The family campground on the north ridge has 31 individual sites with 16 electrical hookups. A group camp has 20 tent sites. Reservations can be made for some of the family sites and are suggested for the group camp. Down the ridge from the campgrounds are a series of picnic spots with water and a shelter provided.

Surrounding Area

Besides Nelson Dewey State Park, you can see more of the Mississippi River region by driving north to Wyalusing State Park near Prairie du Chien. Villa Louis, an old elegant river mansion just north of Prairie du Chien, is run by the State Historical Society. The scenic Great River Road and the historic Pioneer Trail highways intersect at Cassville.

About 20 miles southeast of Nelson Dewey State Park is St. John Mine, an authentic lead mine in Potosi. The Mining Museum in Platteville also features a mine tour and a train ride. You can see figures from the Old and New Testaments constructed of stone, glass, marble and petrified wood at the Dickeyville Grotto (daily tours). First Capitol–Belmont Mound State Park and the Pecatonica State Trail are about seven miles east of Platteville. The park bulletin board has additional information about area side trips.

NEW GLARUS WOODS STATE PARK

Green County. One mile south of New Glarus on Highway 69. Highway map index: 10-F.

Main Attraction

In the early 1800s, the present site of New Glarus Woods State Park was along the famous "Old Lead Road." The route was originally traveled by Winnebago Indians and later used by ox teams to haul lead from local mines to Milwaukee and the Great Lakes.

The park's proximity to the Sugar River Trail makes it a popular destination for bicyclists, and primitive campsites have been developed for their use.

What is now New Glarus Woods was then a dense forest, said to be as large in area as the famous Black Forest in Germany. Tales passed down through generations recall the site as the "loneliest and wildest" part of the entire route from Mineral Point to Milwaukee, "where fierce timber wolves would pursue both driver and oxen."

New Glarus Woods State Park is meant to be taken at a slow pace. First of all, many of its visitors are bicyclists who probably have ridden on the nearby Sugar River State Trail before pedaling over here. They're accustomed to observing the world just as fast as their legs will let them. Second, the park is close to New Glarus, a small town that displays its Swiss heritage with such fun and flair that most park visitors aren't in a hurry to leave.

Things To Do

After your tent is up or the picnic supplies are packed away, you can explore part of the park on the hiking trail (over one mile long) or take your time reading the interpretive labels on the .4-mile Basswood Nature Trail. The nature trail starts near the picnic area behind the shelter.

New Glarus Woods State Park, following a recent

land purchase, is planning to expand. The trail system may be enlarged to about five miles total. One trail will meander along a ridgetop and others will wind through the woods. These trails will serve as the cross-country ski loops during winter. No snowmobiling is allowed in the park. New Glarus Woods will also sponsor an active naturalist program on summer weekends that may include guided "bike hikes" on

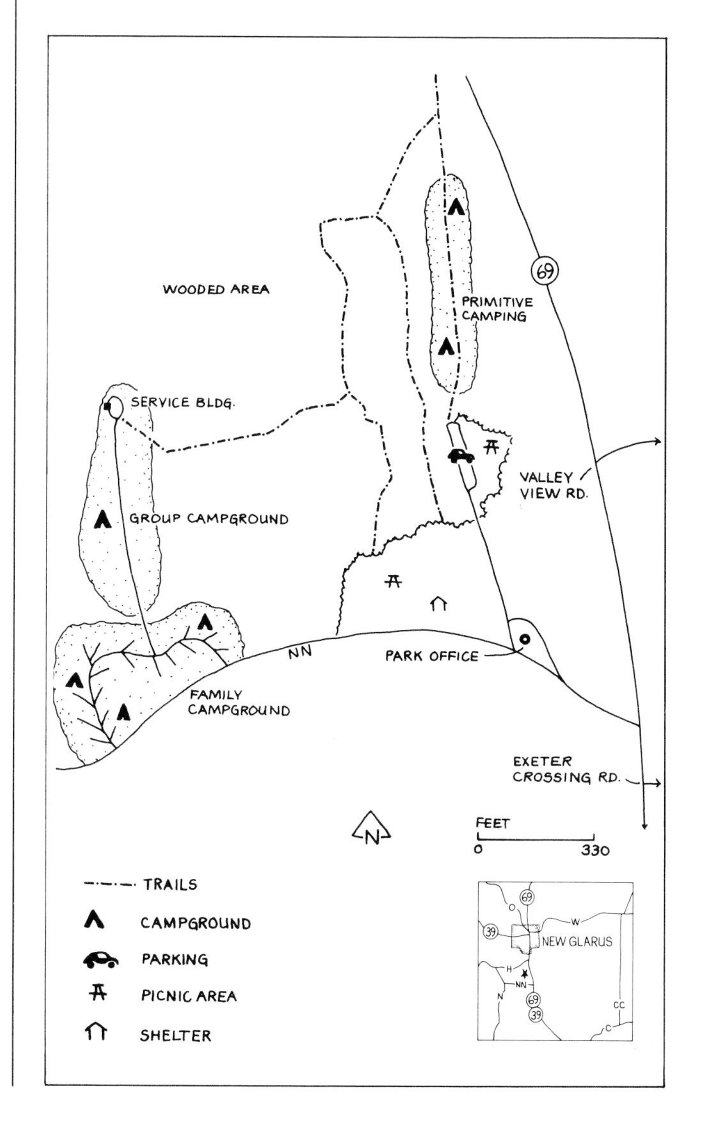

Camping in Wisconsin parks can be a peaceful getaway for those who love the natural world.

the Sugar River Trail. The park's development plans are scheduled to be completed by the early 1990s.

Facilities

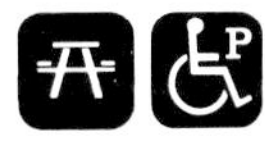

The park itself invites visitors to relax. The 18 family campsites (no showers or electricity) are wooded and shady—a pleasant place to lay back after a day on the bike trail. On summer weekends and other peak times, bicyclists can set up camp in one of the primitive sites developed for their use. Organized groups (120 maximum) may use the group camp, but need to make reservations ahead of time.

The campground may increase in size to 50 sites with the possibility of showers and electrical hookups (depending on budget and usage considerations).

Surrounding Area

The first Swiss immigrants to the New Glarus region followed the Old Lead Road in the 1840s, which cuts through the south side of the park. Today, Swiss habits, foods, cultural activities and architecture have continued to enrich the village since the Swiss colonization.

Each year New Glarus renews its traditions with numerous weekend Swiss festivals. Depending on when you visit, you might see the Wilhelm Tell Drama, the Heidi Festival or the Volksfest, among others. Include the New Glarus Historical Village Museum in your plans during your stay in the area. To get the true flavor of local Swiss heritage, try some flavorful Green County cheese or one of the specialties of the nearby restaurants.

New Glarus Woods State Park lies in the midst of several other state recreation lands. Some of these include the Military Ridge and Sugar River state trails, the Browntown–Cadiz Springs State Recreation Area and Yellowstone Lake State Park.

PECATONICA STATE TRAIL

Lafayette and Grant counties. 10 miles, presently between Belmont and Calamine. Highway map index: 10-E.

Main Attraction

The Pecatonica State Trail runs through the scenic valley of the Bonner Branch of the Pecatonica River. The 10-mile trail swings from side to side of the Bonner Branch, crossing the stream 24 times. The valley becomes deeper, steeper and more wooded in the eastern part, widening into a marshy area where Bonner Branch joins the Pecatonica River just west of the village of Calamine.

Things To Do

The gravel- and cinder-surfaced trail is open to hikers, bicyclists, snowmobilers and cross-country skiers. Final surfacing is not completed yet, but mountain bikes can be used currently. Motor vehicles of any type and horses are not allowed. Trail users can park at either end of the Pecatonica. Eventually the trail will extend seven miles further west to Platteville, with rest stops spaced along the way. The trail is laid out on the old Milwaukee Road railroad bed. Angling through valleys with the rolling hills of southwestern Wisconsin on either side, you'll see rich farmland and will probably pedal past some of Wisconsin's finest as they munch their grassy lunch. Keep an eye out for patches of native prairie grasses along parts of the old right-of-way. These remnants have never been plowed under like the rest of southern Wisconsin's original "sea of grass." As you follow the course of the stream, you'll notice scattered outcroppings of rock. If you look closely, you might spot a garter snake or other native resident sunning itself on a warm afternoon. You can wet your line in Bonner

The trail swings from side to side, crossing the stream 24 times as it angles through valleys with the rolling hills of southwestern Wisconsin on either side.

Branch for smallmouth bass and other fish. Channel catfish can be caught near the Pecatonica River.

Flora and Fauna

The Pecatonica Trail corridor is home for pheasant, quail, song sparrows and other birds. White-tailed deer, fox, mink and muskrat also live in the area.

You'll see mostly oaks, maples and other hardwoods in the woods along the gently sloping trail, with willows and cottonwoods in the lowlands. In season you can pick raspberries, blackberries and wild grapes.

Surrounding Area

First Capitol State Park and the Belmont Mound picnic grounds are close to the Pecatonica State Trail. Stop in for a picnic or just to look around. There is no camping available on the trail, but four state parks in the region have campsites: Governor Dodge, Yellowstone Lake, Nelson Dewey and Wyalusing. Ask any of the park rangers about other back-road bike routes and visitor attractions in southwestern Wisconsin.

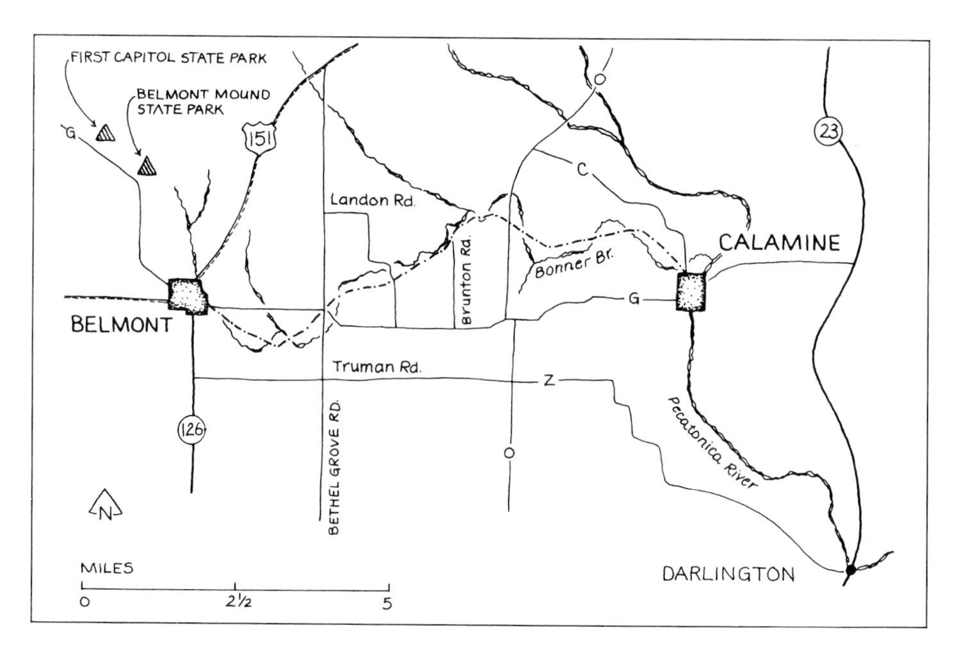

SUGAR RIVER STATE TRAIL

Green County. 23 miles, between New Glarus and Brodhead. Headquarters is in the remodeled railroad depot off Highway 69 in New Glarus.

Main Attraction

Picture yourself cruising on your bicycle through the fertile farm and meadowlands of southern Wisconsin on the Sugar River State Trail. Wildflowers bloom along the trail, the sun is warm, your companions congenial. The 23-mile trail has plenty of places to stop for a break, and the route is so pretty that you're glad you remembered to bring your camera.

Things To Do

The trail headquarters in the restored railroad depot in New Glarus is worth a few photos. Bike rentals, driver-only shuttle service and concessions are available at the depot. A public swimming pool is just one block north of the depot. You can camp in nearby New Glarus Woods State Park, which has 14 primitive bicycle campsites, 18 family sites and a large group camp area.

New Glarus is the center of "America's Little Switzerland," and the community is proud of its Swiss heritage. The town hosts several festivals each year, including the Wilhelm Tell Drama, Heidi Festival and Volksfest. Many shops and homes are styled in traditional Swiss architecture. Make sure to stock up on some of Green County's famous cheese and locally made sausages in New Glarus before heading home.

It's a six-mile jaunt between New Glarus and Monticello, and all but the last mile and a half runs through the New Glarus Public Hunting Grounds. Watch for pheasants, mourning doves and other birds as they munch on the elderberries, wild grapes and wild plums that grow along the trail.

Monticello provides a trailside restroom, water and parking for bicyclists. There's a picnic ground and shelter on Lake Montesian and a public pool on Main Street. The annual homecoming and chicken barbecue is in July. Monroe, the "Swiss Cheese Capital of the USA," is 12 miles south of Monticello on Highway 69.

Between Monticello and Albany (10 miles), the trail cuts through the Albany Wildlife Area. Pheasants,

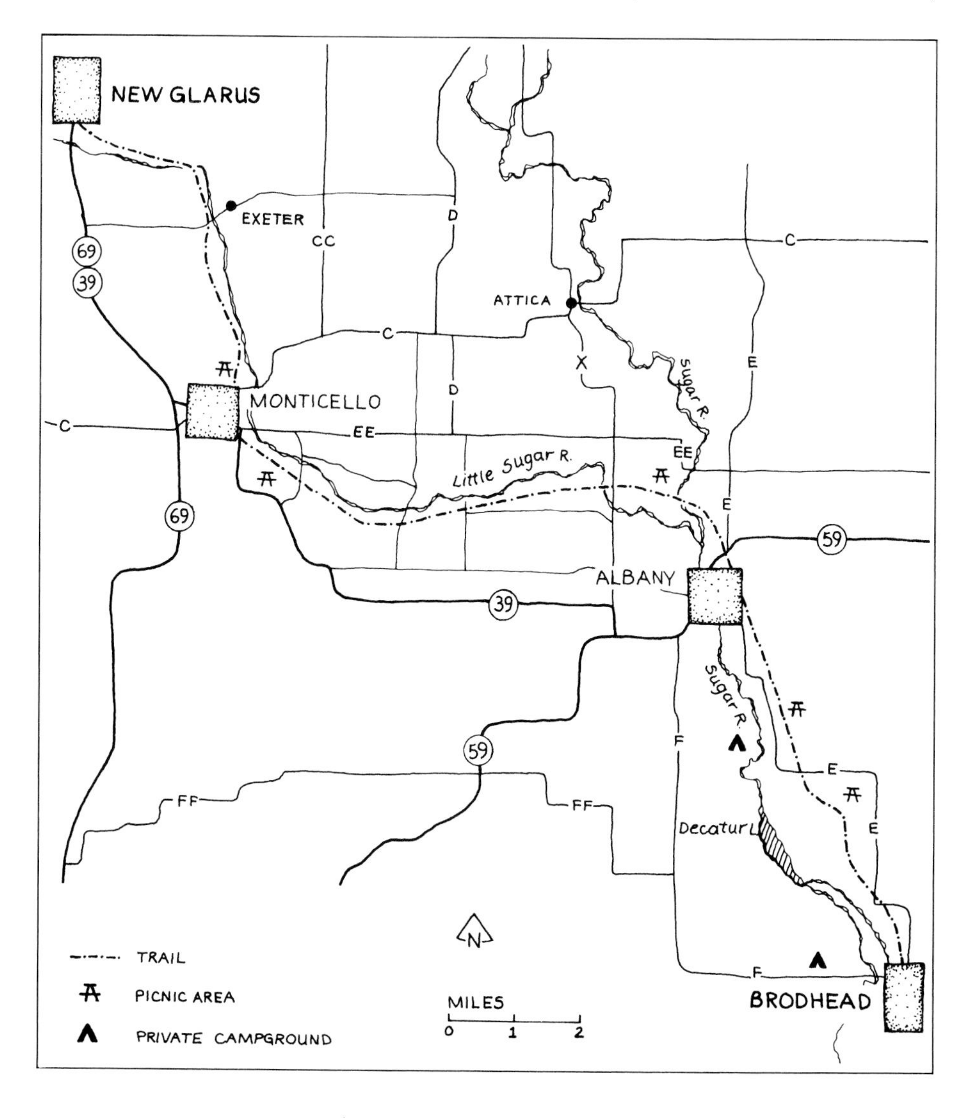

A level trail and a variety of lush scenery await cyclists on the Sugar River Trail.

ducks and other wildlife are hunted here during the season, and fishing can be good for smallmouth bass, walleye and occasional trout. The trail's longest bridge (there are 14 bridges) crosses over the Sugar River in the wildlife area.

Albany provides a trailside restroom, water and parking. Three local parks and a community forest with hiking trails make for tempting trail detours. Fishing, waterskiing and canoeing are some of the other area distractions. Albany celebrates Yesteryear Day and Memorial Day weekend and hosts a country-and-western/bluegrass music festival the third Sunday each July.

14 bridges, including a 112-foot covered bridge, cross the Sugar River as trail users wind through wildlife areas, wetlands and prairie remnants. Check with the several trail towns and villages to see when a festival is planned.

The seven-mile stretch from Albany to the southern end of the trail in Brodhead features a distinctive covered bridge over Norwegian Creek. The 112-foot replica was built as a cooperative venture by the Wisconsin DNR, the Brodhead Jaycees and local volunteers.

Trail users can take advantage of Brodhead's parks and public swimming pool. The old railroad depot has been restored and is now the Brodhead Historical Museum. Bicyclists can camp in a private campground near town and can explore the area on marked bicycle routes on secondary roads. One of these routes leads to the "Half Way Tree" (2.5 miles south of downtown), used by Indians to indicate they were halfway between Lake Michigan and the Mississippi River.

The Sugar River Trail, a former Milwaukee Road branch rail line, is mostly level, passing by rolling farmland, rock outcrops, woodlands and lowlands. Watch for the stretches of prairie remnants along the right-of-way. The trail has become a wildlife corridor and you might spot deer and a variety of small game and birds. The trail is used by hikers, snowmobilers and cross-country skiers during the winter. Horses and motorized vehicles are not allowed.

The trail is part of the National Recreation Trail System, the Wisconsin East-West Bikeway and Wisconsin's Ice Age National Scenic Trail. The Ice Age Trail is a 1,000-mile footpath (partially completed) that traces the furthest advance of the last glacier in the state.

A trail admission card is required for bicyclists aged 18 and older, and is valid on all Wisconsin state trails. Cards are available at the trail headquarters in New Glarus, at New Glarus Woods State Park and at outlets in communities along the trail. You can also buy a Sugar River Trail guide booklet at the headquarters.

TOWER HILL STATE PARK

Iowa County. Drive south of Spring Green for about two miles on Highway 23 (crossing the Wisconsin River). Turn east (left) onto County C for one mile. Highway map index: 10-E.

Main Attraction

The broad Wisconsin River valley stretches below as you take in the vista from the historic shot tower at Tower Hill State Park. Most of the blufftops and their steep slopes are blanketed with hardwood forest. But here, near the shot tower, you can stand amidst a sturdy grove of white pines. Inhaling their scent adds a northwoods flavor to this intimate park.

The shot tower was used to manufacture millions of pounds of lead into ammunition for use throughout the Wisconsin Territory and the upper Midwest in the early 19th century. Original construction began in 1831. Two men dug a vertical shaft through 120 feet of the sandstone bluff, using only ordinary mining tools—picks and crowbars. They then dug a 90-foot horizontal tunnel at water level to connect with the shaft.

The DNR and the State Historical Society have reconstructed the smelter house and wooden shot tower that originally crowned the sandstone shaft. Here, visitors can see a five-minute film that shows the lead shot manufacturing process. You can also examine exhibits and artifacts from the years that the tower was in operation (1833 to 1857).

To make ammunition, lead was transported by horse from southwestern Wisconsin lead mines to the shot tower. The lead was melted in the smelter house on top of the cliff, then dropped down a 180-foot shaft (the top 60 feet of the shaft was made of wood; the rest of the shaft was cut through sandstone).

The drops of lead assumed a spherical shape in

falling and landed in a three-foot-deep basin of water, which both cooled the shot and broke the fall. The shot was hauled by horsepower on a track to the finishing house, which was on the riverbank.

To many visitors, the peaceful ambience of Tower Hill is its main asset now. Families and small groups are the primary users, and they like to come back often to camp, hike or picnic. The park's small size (77 acres) and the lack of swimming facilities keep the crowds away, but that's okay with the "regulars."

Things To Do

The section of the Wisconsin River south of Prairie du Sac to the Mississippi River is a favorite of canoe-

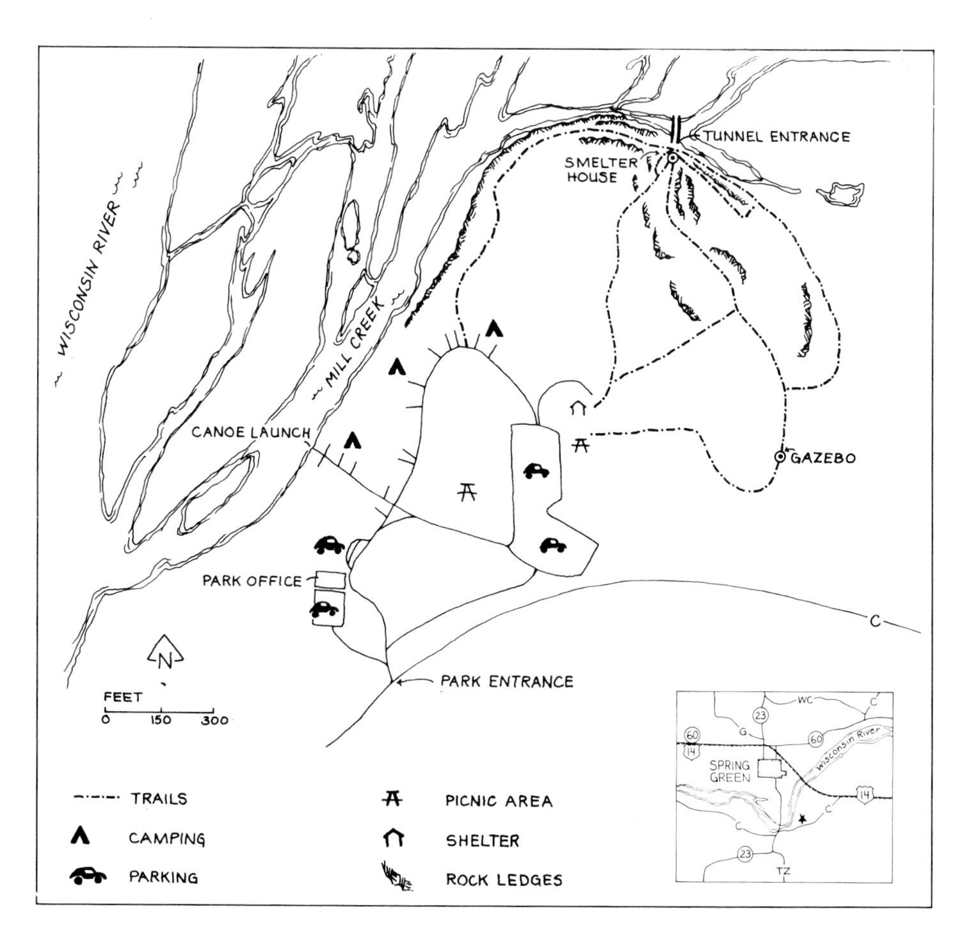

ists for its wild scenery and quiet water. Though the river, now known as the Lower Wisconsin State Riverway, is easily canoed, it's dangerous for swimmers. The current (three to five miles per hour) and changing river conditions can make a deadly combination. At high water, the current digs holes in the sand bottom. During normal water levels, sand drifts into the upstream ends of these holes, resulting in steep drop-offs.

Tower Hill combines history with gorgeous Wisconsin River scenery. The area around the park is full of fascinating natural areas and tourist attractions.

Canoeists aren't the only active visitors who enjoy Tower Hill; bicyclists have also discovered the park. Southwestern Wisconsin is blessed with an abundance of scenic back roads that can challenge and delight bicyclists with hills, curves and visual surprises. The park is a convenient stopover for bicycle vagabonds who are on overnight expeditions or who just want to find a quiet place for a break.

Tower Hill's hiking trails (about two miles) wind through the wooded bottom lands and uplands of the park. The Old Ox Nature Trail is a short loop marked with interpretive signs, leading up to the shot tower and smelter house. If you hike down to the base of the bluff by the wooden bridge, you can hike into the tunnel that leads back to the shaft.

Facilities

Tower Hill has a large picnic area and playground near the campground. There's plenty of space for volleyball and other games. The shelter building can be reserved for your group if you contact the park office ahead of time.

The park's 15 wooded campsites (no showers or electricity) are available on a first-come, first-served basis. Two of the sites overlook Mill Creek, a tributary of the Wisconsin River. Canoeists can easily paddle the short distance up Mill Creek to reach the park, or use Tower Hill as a put-in point for river trips.

Surrounding Area

The area around Spring Green is full of things to see and do. Nearby state recreation lands include Governor Dodge and Blue Mound state parks and the

Military Ridge State Trail. The Spring Green restaurant, which was designed by Frank Lloyd Wright, is about half a mile from Tower Hill on County C. The American Players Theater, an outdoor Shakespearean theater, is also near the park on County C. Matinees and evening performances are presented throughout the summer and early fall.

If you still have time to explore after Shakespeare and Frank Lloyd Wright, drive south of Spring Green on Highway 23 to the House on the Rock. This unique and famous attraction is open during the spring, summer and fall. Tower Hill State Park personnel will be able to give you further details about these attractions.

WILDCAT MOUNTAIN STATE PARK

Vernon County. Three miles east of the village of Ontario on Highway 33. Highway map index: 8-E.

Main Attraction

Wildcat Mountain State Park is part of southwestern Wisconsin's Driftless Area, a region of high scenic bluffs and long narrow valleys untouched by the four glaciers that ground through the state. The 3,740-acre park attracts action-oriented visitors who come to hike, horseback ride, ski or canoe.

Things To Do

The slow-flowing Kickapoo River, which meanders through the park, is ideal for leisurely canoeing. Famous among canoeists, the 125-mile stream flows past farmlands and hemlock-shaded limestone and sandstone bluffs. Wildlife and wildflowers are abundant, especially within the park and the Federal Army Corps of Engineers land, which extends south of Wildcat Mountain down to La Farge. The river originates at Wilton and is canoeable to Wauzeka, where it empties into the Wisconsin River.

The gentle river twists and turns so much that the Algonquin Indians called it "Kickapoo," which means "he who goes there, then here." The stream can become dangerous in a hurry during heavy rains, though, overflowing its banks and posing a threat to unwary canoeists.

Canoe landings are located in Ontario and in the lower picnic area in the park, which is a common starting and stopping point for river trips. You can also put in at numerous access points at bridge crossings along Highway 131. Camping facilities are available in the park and at various private and public sites along the route. Five area outfitters provide canoe rental and shuttle service. Check at the park office for details about camping and rentals.

The best fishing at Wildcat Mountain is for brown trout in Billings Creek, a tributary of the Kickapoo River. The upper portion of the Kickapoo has very few game fish in it, but the tributaries do have populations of trout.

Hikers are able to enjoy the park's rugged limestone-capped bluffs and green valleys on over four miles of trails. The 1.3-mile Hemlock Trail is a self-guided nature loop accessible from the lower picnic area. The trail cuts through the Mt. Pisgah Hemlock–Hardwoods State Natural Area, climbing the hill up

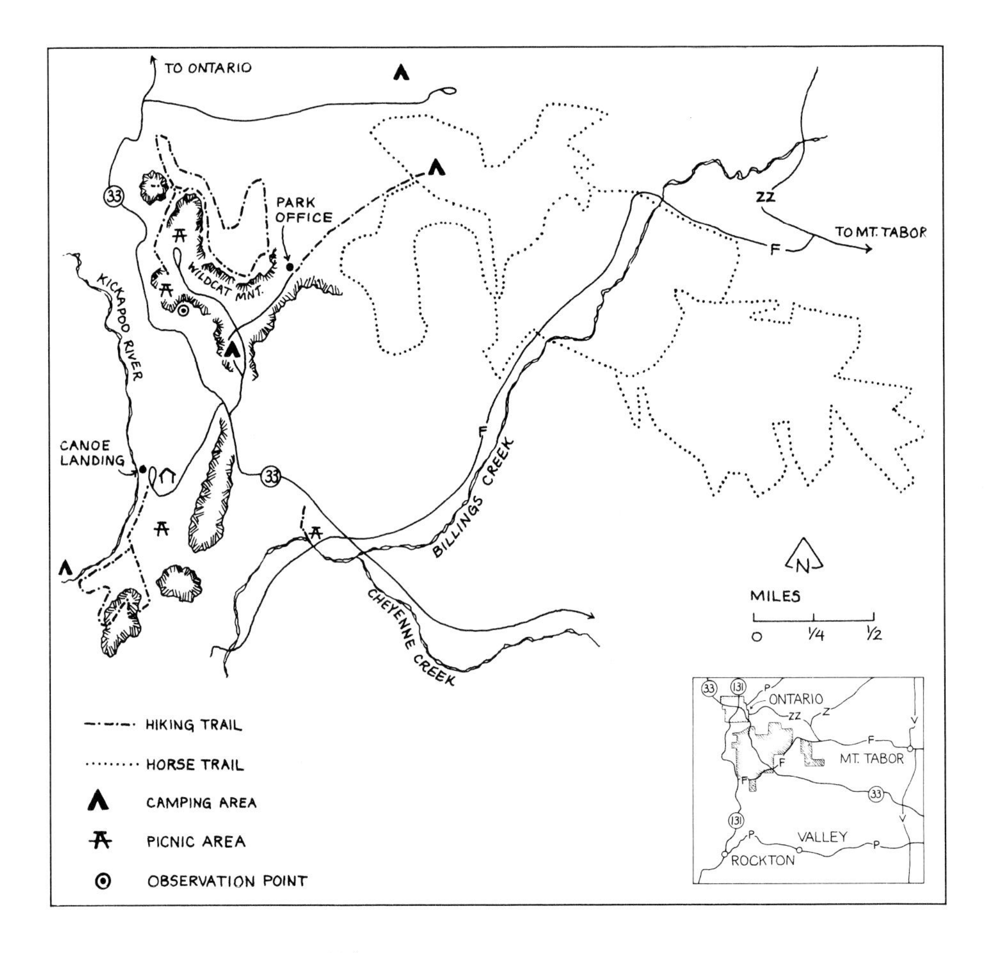

to an observation point. The 2.8-mile Old Settler's Trail begins in the upper picnic area. The most popular observation point in the park is also in the upper picnic area. From here, you might be able to spot some canoeists on the Kickapoo River below or compose a photograph that captures a portion of the panorama that stretches into the distance.

The rolling hills and deep valleys of Wildcat Mountain make the park a favorite among horseback riders. Two connecting loops form the 12-mile Wildcat Mountain Horse Trail, a visual treat for riders. You'll crest bluffs with long vistas of the park and distant scattered farms. Then you'll wind downhill through woods and cross open fields, mostly away from main-use areas. A large part of the park is a wildlife refuge. Wildlife is plentiful, as quiet riders will see. Deer are very common and ruffed grouse will often flush near the trail. A wide variety of songbirds live in the grasslands, forest edge and in the woods.

Fall may be the most spectacular season at Wildcat Mountain because of the sweeping views and brilliant colors. Winter, though, may be the most fun. Seven miles of cross-country ski trails and five scenic overlooks add up to a pleasant outing for beginning and intermediate skiers. You may even experience a day when the sun is warm on your flushed cheeks, the air is fresh and clear and your ski wax matches the snow conditions. Take advantage of such good fortune and promise yourself to ski all the way out to each one of the five overlooks. The trail starts and ends at the upper picnic area with a rest stop midway, where you can continue or take the short trail turnaround.

If you are visiting Wildcat Mountain State Park in the winter, ask for directions to the Ice Cave Trail (on County F near Highway 33). The ice cave is shallow with a spring over the top. In winter, the spring flow freezes into a giant icicle, 16 to 18 feet in diameter. Unusual images, such as this, and the combination of the river, valleys and blufftops make the park a captivating destination in any season.

Wildcat Mountain sports a horse trail campground and a 12-mile bridle trail. It crests bluffs with long vistas, descends through woods and crosses meadows. But you don't need a horse to enjoy the visual feast the park provides.

(continued)

(overleaf)

Bluffs and valleys characterize southwestern Wisconsin, untouched by the glaciers. Wildcat Mountain provides an extensive panorama of the area.

Facilities

Wildcat Mountain has one of the only horse-trail campgrounds in the state park system. Eight campsites are nestled in a valley northeast of the park office. Facilities include drinking water, picnic tables, fire rings, a corral, hitching posts, parking pads and loading ramps. Many riders prefer spring and fall outings. When the park's mixed hardwood forest hits its color peak in October, a local horse club sponsors a Fall Colorama Ride. There are no horses for rent in the area.

The park has family and group camping as well as horse camping. The 30-unit family campground has no showers or electricity. Reservations are accepted for half of these sites and for the 75-person group campground. Naturalist programs are presented on Saturday evenings from Memorial Day through Labor Day.

WYALUSING STATE PARK

Grant County. 12 miles south of Prairie du Chien on Highway 18; across the Wisconsin River bridge, turn west on County C. Highway map index: 10-D.

Main Attraction

One of Wisconsin's most scenic parks lies at the junction of the Wisconsin and the Mississippi rivers. From the many overlooks along the park bluffs, you can view the patchwork of forested bottom land and river scenery as did the French explorers Marquette and Joliet in 1673.

Three of the Indian cultures that lived here were mound builders. Mounds were built in many shapes (deer, bear, bird, turtle, linear and conical) for burial, ceremonial or other reasons. These groups were the builders of many mounds seen on Sentinel Ridge and other parts of the park. Those visitors who wish to find out more about burial mounds may want to drive across the Mississippi River to Marquette, Iowa (across the river from Prairie du Chien), to visit Effigy Mounds National Monument.

Wyalusing State Park is in the Driftless Area of the Midwest that escaped the effects of four continental glaciers. The 500-foot park bluffs, untouched by crushing ice, were carved out of limestone by the eroding river waters. Forested ridges and deep valleys contrast with the sloughs, bays and backwaters of the rivers.

Things To Do

This is a hiker's park. Over 16 miles of trails wind through the 2,654-acre park from blufftop to bottom land and up again. The bluff trails are dotted with overlooks boasting panoramic views of the river valley. Some of the trails are steep, requiring hikers to climb steps. To start your Wyalusing hikes, try the

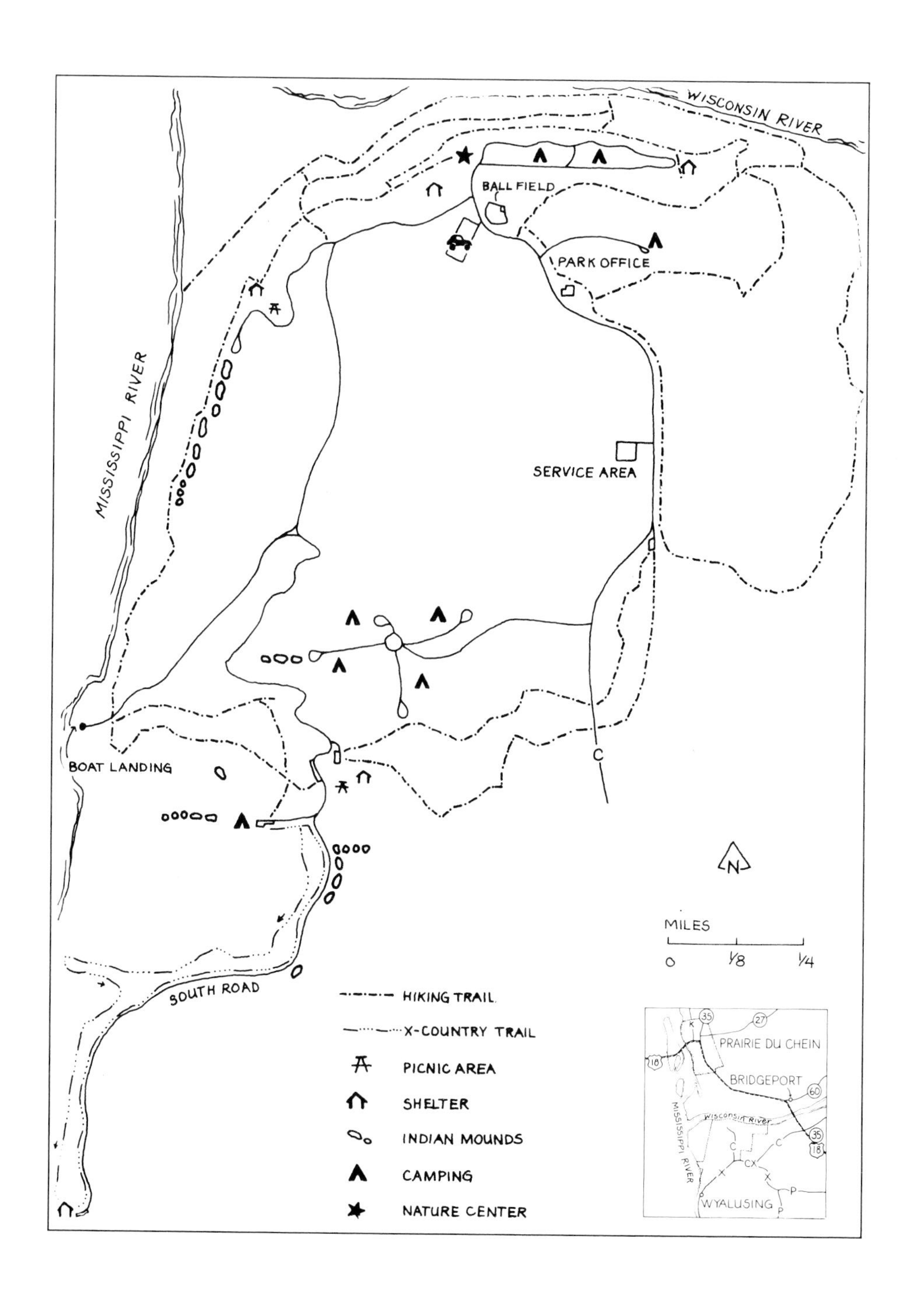
WISCONSIN RIVER
BALL FIELD
PARK OFFICE
MISSISSIPPI RIVER
SERVICE AREA
C
BOAT LANDING
SOUTH ROAD
N
MILES
0
1/8
1/4
HIKING TRAIL
X-COUNTRY TRAIL
PICNIC AREA
SHELTER
INDIAN MOUNDS
CAMPING
NATURE CENTER
35
27
K
PRAIRIE DU CHEIN
18
BRIDGEPORT
60
MISSISSIPPI RIVER
Wisconsin River
C
CX
X
P
WYALUSING

self-guided Sugar Maple Nature Trail to learn about the plants, animals and geology of the park. This trail has a short branch path that leads to Pictured Rock Cave. A waterfall tumbles from the top of the overhang and freezes in winter. Hikers can still find ice protected in the shaded parts of the cave toward the end of May.

The Old Wagon Road Trail follows a seasonal stream all the way down to the Wisconsin River where it joins with the Old Immigrant Trail. It also passes what was once the small settlement of Walnut Eddy, a stopover for farmers and ferrymen during the 1880s. The Old Immigrant Trail was used by westward-bound settlers and led to a ferry across the Mississippi River. The heavily wooded Sand Cave Trail winds past a small waterfall and leads to beautiful Sand Cave. Some of the trails can be strenuous, so take your time to observe and explore. Plan to stop for a trail lunch on a bluff, or a rest break in one of the park's picnic areas spread generously throughout the park. These trails, and the other scenic paths in Wyalusing, can be buggy, too. Don't forget your mosquito repellent.

The park naturalist schedules guided hikes and evening programs on the weekends from Memorial Day through Labor Day. Look for the list of activities posted on the bulletin boards throughout the park. The nature center is located in the concession shelter building next to the Wisconsin Ridge Campground. The naturalist can point out some of the park's most unusual attractions, such as the two designated natural areas, the Wyalusing Walnut Forest and the Wyalusing Hardwoods Forest.

You'd want to have a park where the Wisconsin River meets the Mississippi River, and at Wyalusing the 500-foot bluffs, the forested ridges and deep valleys make this a perfect spot.

Besides hiking and camping at Wyalusing, the backwaters of the Mississippi and Wisconsin rivers offer some excellent sportfishing. Bass, northern pike, walleye and panfish provide most of the action. Boats may be rented from private sources near the park and launched at the park's boat landing. A canoe trail begins at the boat landing and follows along the river sloughs near the park. This is an excellent way to observe waterfowl and river plants and animals. One loop is 9.75 miles, and the other two loops are about six miles each. Maps are available at the park

Hiking Wyalusing's bluffs can be a challenge, but the scenery is extraordinary.

office. The backwater areas are fun to explore by boat or canoe, and it's not hard to let yourself slip back in time and imagine being here 300 years ago.

Even without a boat or canoe, you can still enjoy the Mississippi River. Two miles south of the park, in the Wyalusing Recreation Area on County X, there is a county-operated beach, boat landing and picnic grounds. The state park has no designated swimming area and no lifeguards are on duty.

Come to Wyalusing for a crisp winter outing. When the snow cover is deep enough, the hills are great for sledding and tobogganing. Ice fishing draws frequent winter park visitors. The backwaters of the Mississippi River keep anglers busy trying to catch northerns, bluegills and crappies. Cross-country skiers tour on the 3.5-mile Mississippi Ridge Trail that follows the heavily wooded crest of the bluff bordering the river. Winter campers can choose from several campsites (some with electricity) that are kept open all year. Water is available near the office.

Some winter visitors prefer to take to the trails on snowshoes or on foot. Maybe you will discover a frozen waterfall or experience the tranquility of hiking among snow-covered Indian mounds. The path to Point Lookout is cleared through the winter to let visitors take in the impressive view.

Flora and Fauna

Early morning and late afternoon hikes can be the most fruitful for observing wildlife. Bring your camera or binoculars and try to spot some of the park's wildflowers, birds and animals. You might hear a pileated woodpecker, see a hawk gliding effortlessly above the ridgetops or sight a deer feeding among the giant bottom-land trees.

Winter is an ideal time to observe wildlife. Deer are often spotted along park roads and you might see a flock of wild turkeys or a soaring bald eagle. The bugs are gone and it's easy to identify natural residents by their telltale tracks.

Ask at the park office for the bird checklist and information about the mammals and reptiles that inhabit the park.

Facilities

For campers, Wyalusing maintains two family campgrounds, a permanent indoor group camp and an outdoor group tent site. The two family campgrounds have a total of 132 sites, 32 with electrical hookups. Showers are available. The indoor camp (capacity 108) has four dorms and a main lodge with kitchen and dining facilities. The outdoor group camp has space for 130 campers. Contact the park office for camping details and reservation information for the group camps and the family campgrounds.

Campers, hikers and picnickers can buy supplies and souvenirs at the concession stand near the Wisconsin Ridge Campground. You can also rent canoes, bicycles and other sports equipment.

Surrounding Area

Two nearby attractions are worth a side trip. Villa Louis is an elegant mansion built more than a century ago at Prairie du Chien by Wisconsin's first millionaire. The mansion, noted for its period furnishings, is owned and operated by the State Historical Society of Wisconsin. Stonefield Village, another State Historical Society of Wisconsin site, is a reconstructed 1890 village that re-creates the lifestyles of farmers, merchants, villagers and craftspeople. The village, part of Nelson Dewey State Park at Cassville, is a short drive south of Wyalusing. Wyalusing State Park, incidentally, is at the end of the 92-mile Lower Wisconsin State Riverway, a scenic corridor of river and bluff lands that stretches from Prairie du Sac to the Mississippi River.

YELLOWSTONE LAKE STATE PARK

Lafayette County. Eight miles west of Blanchardville on County F. Highway map index: 10-F.

Main Attraction

Yellowstone Lake State Park is on a man-made lake in the unglaciated hill and valley area of southwestern Wisconsin. The total Yellowstone area (2,600 acres) includes the lake, the park and a wildlife reserve.

Things To Do

The park's main attraction is the lake. Visitors fish for largemouth bass, muskie, northern pike, panfish and other varieties. Licenses are sold at the park office. There are three boat launching ramps on the north shore, and rowboats, paddleboats, canoes and motors may be rented at the concession stand. Motors are allowed on the lake except in the waterfowl refuge, marked off by buoys, at the west end of the lake.

Yellowstone Lake has a good swimming beach with lifeguards on duty almost every day during summer months. Check the sign at the guard stand for the lifeguard's schedule.

Take a hike along part of the park's trail system or explore the wildlife area. The ranger can point out good hiking areas.

Pick a sunny day, pack a lunch and head for the lake. Take a hike to work up an appetite, then settle in at the beach to enjoy the view and cool off in the water.

Yellowstone Lake is a lively spot in the winter, and one of the more popular sports is ice fishing. Sometimes as many as 150 shanties dot the lake. Shanties must have the owner's name and address on the outside and must be removed by March 5. An annual fish-a-ree, sponsored by the Lafayette County Sportsmen's Clubs, is held the first Sunday in February and usually draws a crowd of eager anglers.

Cross-country skiing and snowmobiling are allowed on marked trails only, but hiking and snowshoeing are okay anywhere. Currently, the park maintains 2.5 miles of ski trails and eight miles of snowmobile trails within the park and wildlife area. The snowmobile trail connects with Lafayette County trails.

Facilities

Reservations are accepted for about half of the 130 individual campsites at the park, of which 36 have electrical hookups. Showers are available. The campground has about a dozen walk-in tent sites for those who prefer more privacy. Reservations are required

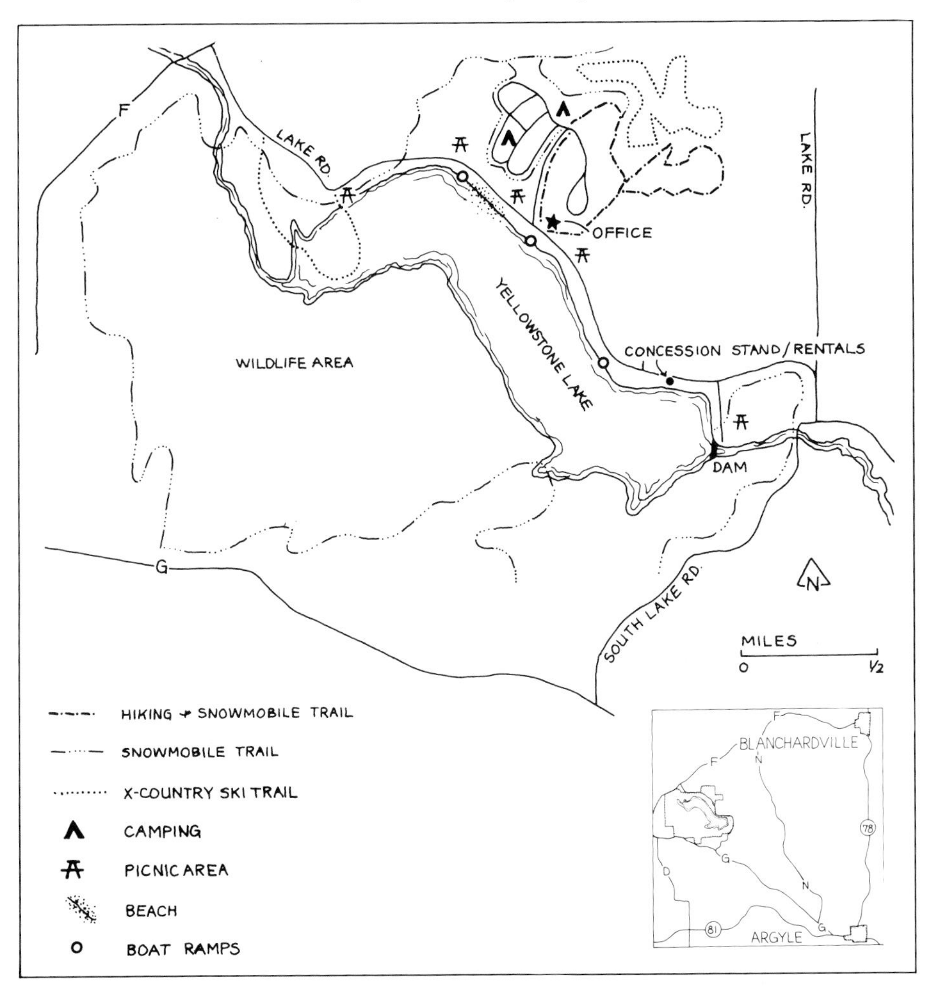

for the 200-person outdoor group camp. Camping supplies and laundry facilities are available in Argyle, Blanchardville and Darlington, or you can buy smaller items at the park concession on the north shore of the lake. The campground is spread out on a hillside, with good views of the nearby lake. Winter camping is permitted in a restricted area, so check at the office for special instructions.

If you are visiting Yellowstone Lake for the day, you might choose to picnic in one of the designated areas or simply stop at one of the tables along the park road. The picnic area below the dam has drinking water and playground equipment, but for a view you can't beat the tables by the beach.

Surrounding Area

There is a lot to do in the Yellowstone Lake area. The Badger Mine and Museum in Shullsburg is 30 miles from the park. Guided cave tours are available at Cave of the Mounds, four miles west of Mt. Horeb. Mineral Point is a hilly town known for its historic buildings, while New Glarus has many Swiss festivals.

Within a circle of Yellowstone Lake are First Capitol, Governor Dodge, Blue Mound and New Glarus Woods state parks. Also nearby are the Pecatonica, Sugar River and Military Ridge state trails, and the Browntown–Cadiz Springs State Recreation Area.

INDIAN HEAD COUNTRY

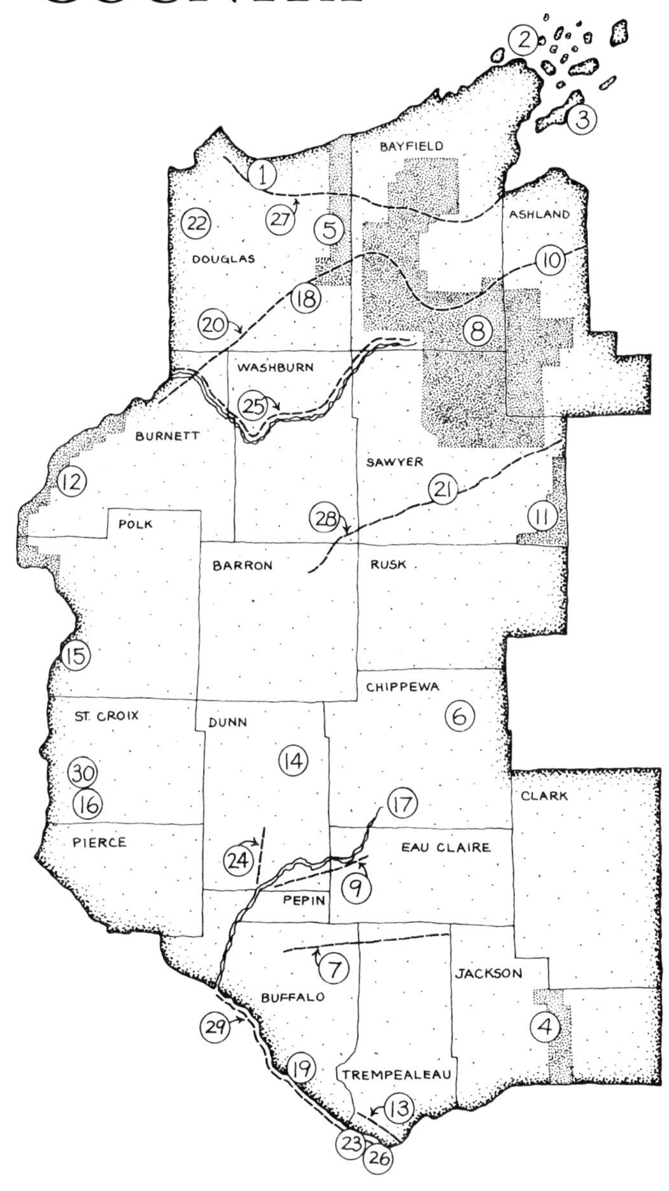

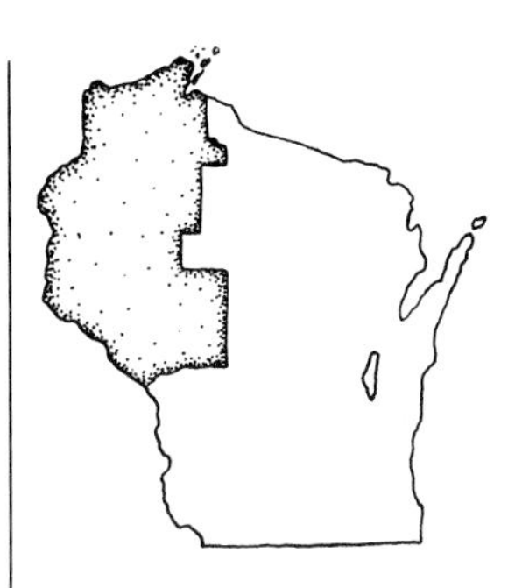

1. Amnicon Falls State Park
2. Apostle Islands National Lakeshore
3. Big Bay State Park
4. Black River State Forest
5. Brule River State Forest
6. Brunet Island State Park
7. Buffalo River State Trail
8. Chequamegon National Forest
9. Chippewa River State Trail
10. Copper Falls State Park
11. Flambeau River State Forest
12. Governor Knowles State Forest
13. Great River State Trail
14. Hoffman Hills State Recreation Area
15. Interstate State Park
16. Kinnickinnic State Park
17. Lake Wissota State Park
18. Lucius Woods State Park
19. Merrick State Park
20. North Country National Scenic Trail
21. Ojibwa State Park

(continued on next page)

AMNICON FALLS STATE PARK

Douglas County. 10 miles east of Superior on Highway 2, one-half mile past the Highway 53 junction. Highway map index: 2-C.

Main Attraction

The rambunctious Amnicon River tumbles over a striking series of waterfalls and cascades in the heart of Amnicon Falls State Park. The warm-water river is an important spawning stream for fish from Lake Superior.

The river flows 30 miles north from its headwaters in central Douglas County to its mouth on Lake Superior. Its root beer color comes from decaying vegetation and tannic acid leached from headwater swamps and bogs.

The park and surrounding area lie on ancient lava flows that gushed from cracks in the earth in the Lake Superior region over one billion years ago. In time, a huge block of lava settled downward, or faulted, in this area following a great earthquake. The geological feature is known as the Douglas Fault, and is best observed in Amnicon Falls State Park. Seas had deposited sandstone over the underlying lava before the earthquake. Today the Amnicon River is still eroding the sandstone and exposing the lava, or basalt. Interested visitors can learn more of the park's tumultuous past by asking for a special booklet on the topic in the park office.

In the park, the river splits into two streams and plunges over three waterfalls (each is about 30 feet tall). The river splits over a fourth falls during heavy water flow. There is even an unnamed waterfall in the park. Located on the right side of the road near the covered bridge parking lot, this falls disappears when the stream dries up.

(overleaf)

The seasons only add depth to an appreciation of the state's public lands, and if you meet winter on its terms, the rewards can be many.

(continued from previous page)

22. Pattison State Park
23. Perrot State Park
24. Red Cedar State Trail
25. St. Croix National Scenic Riverway
26. Trempealeau National Wildlife Refuge
27. Tri-County Recreation Corridor
28. Tuscobia State Trail
29. Upper Mississippi River National Wildlife and Fish Refuge
30. Willow River State Park

Things To Do

During spring, Lake Superior walleye, smelt and rainbow trout (also called "steelheads") migrate up the Amnicon to spawn. Coho salmon (or "silver salmon") spawn here in the fall. Chinook salmon, recently stocked in the river, spawn during autumn as well. Anglers also occasionally catch northern and muskie. Successful fishing on the Amnicon means being in the right place at the right time. Add luck to the formula, too. Check at the park office for current information on seasons, size and bag limits.

The covered footbridge has become a symbol of the park. Hikers linger here on their way to the island across the Amnicon River. The bridge is a favorite of photographers who frame it in their compositions or

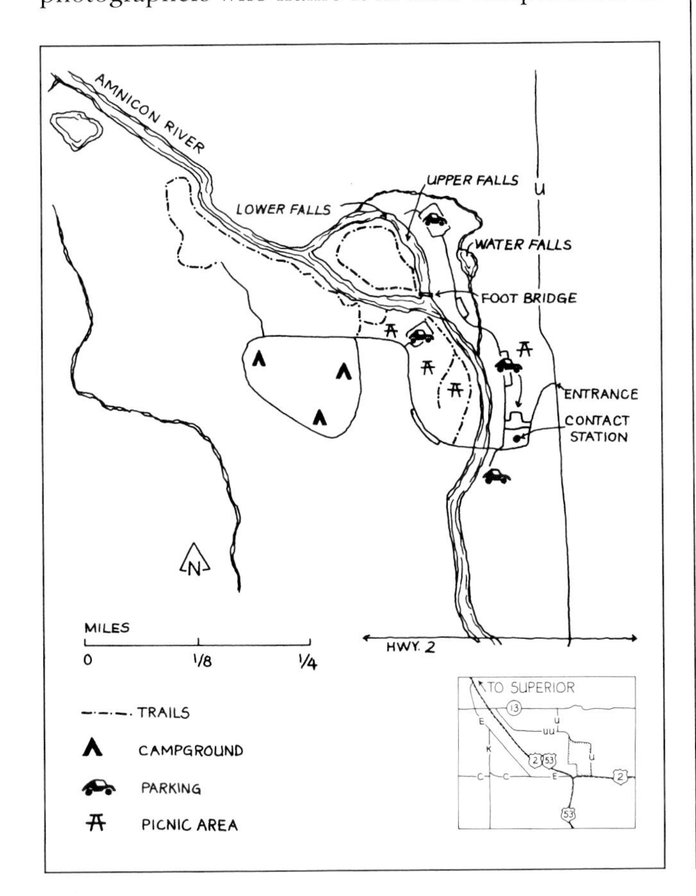

The Amnicon River tumbles through a rocky gorge providing a series of waterfalls and rock formations to explore.

shoot from it while photographing the waterfalls. You can hike around the perimeter of the small island to view the falls and the rocky river gorge.

On the other side of the river, the three-quarter-mile Thimbleberry Nature Trail begins near the campground. Besides learning about the 825-acre park's ecology and natural history from the interpretive signs, you'll be able to hike along the river and through part of Amnicon's forest.

Amnicon Falls State Park has no designated swimming beach. Diving or jumping from the cliffs is not permitted and violators are issued citations. The danger from hidden rocks and fluctuating water levels makes this ban necessary. Swimming is permitted in the river pools below the waterfalls, though no lifeguards are on duty.

The river cascades over a series of falls as it flows toward Lake Superior. Runs of smelt, walleye, trout and salmon swim up the river to spawn. Put yourself somewhere in the middle of all this and enjoy.

Amnicon Falls is a seasonal park that usually opens the first weekend in May and closes the first weekend in October. Off-season visitors can park outside the entrance gate and hike, ski or snowshoe in the park. There are no snowmobile trails on park grounds, though the surrounding area features hundreds of miles of snowmobile (and cross-country skiing) routes. The park is along the route of the Tri-County Recreational Corridor, a 60-mile multi-use trail between Superior and Ashland.

Flora and Fauna

As you hike the nature trails you may spot a deer or porcupine in the woods or see evidence of beaver activity near the river.

Facilities

The park's 36-site rustic campground (no showers or electrical hookups) includes two walk-in sites, two double-unit sites, and one modified site for disabled visitors. A playground is located on the west side of the campground. You can buy camping or picnic supplies in Superior, or just outside the park on Highway 2.

Surrounding Area

Northwestern Wisconsin is famous for its forests, lakes and trout streams. Around Amnicon Falls State Park, you can explore a number of county forests and parks as well as nearby Chequamegon National Forest. State recreation lands close to Amnicon include the Brule River State Forest and Pattison and Lucius Woods state parks (Lucius Woods is now operated by Douglas County). You may also wish to visit the state fish hatchery in the Brule River State Forest. The

North Country National Scenic Trail (a 3,200-mile corridor extending from Crown Point, New York, to the Lewis and Clark National Historic Trail in North Dakota) cuts across this part of the state south of the park.

Duluth, Minnesota, and Superior, Wisconsin, a short drive west of the park, are twin ports on Lake Superior. Both cities feature beaches, charter boat fishing, museums and tours of historic ships. If you take the harbor cruise, you'll see the world's largest grain elevators and coal and iron ore docks. Drive east of Superior on Highway 13 for a scenic auto tour of the Bayfield peninsula. The town of Bayfield is the gateway to the Apostle Islands National Lakeshore.

APOSTLE ISLANDS NATIONAL LAKESHORE

Ashland and Bayfield counties. Headquarters is in Bayfield; 23 miles north of Ashland on Highway 13. Highway map index: 1-D.

Main Attraction

From the sky, the Apostle Islands resemble water lilies in a pond. From water level, they form a maze of forested coastlines amidst the twisting channels of Lake Superior. Lying off the tip of the northern Wisconsin mainland, the cluster of green-cloaked islands reminded early French missionaries of a cluster of men—the twelve Apostles. The name stuck, though there are 22 islands, not 12, and none of them are named for Christ's disciples.

The Apostle Islands National Lakeshore includes 21 of the 22 Apostle Islands and a 12-mile stretch of wild Bayfield Peninsula coast. Created in 1970, the lakeshore is administered by the National Park Service.

The islands were formed during the Ice Age, when glaciers scoured the bedrock and gouged deep channels through the overlying sandstone. The rock formations matured into forested islands when the meltwater filled the glacial basin.

The lake (over 30,000 square miles) and the islands touch the spirit of a wanderer in subtle fashion. Gulls wheel and squawk over a deserted beach, an incoming storm roils the sky with an ominous majesty, or dawn bestows a sense of calm when the sun rises on a quiet lake.

The islands, ranging in size from 3 to over 14,000 acres, possess mystery and fascination. Each has its own story and unique attractions: Hermit Island, it was whispered, has a buried treasure; Stockton Island has black bears, sandhill cranes, and, in the bog, pitcher plants that trap and digest insects; six islands have lighthouses; some have abandoned brownstone quarries. Gull and Eagle islands are breeding grounds for herring gulls; Eagle and Cat islands have great blue heron rookeries and Long Island is home to the endangered piping plover, Wisconsin's rarest breeding bird. And Devils Island is famous for its lake-battered sandstone cliffs, arches and caves.

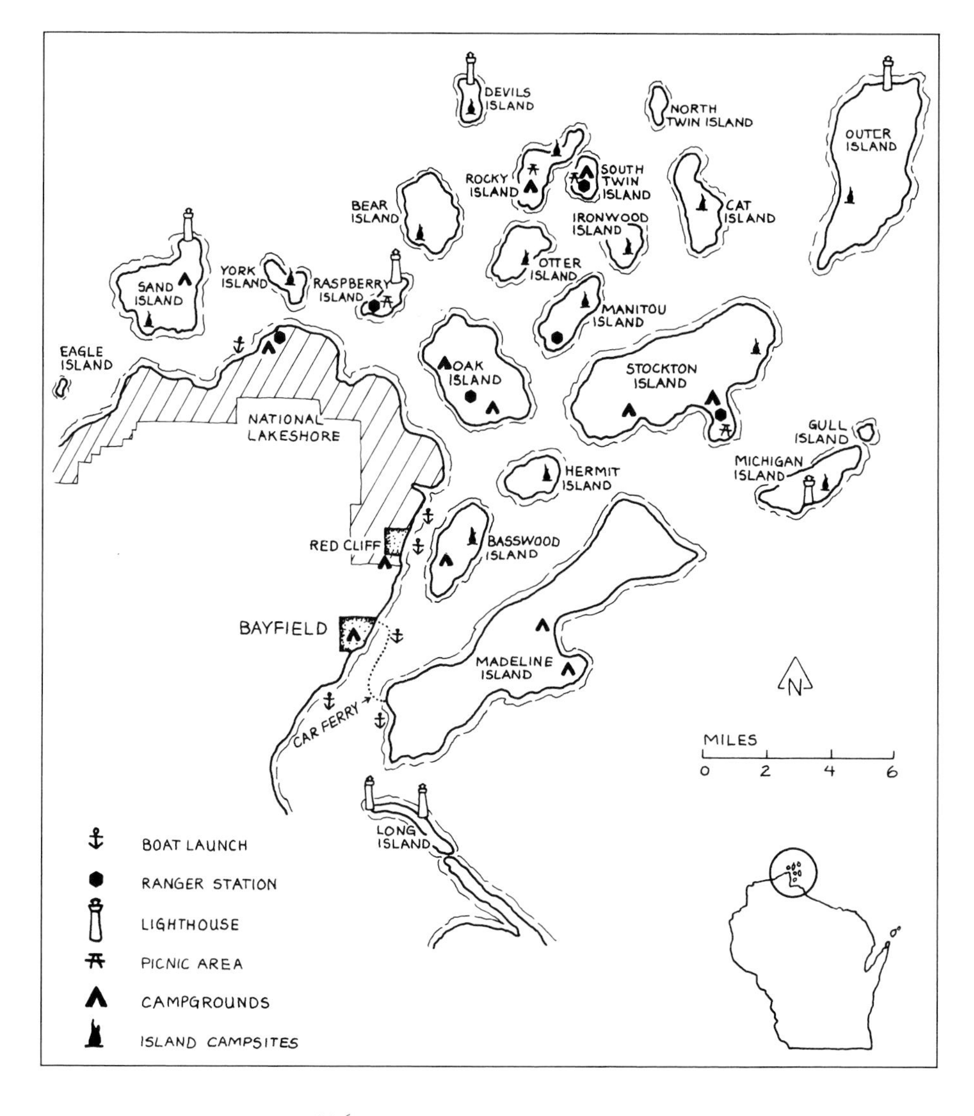

Things To Do

To begin your visit to the islands, stop at the Apostle Islands National Lakeshore Visitor Center, located in Bayfield's old county courthouse. Audiovisual programs and exhibits portray the park's human and natural history as well as its recreational opportunities. You can also get details about camping, hiking, fishing, and boating in the islands.

The Little Sandy Bay Visitor Center is on the mainland portion of the lakeshore. To drive there, head north of Bayfield on Highway 13 and turn right on County K, following the signs. This visitor center also provides exhibits about aspects of the park's story. Visitor centers on Stockton and South Twin Islands are open in the summer, as are ranger stations on several other islands. A variety of summer programs and activities are scheduled on the mainland and on some of the islands throughout the summer. The park newspaper, *Around the Archipelago*, lists such events as boat tours, guest speakers, guided island hikes and campfire programs.

The Hokenson Brothers Fishery, at Little Sandy Bay, is a restored commercial fishery that depicts a small family fishing operation of the 1930s. You can explore the fishery complex and see the *Twilite*, one of the family's original fishing boats. The rustic buildings and historic artifacts are maintained as a museum by the National Park Service.

Each of the 21 islands has its own story and unique attractions to explore. An island excursion may only whet your appetite for more of the clean air, clear water and lush island scenery.

To experience the rest of the lakeshore, you need to go by boat. No matter what type of watercraft you use to tour the islands, an outing on Lake Superior is a pleasure: the air is fresh, the island scenery is exceptional and the lake remains relatively unpolluted. There are many ways to explore the Apostles. Excursion trips through the Apostle Islands Cruise Service leave from Bayfield daily in summer. You can choose from a variety of trips offered: short trips that circle some of the nearest islands, longer tours that pass many islands and include brief stops, sunset cruises and other tours. Park naturalists offer guided hikes on Stockton Island. You can also join the interpretive tours of the Raspberry Island Lighthouse,

To explore the islands you need a boat. A ferry service provides crossings and other types of watercraft can be rented.

and the Manitou Island Fish Camp (a restored commercial fish camp that features demonstrations of fishing tools and techniques).

Visitors who wish to explore or camp on islands that aren't part of an established cruise may take the Apostle Island Water Taxi. The taxi provides shuttle services from Bayfield to any island for one to six passengers. Schedules and rates for all island cruises are available from the visitor center in Bayfield.

Sailing, fishing, boating, and scuba diving are popular lakeshore water sports. The lake is usually too cold for swimming, except in shallow protected bays. No lifeguards are on duty within the National Lakeshore.

Boat launch facilities are available at Little Sandy Beach and at several locations outside the National Lakeshore boundary. Marinas in the Bayfield–Madeline Island area offer equipment, gear, fuel, mooring and storage for boats up to 60 feet long. Many of the islands have public docks; check the lakeshore map for locations.

Weather conditions can change swiftly in the Apostle Islands. A calm sunny day can turn ugly in a hurry. Even in the summer the lake's waters are dangerously cold. Lake Superior has a long history of violent storms and many shipwrecks (about 125 around the islands). Before you set out, get the appropriate nautical charts and find out the current weather forecast from the Coast Guard, island ranger stations or marine radio.

You can rent power- and sailboats and arrange full- and half-day sailing and fishing charters at area marinas. There is no inland fishing on the islands, but Lake Superior provides good sportfishing for lake, brown and rainbow trout, and other salmon species. Mainland streams harbor brook, rainbow and brown trout, and spawning salmon.

Winter's beauty, though harsh at times, attracts those who wish to experience the islands off-season. Cross-country skiing, snowshoeing, ice fishing and winter camping grow in popularity each year. Snowmobiles are not permitted on the lakeshore's islands or mainland unit, but there are over 350 miles of marked snowmobile trails in the surrounding area. Travel on the lake ice is permitted, but conditions can be unpredictable and hazardous. If you'd like to winter camp, register at the park headquarters in Bayfield.

(continued on next page)

Start your investigation of the Apostles in picturesque Bayfield.

Flora and Fauna

Island wildlife populations differ from those on the mainland and often vary between islands. While large animals like deer, black bear and coyote can swim between the islands or cross on ice, smaller animals like mice or red squirrels were probably carried to the islands aboard canoes, boats or drifting debris. Bird life is abundant here because of the mixed forest habitat and because the islands are part of the spring and fall migratory flyway. Over 230 species have been spotted, including bald eagles and loons.

Facilities

The 21 islands that form the Apostle Islands National Lakeshore are preserved as a wilderness. Many islands have designated campsites and hiking trails, though. Backcountry camping for experienced campers requires a free permit, available from mainland or island ranger stations. Wear sturdy shoes for hiking and be prepared for cool, rainy weather. Biting insects are common from early June to mid-September. Insect repellents are useful, but clothing that covers exposed skin is the best protection. The lake water looks clear, yet it should be boiled for at least five minutes before drinking. Outfitters in Bayfield can help you plan an island camping trip. Ask at the Lakeshore Visitors Center for the list of public and private campgrounds in the surrounding area.

Surrounding Area

(opposite page)
Madeline Island is not part of the national park, but shares the scenic features that make the islands special. It has its own state park.

Madeline Island is the largest island in the Apostles and is the only one that is not part of the National Lakeshore. Car ferries cross from Bayfield to La Pointe (the island's only town) on a regular basis from spring breakup to winter freeze. Schedules are available at park headquarters. Island attractions include the Madeline Island Historical Museum, an old Indian burial ground, an airport, golf course and marina. Bus tours are available or you can explore the island by car or bicycle. Big Bay State Park and Big Bay Island Park (run by the township) both have campgrounds (no showers or electricity) and share

a beautiful sandy beach that curves for over a mile along Lake Superior.

Madeline Island has a long, colorful history. French explorers "discovered" it in 1659, though the Ojibwa Indians had lived here since the 1400s. The area where La Pointe stands now represents one of the earliest Indian settlements, fur trading posts and Christian missions in the interior of North America. At various times in its history, the flags of France, England and the United States have flown over the island.

Bayfield was founded in 1856, taking advantage of the protection the islands afforded this natural deep-water harbor. Soon the resources of the islands—the fish, forests, brownstone (sandstone) blocks—were taken in great quantity. Scenery, another of the islands' resources, helped to inspire the growth of tourism in the region in the early 20th century. Bayfield is a distinctive hillside village with a mixture of eye-pleasing architecture (a 50-block area of town is listed as an historic district in the National Register of Historic Places). Ask the chamber of commerce for information about walking tours, festivals, fish boils, etc.

Commercial fishing for lake trout, whitefish, herring and smelt is important to the area's economy. You can watch the commercial fishermen dock in Bayfield after their day's catch and then buy fresh fish from local markets.

After your Apostle Islands adventure, take a drive around the Bayfield Peninsula. As you head north of Bayfield, you'll come to the Red Cliff Indian Reservation (campground, boat launch and marina). Stop at the Buffalo Art Center to see the exhibits and artifacts that tell the story of the Ojibwa Nation and browse the handcrafted items in the gift shop. Other Bayfield Peninsula attractions include the Chequamegon National Forest, the coastal towns of Cornucopia and Washburn, and the festive entertainment of the Lake Superior Big Top Chautauqua (near Bayfield). Ask at the local chambers of commerce for details.

BIG BAY STATE PARK

Ashland County. From La Pointe (on Madeline Island), drive east on County H for five miles to Hagen Road and the park entrance. Highway map index: 1-D.

Main Attraction

The indefinable fascination with small islands makes the picturesque Apostles especially alluring to venturesome travelers. Twenty-one of the 22 Apostle Islands (plus a mainland section) form the Apostle Islands National Lakeshore. Madeline, the largest island, is not part of the lakeshore, but is the home of Big Bay State Park.

Madeline Island is about 14 miles long and 3 miles wide. The island's 45 miles of roads lead auto and bicycle tourers to many Lake Superior vistas. Though the French were the first Europeans to settle here (in 1693), the Ojibwa (Chippewa) Indians had lived on the island since the late 1400s. Today the island is the only one of the Apostles that has year-round residents (its population of under 200 swells to 2,000 during the summer).

When Madeline Island reappeared from under the last glacier (about 15,000 years ago), Big Bay Lagoon was a large, shallow, open bay. Shoreline currents and waves soon built a barrier beach across the middle of Big Bay and later formed another barrier beach across the mouth of the bay. The lagoon that you see today lies between the two barrier beaches.

You can reach Madeline Island by boat or private plane. Ferryboats run on regular schedules between Bayfield and La Pointe from April to December.

Things To Do

Big Bay State Park has a long, curving 1.5-mile sand beach that always seems to have room for beachcombers. Swimming is possible in the cold waters of Lake Superior, but only in shallow, protected bays. Though Big Bay is mostly shallow near the beach, the water is stimulating, even in August.

Just behind the beach is a lagoon that is calm enough for canoes. You can fish for northern pike in the lagoon or for lake, brown and rainbow trout in Lake Superior. If you didn't bring your boat or don't want to rent one, the Bayfield Trollers Association offers full-day, half-day and overnight deep-sea charter fishing trips.

No launching facilities are presently available at the park, although boats can be launched at the pub-

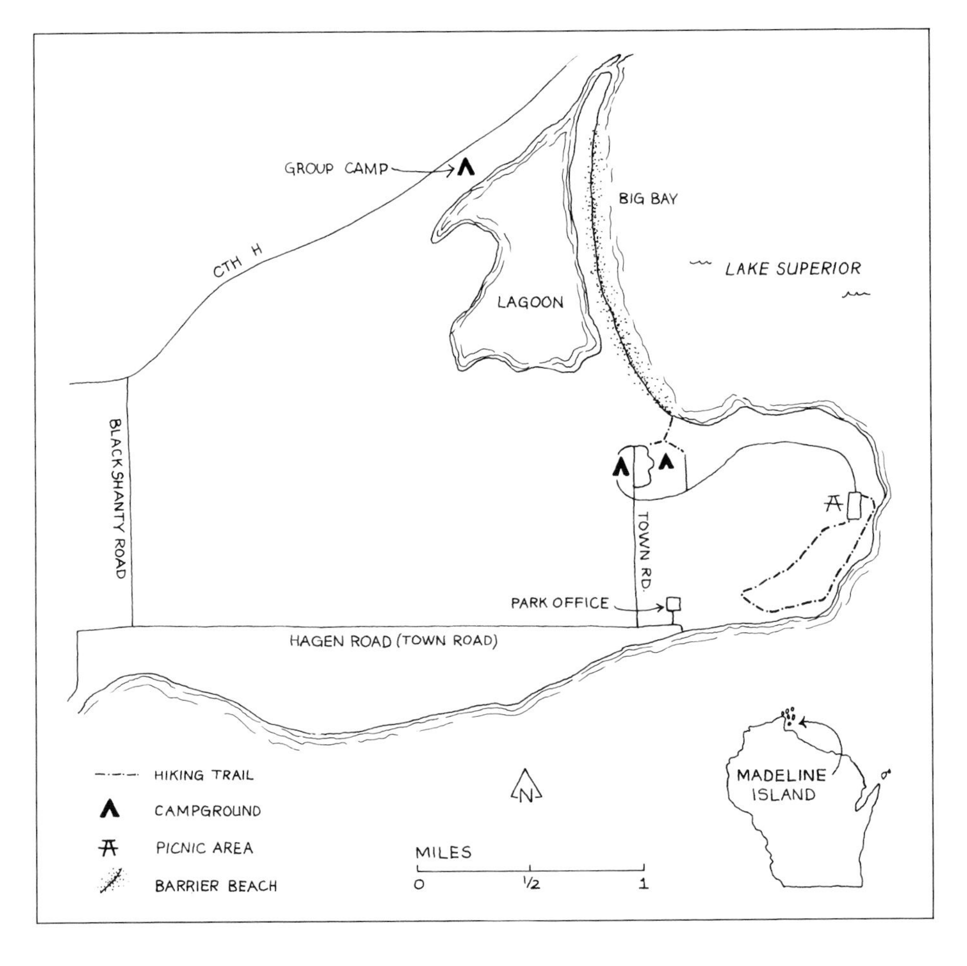

lic landing in Bayfield or at the privately operated landing on Madeline Island. The four marinas in the Bayfield–Madeline Island area have a good selection of equipment, gear and fuel. Mooring and storage for boats up to 60 feet are also available.

Hundreds of boaters enjoy the relatively sheltered waters of the Apostle Islands each season, and the sailing is considered to be some of the best in the country. But Lake Superior is large and dangerous, with a long history of violent shipwrecks. Even on calm days, boaters should keep an eye on the weather. Consult the United States Coast Guard Station at Bayfield for the current weather report and Lake Superior navigation information.

To see the island's most dramatic scenery, drive to the end of the park road to the Big Bay Point Picnic Area. You can eat your lunch to the accompaniment of Lake Superior lapping at the island's rocky shore. The loop trail beyond the picnic area is an exciting hike. You'll see caves (at water level), ledges and unusual sandstone formations sculpted by weather and wind. Ask the park manager about other trails and the Big Bay Sand Spit and Bog Natural Area.

The beach here is roomy and the scenery is dramatic. There's calm water for canoeing and open water for sailing. And, swimming in Lake Superior is nothing if not stimulating.

Big Bay State Park is striking when autumn colors contrast with the blue of Lake Superior. This is the peak time to hike in the forest or watch the migrating flocks in the park's marshy wildlife refuge. Because of the lake's warming influence, autumn lingers in the Apostle Islands. Campers usually will have no problem in the fall finding sites in the area. The park closes prior to the deer hunting season, but the public can still enter.

Flora and Fauna

Great blue herons are a common sight. The thump of their great wings and their gracefulness in flight are awe-inspiring no matter how many times you see them.

Facilities

The 2,358-acre park recently enlarged its family campground to 55 sites (no showers or electricity).

There is also a 20-person indoor group camp available by reservation. To ensure getting a family campsite during the busy summer season, make reservations before boarding the ferry. A short trail connects the state park family campground to the beach.

The other campground, at Big Bay Island Park, adjoins the state park on the north side of Big Bay. The

The rugged shoreline of Madeline Island has been battered and sculpted by weather and wind.

44 campsites are rented on a first-come, first-served basis. The park, operated by the town of La Pointe, has a picnic area and large sandy beaches. The township also maintains a picnic area and swimming beach about one half mile from the ferry dock in La Pointe.

Surrounding Area

Madeline Island also boasts a golf course designed by Robert Trent Jones. The Madeline Island Museum in La Pointe is affiliated with the Wisconsin State Historical Society and has collections of local artifacts from Indians, settlers, and the logging, fishing and trapping industries. An Indian burial ground is near the marina, just half a mile from the ferry dock. Some of the markers are more than 200 years old.

The park doesn't maintain snowmobile or cross-country ski trails, though there are trails everywhere on the island. Just getting to the island in the winter is an adventure. When the ferry is not operating, a motor-driven wind sled offers transportation between Bayfield and La Pointe until the ice is strong enough to drive vehicles across on a plowed ice highway. Winter visitors can enjoy ice fishing on the lake and downhill skiing at Mt. Ashwabay near Bayfield. The Mt. Valhalla Recreation Area in the Chequamegon National Forest (on the mainland) features groomed trails for cross-country skiers and snowmobilers.

After your day trip or camping expedition to Big Bay State Park, you'll find plenty of attractions in the Bayfield area to tempt you to stay. You could start by picking up a map of Bayfield and going on a self-guided walking or driving tour of this hillside coastal town. A 50-block area of Bayfield is listed as an historic district in the National Register of Historic Places. Fifty-two local structures of special historical and architectural importance are included in the Register.

Bayfield is famous for its orchards, commercial fishing industry and an active artist community. The Lake Superior Big Top Chautauqua presents old-time tent shows of popular historical musicals with a regional flavor. Bayfield also sponsors several special celebrations each year. Stop at the Chamber of Commerce office to get details about what you can see and do in the area.

Bayfield is the gateway to the Apostle Islands National Lakeshore. If you're interested in exploring the Apostle Islands, excursion trips leave daily from Bayfield and Little Sandy Bay in the summer. In Bayfield, the Apostle Islands Cruise Service features long and short sightseeing tours in addition to a camper shuttle to Stockton Island and charter service to any other island. The Apostle Islands National Lakeshore Headquarters in Bayfield is a good information stop for details about boating, camping, scuba diving and sightseeing among the islands.

BLACK RIVER STATE FOREST

Jackson County. Headquarters is in Black River Falls at the Interstate 94 and Highway 54 interchange.

Main Attraction

Buttes and bluffs, forests and flowages highlight the multi-use Black River State Forest. Settlers came here to log white pine. Today the forest is managed for timber, wildlife and recreation.

The 65,782-acre forest, established in 1957, is unique among Wisconsin's state forests because of its geological features. The forest lies on the edge of the glaciated central plain, east of the rugged driftless region (lack of glacier debris, or drift) that was missed by the last glacier. Looking east from the top of Castle Mound, you can see what was once the bed of Glacial Lake Wisconsin. The Winnebago Indians have used this land as a meeting ground for centuries. The sandstone bluffs and buttes served as landmarks for travel in the vast forest for both the Winnebago people and European explorers, traders and settlers.

The Black River, so named because of the water's iron content, has cut its channel down through the sandstone to expose the older granite. This window of exposed granite, called an inlier, is 40 miles long and gives this section of the Black River a special character that canoeists enjoy.

Things To Do

The Black River, and East Fork of the Black River, can provide good canoeing in the spring and early summer. Above Hatfield, from Highway 95 to Lake Arbutus, the Black River is rated expert in high water. In low water, the many rocks and rapids make for slow going.

A common canoe trip covers a 24-mile river stretch from Lake Arbutus to Hoffman Wayside on Highway

54. This route usually takes one full day with an overnight camp at Hawk Island canoe campsite. Otherwise, camping is available on sandbars or islands in the river channel, or on private property with the landowner's permission. Canoeing conditions depend on the weather and how many gates are open

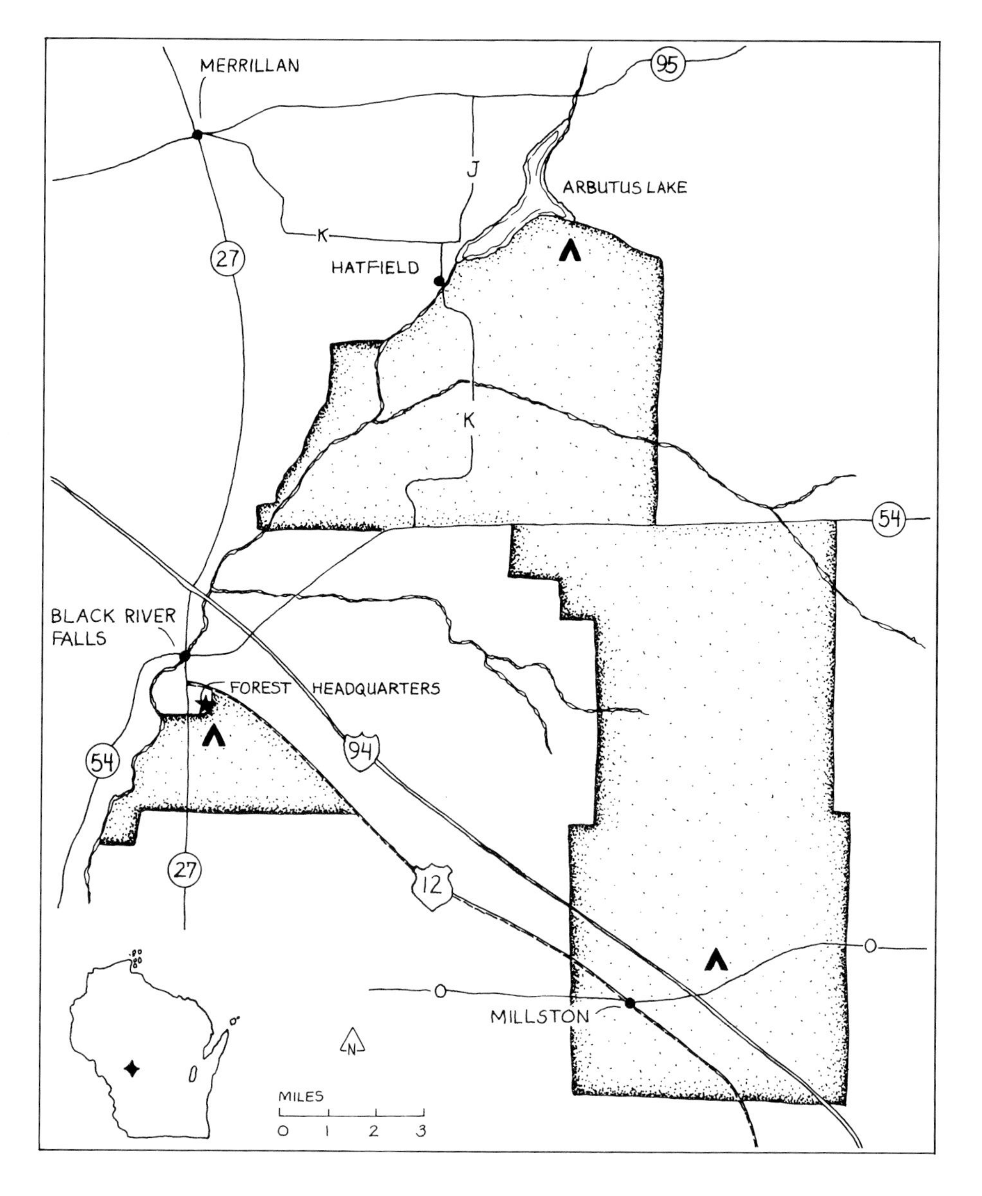

on the Black River Falls dam. For details about canoe landings, portages, rapids and water levels, ask at the forest headquarters in Black River Falls.

Backpackers and hikers can explore the forest on a combination of trails. At Castle Mound you can follow the self-guiding nature trail up to the lookout, or hike down to the Perry Creek picnic area with its pretty gorge. You can also trek the many miles of unmarked woods trails and the county and state forest snowmobile trails. Other good places to go are Wildcat Mound and Wildcat Flowage, and the scenic bluffs overlooking the Black River in the northwest part of the forest. The cross-country ski trails, four miles east and one mile north of Millston, traverse a series of ridges with great views. *(continued on next page)*

All levels of cross-country skiers will enjoy the views from the snow-covered bluffs as they slide along the excellent groomed trails.

You can swim in the forest at Robinson Beach and at Pidgeon Creek. Picnic areas are sprinkled throughout the forest at each of the campgrounds and beaches. Some visitors prefer to take a lunch break at one of the flowages while observing wildlife or panfishing. The best game fishing in the forest is on the Black River and at Lake Arbutus near Hatfield. You can try for walleye, bass, northern, muskie and panfish. The Oxbow Ponds Area offers trout fishing, which is especially popular early in the season.

Winter is no less enjoyable than summer at Wisconsin parks if you prepare for the cold and smile.

About 35 miles of ATV trails have been developed in the forest that connect with Jackson County Forest trails to provide over 60 miles of marked routes. The trails also connect the area towns of Black River Falls, Hatfield, Pray and Millston.

Hunters like the Black River State Forest because of its large deer population and the thousands of waterfowl that frequent the flowages. You're welcome to use the designated campgrounds or you can camp off-site during the deer gun season by getting the required permit (free) at the DNR office. Find out which sections are closed to hunting.

Snowmobiling and cross-country skiing are the most popular winter sports here, while snowshoeing continues to attract a small but loyal minority. The snowmobile trails run mostly north and south through the forest and link with county and private trails. The forest's 46 miles of groomed trails are favorites among snowmobilers from Wisconsin and neighboring states who like the long, scenic routes through woodlands and over rolling terrain.

The Black River State Forest cross-country ski trails are among Wisconsin's finest. Competitive skiers train here because many of the loops in the 27-mile system are widened to accommodate skaters. Both experts and beginners will be challenged by these trails as well as treated to several scenic views of the forest and its snow-covered buttes and bluffs.

The forest maintains two trail systems known as the Smrekar Loops and the Wildcat Loops. All trails are groomed weekly. Two parking lots are provided: Wildcat lot (about four miles northeast of Millston on North Settlement Road) and Smrekar lot (about four miles east of Millston on County O, then north about one mile on Smrekar Road). Two rest areas, marked on the ski map, have adirondack shelters, small shelters, small fireplaces and picnic tables. Drinking water is available at the Central Trail shelter and at the Wildcat parking lot. The Ridge, Norway Pine, and Wildcat trails are quite steep in places and are recommended for experts.

Of photographic interest is an old cemetery just south of the junction of the Central and North trails. You'll also find a root cellar and an old well (no water) that have been restored on an early farmstead along the East Trail. Skiers can pick up narratives at the Smrekar parking lot for the self-guided nature loop on the Central Trail.

The Black River has cut a channel through the sandstone to expose the older granite, which gives this stretch of river a special character that canoeists enjoy.

Flora and Fauna

The 3,700-acre Dike 17 Wildlife Area in the forest attracts hundreds of ducks and geese each fall to 20 nearby flowages. The flowages, built in the 1930s, are also good spots for observing sandhill cranes and sharptail grouse. You can climb the observation tower to photograph the wildlife or just to watch. Over 2,000 acres of Dike 17 are designated as a wildlife refuge. Some of the endangered and threatened wildlife species found here include the bald eagle, osprey, eastern massasauga rattlesnake, Cooper's hawk and Blanding's turtle.

Facilities

There are three family campgrounds in the forest: Castle Mound, on Highway 12 one mile east of Black River Falls; East Fork, two miles southeast of Hatfield along the East Fork of the Black River; and Pidgeon Creek, two miles northeast of Millston. None of the campgrounds (101 total campsites) have showers or accept camping reservations. Castle Mound has six campsites with electrical hookups.

A group camp near the East Fork Campground is available on a reservation basis and can accommodate 100 people. The group camp shelter (electricity and heat) is also reservable in the winter. Local camping areas are in Jackson County Park, and Clark County Park on Lake Arbutus. Check with local chambers of commerce for information about area private campgrounds.

Primitive camping is allowed for backpackers, but you must get a permit before setting out and may camp only at the areas designated on the permit. Pick up a permit and state forest map showing roads and marked trails at the DNR office on Highway 54.

During the winter you can camp in the Castle Mound and Pidgeon Creek campgrounds, though there are plenty of local accommodations available if you don't want to go to extremes to rough it.

Surrounding Area

The region surrounding the Black River State Forest offers a number of other outdoor recreation lands. These include the Buffalo River, Great River, La Crosse River and Elroy-Sparta state trails; Mill Bluff and Buckhorn state parks; the Meadow Valley State Wildlife Area and the Necedah National Wildlife Refuge. While visiting the Black River State Forest, you can find any needed services in Millston, Hatfield or Black River Falls.

BRULE RIVER STATE FOREST

Douglas County. Headquarters is about one mile south of Brule on Highway 27.

Main Attraction

Long famous as a trout stream, the Brule River is also considered a favorite for its canoeing and forest scenery. Visitors can combine hiking, tubing, camping, canoeing, boating or backpacking in the 40,000 acres of state land in the Brule River State Forest.

For centuries before the Europeans arrived, the Indians used the Brule as a link between Lake Superior and the Mississippi. In 1680, Daniel Greysolon, Sieur du Lhut (Duluth, Minnesota, is named for him) recorded his journey up the Brule from Lake Superior. Missionaries and fur traders followed him as the white man's presence grew in this region.

The forest was established in 1907, when Frederick Weyerhauser deeded over 4,000 acres to the State of Wisconsin to be used for forestry purposes. Today it's managed for timber production, recreation, wildlife, fisheries and watershed protection. The Brule is one of the best-known rivers east of the Mississippi. Five U.S. presidents have fished here.

Things To Do

There are no designated swimming beaches, though some visitors enjoy swimming at Little Rush Lake on the eastern edge of the forest. Public beaches are available at Lakes Minnesuing and Nebagamon near the forest. Picnic areas are located at the mouth of the Brule River overlooking Lake Superior, near the Bois Brule Campground and at the St. Croix Lake boat landing.

Hikers and backpackers often explore the forest on the 26-mile Brule-to-St. Croix Lake Snowmobile Trail. This was a major portage trail for Indians, explorers

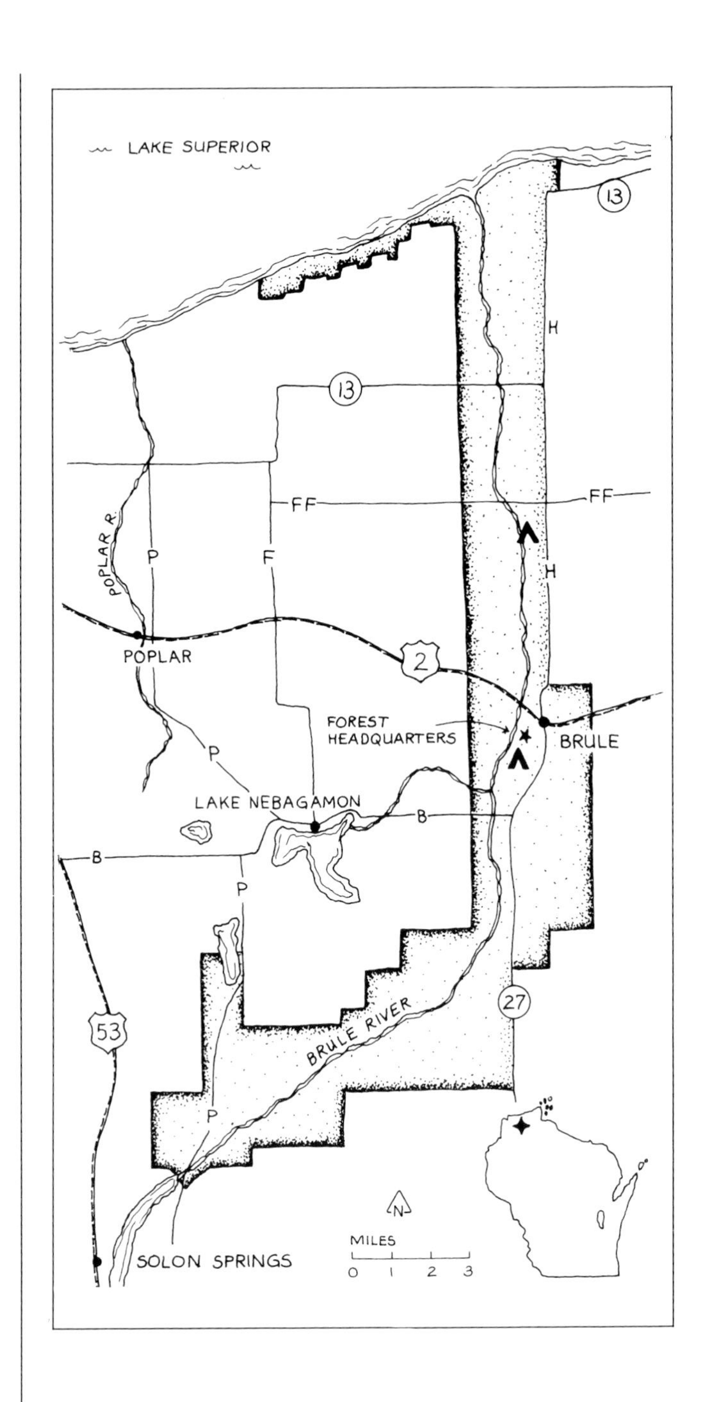
LAKE SUPERIOR
13
H
13
FF
FF
POPLAR R.
P
F
H
POPLAR
2
FOREST HEADQUARTERS
BRULE
P
LAKE NEBAGAMON
B
B
P
27
53
BRULE RIVER
P
N
MILES
0 1 2 3
SOLON SPRINGS

and fur traders. It crosses a continental divide and links the Mississippi River–Lake Superior waterways. You can also hike on the interpretive trail at the Bois Brule Campground, the cross-country ski trails or the logging roads. The interpretive trail is steep in parts, but the overlook of the Brule River Valley from the top of Stoney Hill is worth the sweat. Backpackers can camp overnight in the forest, but they must first get a free permit from the forest headquarters. Those hikers interested in the study of natural plant communities can ask at the headquarters for information about the two natural areas in the forest.

The Brule is one of the finest trout streams and one of the best known rivers east of the Mississippi. Five U.S. presidents have fished here. Also, the surrounding forest provides a host of recreational opportunities.

The upper and lower Brule, divided approximately by the Copper Range (near the Copper Range campground), are like two different rivers. The upper Brule flows slowly through a broad, flat, bog-filled valley, with towering spruce, cedar and tamarack. The snow and rain that fall on the surrounding sandy country sink deep into the ground and rise again in the form of clear, cold springs that form the Brule River. This 30-mile section falls an average of three feet per mile. Stones Bridge, where County S crosses the Brule, is the most popular put-in point for canoe trips.

About four miles from Stones Bridge is Cedar Island, where President Calvin Coolidge spent the summer of 1928. The first real rapids of the trip are below the island.

Winneboujou, where County B crosses the river, is a scenic two-mile stretch with some beautiful summer homes beneath the large pines. Near here is Hall's Rapids, followed by a series of rapids downstream. The last of these is called Little Joe Rapids, an exciting pitch that you may examine from the right bank ahead of time. The passage between the rocks is narrow and close to the right bank, requiring skillful canoe handling to run it. After Little Joe Rapids is the ranger station, the Bois Brule campground and a canoe landing. Between here and the Copper Range campground there is a quiet stretch called the meadows.

The lower Brule, from Copper Range to Lake Superior, is a fast-moving river of almost continuous rapids and steep red-clay banks. It flows through a deep narrow valley covered with a forest of aspen, birch and balsam fir. In this stretch of 19 miles, the river drops 328 feet, an average drop of 17 feet per mile. This is a challenging part of the river where kayaks are more common than canoes. Be prepared for spills.

(opposite page)

Canoeing and the Brule River go together, offering a variety of scenery and water conditions.

The Brule River flows north and empties into Lake Superior. For big-water lovers, this is an ideal spot to spend a sunny afternoon on the beach, or romp in the lake's chilly water for a while. Fishing is always popular here, and you can launch your own boat or try charter boat fishing from the Superior-Duluth area.

Forest personnel will be able to give you details about successful trout fishing on the Brule River.

Hunting and trapping (in season) are allowed on all public lands within the forest boundaries except in a small waterfowl area north of Highway 13. The wildlife managers at the headquarters can offer tips on where to hunt in the forest, even if you only want to shoot photographs.

Winter recreation in the forest involves mostly snowmobilers and cross-country skiers. The Brule–St. Croix Lake Snowmobile Trail is 26 miles long with parking lots near Solon Springs and south of Brule on Highway 27. Cross-country skiers can enjoy the forest on 6.7 miles of groomed trails on the west side of the Brule River. The trail head parking lot is on After Hours Road, off Highway 2. You can also ski on unmarked trails throughout the forest.

Flora and Fauna

It's hard to visit the Brule River State Forest without seeing wildlife. The bogs, barrens, boreal forest and farmland support a wide variety of birds and mammals. Deer, ruffed grouse, migrating geese, snowy owls (during winter), bald eagles and ospreys can be observed in the forest. The upper Brule River Valley and adjacent scrub oak/pine forests support some of the highest deer populations in northern Wisconsin.

The Brule River is home to resident brook, brown and rainbow trout. It's also a major spawning stream

for migratory brown and rainbow (steelhead) trout from Lake Superior. In recent years, coho, chinook and pink salmon have also migrated up the Brule River from Lake Superior for spawning.

Facilities

There are two camping areas in the forest. The Bois Brule campground is about one mile south of Highway 2 on the road to the Brule Ranger Station. This area has 23 campsites with a canoe landing, picnic ground and a 1.7-mile self-guiding nature trail. The Copper Range campground is located near the Brule River, four miles north of the village of Brule on Highway H. There are 17 campsites here with canoe access. Neither campsite has electricity, and both require a sticker and a camping fee. All camping is on a first-come, first-served basis.

Surrounding Area

It's easy to combine a visit to the Brule River State Forest with side trips to three nearby state parks. Lucius Woods State Park features a tall stand of virgin timber, while Amnicon Falls and Pattison state parks each have scenic northwoods waterfalls. Other nearby public recreational lands include several county forests, the Chequamegon National Forest, and the Apostle Islands National Lakeshore. The North Country National Scenic Trail, a 3,200-mile route from Crown Point, New York, to the Lewis and Clark National Historic Trail in North Dakota, passes through the Brule River State Forest.

BRUNET ISLAND STATE PARK

Chippewa County. In Cornell, turn north from Highway 64 onto the park entrance road. Highway map index: 5-D.

Main Attraction

Brunet Island is a river island park named for Jean Brunet, an early pioneer in the Chippewa River region. Born of nobility in France, Brunet was respected by Indians and whites as a guide, explorer, teacher, missionary, engineer and peacemaker. The 1,032-acre park was created where the Chippewa and Fisher rivers join above Cornell.

West of the island, across the Chippewa River, is the beginning of a segment of the Ice Age National Scenic Trail. This 1,000-mile trail, when completed, will curve across Wisconsin as it traces the farthest advance of the last glacier. From Brunet Island, the trail winds westward through the Chippewa County Forest and private lands to the eastern boundary of the Chippewa Moraine Unit (one of nine units of the Ice Age National Scenic Reserve). The trail crosses forested glacial ridges and rushing streams, passing by several beaver ponds and undeveloped lakes. Primitive camping is allowed along the trail in the Chippewa County Forest. You can cross-country ski or snowshoe on the Ice Age Trail during the winter.

Things To Do

On the island, you can hike on the Pine, Timber and Clubmoss trails. The Clubmoss is a three-quarter-mile nature trail with interpretive signs describing some of the plants, trees and landforms that you'll hike past. For a longer hike, try the Nordic Trail loop, which starts on the mainland next to the park headquarters.

Whether you camp or picnic at Brunet Island, bring

The Chippewa Flowage is one of the best fishing waters in the state, offering muskie, northern, smallmouth bass, walleye, catfish and panfish. Brunet Island State Park is a lovely spot to begin your fishing expedition.

your fishing pole with you. The Chippewa Flowage, one of the best fishing waters in the state, is a good spot to angle for muskie, northern, walleye, catfish, smallmouth bass and panfish. You can launch onto the flowage from the park boat ramp on the east side of the island. At night, many boaters tie up in the mooring area on the island's west side between the two campgrounds. The park recently constructed a floating pier that is accessible to disabled visitors.

Brunet Island is a fun place to go canoeing. You can circle the island and wander in its bays and lagoons, or spend the day scouting the Chippewa Flowage. Canoes were the main form of transportation around here before roads, and it's fun to fantasize

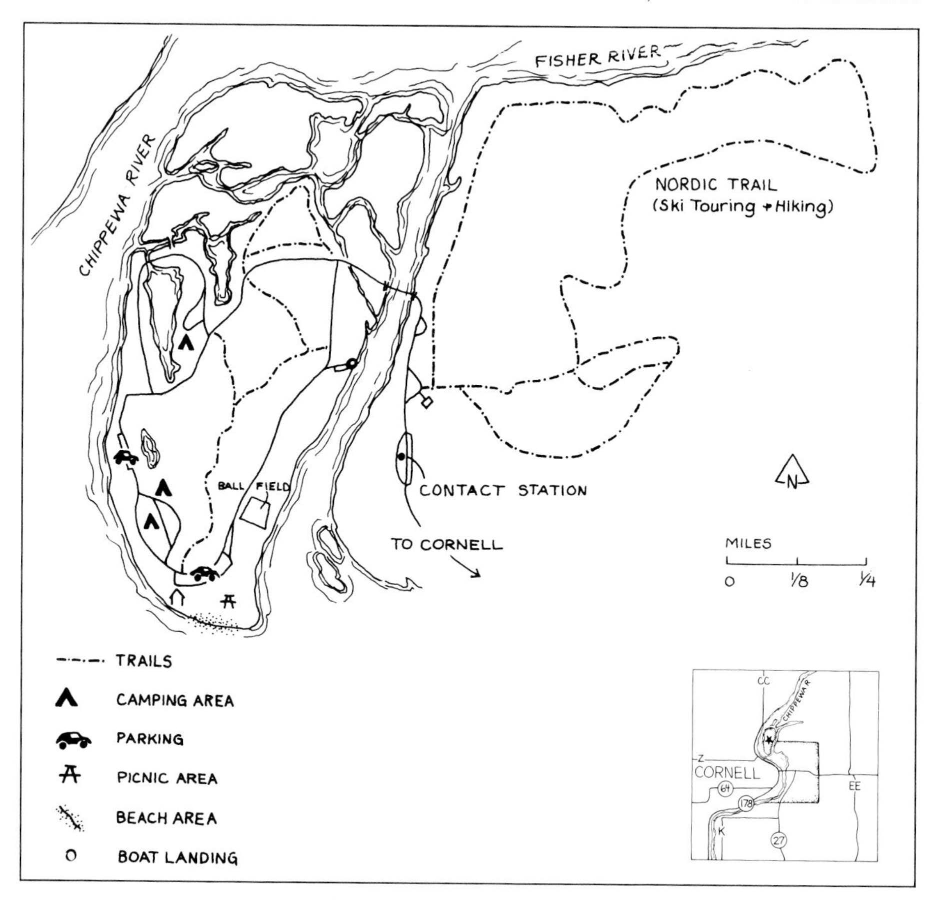

(with or without kids) about Jean Brunet's times, when he first paddled upstream to this area in the early 1800s.

Cross-country skiers and hikers have the park to themselves during the winter. There are four miles of designated ski trails that start near the park headquarters parking lot, though you can wander off the trail if you choose. Snowmobiling is not allowed in the park, but a trail starts one mile west of Cornell, connecting with about 45 miles of trails in the Chippewa County Forest. Ice fishing, snowshoeing and ice skating are other winter pastimes around the park.

Flora and Fauna

While hiking the park's six-mile trail system, you have a good chance of spotting some of the large local deer population. Deer frequent the park at dawn and dusk to feed on the mowed grass and often wander through the campground. Great blue herons are often observed on the backwater lagoons near the north campground. You might also see bald eagles circling above the river in search of a meal.

Facilities

Campers can choose a site on a first-come, first-served basis from two campgrounds on the island. Of 69 sites, 24 have electrical outlets. Drinking water is available, but there are no showers or laundry facilities in the park. You'll find laundromats and camping supplies in Cornell.

Brunet has a spacious beach-picnic area stretching around the south end of the island. There is a large log shelter as well as horseshoe courts, a ball field and a playground. Lifeguards are on duty during the summer.

Surrounding Area

The area surrounding Brunet Island offers a lot to do for visitors who want to explore beyond the park. Cornell has several golf courses, and there is a field archery range just east of the park on the Chippewa River. The Chippewa County Forest, west of Cornell,

The backwater lagoons and wetlands here yield a rich variety of plants and animals to those who look closely.

is a 44,500-acre tract of wild country laced with recreational trails for snowmobiles, ATVs and hikers. It is a prime hunting area with many small lakes and good fishing. Lake Wissota State Park and the Chequamegon National Forest are both short drives from Brunet Island.

BUFFALO RIVER STATE TRAIL

Buffalo, Trempealeau, Jackson and Eau Claire counties. 36.4 miles, from Mondovi to Fairchild.

Main Attraction

The Buffalo River State Trail is a multiple-use track that parallels the Buffalo River for much of its length. The route's scenery is a mixture of marsh, wooded hills and farmland.

Things To Do

Multiple-use means that hikers, horseback riders, snowmobilers and ATVers all share the former railroad right-of-way. Currently, the route is not surfaced for bicycles, though mountain bikes might be able to handle the rough terrain.

Some hikers (and other users, too) carry a fishing pole to try the trout fishing along the trail. Berry picking can be good in season. Observant hikers may notice the native prairie grasses that still thrive in spots along the path.

This trail is open to hikers, snowmobilers, horseback riders and ATVers, although there are seasonal restrictions. So choose your conveyance and enjoy the Buffalo River scenery.

Trail users should be aware of the special seasons on the Buffalo. Horseback riders and ATVers may use the trail from May 15 to November 1, while snowmobilers can run from December 1 to March 15. The Buffalo River State Trail is open for hunting during established hunting seasons. The DNR asks that all trail users stay on the trail grade in order to avoid nearby privately owned land. The trail is closed to horses and vehicles from March 15 to May 15 to prevent damage during the spring thaw.

Surrounding Area

The trail communities of Fairchild, Price, Osseo, Strum, Eleva and Mondovi are good pit stops for food and relaxation. You can find visitor services or a local park in each town. Camping facilities along the trail include the Trempealeau County Campground in Strum and a private campground near Osseo. The Red Cedar State Trail and the Black River State Forest are short drives away from the trail.

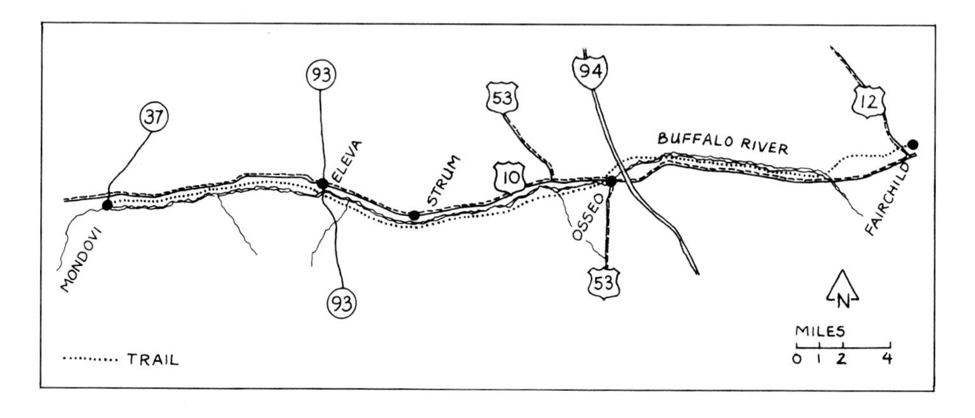

CHEQUAMEGON NATIONAL FOREST

Bayfield, Sawyer, Ashland, Price, Vilas and Taylor counties. 845,000 acres. Forest headquarters is in Park Falls; district offices are in Park Falls, Glidden, Washburn, Medford and Hayward.

Main Attraction

You don't have to know how to pronounce "Chequamegon National Forest" in order to enjoy its lakes, rivers and trails. Some first-time visitors could probably tell you where the muskies are biting before they could say the name correctly, much less spell it.

To sound like a native, say SHO-WAH-MA-GON. If you really want to impress your friends, casually mention that the lyrical name derives from the Ojibwa (Chippewa) Indian language and means "place of shallow water." The reference is to Chequamegon Bay, which extends from Ashland into Lake Superior.

Glacial history is important to the Chequamegon. The ice sheets sculpted the land surface, planing off hilltops and filling in valleys. The region's lakes are also a glacial legacy. As the glaciers retreated, meltwater filled hollows in outwash gravel plains to form some lakes. Others, called kettles, were formed when giant ice blocks melted in kettle-shaped depressions in the earth.

The Dakota (Sioux) Indians were forced westward from this region by the Ojibwas in a series of battles. Radisson and Groseilliers, the first European explorers in northwestern Wisconsin, also originated the fur trade in this region. Wisconsin's logging industry began in the Chequamegon area in the late 1820s when a fur trader named Lockwood got permission to cut timber in the Chippewa River Valley from the Ojibwa and Dakota Indians.

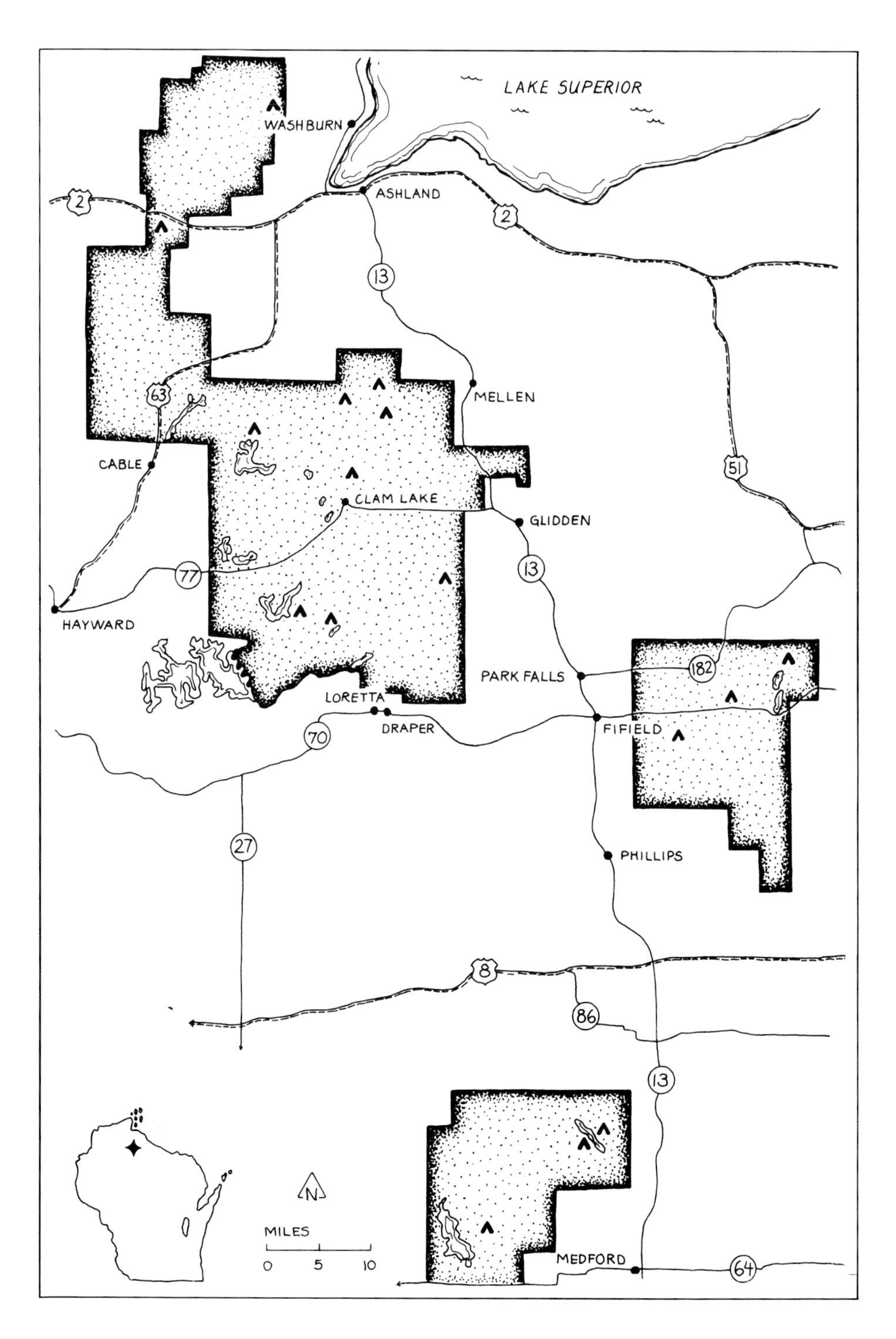
LAKE SUPERIOR
WASHBURN
ASHLAND
2
2
13
63
MELLEN
CABLE
CLAM LAKE
GLIDDEN
51
77
13
HAYWARD
PARK FALLS
182
LORETTA
DRAPER
70
FIFIELD
27
PHILLIPS
8
86
13
N
MILES
0
5
10
MEDFORD
64

The logging era lasted until the turn of the century. By 1924, the once-vast forests of the northwoods were mostly reduced to stumps and rocks, and were ravaged by forest fires. Farmers settled on the cutover land, struggling to work it into fertile soil for planting. The Chequamegon National Forest was created in 1933 as an effort to conserve timber and protect navigable streams. Today, the forest is managed to provide a variety of natural products and public services including timber, water, mineral and wildlife resources, as well as outdoor recreation.

Things To Do

The Chequamegon National Forest boasts 632 miles of rivers and streams and 411 lakes (over 10 acres in size). There's plenty of elbow room for hunting and fishing in the forest, which is divided into three sections in northwestern and northcentral Wisconsin. Visitors need a valid state hunting, trapping or fishing license for those activities and must follow all state laws and regulations concerning the harvest and preservation of game and nongame species in the Chequamegon.

Black bear and white-tailed deer are the big game animals hunted in the forest. Ruffed grouse benefit from the Forest Service practice of seeding old logging trails to clover. Waterfowl hunting is limited and considered average at best, though the forest has developed a number of shallow impoundments to improve local waterfowl habitat.

People have landed trophy and legal-size muskies from the forest lakes. You can also try for northern, walleye, small and largemouth bass, trout and panfish. Rainbow, brook and brown trout provide good action in about 13 trout streams. Public access to fishing water varies from developed boat landings to walk-in sites.

Whether hunting or fishing, keep in mind that there are many parcels of private land scattered throughout the forest. These areas are marked in white on the National Forest Recreation Map. To get information about specific hunting grounds, streams, lakes or spring ponds, contact the closest district office.

The forest is gaining in status among canoeists. Modern-day voyageurs can paddle down rivers that the Indians, missionaries, traders and loggers might still recognize. The main canoeing rivers include the Bad, Jump, Yellow, Chippewa, Flambeau and Namekagon. Canoeists most frequently choose the Chippewa, Flambeau and Namekagon for their river outings. The Namekagon is part of the National Wild and Scenic Rivers System (St. Croix National Scenic Riverway), flowing from Namekagon Lake within the forest boundary.

The forest provides a variety of family recreation possibilities, few more rewarding than a walk in the woods.

The upper reaches of all these rivers are often quite shallow from mid-summer through fall when the water is at its lowest. Portages around the shallow stretches vary from a few feet to several tenths of a mile, depending on the length of the shallow rapids. Canoe rentals are usually available in the larger communities near the rivers. Check with local chamber of commerce offices for details about camping, lodging and other services. The forest district offices can help you with route planning and provide details on river conditions.

Several campgrounds have interpretive or long-distance hiking trails nearby. The Chequamegon National Forest maintains about 200 miles of hiking (nonmotorized use) trails, though there is also an expansive network of multiple-use trails. The Flambeau Trails, for instance, are used by hikers, horseback riders, hunters, snowmobilers and ATVers.

Three forest trails have national significance. The Ice Age National Scenic Trail traverses the state, following the ridge of hills left by the most recent glacier and connecting the nine units of the Ice Age National Scientific Reserve in Wisconsin. A 41-mile segment of the trail cuts through the forest. The North Country National Scenic Trail is part of a 3,200-mile-long system (60 miles through the Chequamegon) that stretches from Crown Point, New York, to the Lewis and Clark National Historic Trail in North Dakota. The Rock Lake National Recreation Trail (near Cable) provides a network of loops for cross-country skiing and hiking.

First learn how to pronounce it, then enjoy the rivers and lakes. Fishing is almost always good, and when the rivers are high, the canoeing is choice. Hikers and backpackers can choose from three forest trails of national significance.

The forest features about 57,000 acres of semi-primitive (nonmotorized) areas divided into 12 parcels. Two wilderness areas, Rainbow Lake and Porcupine Lake, protect about 11,000 acres of forest with over 20 undeveloped lakes. You can get maps and further details about the semi-primitive and wilderness areas at any of the forest offices.

More skiers, hikers and snowmobilers are discovering the Chequamegon each winter. The forest has established a system of over 175 miles of snowmobile trails and about 75 miles of cross-country ski trails. Skiers have nine trail systems to choose from, ranging from the popular Rock Lake loops to the less well-known Penokee Mountain Trail. The Teuton and Valkyrie trails originate at the chalet of the Mt. Valhalla Recreation Area seven miles northwest of Washburn (off County C). This area was once used for training by the U.S. Olympic Ski Team. In addition to the designated skiing and snowmobiling trails, there are hundreds of miles of unplowed roads and ungroomed paths available to the adventuresome.

The forest offices can help you to plan a winter outing. They'll provide information about conditions and forest attractions (in any season). Check with local chambers of commerce about lodging, downhill skiing, etc.

Facilities

Camping facilities are extensive in the forest, with 24 campgrounds divided among the five ranger districts. The campgrounds, all located along lakes, vary in size from 3 to over 90 family units. Visitors who like to camp without a lot of neighbors can choose one of several isolated developed campgrounds or they can camp anywhere throughout the forest. Camping away from developed campgrounds, called dispersed camping, should be attempted only by those experienced in "no-trace camping." This means camping at least 50 feet away from any trail or water's edge, leaving a site with no trace of your presence and packing out all that you pack in.

Sites in the developed campgrounds are available on a first-come, first-served basis (a fee is charged). Many of the campgrounds have nearby picnic areas, boat launches and swimming beaches. The Mondeaux picnic area has concession facilities. Group camping is available by reservation in the forest. One campground (Chippewa) has showers, flush toilets and dumping station; seven have campsites designated for disabled visitors. Contact the forest headquarters for details about group camping and specific campground facilities.

Surrounding Area

Those who are looking for side trips may wish to visit Copper Falls and Ojibwa state parks; the Tuscobia and Bearskin state trails; and the Flambeau River, Northern Highland and Brule River state forests. The Red Cliff, Lac du Flambeau, Bad River and Lac Courte Oreilles Indian reservations are also near the forest. The Apostle Island National Lakeshore and the scenic Lake Superior coastline are north of the forest.

CHIPPEWA RIVER STATE TRAIL

Dunn and Eau Claire counties. 22 miles, from Eau Claire to the Red Cedar State Trail junction (about eight miles north of Durand). Highway map index: 6-C.

Main Attraction

The Wisconsin DNR, long a leader in converting abandoned railroad grades into state trails, has an idea for a new trail designed to promote even more fun with your bicycle. If funding and land acquisition proceed smoothly, the 22-mile Chippewa River State Trail should be in use by the early 1990s.

When this is completed, you'll be able to bike from Eau Claire to Menomonie through two of Wisconsin's most scenic river valleys.

The proposed trail will be developed on the abandoned Milwaukee Road Railroad right-of-way along the Chippewa River. The route will start in Eau Claire, already known as a scenic city for bicycle touring, and will stretch southwest to the mouth of the Red Cedar River. The Chippewa River and Red Cedar state trails meet at this point. Bicyclists can then cross the Chippewa River on a 840-foot trestle (refurbished for bicycles) and continue their ride north on the 14.5-mile Red Cedar State Trail into Menomonie. That would make a 36.5-mile bike route from Eau Claire to Menomonie through two of Wisconsin's most picturesque river valleys. The combined trail might attract 60,000 bicyclists and hikers each year, due to its proximity to the Twin Cities metro area.

In time, the Chippewa River State Trail may be expanded another 24 miles northeast of Eau Claire to Cornell. The route, still shadowing the Chippewa River upstream, would cut through Chippewa Falls and connect with Lake Wissota and Brunet Island state parks. At the other end of the trail, an extension from the Red Cedar–Chippewa River Trail junction southwest to Durand may be developed. No definite plans exist for either idea yet.

Surrounding Area

The Eau Claire–Chippewa Falls area prospered during the lumbering era of the late 1800s. The Chippewa River Valley was the world's number-one source of white pine in the 19th century. Museums and local celebrations still reflect the cities' logging heritage. Contact the chambers of commerce for further details about the attractions and special events in these two towns. Camping is available at Lake Wissota State Park and at several nearby private campgrounds. The Buffalo River State Trail and the Hoffman Hills State Recreation Area are both within short driving distances of Eau Claire.

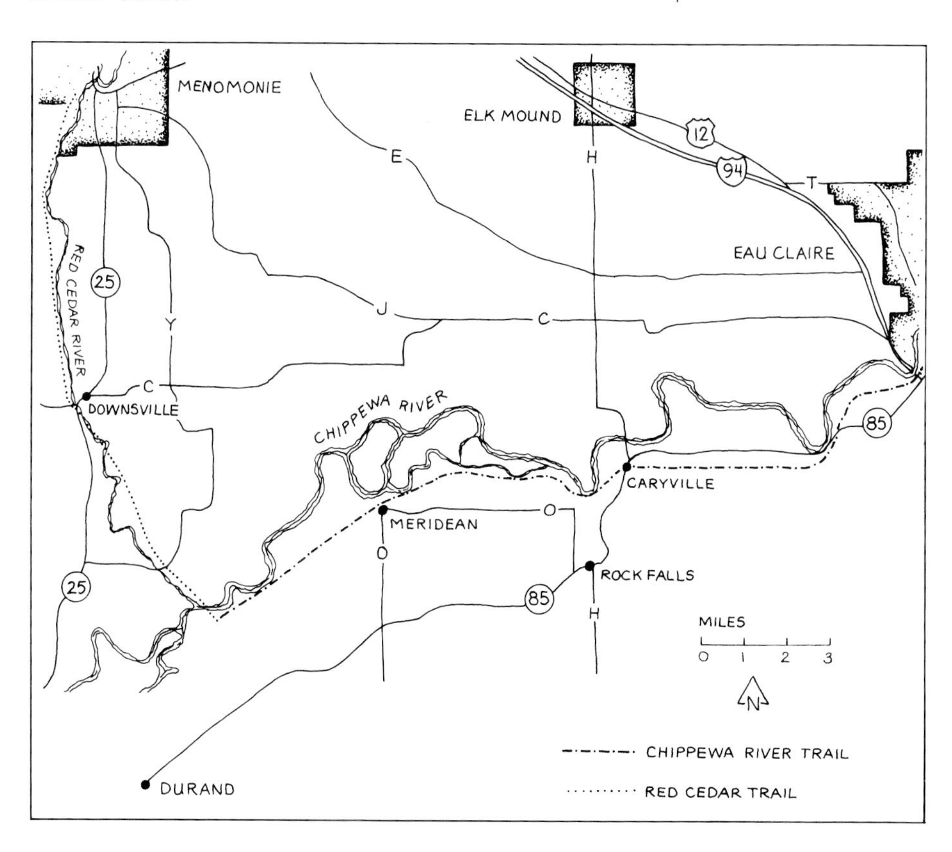

COPPER FALLS STATE PARK

Ashland County. About four miles north of Mellen; turn off Highway 13 (right turn) onto Highway 169, following it to the park entrance. Highway map index: 2-E.

Main Attraction

Rivers, canyons and waterfalls highlight Copper Falls State Park. The park is named for the 30-foot falls on the Bad River as it cuts through about two miles of steep-walled cliffs on its way north to Lake Superior. A little further downstream, Tyler's Forks of the Bad River joins the Bad River by plunging 31 feet over Brownstone Falls into the Bad River Gorge. Chippewa (Ojibwa) Indians showed surveyor John Tyler the falls in 1871, and the site has been a popular attraction since then.

The river meanders for more than eight miles through the park. A quarter mile is closed to public access because of erosion potential. You can see this scenic area from the park trails.

Things To Do

The 2,400-acre park is best experienced by foot. About seven miles of hiking trails, including a self-guided nature loop that offers cliff-top views of Copper Falls and Brownstone Falls, allow exploration of most of the park. The sheer walls of the rugged gorge plunge 60 to 100 feet down to the swiftly flowing water. You'll be able to escape the more popular trails near the waterfalls to fish or hike in the wilder settings elsewhere in the park, such as the Red Granite Falls area. This stretch of cascades and pools is in the southwestern corner of the park.

One trail connects Murphy and Loon lakes, the only lakes in the park. Another trail explores both falls from the other side of the river. Take this trail

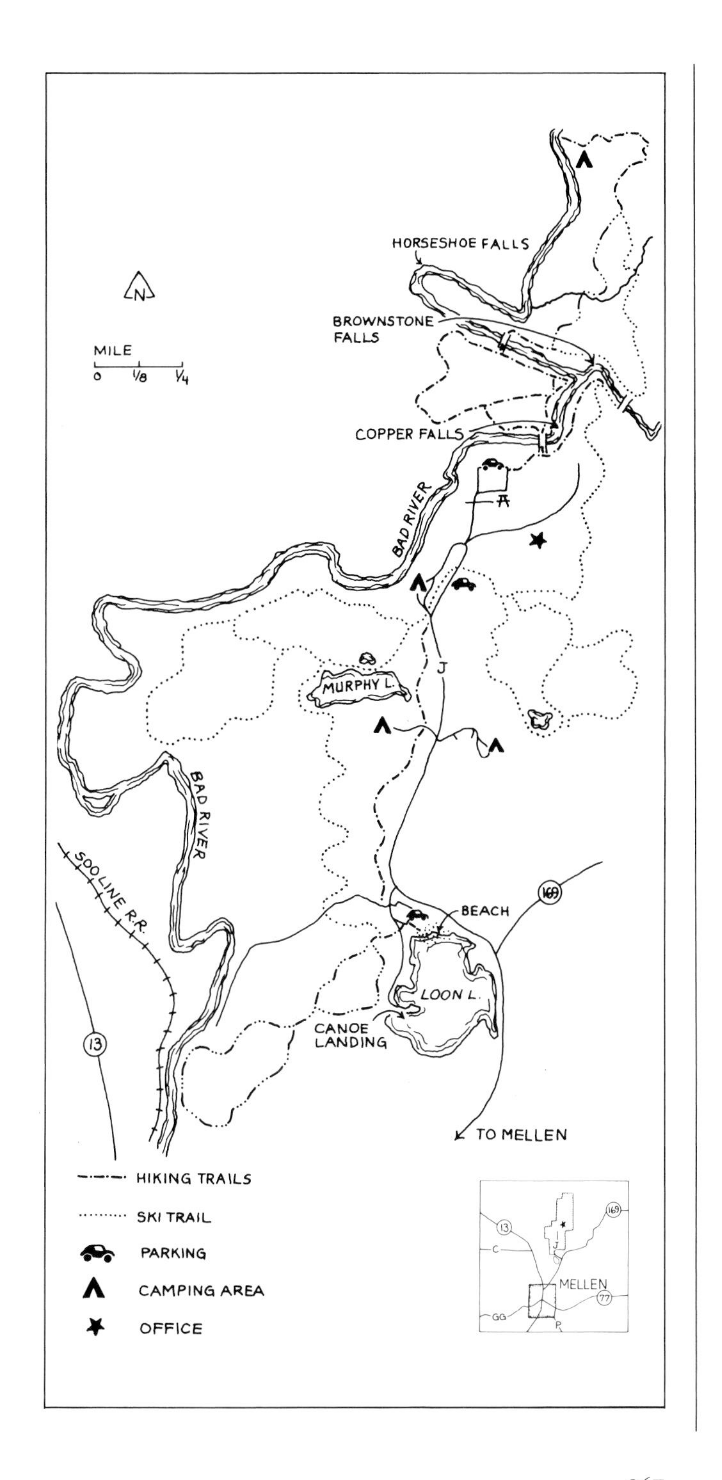
HORSESHOE FALLS
N
BROWNSTONE
FALLS
MILE
0
1/8
1/4
COPPER FALLS
BAD RIVER
MURPHY L.
J
BAD RIVER
SOO LINE R.R.
BEACH
169
LOON L.
CANOE
LANDING
13
TO MELLEN
HIKING TRAILS
SKI TRAIL
PARKING
CAMPING AREA
OFFICE
13
169
C
J
MELLEN
77
GG
P

The sights and sounds of the falls presented against the forest backdrop have drawn people to this place for generations.

from the main parking area and continue past the first footbridge, crossing at the Tyler's Forks footbridge. Listen for the "voices" of the falls. The patient river has been carving this gorge for hundreds of thousands of years, long before man first saw it. The trail follows the river and then turns north, leading to backpack campsites at some large sandstone ledges farther downstream on the Bad River.

The North Country National Scenic Trail cuts through Copper Falls State Park. This is a 3,200-mile trail that meanders through seven northern states, from the Adirondack Mountains of New York to the Lewis and Clark National Historic Trail in North Dakota. Though the trail is not completed yet, interested hikers and backpackers can get information from the park manager at Copper Falls about the segments that run through Michigan's Upper Peninsula and northwestern Wisconsin.

The rivers meander and tumble and the scenery is striking. A hike here is a visual delight as the sheer walls of the gorge plunge 60 to 100 feet to the swiftly flowing river.

Fishing and swimming are the park's water sports. Swimmers can use the sand beach at Loon Lake, near the park entrance. You can fish for rainbow, brown and brook trout in the Bad River and Tyler's Forks. The best fishing is in May, early June and again in the fall. There is a spring (rainbows) and a fall (browns) run of trout from Lake Superior. Loon Lake is fished for largemouth bass, northern and panfish. Small car-top boats and canoes can be launched at the landing at Loon Lake.

Winter at Copper Falls means hiking, snowshoeing and cross-country skiing. The park's six ski trail loops, rated from easiest to most difficult, total 14 miles. You can ice fish on Loon Lake. Snowmobiling is not allowed in the park, but there are extensive county and federal trails (Chequamegon National Forest) nearby.

Flora and Fauna

An after-lunch hike is a relaxing way to acquaint yourself with the park. Listen for the music of the park's songbirds, or the coarse caw-caw of the ravens. Look for large pileated woodpeckers, ruffed grouse, deer, woodchuck, skunk and porcupine. Bears are present in the area, but rarely seen. The park and the surrounding forest consist mostly of hemlock, white cedar, maple, birch, aspen, basswood and white pine.

Facilities

Copper Falls State Park has two campgrounds with a total of 56 individual sites, including four walk-in sites in the south campground. There are no showers in the park, although 13 sites have electrical hookups. The outdoor group camp accommodates up to 100 people (advance registration is necessary). Reservations are accepted for the individual sites and are suggested for the two backpack sites along the Bad River in the northern part of the park. The concession stand in the park shelter sells basic supplies during the summer. Laundry facilities and other services are available in Mellen.

If visiting for the day, enjoy a lunch in the large picnic area overlooking the Bad River. A beautiful log shelter and a playground are close by.

Surrounding Area

Copper Falls is in the heart of Wisconsin's prime fishing area. Scores of lakes offering all kinds of sportfishing are within easy traveling distance. If you like Great Lakes deep-sea fishing, Lake Superior and charter boat fishing for lake trout are only an hour away. Downhill skiers can choose from several excellent slopes in this part of Wisconsin and the Upper Peninsula of Michigan. Even in summer, it's worth a trip to see Copper Peak, a popular ski area with an imposing ski jump, located 15 miles north of Ironwood, Michigan.

FLAMBEAU RIVER STATE FOREST

Sawyer, Price and Rusk counties. Headquarters is on County W at the Flambeau River bridge (17 miles west of Phillips or 11 miles east of Winter).

Main Attraction

The Flambeau River State Forest preserves one of Wisconsin's most fabled northwoods rivers in an unspoiled condition. It is a wilderness area with some virgin timber, the free-flowing Flambeau and four seasons of outdoor recreation.

Though the forest was officially born in 1930, its real beginning dates back to the early part of this century when conservationists tried to preserve part of the rapidly dwindling timber stands for future generations. Today the 88,705-acre forest is most famous for its recreational uses, especially canoeing. But it's also a working forest. The management plan provides for a combination of timber production, aesthetics, wildlife and watershed protection.

The Flambeau River is the focal point of the forest. The North and South forks of the Flambeau River combine within the forest to provide over 60 miles of nearly uninterrupted natural beauty and white-water excitement.

Things To Do

A float down the Flambeau River by canoe, boat or raft has long been considered one of the finest trips in the Midwest. The river offers a unique combination of white water, quiet stretches and untouched northwoods scenery. The northern section of the river is slower-paced while the southern section provides the thrill of roaring rapids and white water.

The North Fork provides a stable flow of water year-round and an easy pace (in the northern reaches) that is ideal for the novice canoeist. There are six canoe landings and 14 primitive canoe campsites along the river. Shuttle services and rentals are available from nearby resorts. You can plan a canoe trip on the North Fork for a few hours or a week-long adventure.

The run from Nine Mile Creek near Highway 70 to Oxbo is about 12 miles. The river's slow pace (Barnaby Rapids is the only piece of fast water large enough to mention) and the forest backdrop make this a good stretch for family canoe trips. Below Oxbo, you'll pass a strip of heavy timber as the river meanders through wild country. When you reach Babb's Island, you'll see the County W bridge. The state forest headquarters is on the north bank of the river just beyond the bridge.

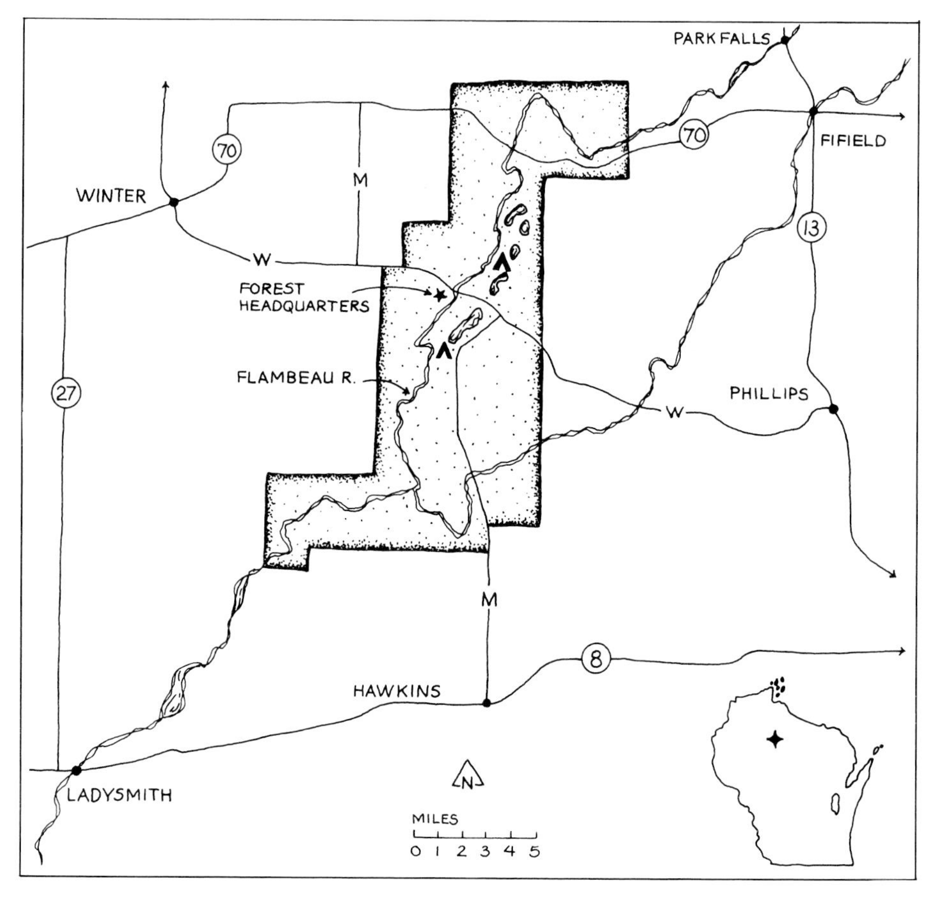

The southern sections of the river provide the challenge of rapids and white water canoeing. The boulder-strewn South Fork fluctuates according to seasonal precipitation. During high water the river is recommended for expert canoeists and kayakers only. During low water, canoeing becomes difficult and some wading may be necessary. There are no campsites along the South Fork.

A trip down this fabled river can provide as much or as little excitement as you wish. Either way, the wilderness scenery and virgin timber stands let you glimpse Wisconsin as it once was.

The most rambunctious part of the Flambeau is below Camp 41, where you can run the Wannigan, Flambeau Falls, Cedar and Beaver Dam rapids. Experienced canoeists study each rapids before shooting them. If you're not sure of your ability to run a particular set of rapids, portage your gear. Below Beaver Dam there are about three miles of fast water until the Big Falls Flowage. Take-out is on the right bank of the river.

You can launch your boat from landings on Connors Lake and Lake of the Pines. The fishing can be good for muskie, walleye, bass and panfish. Ask at the forest headquarters for details about fishing the forest lakes, the Flambeau River and nearby trout streams. Forest personnel can also give you information about public hunting for waterfowl, deer, grouse and other game species.

Hikers can explore the forest on the Flambeau Hills and Oxbo ski trails. You'll also find short hiking loops near the campgrounds. ATVs are prohibited on these trails at all times. An autumn hike is particularly rewarding when it seems like you're the only one in the forest to witness the brilliant colors of the northern hardwoods. Ask at the headquarters for information about the two natural areas that highlight the conifer and hardwood stands in the forest.

Cross-country skiers can tour the forest on two excellent ski trails. The Flambeau Hills Trail (14 miles) and the Oxbo Trail (8 miles) are both groomed and tracked on a regular basis. The Flambeau Hills trail head is located one half mile east of the forest headquarters on County W. The Oxbo Ski Trail begins about one mile east of Oxbo on Highway 70.

The forest grooms over 40 miles of snowmobile trails. The North and South trail systems also link with the Tuscobia State Trail and the Price and Rusk county trails. Parking facilities are provided.

The Flambeau River provides over 60 miles of uninterrupted river scenery through the forest.

A few forest scenic attractions are worth noting. Little Falls/Slough Gundy is a great spot for picnicking, fishing or viewing the white water of the South Fork of the Flambeau River (off County M). You can hear the roaring rapids long before reaching the river's edge. During the high waters of springtime, you may be treated to the sight of a kayaker pitting his skill against the rushing water of the three pitches at Slough Gundy.

Bass Lake, designated as a wilderness lake in 1983, is another special forest attraction. This 94-acre lake

is open for fishing, hunting and sightseeing, but motorboats and vehicles are prohibited. You can park at the end of Bass Lake Road, off Tower Hill Road (from County W).

The forest also boasts a 130-foot-tall white pine tree (13-foot girth) that is over 300 years old. The Big White Pine, one of the last trees of this size left in Wisconsin, is just a short walk from Gill Lane off County M.

Flora and Fauna

The Flambeau River is a magnet for wildlife as well as humans. Along its tree-lined shores you can see deer, raccoon, black bear, otter and other wildlife species. Watch for bald eagles and ospreys, too.

Facilities

Canoe campers may camp for free at designated sites along the river for one night only. Backpackers need a permit for overnight camping. Though there are no specific backpacking trails in the forest, backpackers may hike on the cross-country ski and snowmobile trails as well as some lightly used forest roads. You can get maps, permits and information about canoeing and backpacking from the forest headquarters.

The Flambeau River State Forest operates two 30-unit campgrounds (no showers) on two of the larger area lakes: Connors Lake and Lake of the Pines. All camping is on a first-come, first-served basis. Connors Lake has a developed picnic area (with a shelter) and a large sandy beach (no lifeguard) on the north shore.

Surrounding Area

The region surrounding the Flambeau River State Forest is noted for its lakes and woods. Other nearby recreation lands include Ojibwa State Park, the Tuscobia State Trail and the Chequamegon National Forest.

GOVERNOR KNOWLES STATE FOREST

Burnett and Polk counties. Forest headquarters is in Grantsburg.

Main Attraction

The Governor Knowles State Forest (18,706 acres) stretches like a spaghetti noodle for 55 miles along the banks of the St. Croix National Scenic Riverway. Up to two miles wide, Governor Knowles is a working forest in addition to being a recreation area. Forest management involves timber production, aesthetics, wildlife, fisheries and watershed protection.

The St. Croix National Scenic Riverway is the main recreational focus of the forest. The St. Croix and Namekagon rivers were designated by Congress as part of the National Scenic Riverway system in 1968. The Riverway includes 100 miles of the St. Croix River from Gordon to St. Croix Falls and 100 miles of its major tributary, the Namekagon River. About one quarter mile on each side of the river was set up as a buffer zone. Much of the land along the St. Croix River was owned by Northern States Power Company. Through a cooperative agreement, NSP agreed to donate its land to the National Park Service and the states of Minnesota and Wisconsin. This donation was the nucleus of the new Governor Knowles State Forest.

Things To Do

On a typical day, you can canoe about 20 miles, unless you decide to explore on an island or wet a fishing line in some of the quiet bays and backwaters. The St. Croix River offers good fishing for walleye, sturgeon, northern, smallmouth bass and muskie. There is also good fishing available on the many streams that cross the forest. Brook and brown trout inhabit 11 streams and you can catch northern and panfish in certain sections and impoundments.

The National Park Service maintains several drive-in and walk-in landings and primitive campsites along the St. Croix. Drinking water and firewood are scarce. Canoe rentals, river maps and supplies are available locally (Grantsburg, Danbury, St. Croix Falls and Cushing). To get further details about the National Scenic Riverway, stop at the Highway 70 Information Station (on the Minnesota side) or at the headquarters in St. Croix Falls.

Hikers can explore the forest on two designated trails, each over 22 miles long, at both ends of Gov-

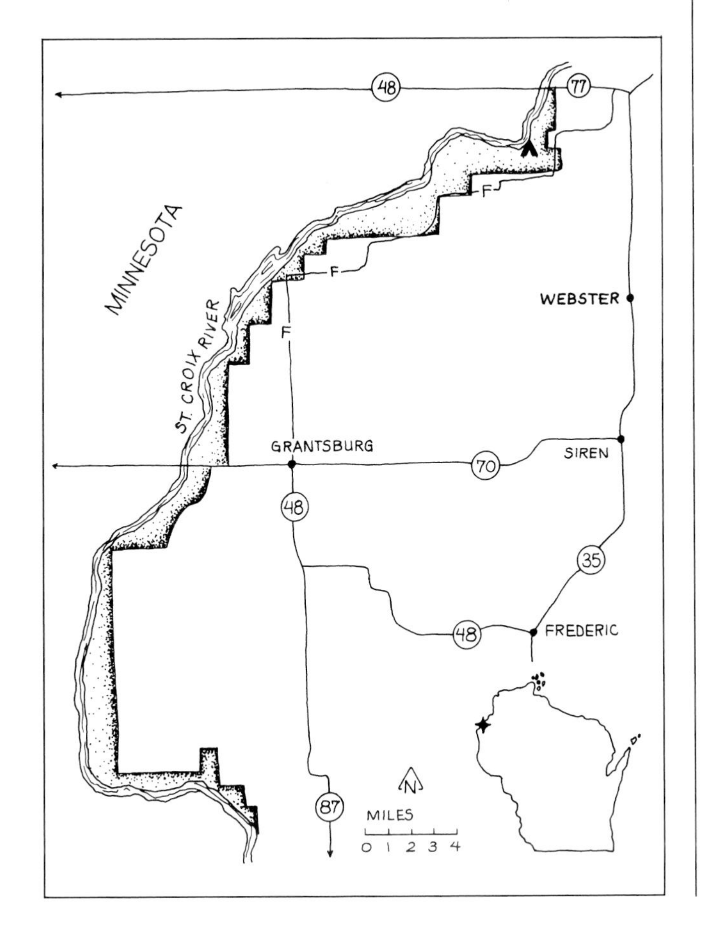

This state forest protects the St. Croix River, which offers good fishing and canoeing.

ernor Knowles. North of the Fish Lake Wildlife Area, the Burnett County Snowmobile Trail enters the state forest and runs for 26 miles south until it joins the Polk County Snowmobile Trail near the village of Wolf Creek. Horseback riders use these trails during the rest of the year. Cross-country skiers can tour part of the forest on the Brandt Pines Ski Trail. This trail, laid out in two loops totaling 10 miles, features a ski shelter. The skier's trail head is about seven miles northwest of Grantsburg.

Backpacking is allowed on forest land, though you need a permit for overnight camping. You can backpack on existing trails or, if experienced, strike off on your own.

Flora and Fauna

Hikers, canoeists and winter visitors might see a wide variety of wildlife in the forest. Bald eagles and about 300 species of songbirds have been sighted in the St. Croix River Valley. You might also spot beaver, otter, mink and muskrat along the river. Hunting is permitted, according to state regulations, for white-tailed deer, black bear and small game.

Facilities

The only forest campground lies in a remote setting at the northern end of Governor Knowles. Designed for organized groups of up to 36 people, the Sioux Portage Group Campground (drinking water, toilet facilities) is available by reservation only. The forest's only picnic area is in the wayside by the Highway 70 bridge on the St. Croix River.

Surrounding Area

The two wildlife areas adjacent to the forest may be of particular interest to bird-watchers and others who enjoy observing fauna on large tracts of public land. The Fish Lake Wildlife Area (south of Grantsburg) and the Crex Meadows Wildlife Area (north of Grantsburg) are both being restored to their original state. Marsh drainage and agricultural efforts, though not successful themselves, decreased waterfowl nesting sites, too. Much of the land was tax delinquent by the 1940s, when the state took it over.

Crex Meadows (30,098 acres) is the larger and more developed of the two wildlife areas. You can enjoy its series of roads and paths for hiking or biking throughout the area. It would be easy to spend a day wandering here, or you can spend an hour driving through. Crex Meadows is a mix of potholes, large lakes, prairie, woods and slough that was once the bottom of a huge glacial lake. Indians hunted and picked wild fruit here when the native tall grass prairie was preserved by natural fires, preventing trees from gaining a foothold.

Today, hundreds of ducks, geese, and sandhill cranes nest in Crex Meadows. You can observe a great blue heron rookery, cormorant nests and several colonies of yellow-headed blackbirds. Deer are common sights. Ospreys and bald and golden eagles also make their homes here. On the prairie, 212 species of true prairie plants have been documented. The Crex Meadows headquarters, just north of Grantsburg, can give you more information.

In addition to the wildlife areas, seven natural areas preserve unusual biotic communities. Interstate State Park, near St. Croix Falls, is the nearest state recreation facility to Governor Knowles State Forest. Just upriver from the forest, the North Country National Scenic Trail crosses the St. Croix River into Minnesota. This is a 3,200-mile route that stretches from Crown Point, New York, to the Lewis and Clark National Historic Trail in North Dakota, passing through Pennsylvania, Ohio, Michigan, Wisconsin and Minnesota along the way.

GREAT RIVER STATE TRAIL

This trail through the lowlands and sandy plains of the Mississippi River valley will soon be linked with other trails to provide an extended route through some of Wisconsin's loveliest scenery.

Trempealeau and La Crosse counties. 22 miles, from Onalaska (north of La Crosse) to the Trempealeau National Wildlife Refuge. Highway map index: 8-C.

Main Attraction

Wisconsin's newest state trail was born privileged. The Great River State Trail's natural good looks come from the broad-shouldered, majestic Mississippi River Valley. It has been well-loved (used) by hikers and bicyclists even before the surfacing was completed. And, because of proposed links with other state trails, it may grow into the longest bicycle route in Wisconsin, which is already a national leader in the development of bicycle trails.

The 22-mile-long trail follows the abandoned Chicago and Northwestern railroad bed and passes through the communities of Onalaska, Midway and Trempealeau. Trail access and parking lots are developed in each of these towns.

Things To Do

The route is mostly level, cutting through the lowlands and sandy plains of the Mississippi River Valley. While riding or hiking, you'll frequently see the distant river bluffs with their exposed rock faces and lush foliage. The trail's 18 bridges cross several waterways including the Black River, Shingle Creek, Tank Creek and Halfway Creek.

Try biking the Great River Trail in autumn. The mosquitoes are gone, the trail is not as busy and the fall colors are brilliant. During established seasons hunters use the trail as an access to other public hunting grounds. Since much of the land adjoining the trail is privately owned, hunters are asked to remain on the trail corridor. Snowmobiling, cross-country skiing and hiking are common winter pastimes.

The Great River State Trail will soon be linked with the La Crosse River and Elroy-Sparta state trails to form an extended bicycle route through Wisconsin's famous "Driftless Area." The southwestern part of the state was missed by the last glacier, leaving a scenic land of rolling hills and streams free of glacial debris, or "drift." Future trail extensions from Elroy to Reedsburg and beyond are possible, depending on land acquisition and budget considerations.

Trail users (aged 18 and older) must pay a State Trail Admission Fee. You can buy either a daily or a seasonal trail permit at Perrot State Park and certain area businesses.

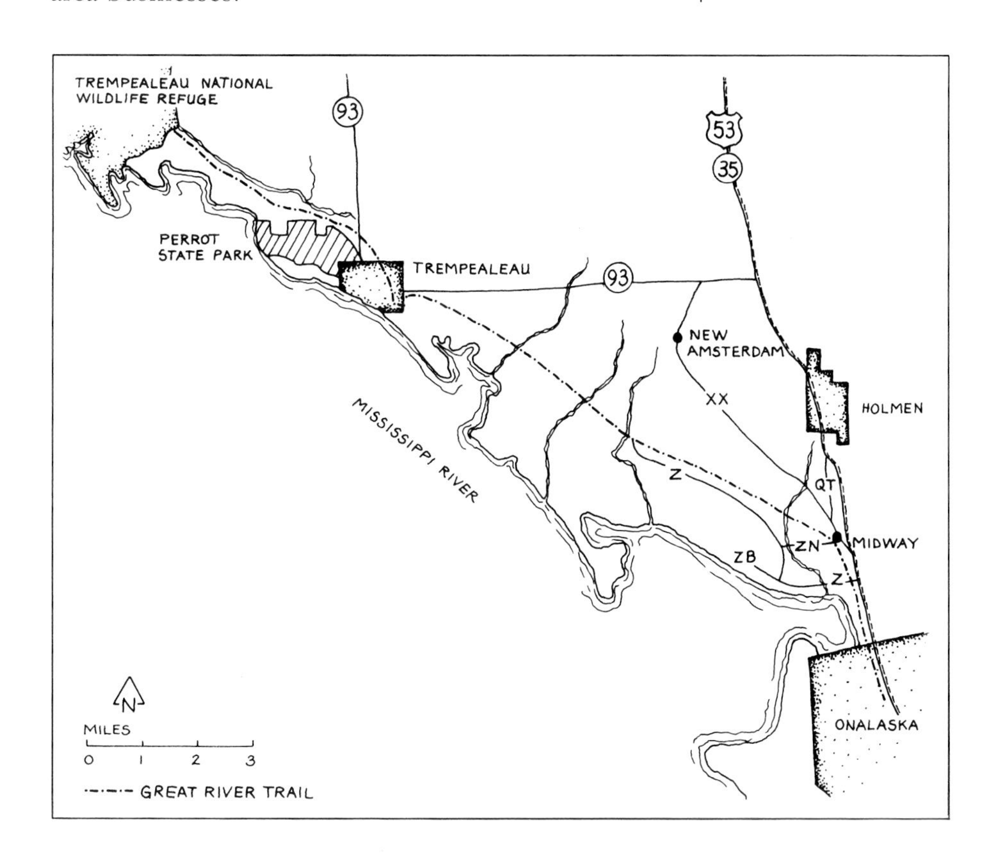

The Great River Trail is never far from a view of the Mississippi.

Flora and Fauna

The bottom lands provide an excellent opportunity to observe the valley's great variety of wildlife. You may spot ducks, great blue herons, egrets, deer and other natural residents. Unfortunately, mosquitoes and flies are also natural residents. Covering exposed skin and using repellents help to make these pests less bothersome.

Facilities

Bicyclists can camp in Perrot State Park, just upriver from Trempealeau along the trail. Take the time for a picnic or a hike up Brady's Bluff for an impressive view of the Mississippi River Valley. You can continue your ride past Perrot State Park to the trail's end at the Trempealeau National Wildlife Refuge.

Surrounding Area

Other nearby recreation areas include Merrick State Park near Fountain City and the Upper Mississippi River National Wildlife and Fish Refuge. Check with local chambers of commerce for details about services, lodging and private campgrounds in the vicinity of the trail.

HOFFMAN HILLS STATE RECREATION AREA

Dunn County. Drive east of Menomonie on Highway 29 to County E. Turn north (left) on County E to Cedar Valley Road. Turn north (left) on Cedar Valley Road and follow the signs to Hoffman Hills. Highway map index: 5-C.

Main Attraction

On many summer days, you can have the view from the top of the 60-foot observation tower at Hoffman Hills all to yourself. The tower, perched on the crest of a 1,400-foot hill, will cost you about a one-mile hike (mostly uphill) to reach it, but the panorama of green, wooded hills rippling into the distance under a broad sky is worth a little sweat.

Richard and Marian Hoffman always felt it was worth the sweat to drive their kids up here from Milwaukee to explore and dream on their land (he was born in Elk Mound). After he retired from his job as a department store executive in Milwaukee, Hoffman donated 300 acres to the state of Wisconsin in 1979. Today, Hoffman Hills has grown to 655 acres.

Things To Do

Hoffman Hills draws the biggest crowds during the winter, when the trail system (over eight miles) is groomed and ready to challenge skiers of all abilities. Though skiers often drive long distances to tour the hills and valleys, the trails are not congested. They wind along hardwood ridges, climb up and down aspen and birch slopes and pass through pine plantations. Most of the trails were cleared by ski clubs, scout groups or other local organizations. The DNR moved the larger trees and constructed the trail bed.

The observation tower was also a volunteer effort.

Take the hike to the crest of the 1,400-foot hill, then climb the tower and enjoy the sweep of the vistas below you. Come back when it snows for cross-country skiing.

The Menomonie Optimist Club began organizing the project in 1984, donating $5,000 in honor of deceased member Greg Schubert (the tower is named for him). Richard Hoffman also donated $5,000 and the DNR matched these funds with $10,000. Navy Seabees from the Twin Cities donated 1,200 hours of labor to build the tower, and the Army Reserve 397th Construction Battalion of Eau Claire furnished the heavy equipment. Area businesses contributed materials and funding, and an Optimist Club member lent a crane for the project.

The result of this community spirit is a tower that lets you view the world above the treetops on the highest point of land in the area. Bring along a snack and a camera and daydream up here for a while. Watch how the clouds cast moving shadows across the hills as the breeze blows them overhead. Sing with the birds if you feel like it. Chances are that no one will hear you, because Hoffman Hills has yet to be discovered in the spring, summer and fall.

(continued on next page)

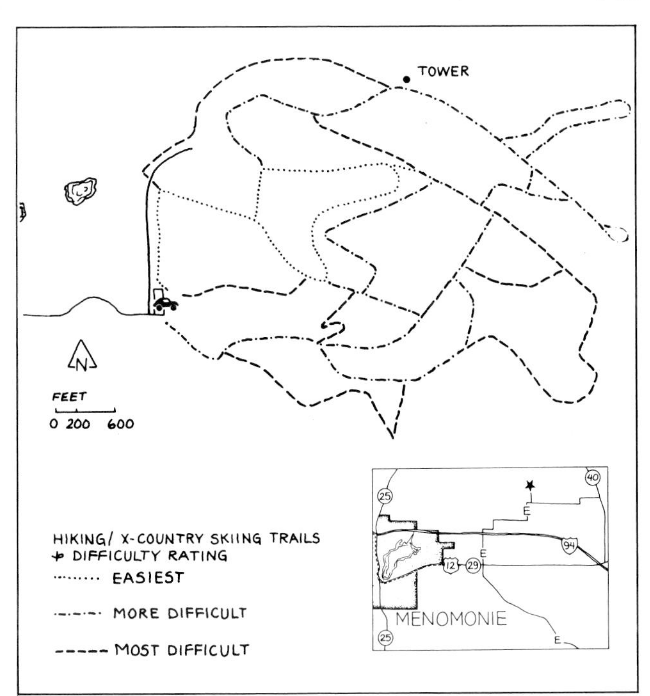

The cross-country ski trails are mowed for hikers in the summer. You can pick berries, listen for the distinctive drumming of a ruffed grouse or try to identify some of the scores of wildflowers found here. Flies and mosquitoes can be pests at times, so bring along some insect repellent. The property is open for the gun deer hunting season in the fall.

As the recreational development of the land continues, two or three additional trail miles will be added. Plans also include some prairie restoration and new self-guided nature trails. Hoffman Hills may

A hike to the observation tower rewards visitors with spectacular scenery coming or going.

evolve into a nature study area complete with classrooms and an interpretive center aimed largely at young people. Though details aren't clear yet, a spring-fed pond may be used for ice skating and by junior anglers. A paddock and trails for horseback riders are other possibilities.

Facilities

The recreation area has two outdoor group camps equipped with a well and rustic toilets to be used by organized youth groups (reservations required). There are no family camping facilities at Hoffman Hills. State parks in the region that do offer camping are Brunet Island, Lake Wissota and Willow River. Kinnickinnic State Park and Red Cedar State Trail are other state recreation areas within relatively short driving distance of Hoffman Hills. For details about private campgrounds and area visitor attractions, contact chambers of commerce in Menomonie, Eau Claire and Chippewa Falls.

INTERSTATE STATE PARK

Polk County. In St. Croix Falls, exit from Highway 8 onto south Highway 35 and follow the signs to the park entrance. Highway map index: 4-A.

Main Attraction

From the Pothole Trail in Wisconsin's Interstate State Park, you can holler to hikers in Minnesota's Interstate State Park across the steep, narrow gorge of the St. Croix River. Though such a border conversation may not be the highlight of your visit, it's just an example of the uniqueness of this park.

It's no accident that both states have a park with the same name across the river from each other. Minnesota and Wisconsin formed Interstate State Park as a cooperative venture in 1900—the first park of its kind in the country. Each park is administered by its respective DNR and operates under its own rules (you need separate vehicle admission stickers for each park, for example).

Interstate's striking scenery had a violent birth. The gorge was cut through the basalt by the incredible power of glacial meltwater. Flowing south from an expansive glacial lake (where Lake Superior is today), the water churned through here with such force and volume that giant, fractured lava blocks were blasted loose and swept away. The resulting steep-walled, rocky river channel is now known as the Dalles of the St. Croix. Weathering over the ages has cracked and split this rock, creating strange formations like the Old Man of the Dalles, a clearly sculpted male profile.

Because of the outstanding glacially formed features of the park, Interstate is one of the nine units included in Wisconsin's Ice Age National Scientific Reserve. The park is also the western terminus of the

1,000-mile Ice Age National Scenic Trail, which traces the furthest glacial advance in Wisconsin.

Things To Do

You can see the Old Man of the Dalles from the Pothole Trail, a short loop that also boasts scenic views of the river. The trail is named for the potholes that were drilled into the lava by turbulent whirlpools of

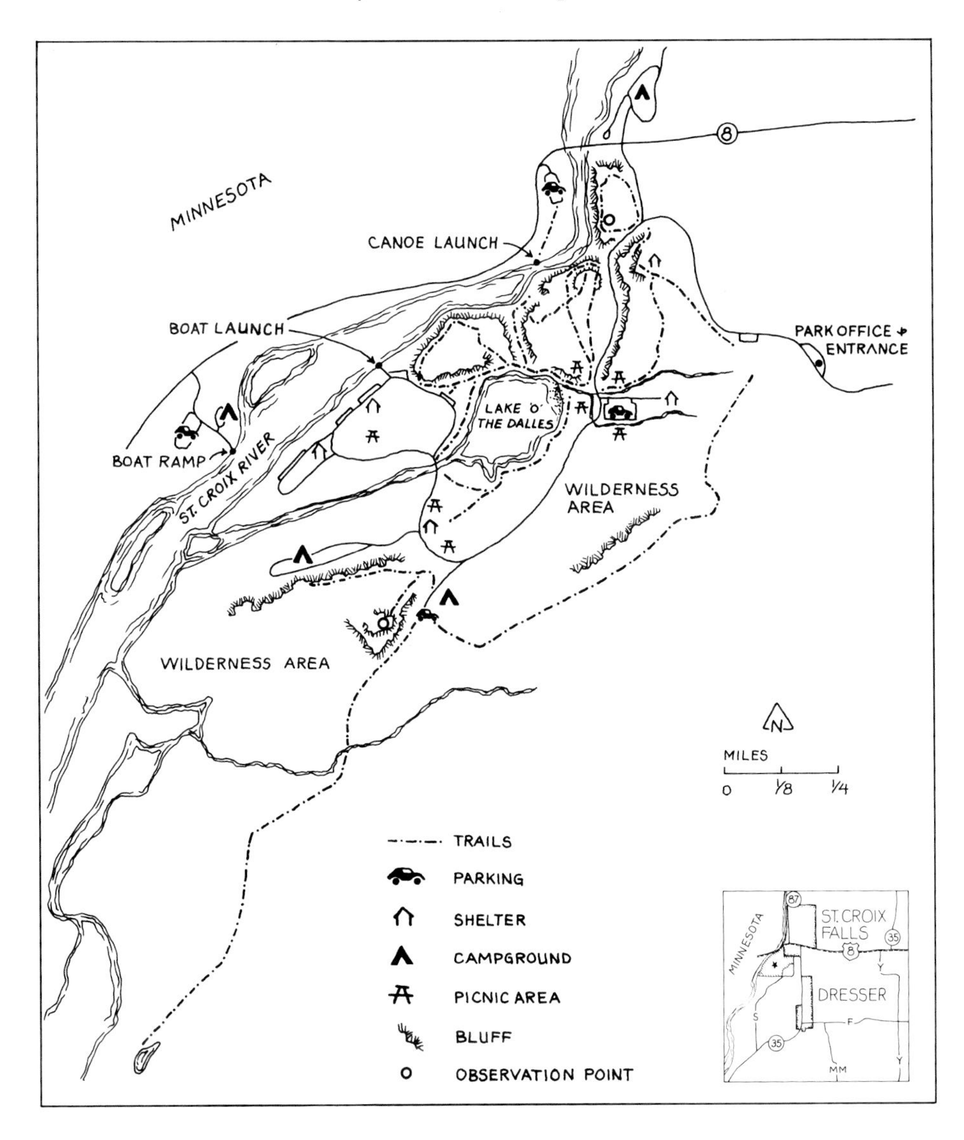

meltwater laden with rocks and boulders. The abrasive mixture of rocks and swirling eddies created potholes up to 25 feet in diameter and up to 80 feet deep. Potholes of all sizes were formed on both sides of the river, though you'll see the best ones on the Minnesota side.

The Ice Age Interpretive Center, near the park entrance, shows what life was like when the world was locked in the icy grip of a great continental glacier. Attractive exhibits depict the story of the Ice Age in a clear, readable style. You'll see bones from extinct Ice Age mammals that roamed the earth over 10,000 years ago and learn about Wisconsin's glacial legacy in a 20-minute film called "Night of the Sun," shown several times daily.

After checking out the Interpretive Center, you can explore the 1,368-acre park on over eight miles of hiking trails. For a good view of the rocky Dalles of the St. Croix, climb the Summit Rock Trail. You'll get a broader vista of the river valley from the Eagle Peak Trail, beginning at the group camping parking lot. The Silverbrook and Skyline trails, the park's most secluded paths, also start near this parking lot.

To find out about Wisconsin's first state park, hike the one-mile self-guided nature trail around the Lake of the Dalles or join in one of the naturalist's programs. Interpretive programs are scheduled on a daily basis from Memorial Day to Labor Day. Guided hikes include exploration of potholes and beaver ponds or investigation of local history and glacial features. Evening programs, scheduled for weekends and holidays, are held in the north campground or in the Ice Age Interpretive Center. Details of all naturalist activities are posted throughout the park.

Interstate features a Vita Course for those who want to get more exercise while hiking. The quarter-mile loop course, including five exercise stations, begins on the east end of the playfield. The park is also the site of two state natural areas: Dalles of the St. Croix River and the Interstate Lowland Forest. Check at the park office for details.

Though the hiking trails and naturalist programs offer excellent chances to experience Interstate, the

(opposite page)

The St. Croix River valley is the attraction at Interstate.

Interstate's striking scenery is even more impressive when you learn of its violent birth. Guided hikes and evening programs will enhance your appreciation of this unique park.

river is the park's focal point. During the legendary logging era of the 19th century, the St. Croix River was a major route for floating logs to the downstream sawmills. The Dalles, where the park is now, was once the site of the world's largest logjam. At least 150 million board feet of logs were stacked upriver for more than two miles like jumbled toothpicks. One hundred seventy-five men worked for six weeks to break the historic jam.

The St. Croix is part of the National Scenic Riverway System with main headquarters and information center in St. Croix Falls. Besides exceptional scenery and a lively past, the river today offers opportunities for boating, fishing and canoeing. The upstream section is faster and more isolated than downriver from the park. Some kayakers and experienced canoeists like to practice their skills on the stretch of fast water below the Highway 8 bridge. There is a boat and canoe launching site on the river just below the Dalles. You can rent canoes and boats from private operators outside the park. If you don't want to provide your own power, a commercial boat line runs guided sightseeing trips through the Dalles from the Minnesota side (in Taylors Falls).

There's good fishing here for most game fish including walleye, northern, muskie and smallmouth bass. You can shore fish on Lake of the Dalles, a small park lake, but there are no boating facilities. The lake has a beach and a bathhouse with lifeguards on duty during the summer.

Winter adds a different quality to Interstate's wild beauty, and cross-country skiing is the best way to explore the park's remote areas. Over nine miles of trails provide scenic skiing for novice and experienced skiers (there are no snowmobile trails in the park). Stop at the Interpretive Center for a ski break.

Flora and Fauna

You might observe beavers at work in the park's southern wilderness area. Deer are also occasionally spotted. Over 200 species of birds, including the bald eagle, either nest in the park or pass through during spring and fall migrations. You can pick up a bird checklist at the park office.

Facilities

Interstate State Park has two family campgrounds with a total of 85 individual sites (showers, no electrical hookups) and an organized group camp for up to 60 campers. Reservations are accepted for the individual sites, and required for the group camp. The park maintains seven different picnic areas and three shelter buildings. Laundry facilities and supplies are available in St. Croix Falls.

Surrounding Area

Both Taylors Falls and St. Croix Falls tempt visitors to linger with special festivals and attractions. Wannigan Days, for example, celebrates the lumbering heritage of the St. Croix River Valley. State fish hatcheries, an alpine slide, and historic buildings are all close to the park. Nearby state recreation lands include Willow River State Park and Governor Knowles State Forest in Wisconsin, and St. Croix Wild River and William O'Brien state parks in Minnesota.

Downhill skiers can choose between two nearby ski areas (both also offer cross-country skiing): Trollhaugen, four miles south of St. Croix Falls, and Wild Mountain, seven miles north of Taylors Falls.

KINNICKINNIC STATE PARK

Pierce County. Exit from Interstate 94 in Hudson, turning south onto County F. Drive about eight miles on County F to Cedar View Road. Turn right (west) onto Cedar View Road for less than a mile to the park's entrance. Highway map index: 6-A.

Main Attraction

The sandy delta at the confluence of the Kinnickinnic River and the Lower St. Croix River attracts a different type of visitor to Kinnickinnic State Park—watercraft campers. The three-quarter-mile beach is an ideal stop for boaters who wish to picnic, swim (no life-guards), play volleyball or just enjoy a sunny after-noon on the sand, and then stay overnight.

The upland woods and prairies at Kinnickinnic are largely undeveloped. There currently are no roads or service buildings, though plans call for development of park roads, picnic areas and hiking trails by the early 1990s. Long-range plans include family and group campgrounds.

The 1,153-acre park was established in 1972. Until the park idea was proposed, the most frequent visitors were the deer, raccoon and other wildlife that came down from the limestone bluffs to drink in the clear St. Croix River. Now the area is preserved for every-body, thanks to three local landowners who wanted to see the Kinnickinnic River gorge and delta become a state park rather than a subdivision for homes.

Things To Do

Kinnickinnic uses a temporary entrance for now. Land visitors must park on Cedar View Road and walk onto the property to hike or bird-watch. No facilities will be available until the next phase of development is completed. Hikers who want to explore the up-lands despite the lack of development can view the two river valleys from dozens of blufftop vantage points. You can also follow the Kinnickinnic River gorge down to the delta.

The Kinnickinnic River is a small cold-water trout stream known for its brown trout fishing. Many anglers use the Fishermen's parking lot on County F (just past Cedar View Road) at the Kinnickinnic River bridge as a river access point.

The Fishermen's parking lot is also a popular take-out spot for canoeists. Within the park, the Kinnickinnic River is a shallow stream during normal water levels. You'll have better luck if you put in at River Falls, about 10 miles upstream from the County F bridge. This is a peaceful run with little development along the river banks. Following a rain, the water level rises and the current is faster, posing a hazard to some canoeists. Canoeists should always check the river conditions before pushing off, especially after

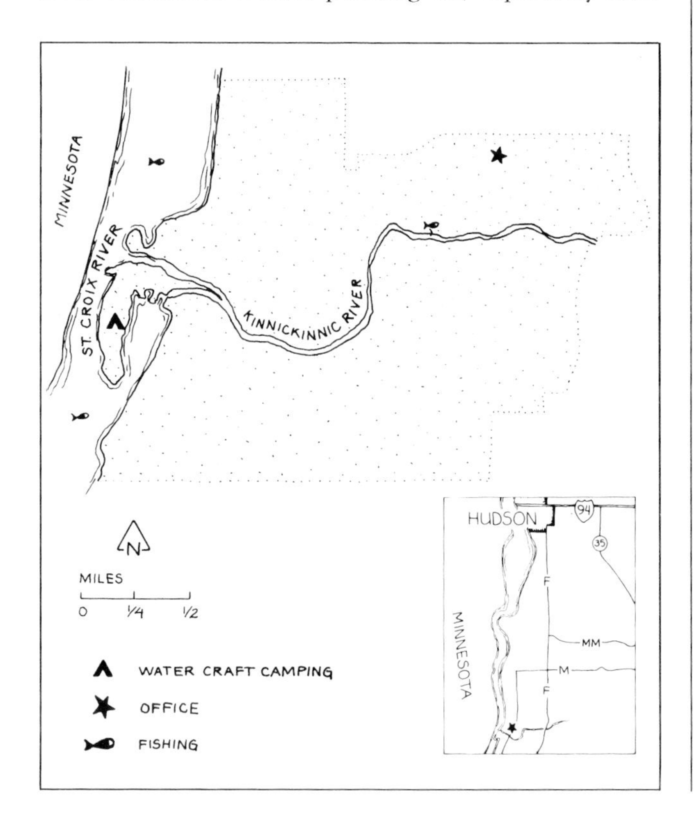

a heavy storm. Those who decide to canoe the shallow river portion through the park will have to travel some distance on the Lower St. Croix because there is no vehicle access for take-outs at the confluence.

The Lower St. Croix is a large, heavily used body of water. The average watercraft length is about 25 feet. Larger craft, such as coal barges and 100-foot yachts, travel on the river as well. Because of the wakes produced by high-powered boats, the river is not very suitable for canoeing (especially on weekends). Canoeists who prefer quieter paddling may wish to plan a trip on the upper portion of the St. Croix National Scenic Riverway, including the Namekagon River, above the St. Croix Falls dam.

This is a place for watercraft campers to enjoy the beach, then stay overnight on their boats or at one of the 12 campsites near the shore.

The St. Croix River is a favorite for fishing, too. The river offers excellent fishing for walleye and smallmouth bass. Public boat launches are located at Prescott, about seven miles downstream from the park, and at Hudson, about 11 miles upstream. There currently are no boat rentals available near the park.

Kinnickinnic State Park, when fully developed, will attract many visitors from the nearby Twin City metro area. The valley is relatively remote, providing a rare opportunity to get away in an increasingly urban region.

Facilities

The Delta Use Area is accessible only by watercraft and is open to boats from about mid-May to mid-October. Boaters who choose to moor overnight must buy a permit from park personnel. Most watercraft campers have boats equipped with on-board sleeping and approved toilet facilities. Boaters with smaller craft can set up camp at one of the 12 tent sites near the beach (toilet facilities provided).

Surrounding Area

Willow River State Park, north of Hudson, is a more civilized park offering family camping, guarded swimming beach, etc.

LAKE WISSOTA STATE PARK

Chippewa County. Drive east of Chippewa Falls on Highway 29, exiting onto County X. Drive east on X to County K and turn north (left). Continue on K to County O, turning west (left) on O to the park entrance. Highway map index: 5-D.

Main Attraction

Lake Wissota is the park's main attraction. The lake was created in 1916–17 when the Chippewa River was dammed, flooding the Chippewa River Valley and the mouth of the Yellow River. The park opened in 1971.

It's fun, while wandering through the park in any season, to imagine what this area was like before "civilization." The Chippewa River Valley was once a vast forest full of moose, cougar, elk, bison, timber wolf, black bear and other wildlife. The Chippewa Indians (Ojibwa) and their ancestors used these animals for food, clothing and shelter. They caught great numbers of fish in the lakes and streams and crafted birchbark canoes for travel. Explorers and trappers also knew these waterways. Later, after the loggers harvested the virgin timber, farmers cleared the land of the huge stumps that remained and tried to turn the land to agricultural purposes.

Things To Do

Some people have a hard time getting past the picnic area near the contact station at Lake Wissota State Park. They stop to enjoy an outdoor meal in the shady grove overlooking the expanse of Lake Wissota and decide to stay there awhile. Most visitors bypass this spot on their way to the beach or campground. That's just fine with those who choose to pass the time on a summer afternoon here, watching the sailboats and water-skiers on the 6,300-acre lake. You'll get a front-row seat for sunset viewing, too.

The Moccasin Trail starts here, hugging the ridgetop past the campground and ending at the swimming beach over one mile away. If you brought your fishing gear along, you can use the stairway to the beach to try some shoreline angling. The beach-picnic area is the park's focal point. On warm days this spot is full of sunbathers, picnickers, boaters and swimmers. The aroma of charcoal and suntan lotion enhances the sights of summer.

The parklands are easy to explore by foot because the trails are mostly flat. Eleven miles of hiking paths follow Lake Wissota's shoreline or wind through the

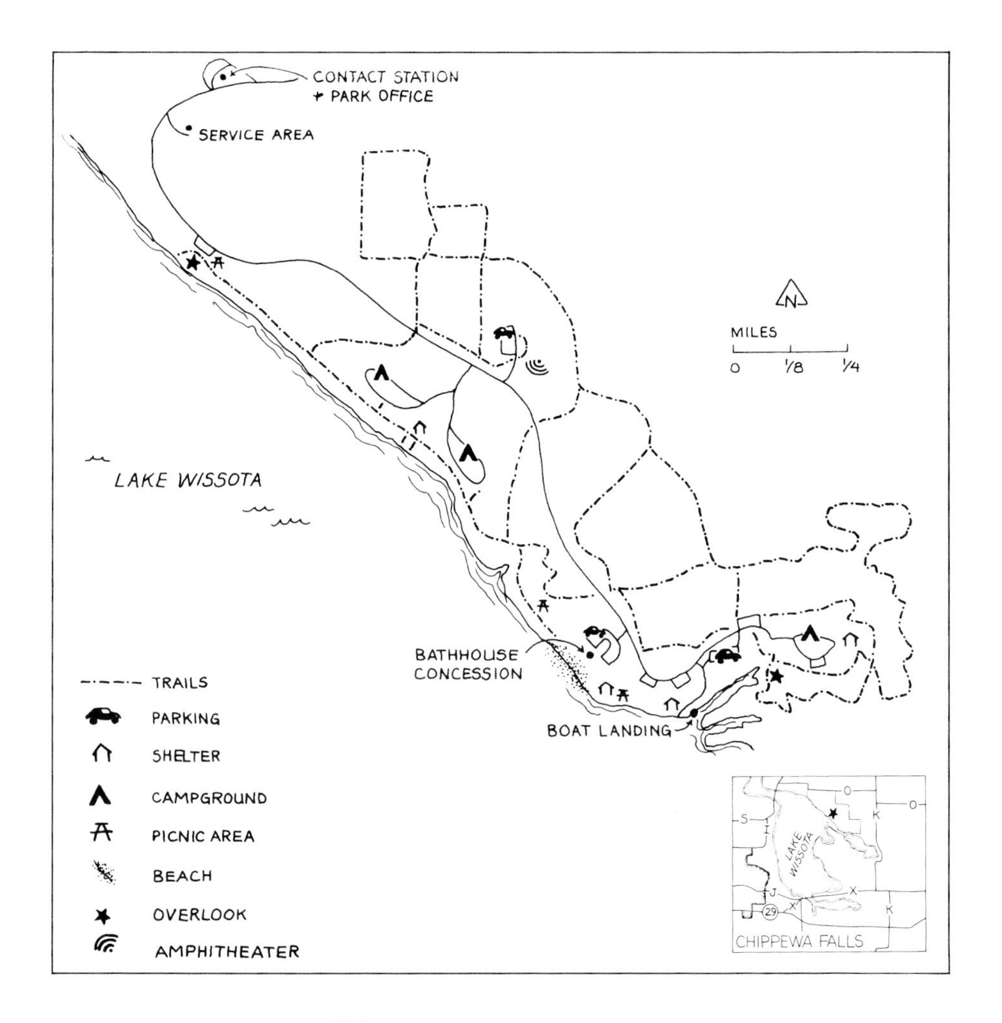

park's prairie, marshes and mixed pine and hardwood forest.

The Beaver Meadow Nature Trail (35 interpretive signs) features an overlook that allows visitors who are unable to hike the one-mile loop to observe the wildlife and the environment of the beaver pond. The park also maintains a three-quarter-mile physical fitness course with 13 exercise stations.

Lake Wissota is the attraction here. You can sail, swim, canoe, fish or boat, then escape the sun on a bike through the woods.

Lake Wissota State Park schedules an active naturalist program throughout the summer. Guided hikes and interpretive activities concentrate on the plants, animals, geology and local history of the Chippewa River Valley. The naturalist also conducts campfire singalongs, bicycle tours and night hikes. Weekend evening programs are conducted in the park's amphitheater. Check the park bulletin boards or at the office for details.

Boaters and canoeists can put in at the two-ramp boat launch near the beach-picnic area. Rentals are available near the park at a nearby resort and marina. Some boaters like to explore the Yellow River bay southeast of the ramps. You can travel a couple of miles here, wandering into the bays and the lower part of the Yellow River. Smaller boats can go quite far upriver when the water level is normal.

Because of its size, it takes a while to learn how to fish Lake Wissota. Many people fish near the highway bridge at the south end of the lake and in the lake's shallow bays. Most of the action is with walleye, bass, northern and muskie, though sturgeon, catfish and panfish are also caught. The lake can get choppy on windy days, so veteran boaters usually keep an eye on the weather. The park has constructed a permanent fishing pier that is wheelchair accessible (near the boat landing). Fish cribs on the lake bottom in front of the pier help attract walleye and largemouth bass.

The park keeps up an active pace in the winter. Cross-country skiers can explore the prairies, woods and lowlands on 7.5 miles of groomed trails. You can snowshoe anywhere in the park except on cross-country ski loops. Lake Wissota's 4.8 miles of snowmobile trails connect with over 150 miles of county

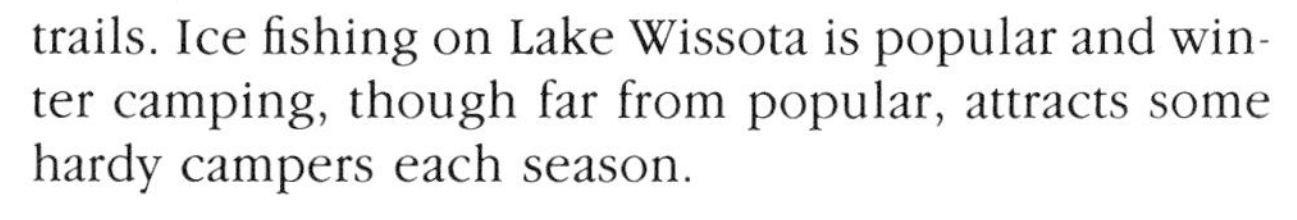

trails. Ice fishing on Lake Wissota is popular and winter camping, though far from popular, attracts some hardy campers each season.

Flora and Fauna

Early-morning or dusk hikes are best for observing the park's wildlife. Over 200 species of birds have been sighted in the park, and deer and other woodland and wetland animals are common. Wildlife checklists are available at the park office.

Facilities

The park's beach area is surrounded by spacious picnic grounds that include a ball field, shelters and play equipment. The beach is guarded during the summer and has a boathouse and concession stand.

The campground at Lake Wissota has 81 wooded family sites with 16 electrical hookups available. Both campground loops have showers and laundry tubs (there is a laundromat in Chippewa Falls). You can buy most supplies at the park concession stand or from merchants in Chippewa Falls and Jim Falls. A playground, shelter (available for groups) and boat mooring area are located between the camping loops.

Two outdoor group camps can each accommodate up to 40 tents. One has a shelter with electricity. Reservations are accepted for both the family and group campground sites.

Surrounding Area

The area around Lake Wissota State Park still has snatches of undeveloped land. Nearby state recreation lands include Brunet Island State Park, Hoffman Hills State Recreation Area and the Red Cedar and Buffalo River state trails. The Chequamegon National Forest and several county forests are also within easy driving distance of the park.

You can explore part of Wisconsin's Ice Age National Scenic Trail and the Ice Age National Scientific Reserve by driving about 20 miles north of Lake Wissota to Brunet Island State Park (in Cornell). The Ice Age National Scenic Trail is a 1,000-mile route that traces the farthest advance of the Wisconsin Glacier. Part of this trail extends westward from Brunet Island State Park to the Chippewa Moraine Ice Age Unit. The Chippewa Moraine is one of nine units in the Ice Age National Scientific Reserve that preserve representative features sculpted by the last glacier. This unit is not yet open to the public. When the 4,000-acre tract is developed, visitors will be able to camp and hike among the many lakes, ponds and hills of this scenic region.

(opposite page)

An early breakfast in the fresh air is a feature common to all the state park campgrounds.

LUCIUS WOODS STATE PARK

Douglas County. Turn east onto Marion Avenue from Highway 53 in Solon Springs. Highway map index: 2-C.

Main Attraction

In Wisconsin, great boreal forests once covered the northern part of the state. A beautiful stand of that virgin pine is preserved here along the shore of Lake St. Croix.

Lucius Woods State Park has one of the most beautiful stands of virgin pine in Wisconsin. Great white and red pines line the shore of Lake St. Croix and the little creek that crosses the park.

The park is near the site of the Bois Brule–St. Croix Portage, the shortest natural water route between Lake Superior and the upper Mississippi River basin. Explorers and trappers, missionaries and soldiers traveled this route between the two great water systems for almost two centuries and the Indians for hundreds of years before them.

Lucius Woods is a small park, but it attracts families and those who are looking for a scenic, uncrowded spot to relax, swim and hike.

Things To Do

A hiking trail follows the creek, letting you see close up the thick, straight and lofty pines that once covered most of Wisconsin. There are picnic tables and a log shelter among the trees overlooking the lake. On the other side of a small rise is the playground and beach area with plenty of space to enjoy a day in the sun.

Lake St. Croix, headwaters for the St. Croix River, is the most popular part of Lucius Woods, offering fishing, boating and canoeing. Swimmers can use the rustic bathhouse by the beach.

The frozen lake is the main winter attraction at Lucius Woods. You can hike, ice fish, ice skate, snowmobile and cross-country ski where conditions allow.

Facilities

The park, operated by Douglas County, maintains a 28-site campground (no showers).

Surrounding Area

The Brule River State Forest is just north of the park, and is worth exploring for winter or summer sports. Pattison and Amnicon Falls state parks, the St. Croix National Scenic Riverway, the Chequamegon National Forest and some large county forests are all close to Lucius Woods. The North Country National Scenic Trail (a 3,200-mile route from Crown Point, New York, to the Lewis and Clark National Historic Trail in North Dakota) passes near the park. The tourist information center in Superior will give you further details on recreation in northwestern Wisconsin.

(next page)

The beach area invites visitors to spend a relaxing afternoon with the right combination of sun and shade.

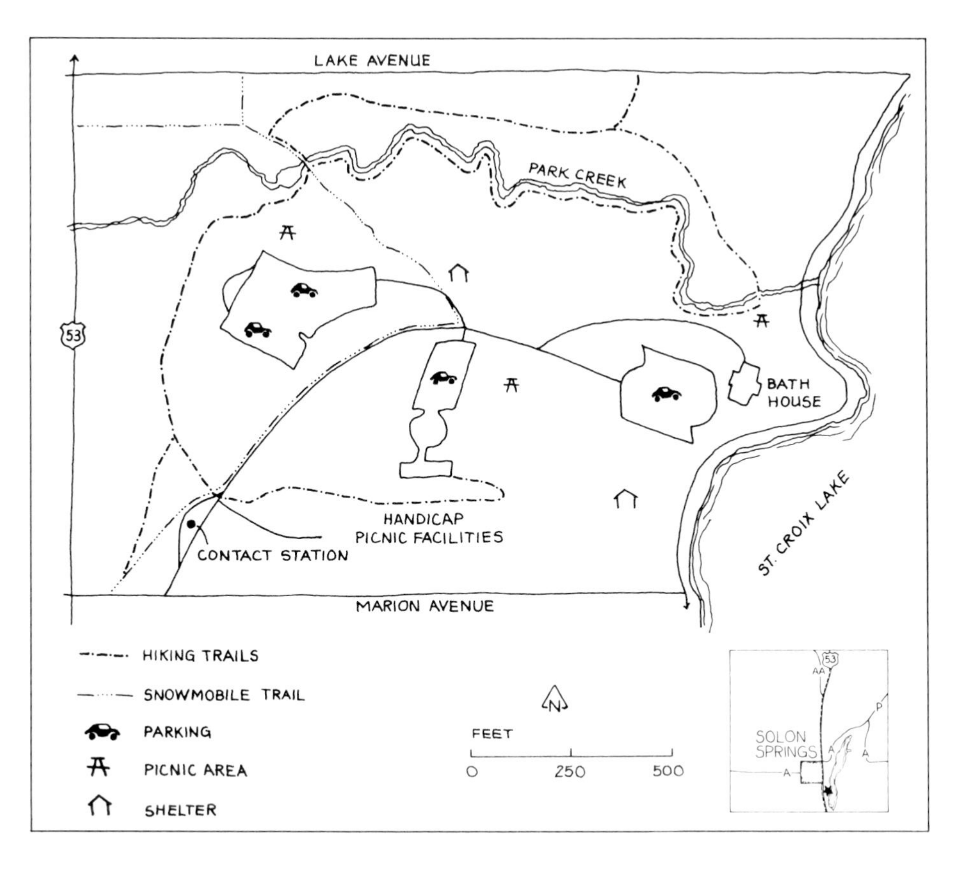

MERRICK STATE PARK

Buffalo County. Just north of Fountain City on Highway 35. Highway map index: 7-C.

Main Attraction

The Mississippi River and its backwaters are a sportsman's dream. Fishing, hunting and exploring could take up most of your time here if you didn't have to work to buy gear or food. But during those times when you can pack your outdoor toys in the boat and feel as worry-free as Tom Sawyer after school, you'll find that Merrick is the state park that is on the most intimate terms with the Mississippi River.

The beauty of this area was preserved when John Latsch of Winona, Minnesota, bought the land and gave it to Wisconsin for use as a park. The name Merrick comes from a famous steamboat pilot and river historian from Prescott, Wisconsin.

Things To Do

Most people bypass Merrick (322 acres) in favor of larger parks with more diversity. That's okay with the loyal group of campers and river lovers who return each year to this water-oriented park. The main reason for their devotion might be the shoreline campsites that let you moor the family boat right at your site. Fountain City Bay is just behind your tent or RV, providing easy access to the Mississippi River (you can launch from one of the two park boat landings).

The bay and river are an endless source of fun and fascination. People flock here to fish during the summer and winter, trying to land walleye, catfish, sunfish or crappie. You can water-ski or wander the backwaters by canoe, sampling just a slice of the great river that the Indians called the "father of waters." If you're quiet and observant, you might spot egrets, great blue herons, muskrats and even playful otters.

(opposite page)

As with many Wisconsin parks, you're never far from a body of water, in this case the Mississippi River.

The park's only hiking path is a one-half-mile self-guided nature loop called the Indian Mound Trail. Merrick is a river bottom, flood plain park located between the Mississippi River and a procession of 500-foot bluffs. The sandstone bluffs are called "hard heads" and comprise some of the most rugged topography in Wisconsin. Thousands of years of erosion by the Mississippi River has separated the Minnesota and Wisconsin bluffs at this point by over three miles. Merrick offers interpretive programs throughout the summer to stimulate and satisfy curiosity about the park and river.

(continued)

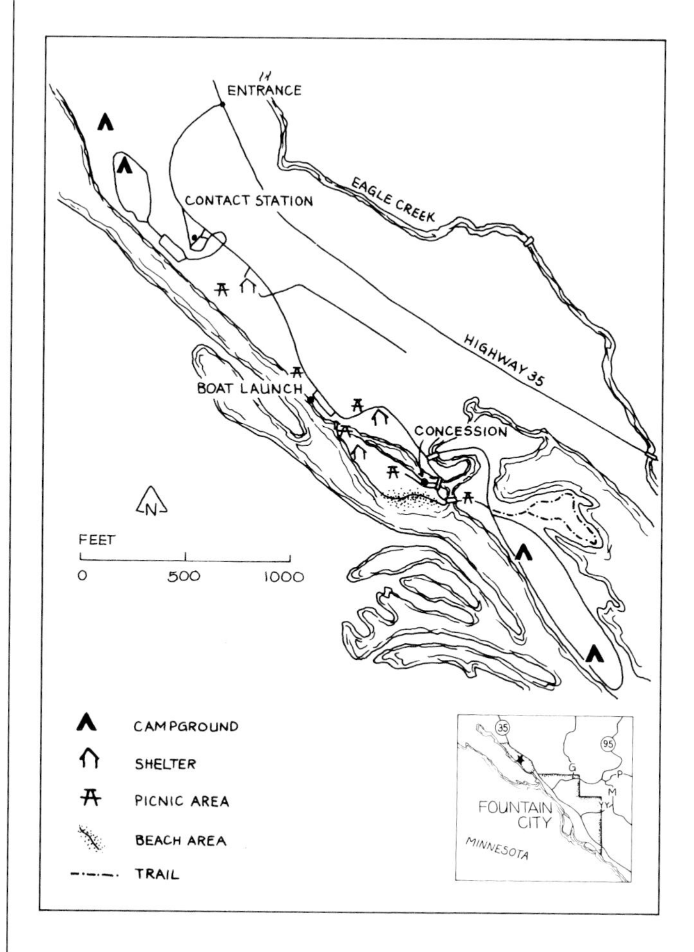

Facilities

You don't need a boat to enjoy the river at Merrick. Shore fishing is good and the park maintains a swimming beach on Fountain City Bay. Picnic sites are plentiful along the shoreline and three shelters are available for use. Supplies (don't forget mosquito repellent) are available in Fountain City.

The park's 76 campsites are divided into two campgrounds. The South Campground (51 sites) has pit toilets and drinking water, while the North Campground (25 sites) has a new toilet/shower building and 15 electrical sites. About half of the park campsites are reservable. You can camp year-round in the North Campground, though the showers are closed during the winter.

You can moor your boat at a shoreline campsite and rise early in the morning to try the fishing on the Mississippi River backwaters.

Merrick's campgrounds are busy well into autumn, especially during the duck and deer hunting seasons. Duck hunters like the convenience of keeping their boats at their campsite and the proximity to good hunting. Deer hunters like to camp here because Merrick lies in the midst of one of the most productive deer hunting areas in the state.

Surrounding Area

John Latsch also donated the land for Perrot State Park (near Trempealeau), downriver from Merrick State Park. Other area state recreation lands include the Great River and La Crosse River state trails (surfaced for bicycles) and the Buffalo River State Trail (not surfaced for bicycles). The Upper Mississippi River National Wildlife and Fish Refuge and the Trempealeau National Wildlife Refuge are both located on the Mississippi River near Merrick and Perrot state parks.

NORTH COUNTRY NATIONAL SCENIC TRAIL

3,200 miles; between Crown Point, New York, and the Lewis and Clark National Historic Trail at Lake Sakakawea, North Dakota. The Wisconsin segment extends from Hurley to the Highway 77 bridge on the St. Croix River (west of Danbury), running through Iron, Ashland, Bayfield, Douglas and Burnett counties.

Main Attraction

Great footpaths, like the Appalachian Trail and the Pacific Crest Trail, inspire those of adventuresome spirit to explore vast slices of America that still resemble our country in its youth. The North Country National Scenic Trail, when completed, will take its place among these giants as the longest continuous footpath in the United States.

The North Country Trail (NCT), created in 1980, is one of eight National Scenic Trails in the National Trails System. It meanders through seven northern states (New York, Pennsylvania, Ohio, Michigan, Wisconsin, Minnesota and North Dakota) along its 3,200-mile route. Although officially administered by the National Park Service, the NCT's development is a cooperative venture shared by a number of federal, state, local and private agencies, which directly manage or will manage segments of the trail.

Though the trail will take years to complete, it's destined to become one of the country's premier hiking/backpacking corridors. The trail's magnitude is hard to imagine, especially considering the diversity of landscapes and points of interest along the way.

The NCT passes through seven national forests, two

national wildlife refuges, Pictured Rocks National Lakeshore, Sheyenne National Grassland and the St. Croix National Scenic Riverway. The footpath also crosses many state and county parks and forests. Hikers will find a variety of historic sites, museums and local attractions throughout the seven trail states.

The trail boasts some of the most scenic terrain in northeastern and midwestern America. From the grandeur of New York's Adirondack Mountains to the sweep of North Dakota's prairies, the NCT seems to promise surprise around every bend. Hikers can wander through the hardwood forests of Pennsylvania, the farming countryside of Ohio, the forests, lakes and streams of Michigan, Wisconsin and Minnesota, and experience the boundless horizons of the Great Lakes. The trail's natural beauty is interspersed with a rich historical heritage that includes old canals and abandoned logging and mining communities.

There's a pioneering spirit among those who volunteer their labor and talents to make the NCT a reality. Maybe it's the scope of the project or simply wanderlust that kindles the desire to be part of such an extensive trail.

The North Country Trail Association (NCTA) is the

main citizen volunteer group promoting the trail. It assists in the coordination of public and private trail construction projects and sponsors trail education programs to increase grass roots support for the completion and maintenance of the NCT. The association also encourages the development of hostels and campsites along the route. The NCTA's headquarters is itself an American Youth Hostel. Housed in a 100-year-old restored schoolhouse in White Cloud, Michigan, the headquarters is strategically located near the halfway point of the trail. If you're interested in becoming a supporting member of the North Country Trail Association, you can contact the group through the address listed in the back of this book.

When this trail is finished it will cross seven northern states and be the longest footpath in the U.S. Investigate the sections open in Wisconsin for a preview.

Nearly 700 miles of the NCT are already completed and open to public use, including segments as long as 95 miles. Another 400 miles of existing trails that follow the NCT route can be used by the public, but have not yet been officially certified as part of the NCT. Connecting sections of varying lengths link the certified segments.

Users should keep in mind that camping facilities, services, fees, rules and regulations are not uniform yet along the trail's length. Even trail width, quality and visitor uses may change from segment to segment. The NCTA has planned an "end-to-end" hike in 1990 to publicize the project and encourage unification of all development efforts.

The NCT enters Wisconsin near Hurley, following a high-potential route and existing trails developed on Iron County Forest lands. It continues along a general route to Copper Falls State Park, where it follows existing trails in the park. Southwest of Copper Falls, the NCT tracks the existing 60-mile "North Country Trail" in the Chequamegon National Forest. This trail helped give birth to the concept of the NCT in the 1960s and gave its name to the entire 3,200-mile route. There's potential for a side trail leading northward through the forest to the Apostle Islands National Lakeshore at the tip of the Bayfield Peninsula.

Leaving the National Forest, the NCT passes through Bayfield County Forest lands and enters the Brule River State Forest, where it follows an existing

trail southward through the forest. A high-potential route continues past Lucius Woods State Park (now administered by Douglas County) and through a state wildlife area before reaching the upper end of the St. Croix National Scenic Riverway. The NCT route parallels the St. Croix River for about 40 miles until it crosses into Minnesota west of Danbury. Some trail users may wish to take advantage of the excellent canoeing on the St. Croix River.

So far, the only certified NCT segments in Wisconsin are in Copper Falls State Park and the Chequamegon National Forest. The 7.8-mile section in Copper Falls State Park leads through a forest to a series of waterfalls on the Bad River. The park maintains two family campgrounds, a group camp area and two backpack campsites in the north end of the park on a side trail off the NCT. Reservations are required for the group camp and are suggested for the family and backpacking sites. For further information, contact the park at the address listed in the back of this book.

In the Chequamegon National Forest, the NCT traverses the northern section, passing through the Rainbow Lake and the Porcupine Lake wilderness areas. The marked trail is open to hiking/backpacking and horseback riding in the summer and cross-country skiing and snowshoeing in the winter. Hikers can set up camp in any of four developed campgrounds that are either along or near the trail. Three Adirondack shelters are also located along the trail. You can find out more information about the campgrounds, off-trail camping and recreation facilities in the Chequamegon by contacting the forest at the address listed in the back of this book.

Northwestern Wisconsin is an outdoor lover's haven. Hundreds of lakes, scores of trout streams and thousands of acres of forest lure visitors in every season. Other state recreation lands near the NCT include the Governor Knowles State Forest (along the St. Croix River, south of Danbury) and Pattison, Amnicon and Big Bay state parks.

(opposite page)

Backpacking Wisconsin trails is the best way to take some of it with you when you're trying to get away from it all.

OJIBWA STATE PARK

Sawyer County. One mile east of Ojibwa on Highway 70. Highway map index: 4-D.

Main Attraction

Ojibwa State Park lies between the Chippewa River on the north and the Tuscobia State Trail on the south. Highway 70 bisects the park from east to west. Some canoeists, hikers and travelers bypass the park without realizing what a peaceful, beautiful spot they've missed.

The park doesn't have the size, facilities or singular scenic highlight that characterize some of Wisconsin's better-known state parks. But it does attract a loyal following who feel its relatively small size (366 acres) and simple tastes give it an intimate atmosphere that higher profile parks don't possess. That's why the Winter Area Lions Club assumed the maintenance and operation of Ojibwa under a lease agreement in 1981 when it looked like the DNR might not have kept the park open.

Things To Do

The park's only designated hiking trail is a four-mile link to the Tuscobia State Trail. Hikers can see many types of timber in the park, ranging from white pine to hardwoods. The land is rough and rocky, with hills, valleys and bogs providing a rich habitat for a variety of large and small wildlife. If you like longer hikes, try the Tuscobia Trail or trails in the nearby Flambeau River State Forest and the Chequamegon National Forest.

After a day on the Chippewa River or the Tuscobia Trail, set up camp in this intimate park and relax beneath the murmuring trees.

The 75-mile Tuscobia State Trail is an abandoned railroad grade used by hikers, horseback riders and snowmobilers. It is not surfaced for bicycles, though the fatter tires of some mountain bikes may be able to handle the trail's soft spots. In winter, snowmobilers use the Ojibwa shelter as a rest stop while riding on the Tuscobia.

The Chippewa River, along the park's northern boundary, is the site of yearly canoe races and a good fishing spot. Visitors try for muskie, pike, bass, trout and panfish. The stony river bottom provides good habitat for fish, but is not conducive to swimming. Hike the river after a storm to experience the sensations of a rain-freshened forest. The feel of the moist leaves on your skin, the smell of clean air and the sound of wind rustling through the woods against the background chorus of rushing water make a pleasant northwoods memory.

Facilities

Ojibwa has six campsites with electrical hookups available. Water, restrooms and grills are in the picnic area. The large shaded picnic area has a solid stone shelter that affords protection when an afternoon thunderstorm rumbles over. Ojibwa State Park is open from May to the end of the gun deer season (about December 1). The park is a Wisconsin Wildlife Refuge, so hunting is not permitted at any time.

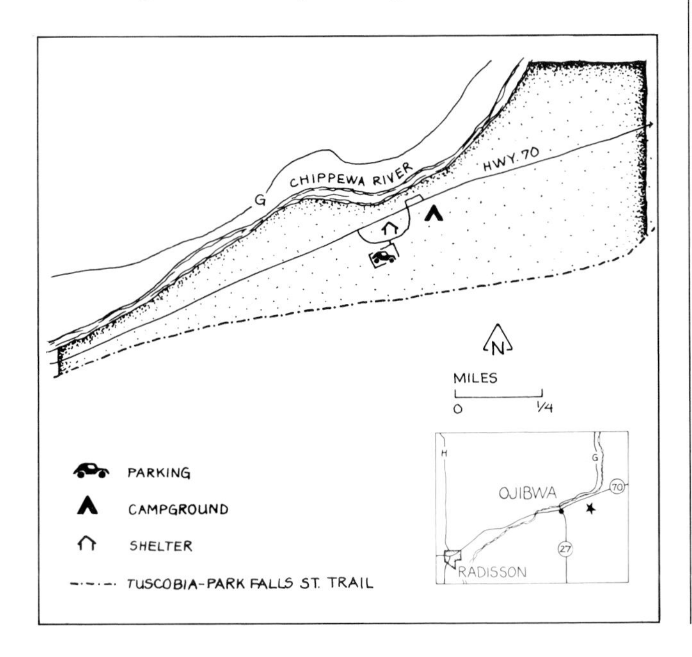

Some hunters like to camp here, though, because of its easy access to nearby hunting areas. Park admission is free, and no vehicle admission sticker is required. All camping is on a first-come, first-served basis (a fee is charged).

The park was established in 1932 as a gift to the people of Wisconsin from Robert W. Baird and his wife, the Ojibwa Sales Company and Northern States Power Company.

PATTISON STATE PARK

Douglas County. About 10 miles south of Superior on Highway 35. Highway map index: 2-B.

Main Attraction

The power and beauty of Big Manitou Falls has entranced people for centuries. The fascination of watching the cataract plunge 165 feet down a steep cliff and listening to its constant roar still inspires people to linger on the overlooks at Pattison State Park. The Chippewa Indians (also called Ojibwa) and their ancestors believed that they heard the Great Spirit's voice in the waterfalls, so they named it Gitchee Manitou.

You can view Wisconsin's highest waterfall (the fourth highest east of the Rocky Mountains) from overlooks on both sides of the river. From these vistas, you'll also see the dramatic gorge that the Black River has carved over the past 10,000 years. The cliff walls are composed of dark basalt, a volcanic rock that formed when great fissures opened in the earth's crust about one billion years ago, spewing molten lava over much of this region. The giant sandstone walls downstream of the falls are relics of ancient seas that once covered the area.

Looking north and west from the overlooks, the cliffs drop off to a broad, forested valley that stretches from the park to the bluffs near Duluth, Minnesota. The valley was created following an earthquake about 500 million years ago when a great block of earth settled downward along the Douglas Fault. Interested visitors can get details about the park's geology (including the glacial period) from the park office.

The Black River begins its northward journey to Lake Superior about 22 miles southwest of the park at the outlet of Black Lake. This is a wilderness lake (walk-in access only) that straddles the Minnesota–

Wisconsin border. In the park, the Black River tumbles over the 30-foot Little Manitou Falls and forms man-made Interfalls Lake (27 acres) before cascading over Big Manitou Falls. Below the park, the Black River joins the Nemadji River for a 10-mile stretch before emptying into Lake Superior. Depending on seasonal precipitation levels, the river can be a raging torrent or a relatively quiet stream.

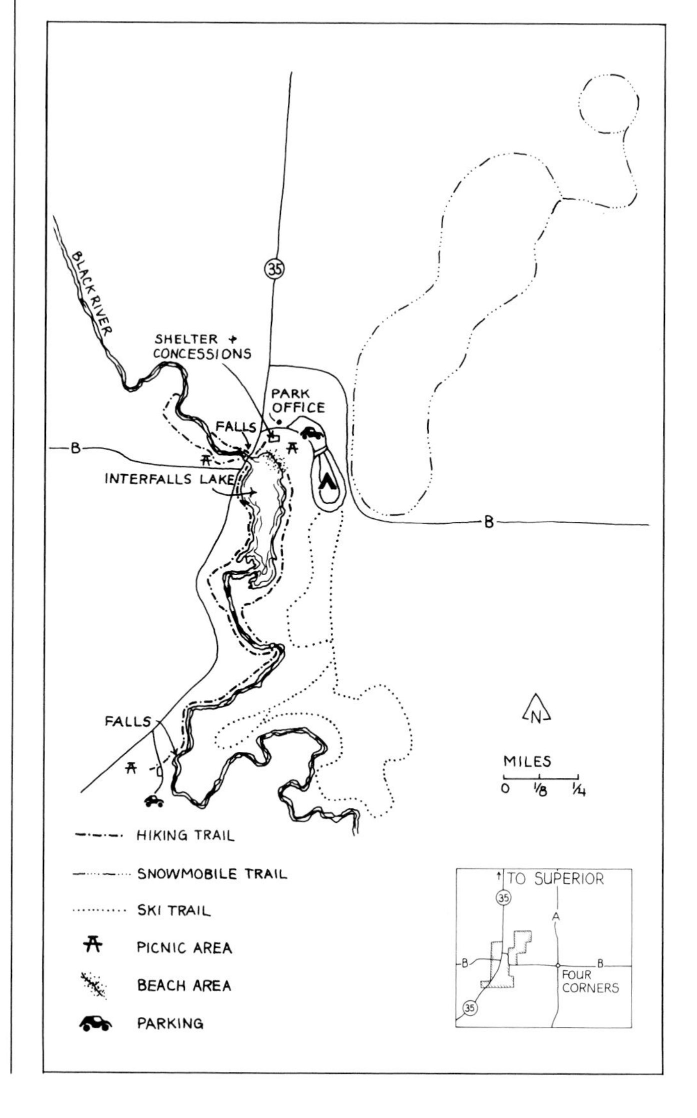

The park belongs to the public because of the generosity of Martin Pattison, an early businessman and community leader from Superior. He became wealthy through dealings in local lumbering, mining and banking (the remains of his Black River lumber camp can still be seen from the park's ski trail). To protect the falls from development, he bought the 660 acres surrounding them and gave the land to the state. The park was created in 1920.

Things To Do

Fishing is not always good at Pattison State Park. Local fishermen catch migrating suckers and redhorse in late spring as they swim upriver from Lake Superior to spawn. Brown and brook trout are native to the river both above and below Interfalls Lake. Rainbow trout are stocked above the lake each year. Steelhead trout (or rainbow) are stocked in the Black River below the big falls. They live in Lake Superior and migrate up tributary streams in the spring to spawn.

Interfalls Lake is not a fishing "hot spot." You might catch bullheads and rock bass, but suckers, chubs and shiners are common. Brown trout and chinook salmon (stocked) migrate into the Black River from Lake Superior beginning in early September. Some of the salmon catches have been up to 20 pounds. Like fishing elsewhere, success involves luck and being in the right place at the right time. Check at the park office for details about fishing regulations, licenses (including trout stamps) and extended seasons for certain species.

The Chippewa Indians thought they heard the Great Spirit's voice in the roar of the 165-foot falls here. They named it Gitchee Manitou.

Whether fishing or exploring, you can hike down to the river bottom below Big Manitou Falls by a one-half-mile trail on the south side of the gorge. This is a dead-end path that is steep in places. The park's two-mile-long self-guiding nature trail circles Interfalls Lake. About halfway around this loop, where it crosses the Black River, you can hike upriver on a .6-mile path that leads to Little Manitou Falls. If you prefer, you can drive to a nearby parking lot and hike a short distance to view Little Manitou Falls. A third waterfall, on Copper Creek in a remote section of the

(opposite page)

Learning about the geology of this park can only enhance your appreciation of the scenery.

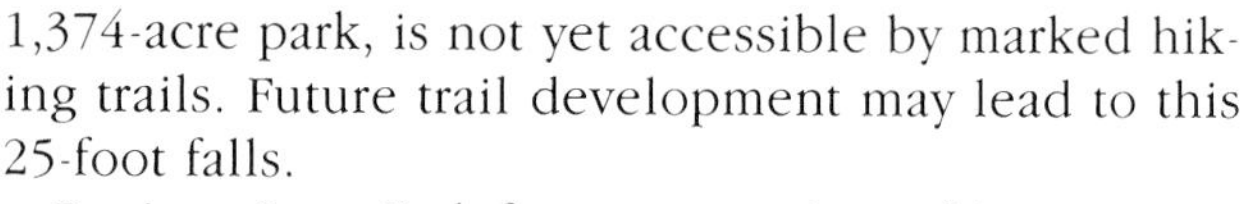

1,374-acre park, is not yet accessible by marked hiking trails. Future trail development may lead to this 25-foot falls.

Pattison State Park features a variety of interpretive displays and exhibits in the shelter building throughout the summer. Scheduled evening programs are also held in the shelter building. The shelter, along with much of the other park developments, was built by the Civilian Conservation Corps (CCC) in the late 1930s. The park office has a booklet that tells the story of the CCC in this area.

Winter visitors can tour the park on 5.5 miles of snowmobile trails and 4.5 miles of cross-country ski trails. They wind through some marshland and are therefore not maintained for hikers during the summer. Maps are available at the park office. Also ask at the office about other snowmobile and cross-country ski trails in Douglas County.

Flora and Fauna

The park is a rest stop for ducks and geese during the spring and fall migrations. You might also spot bald eagles or osprey as they search for fish in Interfalls Lake. Mid-September is usually a good time to observe migrating hawks as they circle the western end of Lake Superior on their southward journey. Deer, beaver and otter are among the wildlife frequently seen in the park. Black bears, bobcats and coyotes are more secretive. Timber wolves have been tracked in Douglas County but are rarely, if ever, spotted in the park. You can pick up bird and mammal checklists in the park office.

Facilities

Camping, picnicking and water sports take place by Interfalls Lake. A large picnic area overlooks the lake and swimming beach. The 59-site campground has showers and 18 electrical hookups (reservations are accepted). You can buy supplies at the park concession or from stores in Superior and the surrounding area. Although no boat launching facilities are provided, canoes and nonmotorized boats that can be

portaged are allowed on Interfalls Lake. The usually low water and rocky bottom of the Black River make it unsuitable for canoeing.

Surrounding Area

Pattison State Park is within easy driving distance of a number of recreational attractions. Area state recreation lands include the Brule River State Forest and Amnicon Falls and Lucius Woods state parks (Lucius Woods is now administered by Douglas County). The Chequamegon National Forest and the St. Croix National Scenic Riverway and Douglas County forests are all nearby. The surrounding region contains hundreds of lakes and over 200 miles of trout streams. The North Country Scenic Trail, a 3,200-mile trail extending from Crown Point, New York, to the Lewis and Clark National Historic Trail in North Dakota, runs south of the park into Minnesota.

Many park visitors plan a side trip to Duluth, Minnesota, and Superior, Wisconsin. These Lake Superior twin ports boast the largest coal and iron ore docks and grain elevators in the world. Both cities feature maritime and historical museums among other attractions. You can take a guided harbor cruise or join in a Lake Superior fishing charter. Stop at the local chambers of commerce for further details as well as directions to some of the scenic area beaches.

PERROT STATE PARK

Trempealeau County. About one mile northwest of the village of Trempealeau. Highway map index: 8-C.

Main Attraction

The combination of imposing river bluffs marching to the horizon, lush lowlands and twisted backwaters have always held a fascination for those who love the Mississippi River. At Perrot State Park, you can survey the fabled river valley from two lofty blufftops, enjoying one of the most striking vistas in Wisconsin.

The first white man to visit here explored the river by canoe. When Nicholas Perrot, a 17th-century French Canadian fur trader, wintered here on his way upriver in 1685–86, he found a vast land "abounding in wild beasts" that included buffalo, elk and cougar. Perrot probably was attracted by Trempealeau Mountain, a 425-foot bluff surrounded by water at the confluence of the Mississippi and Trempealeau rivers.

The "mountain" is also surrounded by colorful legends of several cultures, many of which lay a spiritual claim to it. As with most of the bluffs along the Mississippi River, there are rattlesnakes on Trempealeau Mountain. The Winnebago Indians believed that the snakes guarded their buried tribal ancestors. Reverend D. O. Van Slyke, author of the 19th-century *Garden of Eden*, believed that the rattlesnakes were a divine sign that the Biblical garden was in Trempealeau County.

Things To Do

Far below the summit of Brady's Bluff (520 feet), boats make widening wakes on the river like water spiders on a stream. Most launch from Trempealeau Bay along the river road to sightsee or fish on the river. Good local fishing spots are the mouth of the Trempealeau River (near the boat launch), underneath the railroad trestle, and just downriver from the park behind the lock and dam.

Canoes are at home here. You could spend hours poking into small bays and backwaters on the Trempealeau River or go exploring along the shoreline of the Mississippi. The bottom land is a resting place for thousands of waterfowl, and the silent canoeist with sharp eyes and ready camera can go home with some visual trophies of geese, ducks, herons or egrets.

When viewing the lush foliage of Trempealeau Mountain and the timeless river from Brady's Bluff, the region's nickname of God's Country seems apt. The best views of the legendary mountain are from the steep trails that wind up to the top of Brady's Bluff. Rest at the shelter while on top and look upriver

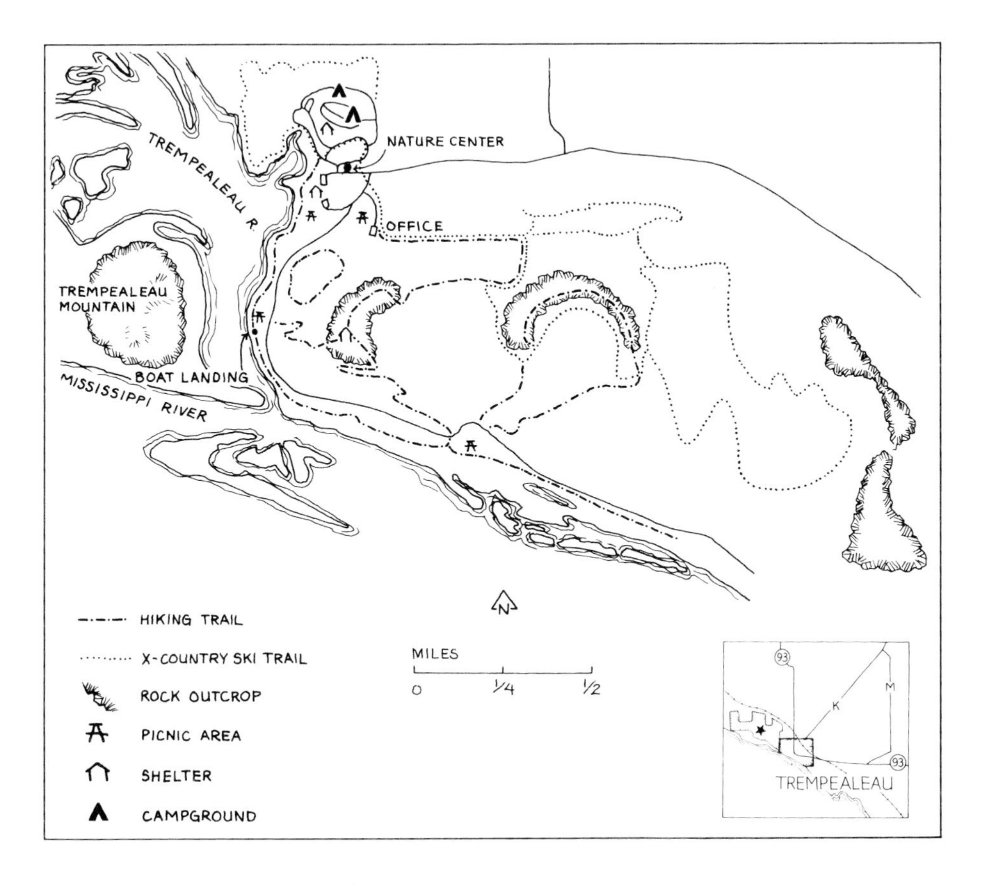

past Trempealeau Mountain. You can see Winona, Minnesota, from here. Downriver is Lock and Dam No. 6, one of many on the Mississippi through which the long river barges pass.

Perrot State Park's four hiking trails wind for eight miles through forests, bottom lands and restored prairie. Pick up a trail map at the contact station or the park office. You can read about the park's geology and Indian history while hiking on the easy Black Walnut Nature Trail or stop to study the Indian mounds when driving along the river road.

If you love the Mississippi River, you'll enjoy the vistas from the blufftops in this park. Then launch your canoe for a closer look.

The park's Indian mounds are reminders of the Native American culture that existed in the area as long ago as 100 B.C. Some of the mounds were built by the Hopewell Indians, who had well-developed crafts of silver and copper and traded extensively with tribes as far away as the Rocky Mountains. The mounds were used for burial, usually containing tools, pipes, weapons and other articles of personal importance to the Indians. Though you can see a number of mounds in the park, many more were destroyed by plowing when some of the park lands were farmed.

Perrot State Park sponsors an active naturalist program. On weekends during the summer, the naturalist schedules guided hikes and evening programs, including slide shows, fireside stories and singalongs. The hikes vary from bluff exploration and night hikes to looking for wildflowers and birdwatching. The nature center, located near the campground entrance, features displays and historical information about the park.

Winter fun at Perrot revolves around cross-country skiing. The park's 8.5 miles of groomed trails vary from hilly to flat, accommodating skiers of all abilities. You can snowshoe anywhere in the park except on the ski trails. Winter camping is gaining in popularity here. Ask park personnel for details about water and which sites are open.

(continued on next page)

The rugged river country provides a challenge to hikers, but the rewards are obvious.

Flora and Fauna

Hikers can literally have a field day identifying the variety of plants and animals in the park while exploring the valleys, upland slopes and marshes. In spring, the woods show off violets, Dutchman's breeches, jack-in-the-pulpits and other wildflowers. Springtime on Brady's Bluff Prairie, a Wisconsin Natural Area, means pasque flowers and puccoon, while autumn ignites the prairie with colorful blazing stars, sunflowers and prairie clovers. Deer and other woodland mammals inhabit the park's hardwood forest; beaver, muskrat, mink and occasionally otters are found on the wetland areas. Over 200 species of birds could be recorded in the park, including the great migrating flocks that visit the area in the spring and fall.

Facilities

Reservations are accepted for some of the 97 campground sites (showers; 36 electrical hookups). Picnic tables are spaced at various shady spots along the river, with a larger picnic ground near the park office and the nature center. The shelter house can be reserved. The park office sells fishing licenses and lends some playground equipment (e.g., volleyball and horseshoe). No swimming is allowed in the park, but there is a public pool in Trempealeau.

Surrounding Area

The surrounding region features other attractions for outdoor lovers. You can visit nearby Merrick State Park (upriver from Perrot) or go bicycling on the Great River and La Crosse River state trails. The Great River State Trail passes through a section of Perrot State Park. The Trempealeau National Wildlife Refuge and the Upper Mississippi River National Wildlife and Fish Refuge are both neighbors of the park.

We're able to enjoy the vistas and wonders of Perrot State Park because of the generosity of John Latsch of Winona, Minnesota. After reading about Nicholas Perrot's adventures here, he bought the land and donated it to the state of Wisconsin for a park in memory of his father.

RED CEDAR STATE TRAIL

Dunn County. 14.5 miles, from Menomonie to the Chippewa River at the Dunnville Wildlife Area. Highway map index: 6-C.

Main Attraction

Bicycles and rivers make a friendly combination. Both encourage you to ignore the traditional ideas of time and look at the world from new angles. It's best to leave your watch in the car before pedaling on the Red Cedar State Trail. Much of the fun of bicycling is to hop off whenever you want to take a picture, rest in the grass or just enjoy the view.

Rivers, like the Red Cedar, also help you to forget about time and to notice details. All you have to do is sit on a riverbank long enough to become mesmerized by the flowing water to know what it's like to feel free of time. And rivers are an endless source of fascination when you get close: water spiders darting back and forth, fish swimming around rocks, and leaves swirling downstream. That perspective is lost as you drive over a bridge, perhaps not even realizing you've crossed a river.

Things To Do

From its starting point at the old railroad depot near Menomonie's Riverside Park (on the west edge of town), the trail hugs the river almost all the way to Downsville, over seven miles downstream. You'll see steep sandstone bluffs and hear the river's voices as it gurgles over the rocks. You might also hear the echoes of inner-tubers as they float down the river. Canoeists enjoy the mostly placid river, too, but you can try that on your next trip. Some visitors do both by canoeing downriver and bicycling back to Menomonie.

The trail towns of Irvington, Downsville and Dunnville reflect the relaxed pace of the river. Irvington, three miles south of Menomonie, is named after George Irvine, who operated a sawmill between 1854 and 1882. A legend describes how a company of French soldiers buried some gold treasure around a bluff south of here, known as the pinnacle, when they were forced to retreat from a menacing band of In-

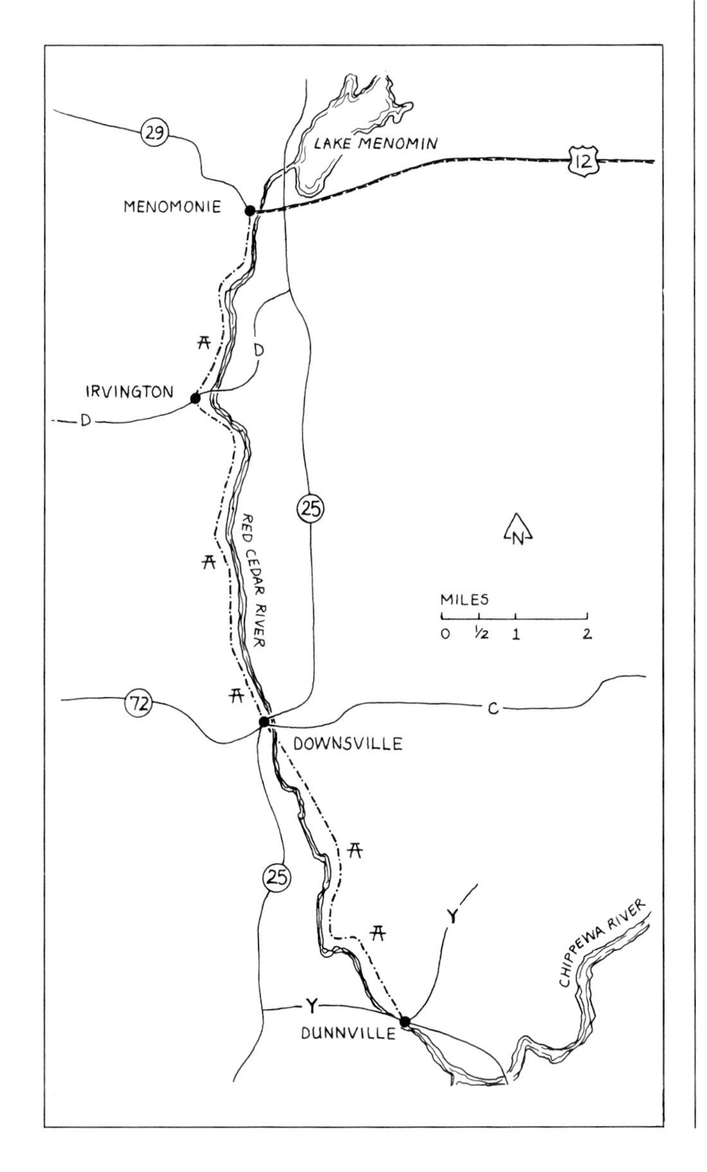

dians. Trail parking is available at the intersection of County D and Paradise Valley Road. The locals say that the bass fishing is good near the Irvington bridge.

Just before Downsville, the trail crosses the Red Cedar River from the west side to the east across a 460-foot former trestle. This is one of 11 trail bridges, the longest of which is the 840-foot span across the Chippewa River at the end of the trail.

Downsville is a convenient rest stop. Highway 25 and County C pass through town, so it's easy to plan a shorter trail ride. There is a parking lot for trail users. Bicycle riders might want to take a break at the Empire in Pine Lumber Museum. The small museum traces the history of lumbering in the area with a collection of artifacts and re-creations of a lumber camp's cook shanty, blacksmith and carpentry shops and bunkhouse.

Logging heritage runs deep in this area. The original railroad that is now the Red Cedar State Trail was built partly as a logging railroad to support the extensive lumber operations in Dunn County. The railroad primarily serviced the Knapp and Stout Company, which grew from a small lumber camp to the largest lumber-producing company in the world in the late 1800s.

Before the railroad steamed in, offering cheaper and quicker transportation, the river was the main method of moving logs to the sawmills. During the spring drive, the Red Cedar would be thick with logs, bobbing and crushing downstream.

You won't see much of the river from Downsville to the end of the trail, but there are other points of interest to grab your attention. South of Downsville (near mile 9) is where the childhood frontier adventures of Caroline "Caddie" Woodlawn took place. Carol Ryrie Brink retold her grandmother's (Caddie) stories in the award-winning children's book, *Caddie Woodlawn*. Caddie's home still stands on part of the original farm, which was designated as Caddie Woodlawn Memorial Park in 1970. This park is south of Downsville along Highway 25.

Four stone quarries once operated near this stretch of trail. Builders and sculptors of the 1880s used this high-quality sandstone (called Dunnville Stone) in such buildings as the Mabel Tainter Memorial Building in Menomonie and for an elegant sculpture in St. Thomas Episcopal Church in New York City.

The hamlet of Dunnville, on County Y near the trail's end, was originally known as Colburn's Landing. It was the county seat for four years until a fire swept through the courthouse in 1858. Menomonie then became the Dunn County seat. Back in its heyday, steamboats carrying passengers and cargo docked at Dunnville and picked up lumber rafts here.

The treasures of Wisconsin trails can be as majestic as a mountain or as dainty as a field of clover.

This trail hugs the Red Cedar River for much of the way. You can ride as others float, and either way the scenery is gorgeous.

The last portion of the trail cuts through bottom lands that form the Dunnville Wildlife Area. The trail ends in grand fashion by crossing the Chippewa River on an 840-foot trestle. The sweeping views of the Chippewa River are photogenic any time of day, but especially so in the warm light of a sunset.

If land acquisition and funding proceed smoothly, you'll be able to continue your bike ride (once across the Chippewa River) southwest to Durand or northeast for 22 miles to Eau Claire. This proposed route, called the Chippewa River Trail, is only in the planning stages and may not be in operation until the 1990s. Future plans for the Red Cedar State Trail include development of rest areas with toilets and drinking water. The old train depot in Menomonie may be renovated into an interpretive center and concession (bicycle rentals, snacks, etc.). Other interpretive activities include guided "bike hikes" and a planned trail booklet.

Visitors 18 years and older must buy a trail permit from April through October. You can buy permits from DNR personnel on the trail, from the DNR office in Menomonie or from some of the local businesses along the trail.

The Red Cedar is a popular cross-country ski trail during winter. The trail is groomed for both skating and diagonal-style skiers. Only the southern 2.5 miles (below Dunnville) are open to snowmobilers, who use it as a connecting link to area snowmobile trails.

The hard-packed, crushed limestone surface of the trail is suitable for all bikes. Even at a relaxing pace, you can bike the 14.5-mile trail in one and a half to two hours. The nearest campground is at Eau Galle County Park, about five to six miles west of the trail's southern end. Bike rental and car shuttle services are not available at this time. The Red Cedar State Trail office in Menomonie can give you information about private campgrounds.

Flora and Fauna

Bald eagles frequent the river a couple miles south on Irvington in late summer and fall, and you might also spot ospreys soaring above the Red Cedar or perched in trees by the riverbank. White-tailed deer, beaver and great blue heron are among the wildlife observed from the trail and along the river, though rabbits, squirrels and songbirds are more likely to be seen. Wildflowers abound along the trail's edge. You'll also bike past sumac, pussy willows and birch and aspen woods.

Surrounding Area

Menomonie hosts a number of festivals and cultural events and is the home of the University of Wisconsin–Stout. Stop at the chamber of commerce to get details about local events and area outdoor activities. Red Cedar State Trail users are within easy driving distance of Eau Claire–Chippewa Falls and the Twin City metro area.

ST. CROIX NATIONAL SCENIC RIVERWAY

Bayfield, Douglas, Sawyer, Washburn, Burnett, Polk, St. Croix and Pierce counties. 252 miles; the Upper St. Croix National Scenic Riverway (including the Namekagon River) runs for 200 miles from the Namekagon Lake dam (Namekagon River) and the Gordon dam (St. Croix River) to the St. Croix Falls dam; the Lower St. Croix National Scenic Riverway runs for 52 miles from the St. Croix Falls dam to Prescott (on the Mississippi River). Headquarters is in St. Croix Falls.

"And so in the aspect of the river, in any of its moods there is always a residual mystery. In its being it is too small and too large, too complex and too simple, too powerful and too delicate, too transient and too ancient and durable ever to be comprehended within the limits of a human life."

Wendell Berry
Recollected Essays

Main Attraction

It seems fitting that there are still wild places that we may never comprehend or dominate. Places, like the St. Croix and Namekagon rivers, where humans are just passing through. These two free-flowing and unpolluted rivers flow through some of the most scenic and undeveloped country in the Upper Midwest.

Wolves and other big game were common when the Dakota (Sioux) and Ojibwa (Chippewa) Indians lived in this river valley for centuries before Europeans came. The country was rich in wildlife, fish, wild rice and other plant foods. It was also rich in beaver, and the Ojibwa allied themselves with the first French trappers and traders. With French-supplied guns, the Ojibwa eventually drove the Dakota onto the plains of southern Minnesota.

After beaver supplies declined, logging took over as the next big industry on the St. Croix. Rivers, like the St. Croix, were once choked with logs. Dams were constructed to build a head of water to float the logs to downriver mills. A logjam in the narrow Dalles (St.

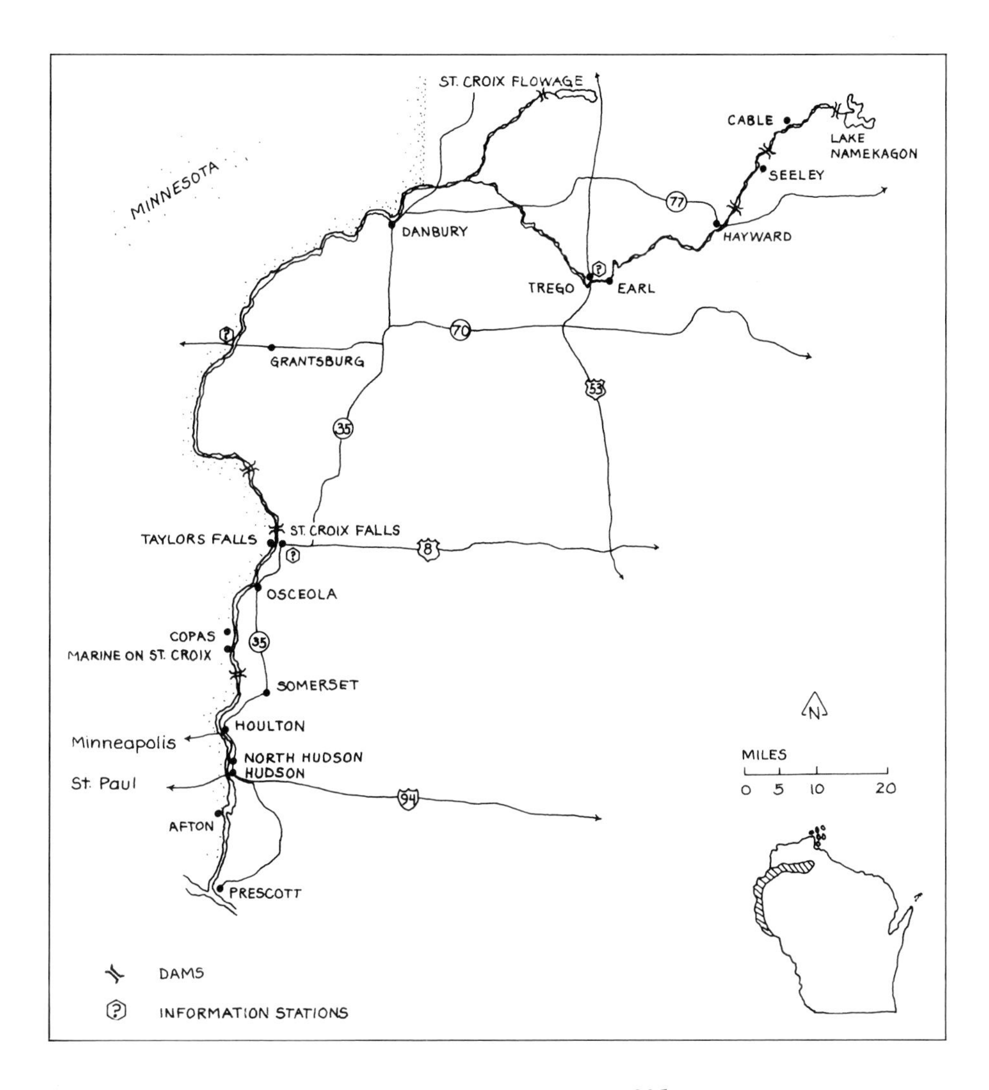

The St. Croix River offers canoeists dramatic scenery and a variety of water conditions.

Croix Falls) in 1886 backed upriver for about two miles and took almost six weeks to clear.

The St. Croix National Scenic Riverway, which includes the Namekagon (its main tributary), was established in 1968 as one of the original eight rivers under the National Wild and Scenic Rivers Act. The Lower St. Croix National Scenic Riverway was added to the system in 1972. The Upper and Lower portions of the riverway offer outdoor lovers a chance to enjoy canoeing, camping, fishing, boating, hiking and swimming in a wilderness-like setting that is within easy driving distance of the Twin Cities metro area. The riverway is managed through the cooperative efforts of the National Park Service, the Minnesota and Wisconsin departments of natural resources and the Northern States Power Company.

Things To Do

You can choose how to experience the riverway, but you should be prepared to do so on the river's terms. Rapids, insects, large water, changing river levels and unpredictable wind and weather conditions can't be controlled but can be planned for. It's good to talk to the National Park Service rangers before pushing off downstream on your river adventure.

Three visitor information stations are located along the riverway. The North District station (on Highway 63 near Trego) and the South District station (on Highway 70, west of Grantsburg) are both open seasonally. The riverway headquarters in St. Croix Falls is open year-round. Each station features exhibits on the natural and cultural history of the area. Depending on which station you visit, you can see a short slide program or movie that introduces the riverway to newcomers. Rangers at each station can help you plan day trips or extended outings on the riverway, answering questions about fishing, boating, river conditions or other aspects of your trip.

The upper St. Croix and Namekagon rivers both are punctuated by rapids that challenge canoeists, though none of the riverway's waters are classified as white water. If you're looking for the excitement of rapids, spring is a good time to canoe the upper Namekagon and the St. Croix above Riverside. These stretches become rocky and more difficult to canoe as the water level drops during summer.

The Namekagon downstream from Hayward and the St. Croix below the CCC bridge are usually canoeable throughout the season. Both rivers are characterized by quiet pools interrupted by easy rapids. Another section of rapids is between Nelson's Landing and Highway 70 on the St. Croix. During spring

It's hard to find free-flowing, unpolluted rivers, but when you do, it's easy to understand why their beauty needs to be preserved.

runoff, these rapids can become moderately hazardous to novice canoeists. Below Highway 70, the St. Croix is wider and slower, making it ideal for novice and family canoeists any time of the season. Check at one of the visitor information stations for current details about river levels and rapids. You can also get a list of area canoe outfitters at the stations (rental and shuttle service available).

Though the Upper Riverway is usually associated with canoeing, you can use a small powerboat on the flowage at St. Croix Falls, Trego and Hayward. Bass, muskie, walleye, northern, sturgeon and panfish can all be caught in the St. Croix. The intimate, swifter-flowing Namekagon is noted for its brown trout fishing. Inner-tubing and hunting (deer, duck, geese and small game) are other popular recreation activities in the river valley.

The Lower St. Croix National Scenic Riverway is wider, deeper, slower and more developed than the Upper. Its flow is controlled by the dam at its upstream end in St. Croix Falls. Downstream, the river rushes through a narrow, steep-walled gorge called the Dalles of the St. Croix. One of the most popular sections of the riverway for easy canoe day trips is from Taylors Falls to the Osceola landing or to William O'Brien State Park. Tour boat rides are available near Taylors Falls and Stillwater (on the Minnesota side).

Below the confluence of the St. Croix and the Apple rivers, the Riverway becomes deeper and slower-paced. Large powerboats are common on this stretch. The valley widens still more for the last 25 miles of the riverway, where the river is known as Lake St. Croix. Powerboating, houseboating, waterskiing, fishing and sailing are the primary water activities on the lake. Special water-use regulations (e.g., slow speed and no-wake zones) apply on the Lower Riverway.

The Lower Riverway and parts of the Upper are busiest on the weekends between Memorial Day and Labor Day. Those who wish to experience some solitude may want to plan a trip during mid-week or in spring or fall.

Flora and Fauna

Off-season outings or canoeing on less traveled sections of the riverway give you the best chance to observe eagles, ospreys and waterfowl (wood ducks, mallards or great blue herons). You might also spot deer, beaver, otter and other wildlife. Black bears live near portions of the Upper Riverway but are rarely sighted. To prevent them from investigating your campsite, keep a clean camp and hang all food packs. Ask a ranger for other suggestions for avoiding unwanted natural visitors (raccoons, for example, are notorious campground raiders).

The more remote, isolated tract of the St. Croix River Valley provides relatively good habitat for the timber wolf. The Wisconsin DNR monitors wolf activity in this region and estimates that 13 animals, divided among three or four packs, live in the northwestern corner of the state. Chances are slim that canoeists will spot a timber wolf.

Facilities

Most camping is at canoe-access primitive sites, though you'll find more developed camping areas within the state parks or private campgrounds located near the riverway. Some lands along the riverway are still privately owned and are off limits to camping and hiking. Canoe groups should ask a park ranger about which campsites are large enough for their needs. If desired, groups can also schedule informal interpretive programs with one of the riverway naturalists. Drinking water is available at many landings. The river water is not safe to drink unless it's treated or boiled for about 30 minutes. There are no user fees within the riverway except for entrance and camping fees charged in state parks and forests. All appropriate Minnesota and Wisconsin watercraft, fishing, hunting and trapping licenses apply.

Surrounding Area

Today, canoeists paddle the same waters that Indians, voyageurs and log drivers knew. Though the riverway is not a wilderness (because the land outside its boundaries has been altered by farming, forestry, highways, etc.), the corridor is preserved in a natural state by a variety of public lands. (Counties, townships and the St. Croix band of Ojibwas also manage portions of the riverway.) The Namekagon River begins in the Chequamegon National Forest and the St. Croix River flows through extensive county forests until it reaches the Minnesota border.

On the Wisconsin side, the riverway is flanked by the Governor Knowles State Forest, the St. Croix Islands Wildlife Area, and Interstate and Kinnickinnic (in development) state parks. The Crex Meadows and Fish Lake wildlife areas and Willow River State Park are all close by the riverway. The Minnesota side is protected by the St. Croix and Chengwatana state forests and by St. Croix, Wild River, Interstate, William O'Brien and Afton state parks.

The parks and forests in both the St. Croix and Namekagon river valleys feature a variety of bicycling, horseback riding and hiking trails. Snowmobilers and cross-country skiers will find hundreds of miles of trails in the region as well. Check with the riverway information centers and the Wisconsin and Minnesota DNR offices (in the state parks and forests) for details about trails, naturalist programs and attractions in the riverway communities.

TREMPEALEAU NATIONAL WILDLIFE REFUGE

Trempealeau and Buffalo counties. Drive about three miles west of Centerville on Highway 35-54, then turn south (left) onto South Prairie Road.

Main Attraction

By the time the Trempealeau National Wildlife Refuge was established in 1936 as "a refuge and breeding ground for migrating birds and other wildlife," the idea of protecting and managing wildlife in national refuges was 33 years old. Besides the indiscriminate use of wildlife, other factors such as drought and the drainage and development of marshes and tidal wetlands also threatened many species.

The Trempealeau NWR has grown from its original 700 acres to over 5,600 acres of marshes, bottom land hardwoods and upland grasslands and forest. The Mississippi River Valley in the refuge area varies from three to six miles in width and is bordered by forested bluffs rising 400 to 500 feet above the valley floor. About 80% of the refuge is made up of wetlands, with the remaining 20% made up of bottom lands and a 700-acre central upland area.

Located on a major north-south flyway, the refuge fills in spring and fall with migrating birds.

Things To Do

Wildlife observation is the main draw for most of the refuge's visitors. The refuge is located along one of the major north-south flyways, providing feeding and resting areas for the great semiannual migrations of ducks, geese and other birds. A five-mile, one-way auto tour offers excellent opportunities for viewing wildlife, especially during early morning and evening hours. White-tailed deer are usually spotted throughout the year.

A self-guided nature trail (about one mile long) is located about halfway around the wildlife drive. You'll hike past interpretive panels that highlight plants and animals found in the refuge. An observation platform, photo blind and scenic viewing areas make it easy to see the refuge and its wildlife from different angles. Several miles of dikes and service roads closed to vehicles are available for hiking. You can also bicycle on the wildlife drive and on all refuge roads closed to motorized traffic. Snowmobiles, trail bikes and ATVs are not allowed on any portion of the refuge.

Parts of the main refuge pool are open to fishing, though certain sections are seasonally posted to pro-

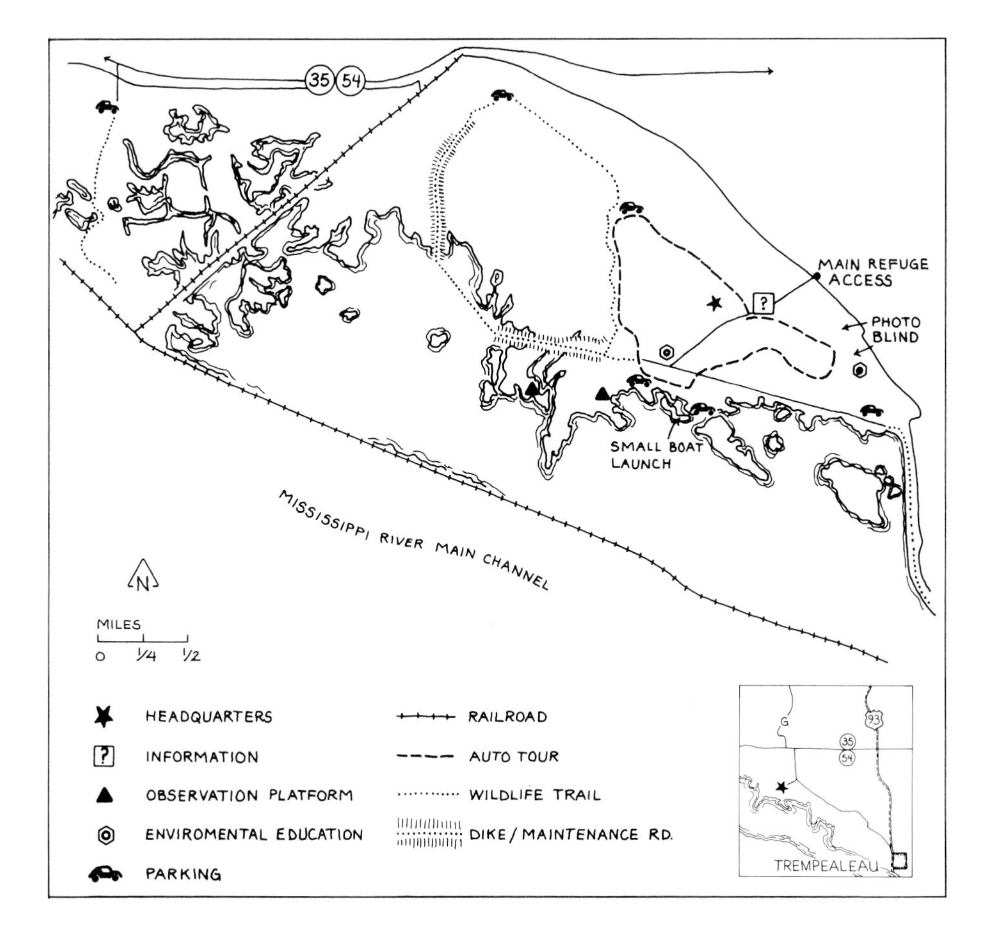

Birdwatchers and photographers will find a visit here most rewarding in the spring and fall as migrating flocks stop for a rest in the protected wetlands.

tect sensitive wildlife areas. A boat launching site with parking facilities is located near Kiep's Island about one mile east of the headquarters. Only electric motors are allowed. You can fish from the bank at the boat landing and from the Trempealeau River dike north of Trempealeau Mountain. The dike can also be reached by hiking from a parking lot east of the headquarters or by boat via the Trempealeau River. Bullheads are the most common catch, though you might land a northern or yellow perch. Ice fishing is permitted throughout the main pool during the winter months.

The refuge is open to small game, waterfowl, and archery and gun deer hunting by special permit. Maps showing open areas and details about refuge hunting are available at the headquarters.

Winter visitors can snowshoe or cross-country ski anyplace on the refuge, though no trails are groomed.

The Fish and Wildlife Service (U.S. Department of the Interior) is implementing a 20-year master plan for the Trempealeau National Wildlife Refuge. Part of the plan involves protecting about 950 acres of wildlife habitat on lands adjacent to the refuge. In addition, two public-use natural areas (about 400 acres) will be created. Interpretive trails and environmental education sites will be expanded. A recreational trapping program and a hunting dog training area will also be started. With these and other improvements, the refuge's annual visitation may jump from about 20,000 to over 50,000 visitors.

Facilities

The refuge has no camping facilities.

Surrounding Area

Perrot State Park, just south of the refuge, offers several miles of groomed cross-country ski trails as well as a campground. Other nearby public lands include Merrick State Park, the Great River and La Crosse River state trails and the Upper Mississippi River National Wildlife and Fish Refuge.

TRI-COUNTY RECREATIONAL CORRIDOR

Douglas, Bayfield and Ashland counties. 60 miles; between Superior and Ashland.

Main Attraction

The Tri-County Recreational Corridor is the first of its kind in Wisconsin. The idea is not new. The Wisconsin DNR has long been a national leader in converting abandoned railroad grades into recreational trails. The Tri-County trail was also created from an abandoned railroad right-of-way. Its uniqueness stems from the corridor's mentors—a private group operating independently of the Wisconsin DNR.

The trail's support group, "Friends of the Corridor," has benefited from the DNR's successes and failures in trail development. The supporters feel that a local group will be more responsive to trail users' needs and will be able to act faster than the state bureaucracy. The success of this project complements the efforts of the DNR, benefiting all those who use recreational corridors. It also adds a scenic segment of trail to the state's trail system, contributing to Wisconsin's national lead in recreational corridor mileage.

This trail provides access to hundreds of miles of other recreational trails, and passes through some of the region's most exciting scenery.

Things To Do

The Tri-County Trail is designated as a year-round, multiple-use corridor that roughly parallels Highway 2 from Superior to Ashland. Trail users can branch off onto hundreds of miles of other recreation trails in northwestern Wisconsin.

Trail development is not completed yet. Current projects involve re-decking bridges, installing guardrails and posting safety signs. Plans call for improving trail head access points and constructing shelters, scenic overlooks and picnic areas. If you're interested in contributing to the development process, contact the Tri-County Recreational Corridor Commission listed in the address section in the back of this book.

The Tri-County trail passes through some of the region's most exciting scenery: Amnicon Falls State Park, the Brule River State Forest and the Chequamegon National Forest. There are campgrounds in each of these areas. Services and supplies are available in Superior, Ashland, Poplar, Brule, Iron River and other nearby communities.

Though development is ongoing, many visitors already are using the trail. During summer, hikers, joggers, horseback riders and ATVers share the corridor. The trail may eventually be surfaced for bicycles, but you'll need a mountain bike to negotiate the soft sections for now. Hunting, snowmobiling and cross-country skiing are the main off-season trail activities.

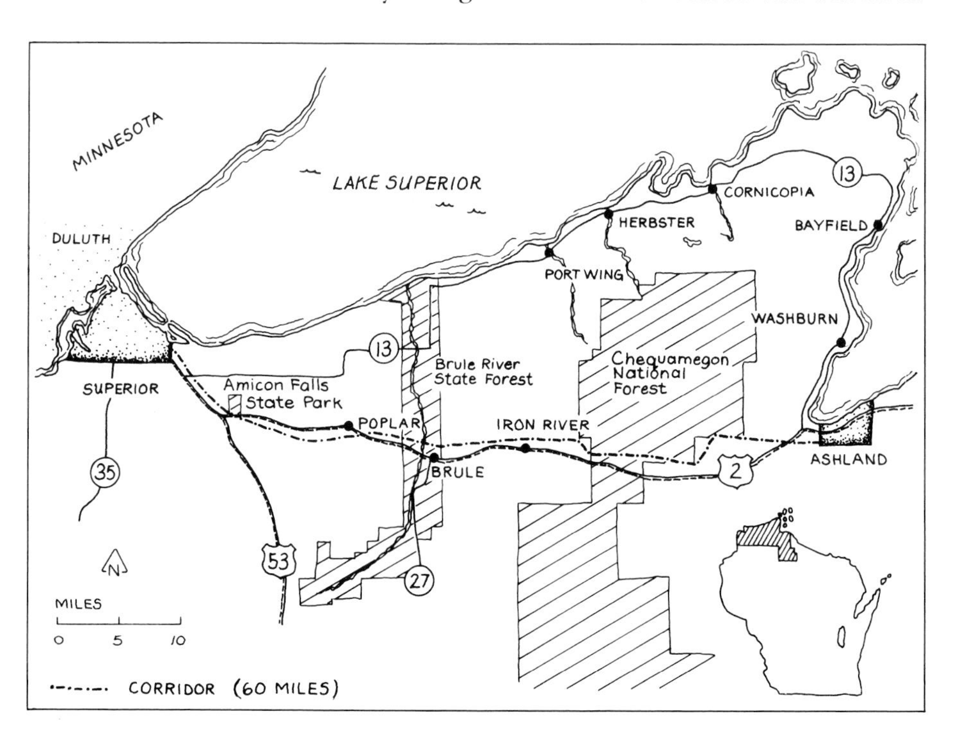

Surrounding Area

While in the area, you might want to explore other nearby public lands. Pattison, Lucius Woods (operated by Douglas County) and Copper Falls state parks are all short drives south of the trail. The North Country National Scenic Trail (a 3,200-mile corridor extending from Crown Point, New York, to the Lewis and Clark National Historic Trail in North Dakota) traverses northwestern Wisconsin, south of the Tri-County trail. Wandering north to Bayfield, you could plan an island sailing or camping adventure in the Apostle Islands National Lakeshore or visit Big Bay State Park on Madeline Island. Sailing, and deep-sea fishing charters are available in Bayfield.

TUSCOBIA STATE TRAIL

Barron, Washburn, Sawyer and Price counties. 75 miles; between Park Falls and Tuscobia (just north of Rice Lake).

Main Attraction

This is Wisconsin's longest trail, and the scenery is the most diverse. Mount up and ride through farmland and woodland, near lakes and wetlands and past rivers and streams.

Wisconsin's longest state trail also has the most scenic variety. If you hike, horseback ride or snowmobile the entire route, you'll pass farmland, forest-ringed bogs, cool lakes and trout streams and mixed hardwood/softwood forest.

The Tuscobia stretches along an abandoned railroad right-of-way that was built in the early 1900s to support the region's logging industry. Many spurs and connecting logging railroads fed a steady diet of hardwood logs (the white pine was largely logged by then) into the mainline for transport to the sawmills in Rice Lake, Park Falls and elsewhere. Farmers tried to cultivate the cutover lands but often failed unless they were lucky or smart enough to settle on the more fertile, flat and stone-free soils.

You can still see evidence of the area's past in the large stumps of white pines and hardwood trees, the traces of spur lines in the second-growth woods and the stony clearings. The trail has four distinct sections, separated by land use, history and geography.

Things To Do

The Red Cedar Valley section (about 13 miles) runs from the western terminus at Tuscobia to Birchwood. Much of this section is part of Wisconsin's 1,000-mile Ice Age National Scenic Trail that traces the farthest advance of the last glacier. On this stretch, you'll pass by farmland, several pothole lakes and marshes and the popular Red Cedar Lake area. You can fish for native brook trout in Tuscobia Creek or for brown trout in the Brill River.

The Blue Hills section, from Birchwood to Radisson (22 miles), is noteworthy because of the relative wilderness and beauty of the region. The present hills are the eroded quartzite roots of ancient mountains that may have rivaled the Rockies in height. Gorges, talus slopes, tumbling streams and lofty overlooks are trademarks of the Blue Hills. In this region of few road crossings, you might spot deer, black bears (rarely seen), bald eagles or ospreys. The Couderay River is known for canoeing and bass fishing. You can plan side trips into Sawyer and Rusk county forests, which cover most of the Blue Hills with over 70,000 acres of public land.

The Chippewa Valley section of the trail (20 miles) extends from Radisson to Loretta. The Chippewa River, popular for canoeing and fishing, is the main recreational attraction on this stretch of the Tuscobia. The trail passes next to Ojibwa State Park, the halfway point of the route and the only state campground along the way. The Brunet River (east of Winter) offers trout fishing upstream from the trail and muskie fishing downstream.

The Northwoods section, from Loretta to Park Falls (20 miles), traverses much of the old northwoods logging region of Wisconsin. Most of this portion of the trail is wild and isolated. The Tuscobia cuts

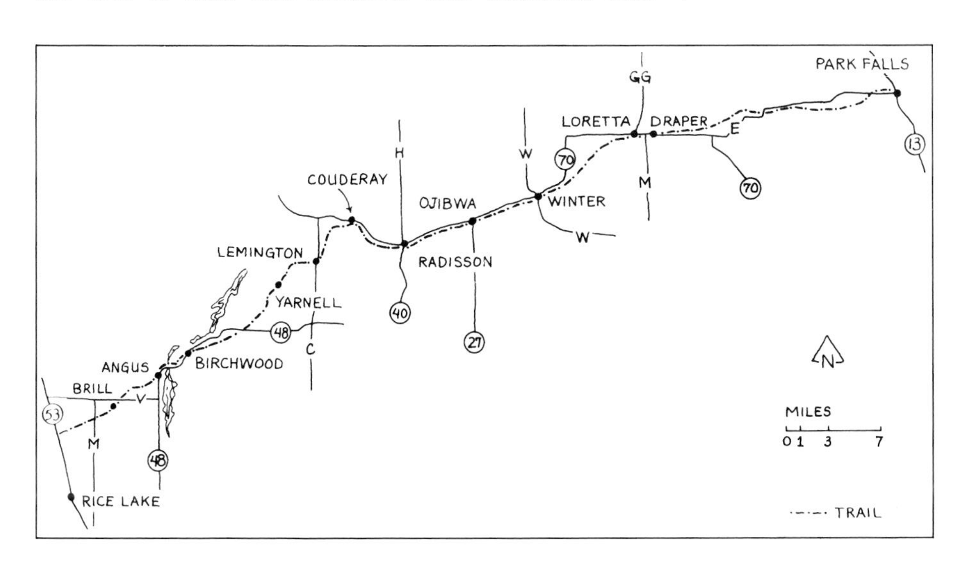

The changes in vegetation across the seasons make repeat visits to Wisconsin parklands worthwhile.

through parts of the Flambeau River State Forest and the Chequamegon National Forest. The Flambeau River attracts canoeists of all abilities because of its wilderness setting and mixture of exciting rapids and slower-paced stretches. Interested trail users may wish to get detailed Flambeau River and Chequamegon forest maps to plan side trips. On this section of the trail, you'll pass hardwood ridges, aspen, alder-willow lowlands and black spruce and tamarack swamps that provide great chances to see deer and other wildlife. Butternut Creek, west of Park Falls, is an excellent trout stream in a picturesque setting.

Most trail users are hikers, horseback riders and snowmobilers (ATVs and motorcycles are not allowed). The Tuscobia is not surfaced for bicyclists and there are many soft and uneven parts. Those visitors who still wish to bike on the trail may want to use a mountain bicycle with wide tires. Whether you explore the trail on foot, horse or snowmobile, be prepared to "rough it" because state facilities (besides Ojibwa State Park) are nonexistent. The Tuscobia is complete except for a few short sections that require detours onto roads that parallel the trail.

Most services are available at Rice Lake, Birchwood and Park Falls, though you can get basic necessities in the other trail communities. Check at local chambers of commerce about area private and public campgrounds.

Sawyer County has developed two snowmobile trails to complement the Tuscobia. The first is a nine-mile loop near Couderay. The second, near Draper, connects the Tuscobia State Trail with the snowmobile trails in the Flambeau River State Forest. Because of the snowmobiles, cross-country skiing is not ideal on the state trail, but there are many good ski trails in the area. Cross-country and snowmobile details are available at the DNR ranger station in Winter.

UPPER MISSISSIPPI RIVER NATIONAL WILDLIFE AND FISH REFUGE

284 miles, from the mouth of the Chippewa River (Wisconsin) nearly to Rock Island, Illinois. Wisconsin counties: Buffalo, Trempealeau, La Crosse, Vernon, Crawford and Grant. Refuge headquarters is in Winona, Minnesota, and the visitor contact station is in McGregor, Iowa. District offices are located in Winona, Minnesota; La Crosse, Wisconsin; McGregor, Iowa; and Savanna, Illinois.

Main Attraction

It seems fitting that the grand valley of the Father of Waters is home to a national wildlife refuge that has the longest boundaries of any in the lower 48 states. The scale of the Upper Mississippi River National Wildlife Refuge (about 200,000 acres through four states) is exceeded only by the vast river itself.

The refuge contains a variety of life zones and climatic conditions. Habitats include wooded bottom lands, extensive marshes, sloughs, ponds, wet meadows and sand prairie. For most of the refuge corridor, towering cliffs and steep, forested slopes line the river valley. Many species of plants and animals normally associated with more southern or northern geography extend their ranges along the Mississippi River Valley. Some 270 species of birds, 57 species of mammals, 45 species of amphibians and reptiles and 113 species of fish are found here.

Eleven dams and locks within the refuge form a series of pools that vary from 10 to 30 miles long. The dams have raised water levels, creating a maze of channels, sloughs, marshlands and open lakes over the bottom lands. Excellent stands of aquatic plants have developed, establishing habitat for waterfowl and other wildlife.

(continued on next page)

UPPER
MISSISSIPPI
RIVER

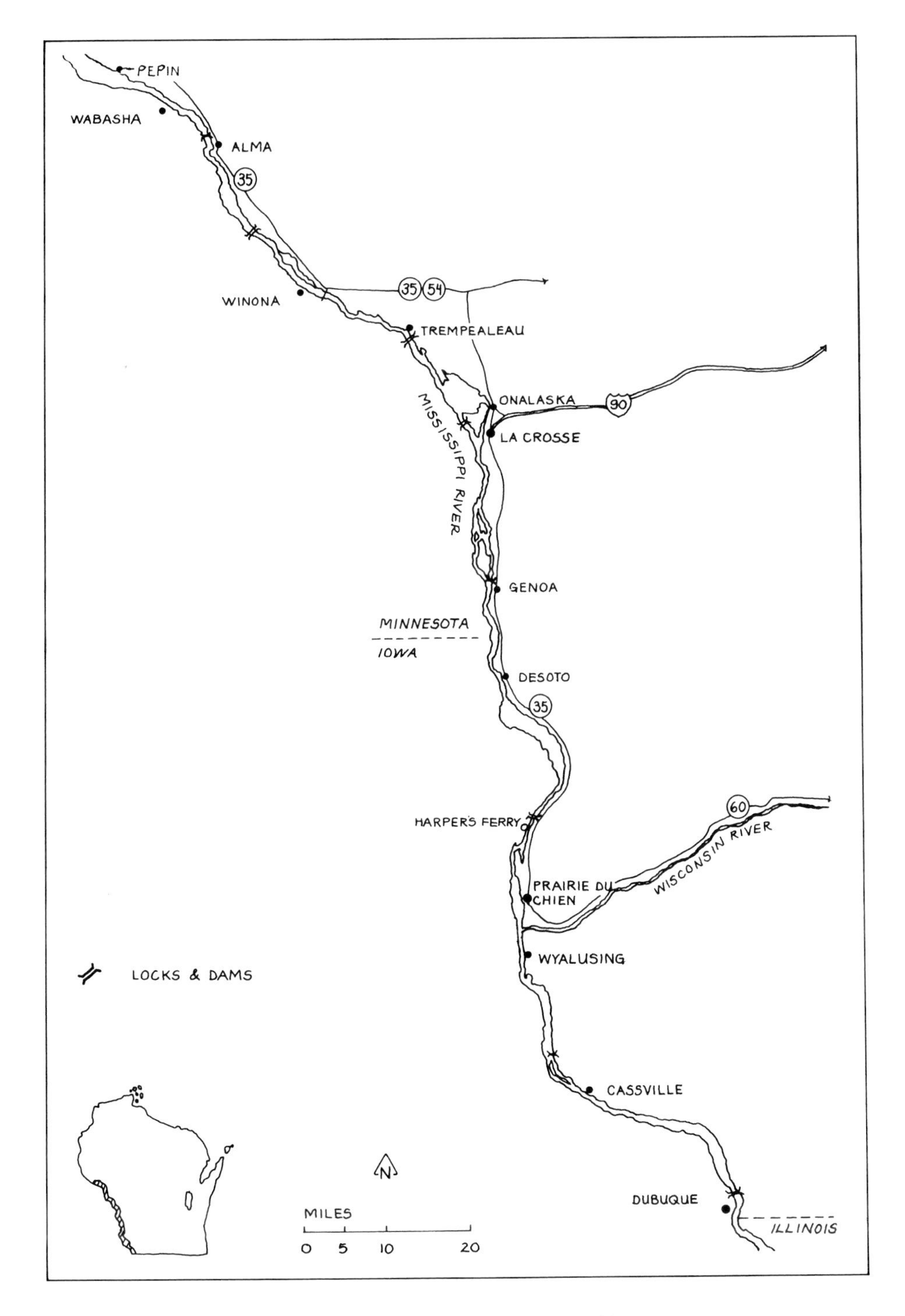

Millions visit the Mississippi River Valley for the wilderness character that remains despite man's presence.

Things To Do

Even considering all of man's changes, the Upper Mississippi River Valley still retains some of the wilderness beauty that the Indians and explorers knew. You can see this for yourself by scrambling to the top of a river bluff. (Wisconsin's Perrot, Wyalusing and Nelson Dewey state parks offer scenic hiking trails that crest river bluffs. The other three states also have their own Mississippi River parks.) The great cliffs still loom above the river. A carpet of woodlands shrouds the cities and other evidences of man's presence. From the peak of a lofty bluff, you can see the valley from the same perspective as the hawks that have circled overhead. The river has endured change yet still seems unspoiled.

The refuge, established in 1924, is primarily managed for wildlife, yet it attracts about three million recreationists each year. The most popular activities include wildlife observation, environmental education, boating, fishing, hunting, bird study and sightseeing. Tracing the history of the river valley is also fun. Signs and markers point out the sites of old Indian battlegrounds, villages, forts, trading posts and the routes of early explorers. Evidence of ancient mound-building tribes is found along the bluffs and bottom lands.

Nature lovers will want to visit during all seasons to view the 270 species of birds, 57 species of mammals, 45 species of amphibians and reptiles and 113 species of fish. Wow.

If you're interested in more details about the river's past, as well as the present, stop at the visitor contact station located on Highway 18 on the north edge of McGregor, Iowa. Lists of refuge birds, mammals, reptiles and amphibians are available here and at the district offices.

Fishing is popular year-round on the Upper Mississippi. Walleye, northern, sauger, bass, perch, crappie, sunfish and catfish are caught below the dams, in sloughs and in channels between islands. A state fishing license is required and state laws apply. Excursion trips and boat rentals are available at marinas, landings or municipal boat yards along the river. The navigation locks will pass your boat through the dams to the next pool. Some visitors choose to experience the river by houseboat (they can be rented from several places along the river). The pace is easy and you can fish and camp where you wish among the channels and islands.

Much of the refuge is open to hunting during state seasons, though 14 areas (over 41,000 acres) are closed for the protection of migratory waterfowl. After duck season, these areas are open to trapping and upland and big game hunting according to state and federal seasons. All state and refuge licensing and regulations apply.

Flora and Fauna

The Upper Mississippi Valley is a major migration route for birds. Thousands of tundra swans stop at favorite resting areas during the spring flight. Large numbers of canvasbacks use the refuge, especially during fall migration. At times, up to 75% of the canvasback continental population may be seen on pools 7 and 8 alone. The bottom lands are a favorite haunt of the wood duck. Thousands of these brilliantly marked birds feed in the protected sloughs and shallows and nest in the hollow trees along the islands and bluffs.

Bald eagles winter in the refuge, usually below the dams or near the mouths of tributaries where fish provide a ready food supply. Striking migrations of other birds can be observed during spring and fall when hordes of warblers, vireos, thrushes and sparrows drift through the trees and shrubs of the river islands and bluffs. You may notice the calls of pileated woodpeckers and whippoorwills in the remote woodlands.

The bottom lands are home to myriads of marsh and water birds such as herons and egrets. Muskrat, mink, beaver, otter, raccoon, skunk, weasel and fox also live here. White-tailed deer and a variety of small game are abundant in the forests.

Facilities

Modern campgrounds are available at various state, municipal, and commercial parks on both sides of the river. In Wisconsin, you can camp at Merrick, Perrot, Wyalusing and Nelson Dewey state parks. Primitive camping on the refuge islands and beaches is permitted for up to two weeks at one site.

The sandbars and beaches along the main channel attract thousands of visitors who are looking for picnicking and swimming spots. To avoid litter problems, carry trash bags for all garbage. Buried litter is usually dug up by animals or floated downstream during high water.

Surrounding Area

Besides the Wisconsin state parks already mentioned, you may wish to bike on the Great River or La Crosse River state trails, or canoe on the Lower Wisconsin State Riverway. Driving is a pleasant way to sightsee in the Upper Mississippi River Valley. A continuous system of highways designated as the Great River Road closely follows the refuge boundaries. For exceptional vistas of the river valley in Wisconsin, drive to Alma, La Crosse and Cassville. You'll also get impressive views at Winona and La Crescent, Minnesota, and at Lansing, McGregor and Dubuque, Iowa. Of course, the scenery that you see atop the Minnesota and Iowa bluffs is of Wisconsin.

WILLOW RIVER STATE PARK

St. Croix County. Three miles east of Hudson on I-94 to Highway 12 exit. Two miles north to junction of Highway 12 and County A. Continue north on A to park. Highway map index: 5-A.

Main Attraction

Three man-made dams on the Willow River form three flowages in Willow River State Park. Though most activities in the park revolve around the water, the river scenery, deep gorges and woodlands are attractions, too. There's also camping, hiking and winter sports to enjoy.

The land that the pioneers knew was virgin prairie. County A, which leads to the park, used to be a trail for Indians traveling to burial mounds above the St. Croix River. The path wound through prairie where buffalo, wolf and cougar lived. A pioneer wrote, "The grass was up to our horses' mouths; they would nip it as we rode." Scattered remnants of the prairie have been restored in the park.

Things To Do

The boat launch is on the south side of Little Falls Lake. No motors are allowed on the lake, making it ideal for fishing, canoeing and sailing. The three lakes contain northern pike, walleye, largemouth bass and panfish. There are brown trout in the lower Willow River, below the Little Falls Lake dam. Canoes and rowboats can be launched on Mill Pond and Mound Pond. Ask a park employee about access points for these two lakes. Whether fishing or looking, a leisurely boat trip is a fun and relaxing change of pace.

The beach area on the south side of Little Falls Lake is the busiest spot in the park. There's plenty of elbow room for throwing a softball, sunbathing or playing in the sand. Lifeguards are on duty in the summer and there is a bathhouse.

Most of the park's developed trails (over eight miles) wind through the woods and open fields below Mill Pond, on the south side of Little Falls Lake. Two of the seven trails are self-guided nature trails (Burr Oak and Hidden Ponds). You can hike along the Lower Willow trout stream or follow the shores of Little Falls Lake. The park's longest path, the Little Falls Trail, passes the gravesites of the William Scott family, the first settlers in this area. The view from here, overlooking the Willow River, is one of the most inspiring in the park.

Willow River State Park's naturalist program is active throughout the summer and designed for visitors who wish to discover more about the history, plants and animals of the area. Program schedules are posted in the park office and on all park bulletin boards. The nature center (near the beach) features attractive displays and a meeting room used for spe-

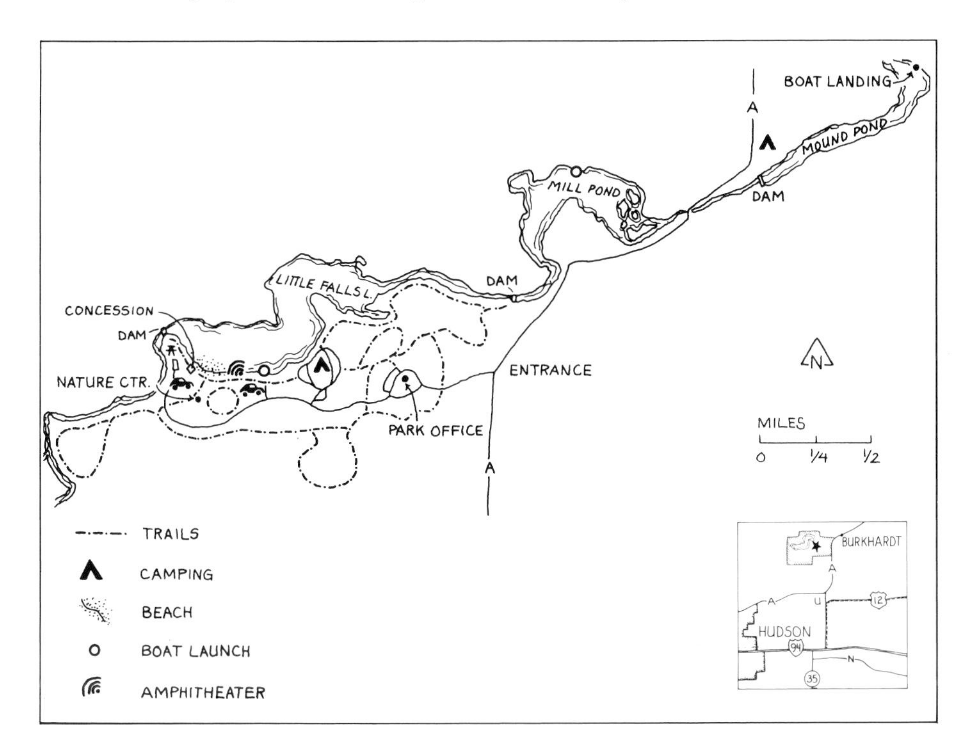

cial classes. The room also doubles as a warming house for cross-country skiers. The nature center is staffed by volunteers, many of whom are members of Wild Heritage, a local environmental education group.

Some of the prairie the pioneers knew has been restored here, and the Willow River flowages deserve serious attention from fishing enthusiasts.

Willow River's trails stay open in winter for cross-country skiing and hiking. Beginning and experienced skiers can use about eight miles of trails. Ice skating, sliding and tobogganing are allowed anyplace where the conditions are suitable.

You can winter camp in one of several walk-in sites in the park. Bring your fishing gear and try ice fishing in any of the three lakes. Snowmobiling is not allowed in the park's interior, but you can use the county trail, which cuts through the eastern portion of the park. The park's three dams are a favorite subject for photographers in the winter when moisture rising from the moving water fashions unusual ice sculptures.

Flora and Fauna

You can fish in any of the lakes, but take some time to observe the scenery and the wildlife, too. Paddling slowly along the shoreline at dawn you might see deer, muskrat, fox or beaver. At any time of day, you can see frogs, birds, wildflowers and plants. Maybe you'll see some species you hadn't noticed when hiking.

Facilities

After a swim you can eat lunch in the picnic grounds overlooking the lake, right next to the beach. You can buy groceries and picnic supplies at the park concession near the beach, or at stores in Burkhardt or Hudson.

The wooded 72-site family campground is also on the south shore of Little Falls Lake. Campground facilities include showers and 19 sites with electrical hookups. At the north end of the park, near the Mound Pond Dam, is a 150-person outdoor group camp. Reservations are accepted for both camping areas.

Surrounding Area

Willow River is one of Wisconsin's most popular parks because of its scenic beauty, large swimming beach and short driving distance from the Twin Cities metro area. Other state recreation facilities in the region include Hoffman Hills State Recreation Area and the Red Cedar State Trail near Menomonie. Kinnickinnic State Park is south of Willow River, near River Falls. The St. Croix National Scenic Riverway, headquartered in St. Croix Falls, flows just to the west of Willow River State Park. William O'Brien and Afton, two Minnesota state parks, are both short drives from Hudson.

In addition to the scenery, the gentle nature of the Willow River makes it a fine spot for family canoeing or boating.

NORTHWOODS

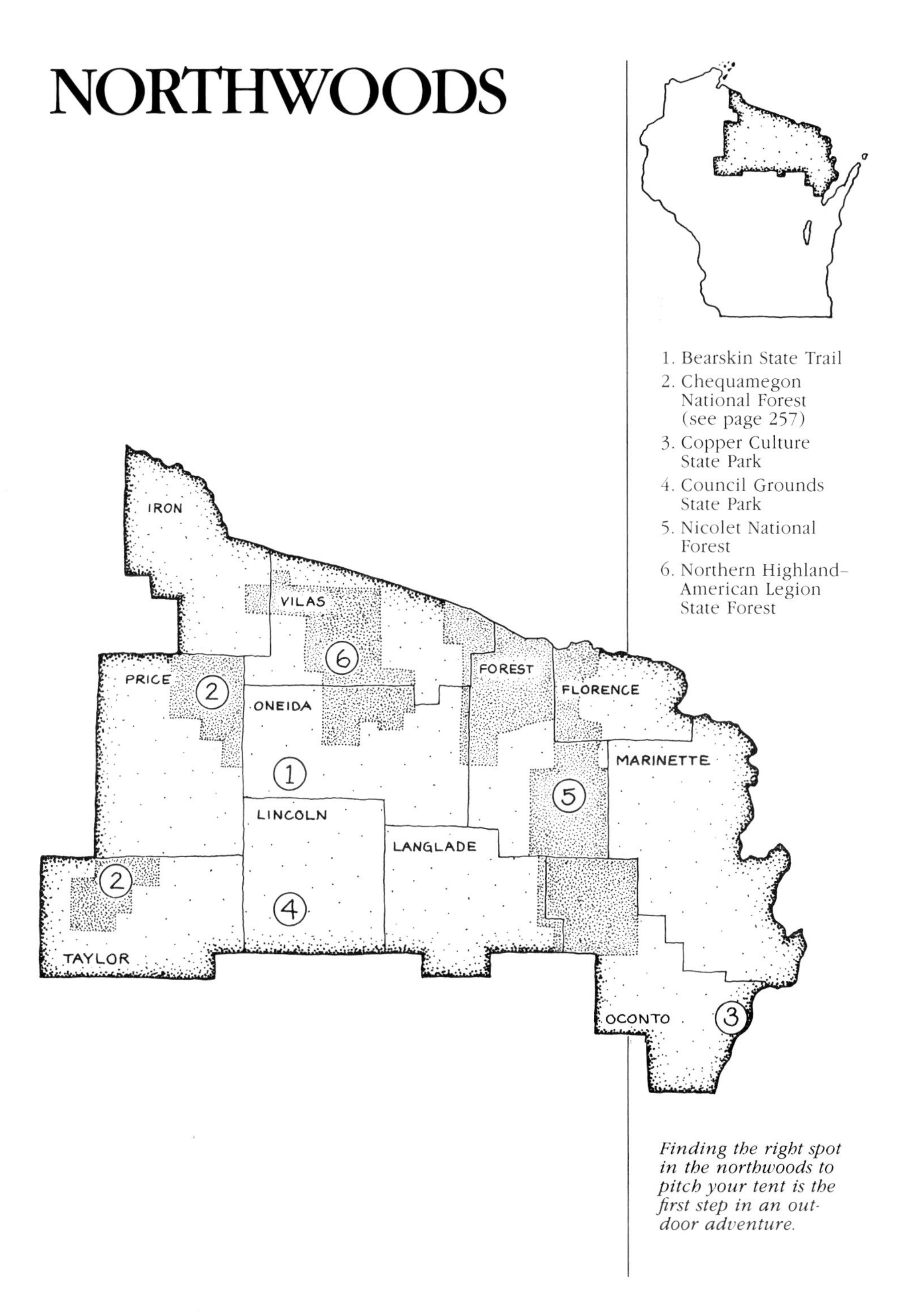

Finding the right spot in the northwoods to pitch your tent is the first step in an outdoor adventure.

BEARSKIN STATE TRAIL

Oneida County. 18 miles; between Minocqua and County K.

Main Attraction

The Bearskin State Trail winds through some of northern Wisconsin's most picturesque scenery. This is a trail that hikers, bikers and snowmobilers enjoy because of its many water crossings and access to several lakes. Two of the creeks that you'll see, Bearskin and Rocky Run, are excellent trout streams.

Things To Do

Because of several road crossings, access to the Bearskin Trail is easy. You can park behind the post office in Minocqua at the north end of the trail, on Blue Lake Road six miles south of Minocqua, or on County Highway K at the south end of the trail. Pack a picnic lunch and pause in the trail rest area on South Blue Lake.

The fishing in this part of Wisconsin is legendary, so as you travel the Bearskin Trail, pack a fishing rod for those places where the trail crosses a trout stream or passes a lake.

Lots of hikers and bikers tote fishing poles while on the Bearskin. You're in the midst of northern Wisconsin's famous fishing country up here, so take a trail break and drop a line in a lake or stream.

Currently, there's a small section of trail that is closed north of Goodnow, but bikers bypass this part on marked town roads. Gas, groceries and other supplies are available in Minocqua, Hazelhurst, Heafford Junction, and at the junction of County K and Highway 51.

Flora and Fauna

The northwoods forest and lake scenery and the chance to spot wildlife from a bicycle make the Bearskin Trail a favorite among families. Bicyclists will pedal past hardwood stands of oak and maple and second-growth woods that have replaced the majestic

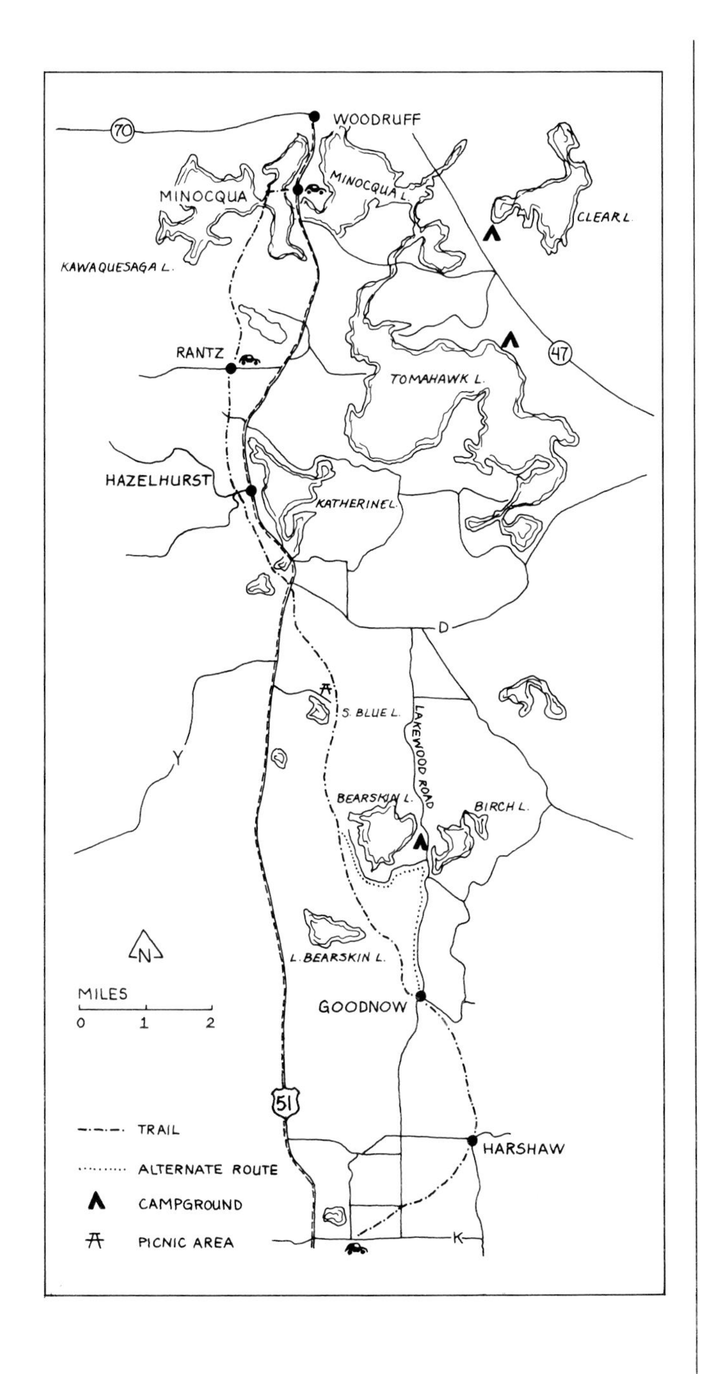
WOODRUFF
70
MINOCQUA
MINOCQUA L.
CLEAR L.
KAWAQUESAGA L.
RANTZ
47
TOMAHAWK L.
HAZELHURST
KATHERINE L.
D
S. BLUE L.
LAKEWOOD ROAD
Y
BEARSKIN L.
BIRCH L.
N
L. BEARSKIN L.
MILES
0 1 2
GOODNOW
51
TRAIL
HARSHAW
ALTERNATE ROUTE
CAMPGROUND
PICNIC AREA
K

The Bearskin Trail travels through country dense with lakes. Pause on the bridges for sweeping views of the wooded shoreline.

white pine forests that were cut down in the late 19th century. Berry hunters like to keep a lookout for blueberry, blackberry and raspberry bushes when they're in season. You can also try to identify the various plant communities as you pass grassy openings or bogs. Lucky bikers may surprise a deer on the trail—and look up in time to see a bald eagle, osprey, hawk or heron.

Facilities

Although public campgrounds are not available along the trail (except those in the state forest), there are private campgrounds in the area. You could easily coordinate a trip on the Bearskin with a more extensive visit to the Northern Highland–American Legion State Forest.

Surrounding Area

The Woodruff-Minocqua area, just to the north of the trail, has many resorts and tourist attractions, among them a popular water-ski show.

For regional tourist information, stop at the visitor centers in Woodruff and Minocqua. To find out more about the bike trail or the Northern Highlands–American Legion State Forest, contact the Trout Lake Forestry Headquarters at Boulder Junction or the Woodruff Area Headquarters (DNR).

COPPER CULTURE STATE PARK

Oconto County. At the end of Mill Street in Oconto. Highway map index: 6-I.

Main Attraction

Copper Culture is one of the state's archaeological parks, currently operated by the city of Oconto. The park is small, but it offers a lot for history buffs. It has one of the oldest cemeteries in the United States with 200 burials. The ones that have been examined contain burial implements of stone, copper, bone and shells, placed in the graves as burial offerings.

The park's name refers to the Old Copper Culture People: nomadic hunters who quarried copper from natural deposits in northern Michigan and Wisconsin. Under repeated heating and hammering, copper nuggets could be fashioned into spear tips, knives, fishhooks, bracelets and other tools and ornaments. The center for the Old Copper Culture was in Wisconsin and the upper peninsula of Michigan, though Copper Culture artifacts have been found in parts of Ontario, Manitoba and Minnesota. You can see some of the artifacts on display in the Belgian homestead in the park.

Archaeology is the attraction at this park. Artifacts found here date from thousands of years ago.

Surrounding Area

This is a peaceful place for a picnic or a walk on the park grounds. Besides the park, Oconto has a large variety of year-round activities for visitors. Local Hollywood Park has a swimming pool, playground and camping facilities. Fishing is good in nearby Green Bay, and the Oconto area is a favorite of hunters for its large and small game. While having fun around Oconto, make sure to find out more about its first residents at Copper Culture State Park.

COPPER CULTURE STATE PARK

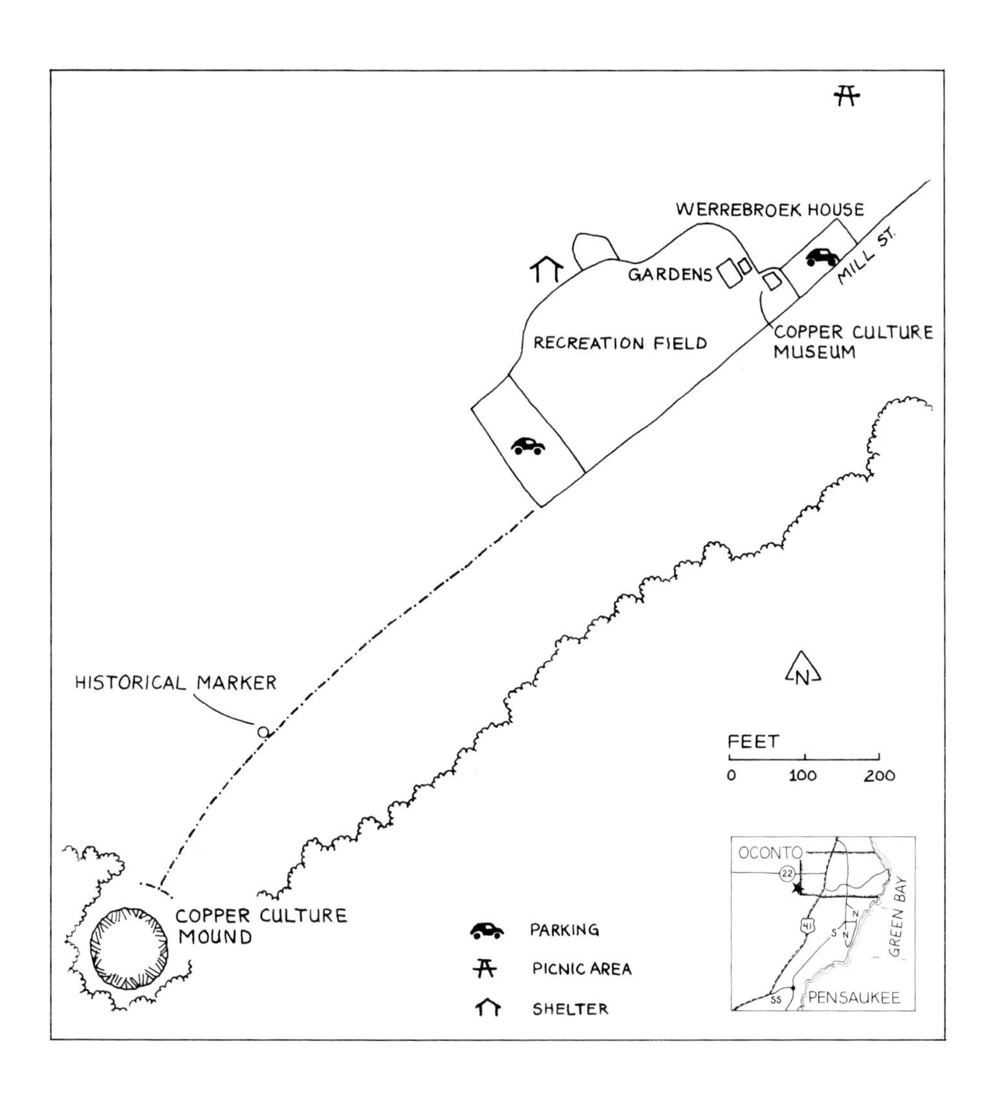

COUNCIL GROUNDS STATE PARK

Lincoln County. Three miles northwest of Merrill on Highway 107. Highway map index: 5-F.

Main Attraction

Council Grounds State Park, on the Wisconsin River, has been a gathering place for centuries. Artifacts found in the park suggest that a Woodland Indian village grew here about 600 A.D. Around 1,000 years later, Ojibwa (Chippewa) Indians established a village in the same area as the prehistoric community. They trapped fur in this region to trade with the French.

The Ojibwa gathered in the present park land for annual tribal festivities. They canoed down tributary streams of the Wisconsin River to meet for many days and nights of celebration. During the logging era, hundreds of rivermen met here each year to sort out some 600 million feet of floating logs for the sawmills downstream.

There's plenty to do on land, and even more to do on the water during all seasons here. Hiking beneath the park's majestic white pines is a good example.

Today, Council Grounds is a gathering place for visitors who like water sports, camping and relaxation.

Things To Do

While the virgin timber in this area fell to the lumberjack's axe in the late 19th century, the white pines in the park, some of them 80 to 120 years old, are still impressive. The largest reach a maximum height of 124 feet with a diameter of 21 inches. Take the time to hike among these forest giants on the Big Pines Nature Trail or in the Krueger Pines Scientific Area. The scientific area is named for the state senator who was a leading conservationist and an advocate of natural resources programs.

After your stroll through the park's big pines, have some fun and try the Vita Course. This exercise and jogging circuit is designed to promote strength, stamina and coordination. Signs spaced along the running trail explain how to correctly perform the exercises. Kids enjoy the Vita Course too, especially if they can outdistance their parents.

Council Grounds visitors benefit from a volunteer naturalist program that sponsors guided hikes and evening activities on Wednesdays, Fridays and Saturdays from mid-June through Labor Day. Schedules

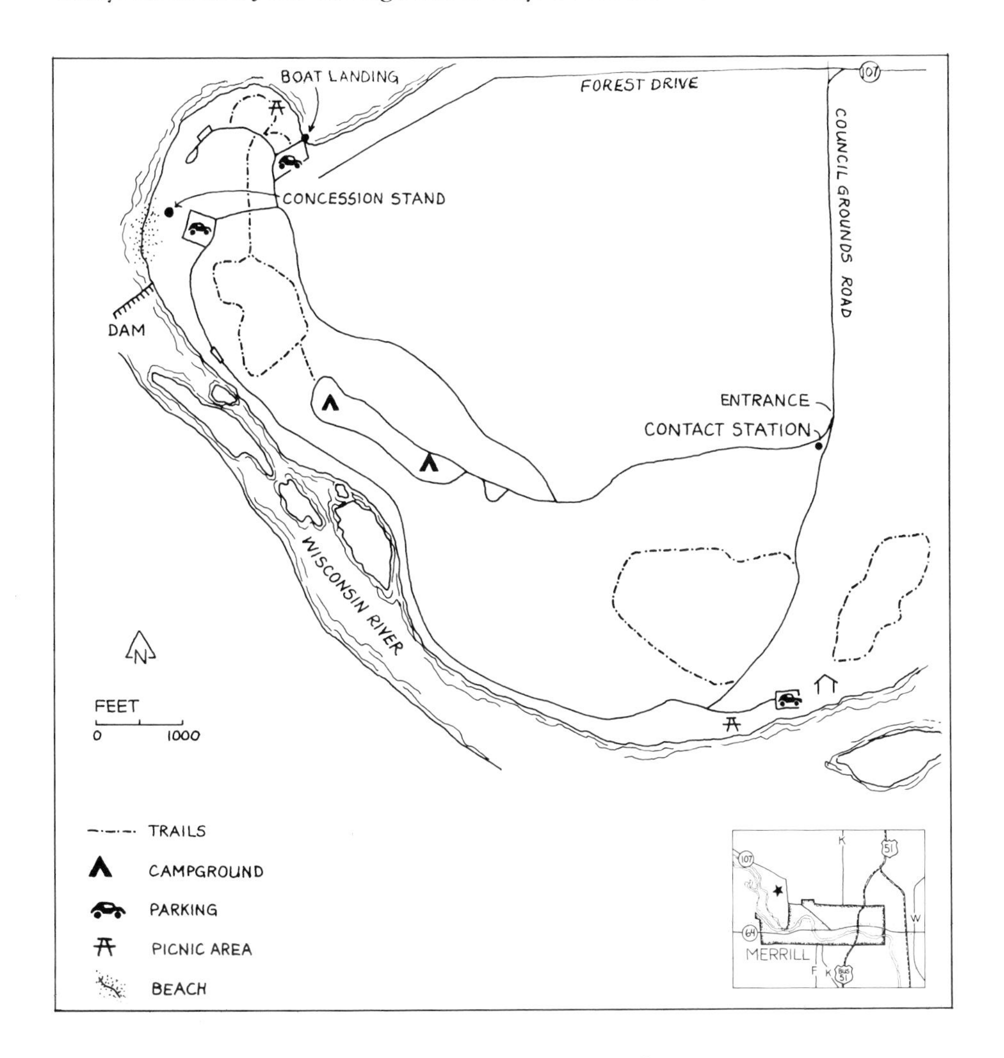

are given to campers and are posted on park bulletin boards. The park is also happy to have a Volunteer Campground Host program. Hosts usually are in the campground from early June to mid-October.

Popular water activities include boating, canoeing, waterskiing, swimming and fishing. A lifeguard is on duty at the park beach during the summer months. The "Mother Nature" concession stand, near the beach, rents canoes, paddleboats and a pontoon boat and sells firewood, snacks and grocery items. Profits from the concession stand, operated by the Merrill Area Jaycees, will be targeted for improvement projects in the park.

The land that is now the park has been a gathering place for centuries. That part hasn't changed as families and other groups gather here for picnics.

Fishing boats can be launched near the north picnic grounds, and anglers try for muskie, northern, walleye, bass and panfish. Canoeing is another favorite pastime here, because it's easy to paddle around the Alexander Flowage or lazily drift below the dam toward Merrill. In winter, the frozen flowage attracts ice fishermen while other snow-time visitors prefer to hike or ski through the park's majestic pines.

Facilities

Two picnic areas serve the park at opposite ends with a modern campground in the middle. Both picnic grounds are spacious. A family can enjoy a rousing volleyball game and not crowd the couple playing frisbee or the daydreamer musing beneath a big tree. Whichever picnic area you choose, you'll have a good view of the Wisconsin River.

Surrounding Area

Merrill has 11 city parks with a variety of facilities. A scenic drive north of Merrill on Highway 107 follows the Wisconsin River to Tomahawk, 25 miles away. There are free water-ski shows in town three times a week. Check the Tomahawk Information Center for time schedules. Wausau, about 15 miles to the south of Merrill, is the home of the Leigh Yawkey Woodson Art Museum, famous for wildlife art.

NICOLET NATIONAL FOREST

Langlade, Oconto, Oneida, Vilas, Forest and Florence counties. 657,000 acres. Forest headquarters is in Rhinelander; district offices are in Eagle River, Florence, Lakewood and Laona.

Main Attraction

The loon's sorrowful, haunting call echoes across Perch Lake at dusk, perhaps snapping a camper out of a campfire reverie. Of the five campsites spaced around the 51-acre lake in this walk-in campground, you may spot only a couple campfires mid-week.

The solitude suits the loons (and campers) just fine. Growing people-pressure forces the loons to retreat to isolated lakes, to the privacy they need to reproduce. They can still find homes among many of the more than 1,200 lakes of the Nicolet National Forest.

The Nicolet National Forest was created in 1933 as a way to help the forests recover. Today the Nicolet is managed to provide a variety of natural products and public services, including timber, water, mineral and wildlife resources, as well as outdoor recreation.

Things To Do

The Perch Lake Campground is one of several non-motorized, walk-in areas that, along with three wilderness tracts, provide more than 33,000 acres for year-round backpacking and primitive camping opportunities in the Nicolet. This particular spot (in the Florence Ranger District) is a favorite in the forest because you can hike in or canoe to the campsites. Perch Lake is also connected by a one-mile trail to the Lauterman Lake Walk-In Campground and Lauterman National Recreation Trail. In addition, the Whisker Lake Wilderness Area (7,500 acres) is just east of the Perch Lake parking lot. As in any of the national forest's primitive or wilderness areas, no drinking water is provided and users must boil, filter or chemically treat their water.

The Nicolet National Forest is known as the "Cradle of Rivers" because six of the seven canoeable rivers that run through or adjacent to Nicolet rise within the forest boundaries. The rivers (Brule, Oconto, Peshtigo, Pine, Popple, Wisconsin and Wolf) each have developed national forest campgrounds either on the river or within a 15-minute drive. The Pine, Popple and Pike (east of Nicolet in Marinette County) are part of the State Wild Rivers System. The

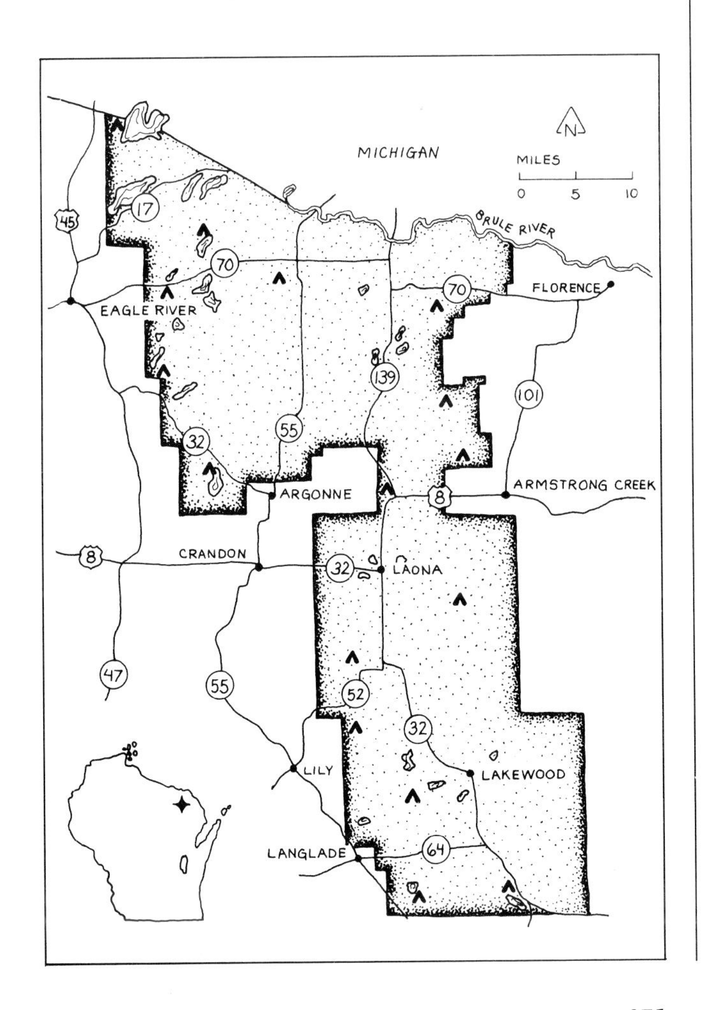

Wolf River is part of the National Wild and Scenic Rivers System.

The river scenery is vintage Northwoods: stretches of tall pines and hardwoods through rock outcroppings, swamps and open meadows. Your chances of observing wildlife or catching fish are good. There's plenty of challenging white water for experienced canoeists, kayakers and rafters, but there are long stretches of quiet water, too. You can get river information about conditions, difficulty, maps and lists of outfitters and guide services from the forest headquarters and the district offices.

The Nicolet National Forest doesn't cater only to those who choose to rough it. Everyone can find some outdoor fun here. Besides its 1,200 lakes, the forest also contains about 1,100 miles of trout streams. Fishing for trout, northern, bass, muskie and walleye is very good. The forest is also noted as a productive hunting area for deer, bear, grouse and waterfowl. Swimming, canoeing, boating and rafting are popular, plus there are more than 80 miles of cross-country ski trails and 520 miles of snowmobile and interpretive trails. Other trails are developed for hiking and snowshoeing.

The Nicolet National Forest maintains at least 11 designated hiking trails. Two of these, the Lauterman and Ed's Lake, are National Recreation Trails. Some are interpretive trails and some double as hunting and snowmobile trails during other seasons. Cross-country skiers also have a variety of trails to choose from. The Lauterman and Anvil trails are the most popular, though others are less crowded.

Hunting is part of the forest's recreation picture, and is part of its wildlife management program, too. General hunting and trapping regulations that apply to the state of Wisconsin also apply to the Nicolet National Forest. For specifics on hunting and trapping regulations and license fees, contact the Wisconsin DNR, Box 7921, Madison, WI 53707 (608-266-1877).

Some areas of the forest are open for hunting and trapping but are closed to motor vehicles. The major walk-in-only zones include the Headwater, Blackjack Springs and Whisker Lake wilderness areas. Not all

(opposite page)

A late autumn frost may greet hunters who come to the forest for a variety of game.

NICOLET NATIONAL FOREST

of the lands within the boundaries of the Nicolet National Forest are publicly owned and may not be open for hunting and trapping. Check with forest headquarters staff in Rhinelander or at one of the district offices to find out details about land ownership.

White-tailed deer is the most popular big game animal hunted in the Nicolet National Forest. The current deer population is about 24,000 animals, with the largest concentration found in the forest's southern section. In the past few years, hunters have harvested about 4,000 deer annually. Bow hunters account for 10% of the harvest, though interest in archery hunting has been increasing steadily each year. The forest black bear population numbers about 400 animals.

There's a place for both animals and man to find solitude in the forest's wilderness areas, and the wild rivers that cross the forest are some of the best in Wisconsin.

Most of the hunting trails in the Nicolet include networks of old roads that have been seeded to a clover/grass mixture and mowed periodically. These trails provide forage for many types of wildlife, including deer and ruffed grouse. The use of dogs for bear hunting and baiting for deer and bear hunting is allowed within most of the forest. Hunters should check with the DNR for specific regulations and for hunting maps.

Flora and Fauna

The forest trails wind through a variety of tree cover, including maple, birch, hemlock, spruce, aspen, balsam fir and pine. These trees are mostly second growth, taking over after northeastern Wisconsin's best timber had been slashed and many fires had devastated the Northwoods by the early 1900s. You can get a glimpse of the forest's former glory by hiking the Franklin Lake Interpretive Trail, where a stand of lofty white pines is preserved.

Facilities

Picnicking, camping and other outdoor recreational activities on Nicolet National Forest land are generally unrestricted. No permits are required, and small campfires are permitted. The only exception is at designated facilities where camping and picnicking are restricted to the sites provided on a first-come, first-served basis. Fees are charged at most developed campgrounds (no electrical hookups provided). No reservations are accepted except for the group campsites.

You can have two types of camping experiences at Nicolet. The Forest Service maintains 27 auto-access and walk-in campgrounds, or you can camp in dispersed camping areas, which are most anywhere on forest land not posted as closed to camping. Visitors in dispersed areas should be experienced "no-trace" campers, meaning that they practice good woodsmanship, leave the campsite as clean as or cleaner than they found it and pack out whatever they pack in.

Visitors may wish to check at the forest headquarters in Rhinelander or at one of the four district offices for details about camping. Some campgrounds are on lakes or rivers known for their good fishing, boating or canoeing. Others may be excellent swimming lakes or near to hiking and hunting trails. The forest offices can also tell you how to get detailed topographic maps of the region. A Forest Visitor Map is for sale for $1.00.

NORTHERN HIGHLAND–AMERICAN LEGION STATE FOREST

Iron, Vilas and Oneida counties. Forest headquarters is at Trout Lake, near Boulder Junction. DNR area headquarters is in Woodruff. Contact stations (open daily June–August) are at Clear Lake and Crystal Lake.

Main Attraction

Even wearing snowshoes, you can work up a sweat hiking through the deep snow to one of the wilderness lakes in the Northern Highland–American Legion State Forest. You're hunting bald eagles today and your camera is poised under your parka. As you scan the treetops for a nest, one of the awesome birds takes off from a tall white pine across the lake to fish in the headwaters of the Wisconsin River. A few quick shots—maybe you caught him.

It wasn't too long ago that the cry "Timber!" echoed through the virgin forests of northern Wisconsin. The present state forest land produced some of the prime pine logs of the Paul Bunyan era. The 220,000-acre forest still produces timber as well as provides for recreation and the protection of wildlife and watersheds.

The forest is in one of the most concentrated lake districts in the world, and the headwaters of both the Wisconsin and Chippewa-Flambeau river systems are here, too.

The forest is in one of the most concentrated lake districts in the world, and is also the headwaters of the two largest river basins in Wisconsin: the Wisconsin River and the Chippewa-Flambeau River systems. The warning cries of loggers have been replaced by the happy sounds of people enjoying the lakes and streams, wild areas, trails and campgrounds in all seasons.

Things To Do

For those who prefer to canoe-camp or backpack, the forest has a lot to offer. A hundred or more canoe campsites are spaced along the many miles of forest waterways. Camping is free, but limited to one night per site with access only by watercraft. Ask the ranger for canoe route maps and information about rapids. It's easy to plan long or short trips because of the network of roads and access points. Rentals, shuttle service, supplies and outfitters are available in the forest communities. Use common sense while canoeing, being aware of wind conditions or fast-forming squalls that can sweep suddenly across some of the larger lakes.

The fishing can be exciting in the forest waters. Try matching wits with the famous muskie, and test your skills at landing one of these spunky trophies. The fishing is good for northern pike, walleye, bass, trout

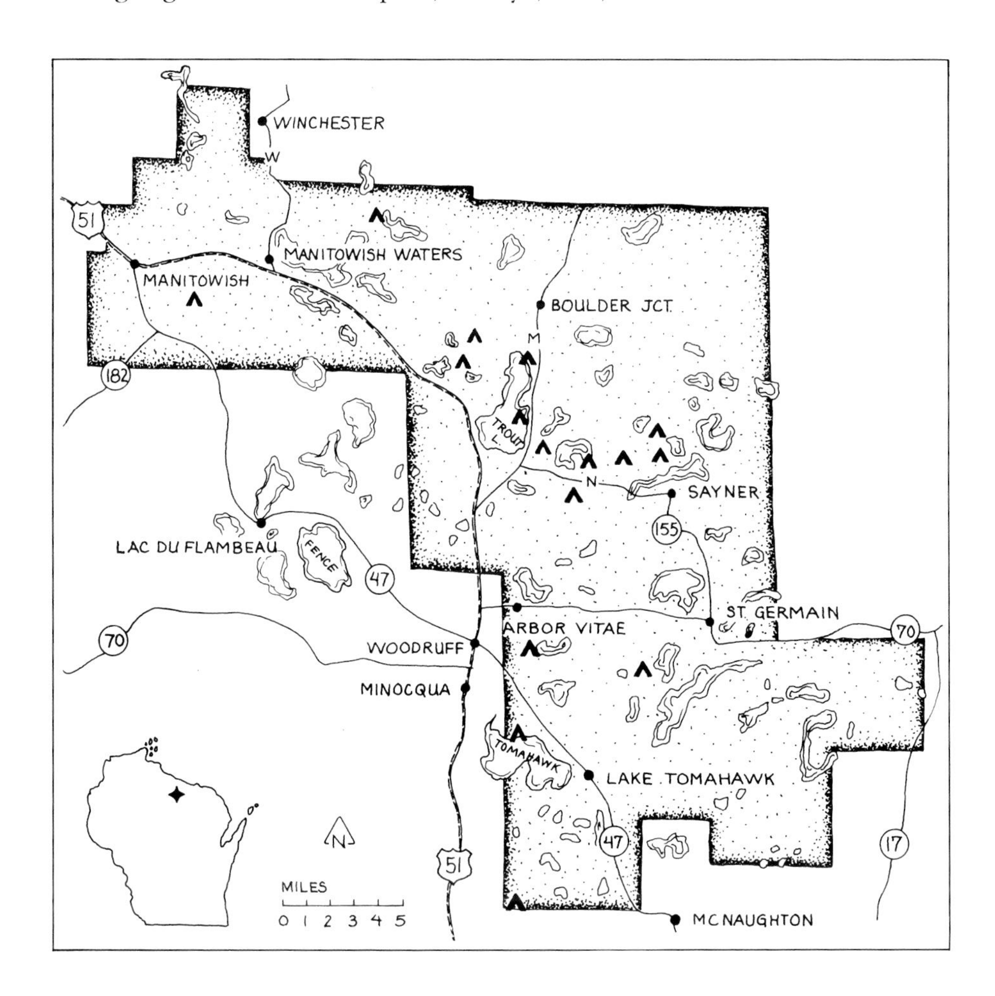

and panfish, too. For some anglers, autumn is the time for a northwoods fishing trip because "that's when the fish bite best." Other outdoor people start to daydream about hunting when the leaves turn. Subject to certain regulations, all state forest land is open to hunting of large and small game. Check hunting regulations for exact opening and closing dates.

The hiker has the chance to see the forest as it has been for hundreds of years. Some knowledge of forest birds will help you to recognize the mound-like nest of the loon while hiking along a lakeshore in spring. Listen for its haunting call.

The state forest has miles of hiking trails, logging roads and self-guided nature trails to explore. Acquaint yourself with the forest beforehand by participating in the evening programs at Crystal Lake Campground, which include guest speakers, slide shows and movies. Details of these weekly summer events are posted in the campgrounds. The rangers can also suggest nearby vistas where you can get a broader view of the forest and lakes. Be sure to ask about trail maps and seasonal hiking conditions.

It's easier to observe and track wildlife when the state forest is buried in snow, but most winter visitors have other tracks on their minds. An extensive network of snowmobile trails links almost all of the regional communities. Cross-country skiers can practice their stride on miles of marked and unmarked forest trails.

If you have the proper gear, consider a winter camping trip in the state forest. Clear Lake Campground stays open during the winter for the hardy few who like their camping snowy, cold and uncrowded. You can try ice fishing for that big one you missed last summer, or tramp through the snowy woods on snowshoes. A camera protected from moisture and cold packs easily for a winter ski or hike. And a picture of a lone skier on a frozen lake with the sun peeking through the trees can tell more about your state forest adventures than a whole season of "fish" stories.

After the snows melt and the trees shade the roads again, come back to camp on a different lake. Bring

(opposite page)

Self-guided nature trails provide information about the forest to help young explorers.

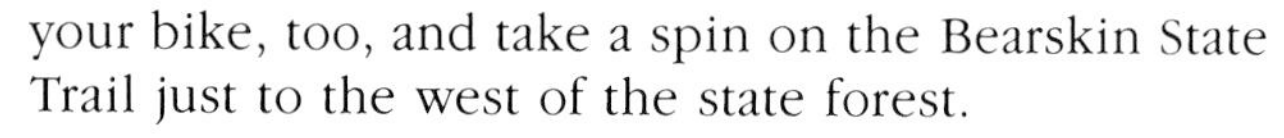

your bike, too, and take a spin on the Bearskin State Trail just to the west of the state forest.

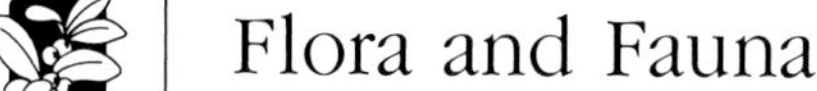

Flora and Fauna

Thousands of state forest acres and more than 60 lakes within its boundaries are classified as wilderness areas or other wild resource zones. Development is limited or prohibited in these zones to preserve their natural state. This is good news to the rare or endangered species that live in the forest, like the spotted salamander and the bobcat. Lucky visitors may spot a soaring osprey or a Cooper's hawk.

Facilities

Individual wilderness campsites with boat or walk-in access are available in the forest. You can backpack on over 30 miles of marked trails, but first you must pick up a free special permit at the Trout Lake Headquarters or at the Woodruff Area Office. Reservations are accepted at the wilderness sites.

Boaters, canoeists and fishermen can enjoy a break at one of the ten recently developed shore lunch sites. All of these lunch sites are on state land and are accessible by watercraft only. Each site has a dock, picnic table and grill, furnished by the Lakeland Chapter of Muskies, Inc. Seven lunch sites are on Tomahawk Lake, and one each on Minocqua, Carroll and Little Arbor Vitae lakes. No fees are required to either launch on these lakes or use the shore lunch sites. The sites, however, are strictly day use with no camping allowed. For more information, contact one of the state forest headquarters or the Greater Minocqua Chamber of Commerce.

Wilderness etiquette prevails at the shore lunch sites as well as at any of the primitive sites in the forest: carry out all nonburnables and leave the site cleaner than you found it.

Most of the 18 family and two group campgrounds in the forest provide boat landings, because there's a lake waiting for you at each campground. Even day-use areas such as picnic grounds and waysides are usually tucked under the trees along a lake or stream.

For a detailed index and map of campsites, day-use areas and trails, write to the DNR at Rt. 1, Box 45, Boulder Junction, WI 54512.

Surrounding Area

If you want to explore the state forest but would like to know where to find a motel, cottage or restaurant, write to the local or county chamber of commerce for information about the area that you'd like to visit.

SOUTHERN GATEWAY

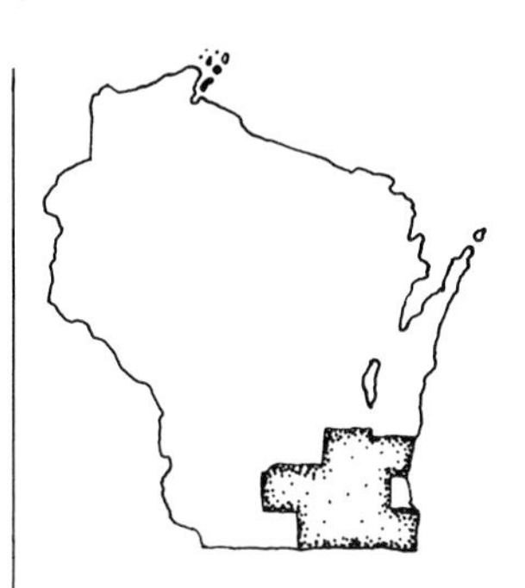

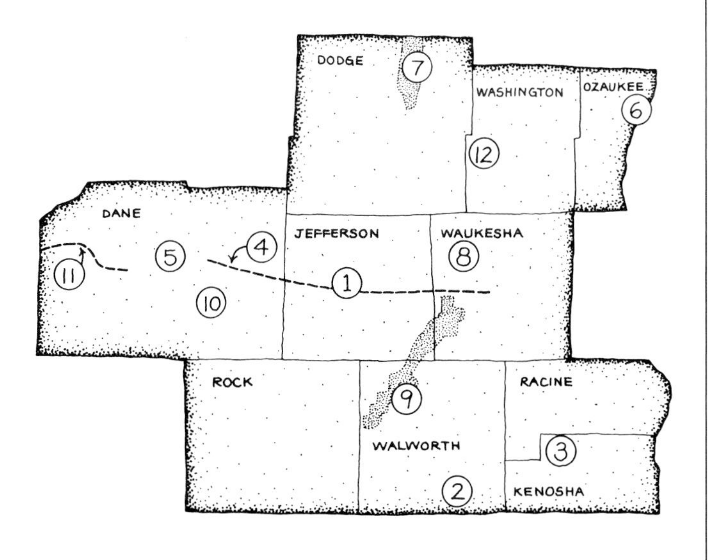

1. Aztalan State Park
2. Big Foot Beach State Park
3. Bong State Recreation Area
4. Glacial Drumlin State Trail
5. Governor Nelson State Park
6. Harrington Beach State Park
7. Horicon Marsh Wildlife Area and Horicon National Wildlife Refuge
8. Kettle Moraine State Forest—Lapham Peak Unit
9. Kettle Moraine State Forest—Southern Unit
10. Lake Kegonsa State Park
11. Military Ridge State Trail
12. Pike Lake State Park

(opposite page)

While nothing can replace the vast forests that were once here, state parklands seek to restore and preserve their beauty for future generations.

AZTALAN STATE PARK

Jefferson County. Three miles east of Lake Mills on County B. Highway map index: 10-G.

Main Attraction

One of Wisconsin's oldest mysteries surrounds the silent stockade at Aztalan State Park. The ancient Indian village still hides most of its secrets following more than a century of probing by archaeologists.

Ponder the mysteries of this ancient Indian village as you enjoy a hike or a picnic on the park grounds.

The lack of enlightening discoveries about the village has prompted some local myths. One story, originated by the settlement's discoverer, N. F. Hyer, in 1836, was that it was the birthplace of the Aztecs. Hyer, speculating that the Aztecs migrated from Wisconsin to Mexico, was responsible for the park's name. Another myth was based on evidence that the people were cannibals. A state historical marker at the park notes that this custom made the Aztalanians "unsatisfactory neighbors" to native Wisconsin tribes. Actually, investigations have shown that cannibalism was not common, and may have been part of a ceremony.

Some scholars think that the people of Aztalan may have been more advanced than the nearby Woodland Indian tribes. The Aztalanians are similar to Indians in the Cahokia Village area of western Illinois (near St. Louis) and could have emigrated to Wisconsin. Both groups of Indians are part of the Middle Mississippian culture who were influenced by the pyramid-building Aztecs of Mexico. The former were characterized by temple mounds, palisaded villages, complex pottery and crafts, an agricultural base and large communities.

The major mystery of Aztalan, occupied from about 1100 to 1300 A.D., is what happened to the village and its people. Local tribes could have destroyed Aztalan or a prairie fire could have forced them out.

Maybe they were killed or absorbed into neighboring tribes. No one knows for sure.

Things To Do

While Aztalan doesn't tell everything it knows about past events, it provides a peaceful setting to contemplate its mysteries and enjoy nature. Today, you can imagine life in the village while picnicking near the partially restored stockade. Because the focus has been shifted from excavation to restoration, parts of the old log stockade around the village site and two large ceremonial mounds have been reconstructed. Beyond the stockade walls to the northwest is a series of nine conical burial mounds.

This is a good place for hiking and taking pictures because of its history and uniqueness. In the future,

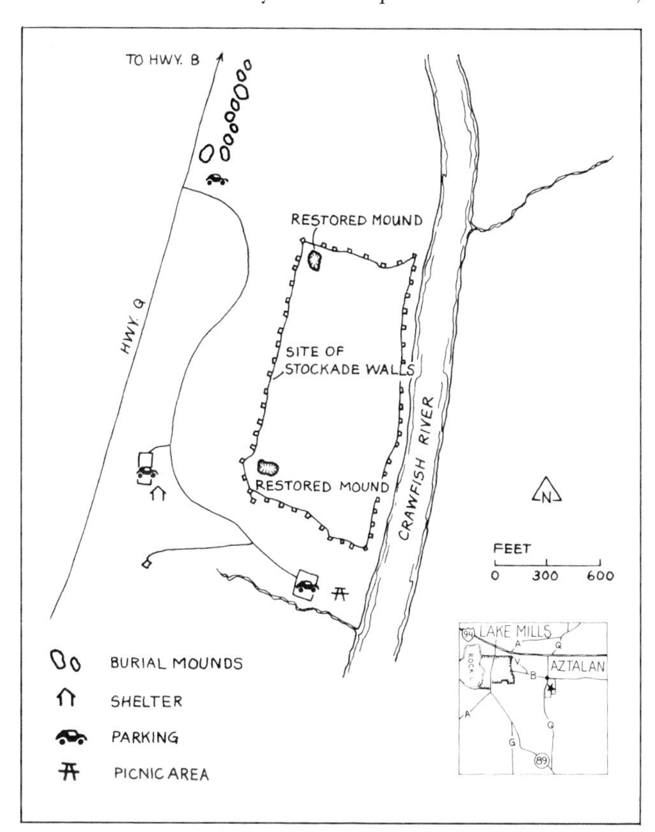

The stockade at Aztalan rises above the grassy field as it did hundreds of years ago.

additional hiking paths are planned as well as the reconstruction of some Indian homes and ceremonial structures. An information center and museum will also be built on the site.

Interested visitors may want to stop at the Aztalan Museum next to the state park grounds. Run by the Lake Mills–Aztalan Historical Society; the museum is the only remaining structure from a once-bustling 19th-century settlement called Pioneer Aztalan. You'll see displays of artifacts, plus articles, maps and documents from Wisconsin's pioneer days. The museum site also features three log cabins.

Flora and Fauna

The 172-acre park is mostly prairie with a small oak woods. Along the Crawfish River are wet shrub communities that contain cottonwood, willow, sumac and burr oak trees. Fishing is generally poor, although you might catch some northern, walleye or catfish.

Facilities

Curiosity about this Indian ghost town attracts thousands of visitors each year, not only to speculate about Aztalan's fate, but to relax as well. Park facilities include a picnic area by the Crawfish River, a group shelter and over three miles of hiking trails. This is a day-use-only park; camping is not allowed. State park admission stickers are not required here.

Surrounding Area

Aztalan is an easy drive from Madison and Milwaukee. The park is in a region that contains a number of other state recreation lands. Governor Nelson, Lake Kegonsa and Pike Lake state parks, the southern Kettle Moraine State Forest and the Glacial Drumlin Trail (with access in Lake Mills) are all nearby side trips from Aztalan State Park.

BIG FOOT BEACH STATE PARK

Walworth County. Just south of Lake Geneva on Highway 120. Highway map index: 11-H.

Main Attraction

Big Foot Beach State Park is on Lake Geneva, one of the largest, cleanest lakes in southeastern Wisconsin. The park is small (272 acres), but the large beach frontage and shaded picnic grounds make it a favorite stop for day visits or camping trips.

Lake Geneva is fed directly from deep springs and from small streams that originate from other springs. Fontana, a town on the western end of the lake, was so named by the French because of the numerous "fountains," or springs.

Lake Geneva may be the most famous lake in southern Wisconsin. It's large and clean, and park visitors will find the beach a wonderful place to spend a day.

Lake Geneva has had several names. The Potawatomi Indians called it "Kishwauketae," meaning "clear water." The French fur traders called it Big Foot Lake, named after the Potawatomi Chief Maunk-suck, or "Big Foot." A frontier surveyor named the lake "Geneva" in 1833. People aren't sure if the name came from a similarity to Geneva Lake in Switzerland, or if the surveyor named it after his hometown of Geneva, New York. However it got its name, Lake Geneva became famous for its beauty. The lake's charm attracted thousands of visitors each season. Then, after the Chicago fire of 1871, the picturesque area around the lake became the playground for Chicago's moneyed families. The Great Depression ended the era of elegance on the lake, but Lake Geneva is as popular today as ever.

Things To Do

Most people come for the water sports. Lake Geneva (5,262 acres) is a good fishing spot for northern, walleye, smallmouth and largemouth bass, brown trout, cisco and panfish. During the summer, anglers try their luck near the shoreline weed beds, or in the deeper waters, where they concentrate on catching walleye and smallmouth bass. Ice fishermen dot the lake in the winter, trying for northern, walleye, cisco or panfish.

The seven-mile-long lake is big enough to accommodate many boats without crowding. High windstorms occasionally blow in from the west, though, making boating difficult on the choppy water as big waves roll into the sandy park beach. Besides fishing, the lake is a natural for sailing, waterskiing, canoeing and powerboating. It's also fun to swim or lie on the 900-foot beach to watch the variety of games that the big and little kids play. Lifeguards are on duty during the summer.

Besides the water activities, try a hike in the park. Big Foot Beach is not large enough for a challenging hike, but there's plenty of room for a leisurely stroll. The park has a surprising variety of plant habitats.

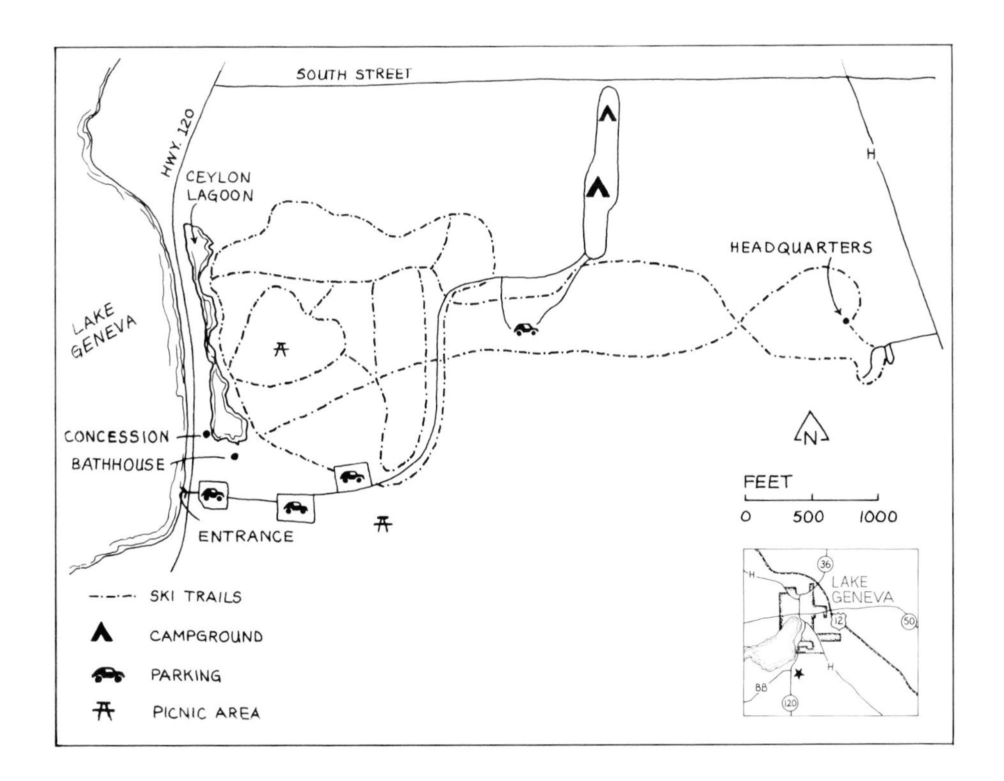

People with feet of all sizes enjoy Lake Geneva at Big Foot Beach State Park.

Hikers will see oak-hickory woods, open fields, prairie remnants, marshes and shorelines. You can hike on over four miles of marked trails, including a short nature path. Cross-country skiers tour on these trails during the winter months.

The woods surrounding the picnic area has paths and openings that are easy to find and interesting to walk along. You could explore the lagoon, cross the arching bridges, or wander barefoot along the lakefront. Hiking along the park road leads past the marsh and open upland areas where you can see cattail and goldenrod. A hike through all these places could last two or three hours if you take the time to explore carefully. The *Visitor*, Big Foot Beach's information paper, carries informative articles about some of the plants and animals you may observe as you wander through the park. If you'd prefer a longer walk, try the 25-mile trail that circles Lake Geneva.

Flora and Fauna

Big Foot Beach is the only state park with its boundaries entirely inside city limits. Besides squirrels and rabbits, the park is home to gulls, hawks and ducks.

Even though it's in town, the park harbors a variety of wildlife: deer, raccoon, fox, muskrat, skunk and flocks of migrating birds.

Facilities

The picnic area is large and shaded, bordering on Ceylon Lagoon. The lagoon was built as a replica of Lake Geneva by the son of Fred Maytag (the washing machine magnate), who once owned much of the park land. The 100-site campground (showers; no electrical hookups) is at the end of the park road in an oak woods. Reservations are accepted for individual sites.

Surrounding Area

Big Foot Beach State Park is an easy drive from both the Milwaukee and Chicago metro areas. Other state recreation land near the park includes the Southern Unit of the Kettle Moraine State Forest and Bong State Recreation Area. Ask at the park office for further details about these state facilities.

BONG STATE RECREATION AREA

Kenosha County. About 6 miles southeast of Burlington on Highway 142. Highway map index: 11-I.

Main Attraction

The Bong State Recreation Area is a unique concept in Wisconsin's state park system. In general, the recreation area has more flexibility in creating special use zones for such activities as hang gliding, model rocket and airplane flying, and land sailing. Traditional recreation activities (camping, swimming, hiking, etc.) take place in other parts of Bong.

The idea for Bong took shape after the Air Force scrapped plans to build a jet fighter base on the present site in the late 1950s. Before the government cancelled the project, tons of topsoil were removed and a 2.5-mile runway was being constructed. The Department of Natural Resources bought 4,515 acres of the abandoned air base for the state's first recreation area. Now the former government land has become a lush oasis of green in an increasingly urbanized corner of the state.

Things To Do

The "disturbed area" (runway site) is designated as a Special Use Zone. In addition to being an ideal place for dirt bikes and snowmobile trails, this flat area may be reserved for a variety of recreation uses. Some of the permitted activities include dog trials, horseback riding, model airplane flying, hot air ballooning, hang gliding, ultralight flying, land sailing, falconry and waterfowl hunting. All activities are rated according to their compatibility and scheduled to avoid potential conflicts. Contact the visitor center for details about what you can do in the 1,200-acre Special Use Zone.

The Molinaro Visitor Center is the best place to begin your visit to Bong. You can get details about what to see and do here and browse through the natural history exhibits. A full-time naturalist regularly schedules guided hikes and seasonal programs for the public and for organized groups (with advance reservations). Private groups can also reserve the center's 100-seat auditorium (a fee is charged)

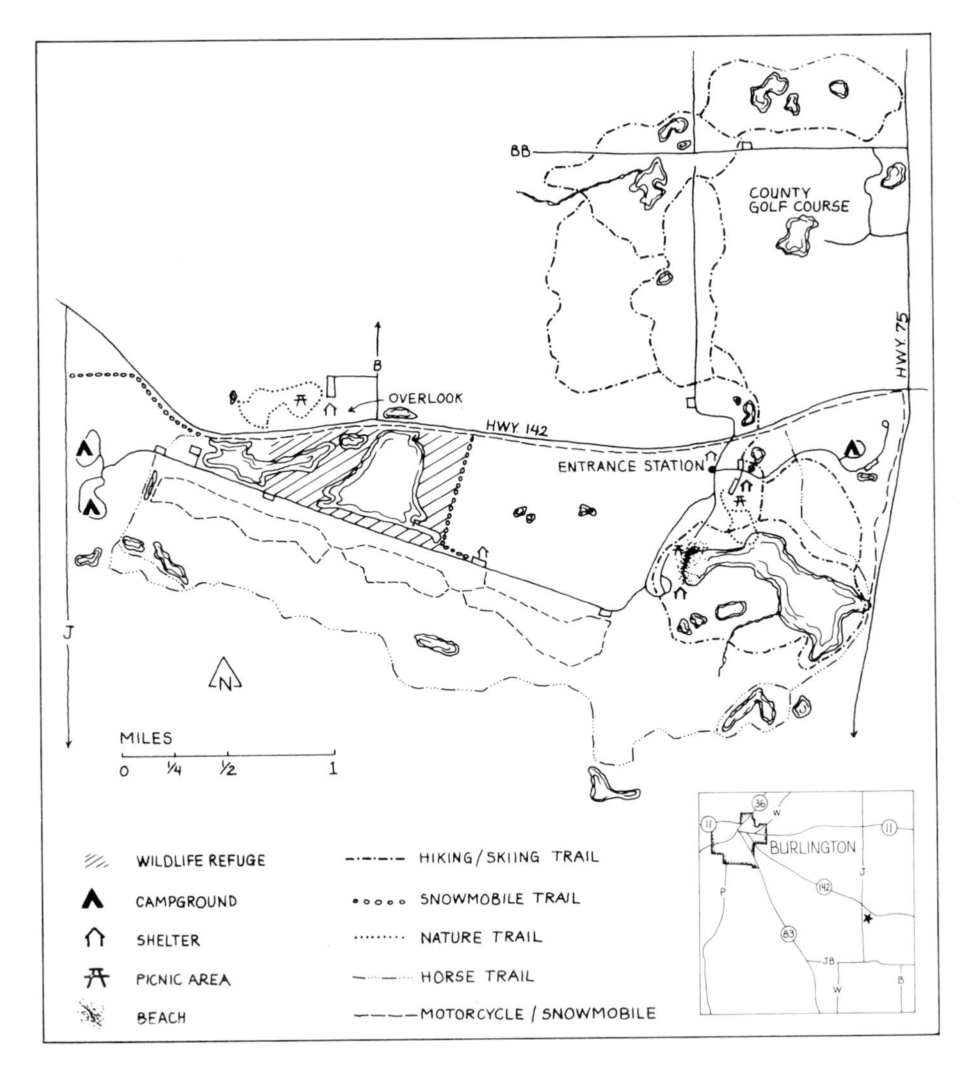

or the 200-seat outdoor amphitheatre. Volunteers play an active role at Bong by assisting with the interpretive programs, conducting research or helping the staff with special maintenance or planting projects.

Horseback riders, snowmobilers and motorcyclists are restricted to marked trails. Horses may be rented from a nearby stable. To get details about horse rental or fee information and regulations about the motorized vehicle trails, call the office or stop at the visitor center.

This place is unique in the state recreation scheme because of its flexibility. Hang gliding and land sailing are but two possibilities here.

Bong has 72 bodies of water. East Lake (150 acres) is the largest of these and is the focal point for water sports. The lake is stocked with yellow perch and northern for those who like to fish. There is a boat landing with parking for access by canoes and non-motorized boats (motors are not allowed on the lake). The beach complex on the lake's western shore includes a 400-foot sand beach and a bathhouse with showers.

Bong is open for hunting during regular seasons for waterfowl, pheasant, deer and small game. Hunting is limited to designated areas and is managed under stringent rules. Ask for the hunting information sheet at the visitor center.

Bong is open all year and attracts many visitors for snow-time fun. Snowmobilers use a marked 6.5-mile trail in the Special Use Zone and five miles of trails along highways 142 and 75. The 14 miles of hiking trails are groomed for cross-country skiers. Other winter sports include sledding, ice skating and ice fishing. Water is available at the Molinaro Visitor Center.

Flora and Fauna

The recreation area's 14 miles of hiking trails range through the prairie, woodland and wetland in the eastern section of the property. A springtime hike is rewarded by the first blooms of the year—white bloodroot and lavender hepatica. In summer, you may spot a great blue heron from a boardwalk trail or breathe in the aroma of sweet clover on a prairie

Hang gliding is one of the unconventional activities allowed at this unique park.

path. Autumn hikers will witness the season's last blooms—goldenrod, aster and gentian. In winter, tracks in the snow show an abundance of wildlife that is easier to overlook during the other seasons.

Bird-watchers are attracted to Bong by the many species that visit or live here. Yellow-headed blackbirds, short-eared owls and a variety of hawks are among the specialties. Waterfowl and shorebirds including terns, bitterns, herons and sandpipers are especially abundant around the wetlands and flowages. A bird checklist is available at the Visitor Center.

You can find out more about local plant and animal life on the two self-guided nature trails. The Grassland Trail (one mile) starts near the Molinaro Visitor Center, and the Overlook Wooded Trail (one mile) begins north of Highway 142 near the western boundary of the recreation area.

Facilities

Families and organized groups can camp or picnic at Bong. Two group campgrounds, called Sunset and Sunrise, can accommodate up to 600 campers. Contact the office for reservation information about the group sites or the six picnic shelters (all with electricity). The family campground, on the west side of the property, has 130 sites (no electricity). Showers are available in the bathhouse on East Lake. Plans call for a new campground that will have electrical hookups and showers.

Surrounding Area

The Bong State Recreation Area, named for an ace World War II fighter pilot from Wisconsin, is less than a one-hour drive from downtown Milwaukee. The Kenosha County Golf Course is just to the east of Bong on Highway 75. Other state recreation facilities in the area include Big Foot Beach State Park, the Southern Unit of the Kettle Moraine State Forest and Havenwoods Environmental Education Center in Milwaukee.

GLACIAL DRUMLIN STATE TRAIL

Dane, Jefferson and Waukesha counties. 47 miles; between Cottage Grove and Waukesha.

Main Attraction

The Glacial Drumlin State Trail is a former rail line recently developed into a biking/hiking route. The trail is named for the glacially formed elongated ridges and oval-shaped hills characteristic of this region. Bicyclists will also pass through wetlands and southern Wisconsin farmland.

Things To Do

The trail starts at Cottage Grove, just east of Madison, and runs to Waukesha, west of Milwaukee. The 47-mile crushed limestone trail can be easily biked in a day by experienced cyclists. Families and those who prefer shorter jaunts can break the route into sections, planning a trip around the communities spaced along the way. Parking lots are located at the trail heads and in Deerfield, Lake Mills, Sullivan, Dousman and Wales. Rest areas are being developed, but not all of them are completed yet.

The history and landforms of Wisconsin are inextricably linked to the Ice Age, and this trail shows off the distinctive characteristics left by the glaciers.

One of the most scenic parts of the trail is just west of Lake Mills on Rock Lake. Stop on the trestle for a good view of the town, lakeshore homes and a good beach. This is a pleasant spot for a trailside lunch.

Two stretches are currently closed: a four-mile gap near Jefferson and a one-mile gap east of Dousman. Future development may connect the Glacial Drumlin Trail with local designated bicycle routes or the Military Ridge State Trail that runs from Verona (southwest of Madison) to Dodgeville.

Winter trail use is open to hikers, snowmobilers

and cross-country skiers. ATVs and other motorized vehicles are prohibited.

Bicyclists 18 years of age and older are required to have a state trail pass in order to use the Glacial Drumlin Trail. You can buy a pass from private vendors, park rangers patrolling the trail, and at Lake Kegonsa State Park or the Kettle Moraine State Forest office.

Surrounding Area

Glacial Drumlin Trail is within easy biking distance of Lake Kegonsa and Aztalan state parks, the Southern Unit of the Kettle Moraine State Forest, and the Lapham Peak Unit of the state forest. Camping is available at Lake Kegonsa and in the Southern Kettle Moraine as well as at private campgrounds in the area. You can buy supplies in the trail communities.

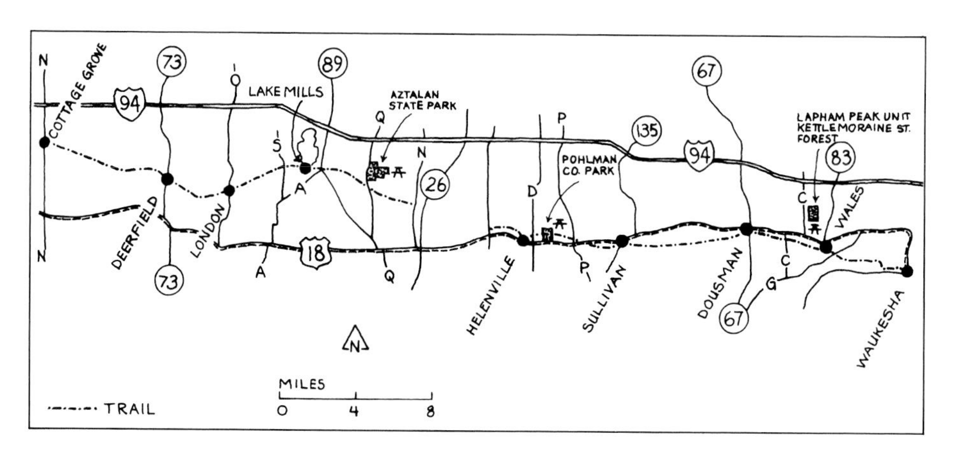

GOVERNOR NELSON STATE PARK

Dane County. Northwest shore of Lake Mendota near Madison. Access on County M. Highway map index: 10-F.

Main Attraction

Governor Nelson State Park is the newest addition to Wisconsin's park system. The 442-acre site is a mixture of wetland, woods and rolling farmland along the shoreline of Lake Mendota.

Spend a day here and investigate the Indian burial mounds preserved in the park. The beach is relaxing, and so is sailing on Lake Mendota.

Before European settlement, Indians lived in the area. The whole Madison region, and in particular the land close to the lakes, contains many mounds, burial grounds and encampment sites. The park has several mounds, probably constructed by Woodland Indians known as the Effigy Mound Builders. The most notable is a 282-foot-long panther-shaped effigy mound. There is also a bird effigy and several conical mounds. Others have been desecrated or disturbed by farming. You can see other mounds in southern Wisconsin at Lake Kegonsa, Devil's Lake, Wyalusing, Nelson Dewey and High Cliff state parks, and at Lizard Mound County Park (Washington County).

Things To Do

Lake Mendota (about 10,000 acres) is the park's focal point. The young park features a 500-foot beach, bathhouses with solar-heated showers, and a four-ramp boat landing. From the park you'll have a grand view of the Madison skyline and the State Capitol across the lake. The big lake attracts water sport lovers, so you'll see a flotilla of sailboats, powerboats and sailboards on the lake. Fishing can be good for northern, walleye, bass and panfish. Besides taking advantage of the beach and lake, visitors can hike, bike, picnic and play open field sports. Winter attracts ice fishermen and ice boaters onto the frozen lake. The trails are marked for cross-country skiers, while snowshoers can explore the park on their own.

(continued)

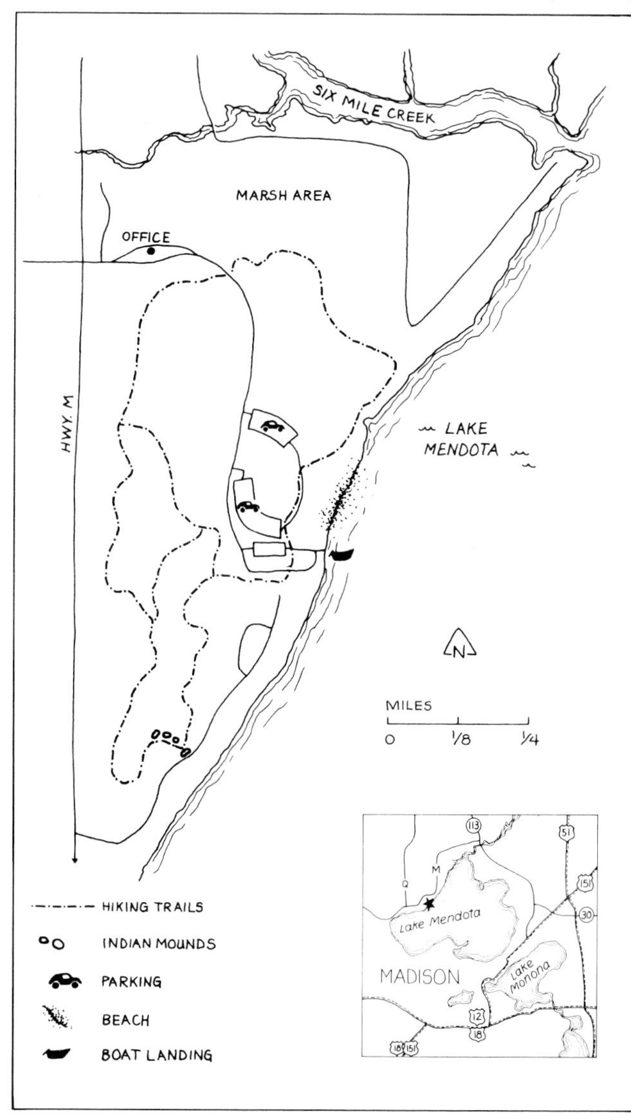

Governor Nelson offers a variety of southern Wisconsin habitats and vegetation.

Flora and Fauna

The hiking trails (with interpretive signs) traverse a variety of park terrain, providing close-up looks at local flora. The wetlands around Six-Mile Creek and Spring Creek support cattail, sedge, canary grass, willow and dogwood. Shoreline tree cover includes some hardwoods and a number of cottonwoods, soft maples, elm, willow and box elder. Inland woods are mostly oak-hickory.

Wildlife habitat in the park is limited to small patches of upland woods, softwood shoreline and the relatively untouched wetland area. You may spot deer, muskrat and a variety of small game. Look for ring-necked pheasant and the many species of waterfowl that frequent the nearby wetlands of Lake Mendota.

Facilities

Governor Nelson State Park, Wisconsin's first urban state park, is maintained as a day-use facility (no camping).

Surrounding Area

Madison is a scenic city famous for its lakes and parks. Lake Mendota is the largest of five metro-area lakes, four of which are connected by the Yahara River. A handful of state parks and biking/hiking trails are within easy driving distance of the city. To get more information about Madison and nearby attractions, write to the Greater Madison Convention and Visitors Bureau, 425 W. Washington Ave., Dept. S, Madison, WI 53703 (or call collect: 608-255-0701).

HARRINGTON BEACH STATE PARK

Ozaukee County. East on County D off Highway 43; Seven miles north of Port Washington. Highway map index: 9-I.

Main Attraction

Wild beach and lowland forest along Lake Michigan in Harrington Beach State Park offer a refreshing switch from city life. Although the park is just up the road from Milwaukee, the park often isn't crowded, even the weekend before Labor Day. The unusual seems to be the norm at Harrington Beach. Lake Michigan is an obvious attraction, but the rugged shoreline of inland Quarry Lake is just as scenic. The lake is an abandoned limestone quarry ringed by cedars.

Things To Do

Fishermen like 26-acre Quarry Lake for its bass, bullhead and panfish. Swimming and boating are not allowed on the lake, but you can hike around most of Quarry Lake on an established trail.

Another trail winds through a forest of ash, maple, birch and quaking aspen as it leads to a view of Lake Michigan. The White Cedar Swamp Nature Trail is accessible from the lower parking lot or from Quarry Lake Trail. The white cedar swamp that the nature trail passes through used to be typical of Lake Michigan shoreline before development. The cooling effect of the big lake encourages cedars and other common northern plant species to grow this far south.

Surf fishing is a growing activity along the mile of Lake Michigan shoreline here. If you're lucky, you might land a salmon or trout to take home.

The park stretches for a mile along Lake Michigan with about a mile of sand beach. This is a great place to forget about what happened yesterday and just lie

(opposite page)

Although the park closes November 1, there's still plenty of time to enjoy the fall color.

back in the sand or brave a chilly swim in the lake (no lifeguards on duty).

After daydreaming on the sand or mounting a beachcombing expedition, try some surf fishing for trout and salmon. Several good catches are made during the summer months. Charter boat fishing is available in Port Washington and in Sheboygan.

Facilities

Harrington Beach has five separate picnic areas in the woods and near Lake Michigan. One small area is on the beach and another is next to the upland parking

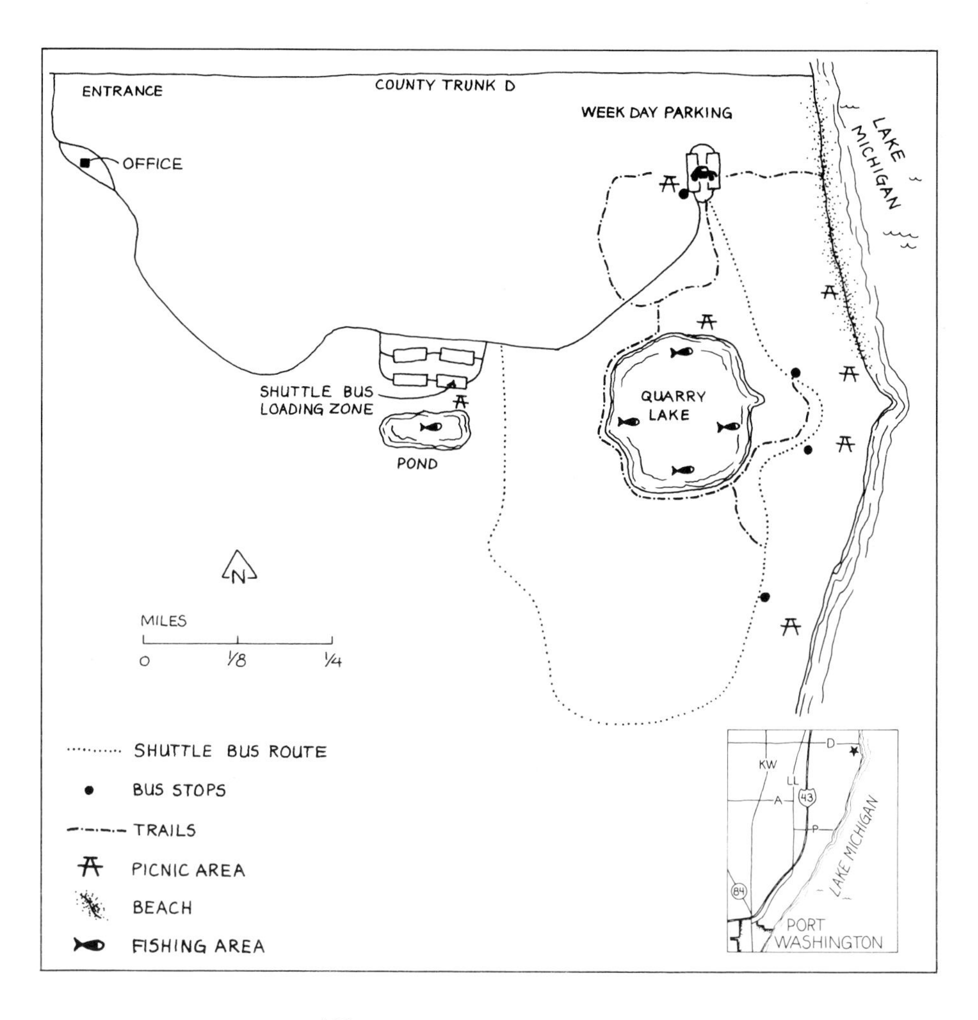

lot at the children's fishing pond. The uplands provide more elbow room than by the beach. There's plenty of space to throw a frisbee or fly a kite with the panorama of Lake Michigan as a backdrop. The park maintains two volleyball courts and two horseshoe courts for visitors. Users should bring their own equipment along, though volleyball nets and horseshoes are available for a small rental fee. The park's three shelter buildings can be reserved. Supplies are available in nearby Lake Church and Belgium.

During busy weekends or holidays, no cars are allowed past the upper parking lot. A shuttle bus takes picnickers and beach bums to the various grassy areas near the lake. Harrington Beach, named for a state employee instrumental in developing new state parks, has no camping facilities. The park is closed from November 1 to April 30. Cross-country skiing and other winter sports are available in Kohler-Andrae State Park to the north, and the Northern Unit of the Kettle Moraine State Forest to the west of Harrington Beach.

HORICON MARSH WILDLIFE AREA AND HORICON NATIONAL WILDLIFE REFUGE

Dodge and Fond du Lac counties. Wisconsin DNR headquarters is one mile north of Horicon on North Palmatory Street, off Highway 33. National Wildlife Refuge headquarters is west of LeRoy off County Z. Highway map index: 9-H.

Main Attraction

The 31,000-acre Horicon Marsh is the largest freshwater cattail marsh in the United States. The marsh is under federal and state management. The northern two thirds is administered as the Horicon National Wildlife Refuge by the U.S. Fish and Wildlife Service, and the southern third is administered as the Horicon Marsh Wildlife Area by the Wisconsin Department of Natural Resources.

The Horicon Marsh is a shallow, peat-filled lakebed created by the Green Bay lobe of the Wisconsin Glacier. Over several thousand years, the original lakebed was transformed into a marsh as silt and organic sediment reduced the depth of the lake basin. The marsh has, for most of its history, been home to an abundance of fish, birds and other marshland wildlife.

Archaeological evidence suggests that man was already here when the marsh was in its infancy. Nomadic hunters, here as early as 12,000 years ago, were followed by other Indian cultures. Most recently, Potawatomis and Winnebagos lived in villages around the marsh. The first white people settled near the Indian communities.

Over the next several decades, the marsh was controlled by special interest groups. Between 1870 and the early 1900s, recreational and commercial hunting dominated the marsh. Shortly after, private and public drainage projects attempted to convert the marsh

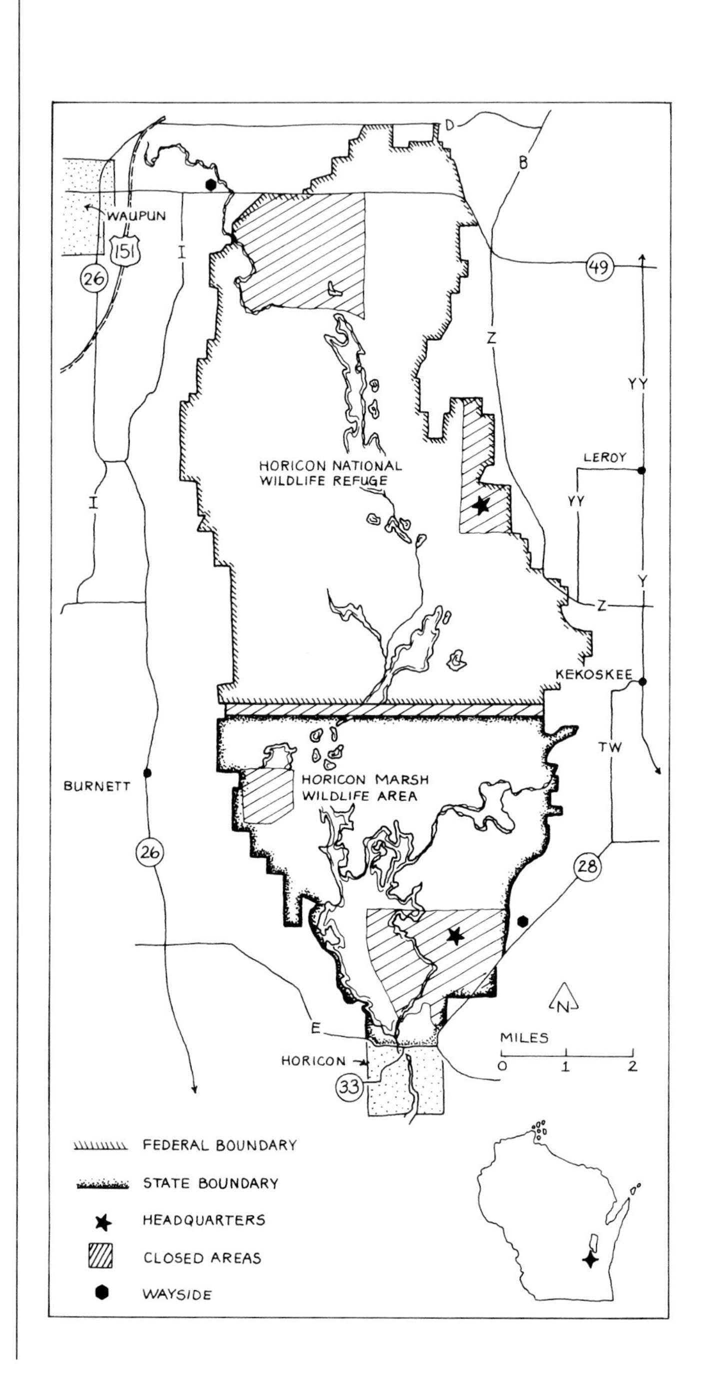
D
B
WAUPUN
151
26
I
49
Z
YY
HORICON NATIONAL
WILDLIFE REFUGE
LEROY
YY
I
Y
Z
KEKOSKEE
TW
BURNETT
HORICON MARSH
WILDLIFE AREA
26
28
N
E
MILES
0 1 2
HORICON
33
FEDERAL BOUNDARY
STATE BOUNDARY
HEADQUARTERS
CLOSED AREAS
WAYSIDE

into productive farmland. This project failed because effective drainage was never attained during periods of high water, and during drought years, much of the peat was destroyed by attempts to burn off marsh vegetation. In the 1920s to 1930s, conservation-minded individuals and groups worked to preserve the marsh for future generations. Their efforts resulted in the protection of the Horicon Marsh, which, in the Algonquin language, means the land of clean, pure water. Today, the marsh is managed to preserve and produce wildlife, and to provide recreational opportunities.

(continued on next page)

Horicon is a major gathering place for migrating Canada geese as well as other species.

Things To Do

The best ways to explore the Horicon Marsh are by canoeing or hiking. The marsh's wetlands, channels and ditches are especially enjoyable by canoe in the spring before the insects hatch, and in the fall, before the hunting season. You can rent canoes in Horicon. Hiking trails wind through the marsh and woods in both the state and federal areas. Fall is the most popular hiking season here, though the trails are open for cross-country skiing during the winter.

The vast marsh is accessible to hikers and canoeists, and spring and fall are the best times to visit. Over 100,000 Canada geese stop here during migrations.

Hunting for deer, pheasant, partridge and small game is permitted in the national wildlife refuge. Similar hunting is permitted in the state wildlife area, including the taking of ducks and geese. Visitors can fish for northern and panfish in the marsh. Both the state and federal portions of the marsh have posted closed areas that limit public access for the protection of wildlife. Stop at the respective headquarters to pick up maps and to get current details about hunting seasons, bag limits, closed areas and regulations. Horicon Marsh is a day-use area. Camping on state or federal land is not allowed.

Flora and Fauna

The marsh is used for resting and feeding by various species of waterfowl during spring (March–April) and fall (September–December) migrations. Over 100,000 Canada geese use Horicon as they migrate between nesting grounds in the Hudson Bay area and wintering areas in southern Illinois, Kentucky and western Tennessee. Visitors will also be able to observe flocks of mallard, shoveler, pintail and other species of waterfowl during the migration.

Horicon is the largest nesting area for redheaded ducks east of the Mississippi River. Other birds that nest here include ruddy ducks, double-crested cormorants and coots. Fourmile Island, a designated state natural area, supports the largest heron and egret rookery in Wisconsin. More than 248 species of birds have been observed on the marsh. Over half of these nest at Horicon, while the others are observed during spring and fall migrations. Only a small number of species are year-round residents.

White-tailed deer, red fox, skunk, otter, coyote and other common mammals inhabit the marsh. Muskrats are plentiful and are managed (by regulated trapping) to help maintain a balance between open water and vegetation for waterfowl nesting.

Surrounding Area

Horicon Marsh Wildlife Area is one of nine units in the Ice Age National Scientific Reserve in Wisconsin. It was selected because it's an excellent example of an extinct post-glacial lake. To see other outstanding examples of the effects of the Wisconsin Glacier, drive east of the marsh to visit Pike Lake State Park and the Northern Unit of the Kettle Moraine State Forest.

KETTLE MORAINE STATE FOREST— LAPHAM PEAK UNIT

Waukesha County. 1.5 miles south of I-94 (Delafield exit) on County C; or two miles north of Highway 18 on County C. Highway map index: 10-H.

Main Attraction

Lapham Peak (1,233 feet) is the highest point in Waukesha County. From the top of the observation tower at the summit, you can see about 16 lakes speckling the countryside like irregular blue jewels on a rumpled green quilt. The sweeping view includes Holy Hill to the north, the highest point in the Kettle Moraine and the site of a Catholic monastery that attracts many visitors annually.

The sweeping vistas from the peak will give you an overview of what the glaciers did to this area of Wisconsin. Then, take a guided hike for a more detailed view.

At 580 acres, Lapham Peak is the smallest unit of the Kettle Moraine State Forest (the Northern Unit covers over 27,000 acres, and the Southern Unit covers almost 18,000 acres). Like the other two units, Lapham Peak highlights the glacial features that give the forest its name.

The peak has had several names. Early settlers called it Big Hill, but later it was known as Stoney Hill, Prospect Hill and Government Hill. Finally, in 1916, it was renamed Lapham Peak, in honor of Increase A. Lapham, a prominent conservationist and scientist in the 1800s.

Lapham Peak and the rest of the Kettle Moraine were sculpted by the Wisconsin Glacier when it spread south from Canada over the state 12,000 to 15,000 years ago. The great ice sheet was two miles thick at its origin, tapering to hundreds of feet at the end. Two fingers of the glacier, the Lake Michigan Lobe on the east and the Green Bay Lobe on the west, grated against each other along a 120-mile junction. This action caused melting and the deposit of rock, sand and gravel between the lobes, forming a moraine (ridge) about 300 feet above the surrounding land. Kettles, or holes, were formed by large hunks of ice in the moraine. This ice eventually melted and the earth above it caved in. The name of the forest, Kettle Moraine, is taken from these outstanding features.

The Ice Age National Scientific Reserve and the Ice Age National Scenic Trail were created to preserve Wisconsin's glacial legacy. The Northern Unit of the Kettle Moraine State Forest is one of the nine Ice Age

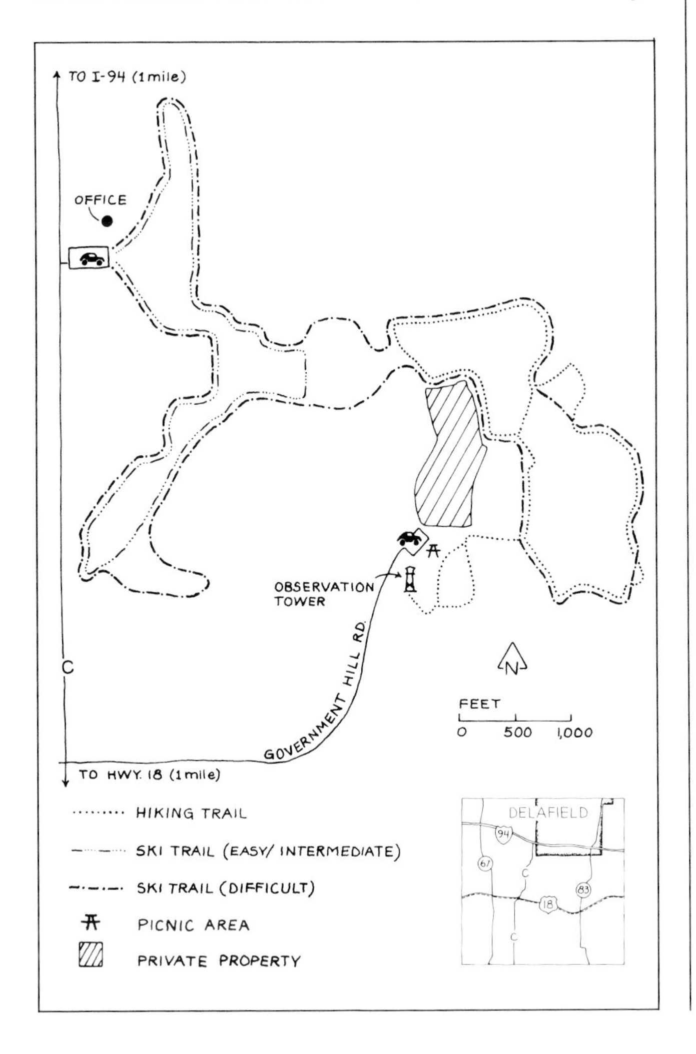

Reserve units. All three sections of the state forest (North, South and Lapham Peak) contain portions of the 1,000-mile Ice Age Trail.

Things To Do

Current development includes picnic areas, a three-acre prairie restoration project and over six miles of hiking/cross-country ski trails. Hikers may spot red-tailed hawks, deer and other woodland wildlife. Guided hikes are the main feature of Lapham Peak's interpretive program, some of which are led by volunteers. Volunteers have also helped clear trails and plant trees in the forest unit. Future development may include a family campground, bridle paths and more hiking/skiing trails.

To experience the beauty, variety and geology of this area, take the time to wander along the Kettle Moraine Scenic Drive. The route connects the three units of the state forest and is marked by green acorn-shaped signs. Pike Lake State Park is also along the drive. Detailed maps of the Kettle Moraine Scenic Drive can be obtained from state park and forest facilities along the way.

Surrounding Area

Lapham Peak is close to several other state recreation properties such as Aztalan State Park, Havenwoods State Forest Preserve in Milwaukee and the Glacial Drumlin State Trail. The trail (47 miles; between Cottage Grove and Waukesha) passes within two miles of Lapham Peak and a spur may someday link the two. Lapham Peak is an easy drive from downtown Milwaukee, only 40 minutes away.

KETTLE MORAINE STATE FOREST—
SOUTHERN UNIT

Waukesha, Jefferson and Walworth counties. Forest headquarters and visitor center is on Highway 59 between Palmyra and Eagle. Highway map index: 10-H.

Main Attraction

Kames, kettles, eskers, moraines and landforms of other curious names make up the glacial topography of the Kettle Moraine Southern Unit. Besides the scenic variety, you can experience the forest with a range of recreational activities that might lure you back for the diversions of another season.

Things To Do

Hiking is the best way to see the glacial formations up close, and there are about 75 miles of trails to explore. A large section of Wisconsin's statewide Ice Age National Scenic Trail enters the Kettle Moraine near the Pine Woods campground. It travels south through the forest along the Scuppernong Marsh, around water-filled kettles and Lake La Grange, leaving the forest at Rice Lake. You can reserve three overnight backpacking shelters along this trail for use year-round.

The Scuppernong hiking trail, in the northern portion of the Kettle Moraine, has three loops that wander into kettles, over kames (conical hills), and through pine and oak forests. It's easy to get to this trail from Ottawa Lake and the Pine Woods campground. The La Grange camp and picnic area has easy access to the John Muir and Nordic trails. The Muir Trail is the more rugged of the two, following moraines (large ridges of gravel) and passing several kettle potholes. The Nordic Trail, designed for cross-country skiing, is the longest trail in the forest, with some good views for hikers.

You can participate in guided nature hikes with the park naturalist or try several self-guided nature trails. The guided hikes cover different aspects of the forest, such as "Animals by Sight and Sound." For more forest background, attend the evening slide and movie programs at the Ottawa Lake Recreation Area. The visitor center has a small museum interpreting the natural history of the Kettle Moraine and a slide show about the glacier. Weekly program schedules are posted on forest bulletin boards.

The four self-guided nature trails each highlight a different aspect of the state forest. The Scuppernong Springs Nature Trail (1.5 miles) features bubbling springs and an historic trout pond. The Wood Duck Kettle Nature Trail (.5 mile) shows off the rugged

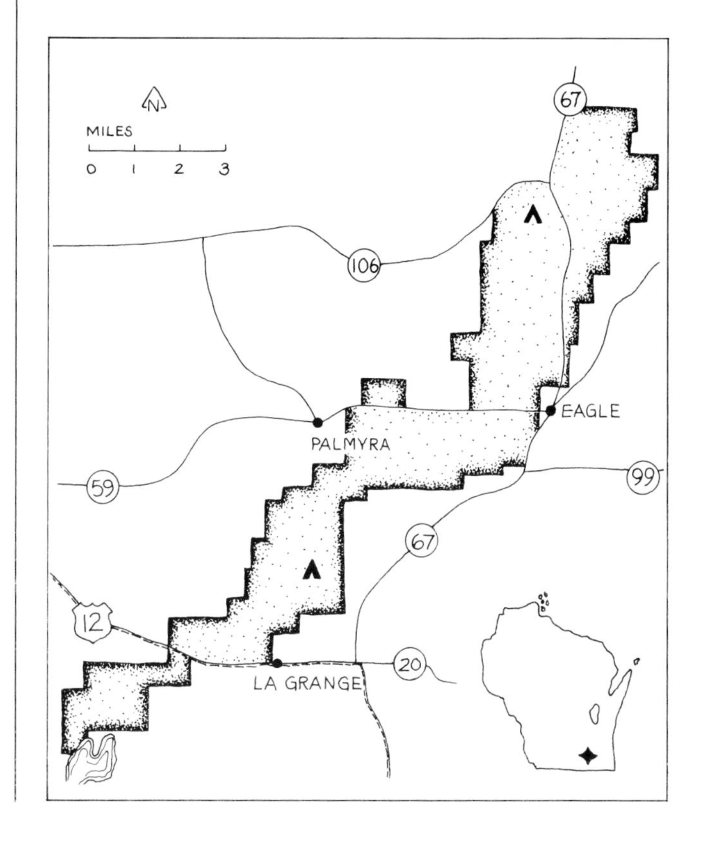

beauty of the Kettle Moraine. The Rice Lake Nature Trail (.5 mile) encircles a pond that attracts bullfrogs, painted turtles, blue herons and mallard ducks. A wildlife observation blind is available for viewing the natural residents of this pond.

The Paradise Springs Nature Trail (.5 mile, paved) is especially designed to accommodate park visitors with physical disabilities. The nature area includes a fieldstone springhouse, trout pond (with fishing pier), meandering brook, wooded areas and interesting wildlife. A cold-water spring flows at a rate of about 30,000 gallons per hour.

The Nordic Trail, although designed for cross-country skiing, is a good choice for hikers exploring the unique topography of the forest.

The rolling wooded terrain of the forest with its visual surprises makes this a favorite destination for horseback riders. Three loops totaling 27 miles are spread throughout the forest. Riders can set up camp at the horsemen's campground near Palmyra. Horses can be rented from private stables nearby.

The main fishing spots are Ottawa, Whitewater and Rice lakes where you might catch walleye, northern, bass or panfish. Each of these lakes has boat launching ramps, but motors are prohibited on Ottawa Lake. There are scores of other good fishing lakes surrounding the state forest. The most popular trout fishing stream in the state forest is Bluff Creek. Access is from a small parking area and fire lane on Hi-Lo Road. Hike north on the fire lane about one half mile to the creek. Brook and brown trout are occasionally caught in the south branch of the Scuppernong River, upstream from the Highway 59 bridge (just east of County Z). Anglers should get trout fishing details at the forest headquarters before casting because some private lands are located on parts of these streams.

The only state-operated target shooting range in Wisconsin is in the Kettle Moraine southwest of Eagle. The McMiller Shooting Center has target practice facilities for archery and different types of rifles and handguns. The state forest also has good hunting areas with a variety of game available. Ask at the forest headquarters for detailed information.

Hiking and horseback riding are probably the best ways to experience the Kettle Moraine as the Indians and settlers did. Perhaps the next best is by bicycle.

(opposite page)

Autumn in the Kettle Moraine offers a brilliant show of color to hikers, and the forest begins to open, exposing more of the geologic features.

The hilly, wooded and winding roads make for scenic biking, but cyclists should be aware that cars use these roads, too. Several regional bike routes use secondary roads within and outside of the state forest. You can park and get bicycle trail information at the general store in La Grange.

The Kettle Moraine Southern Unit (over 17,000 acres) is a popular spot in the winter for ice fishing, tobogganing, hiking, snowmobiling and cross-country skiing. The Ice Age National Scenic Trail backpacking shelters are open for adventuresome winter campers. Snowmobilers can explore the forest on about 46 miles of trails with access to surrounding county and club trails. Good snow patterns and short driving distances to urban areas make the cross-country ski loops the most used trail system in the state. Families and beginning skiers like the Nordic Trail because its level to gently rolling terrain provides for a relaxing tour. The Scuppernong and McMiller trails offer 34 miles that challenge even the most advanced skier. Skiers can experience some rugged backcountry touring on the John Muir Trail.

Hikers and snowshoers, who aren't allowed on the groomed cross-country ski trails, now have their own designated paths. Called the Emma Carlin Trail, the looped routes wind through meadows in rolling oak and pine forest openings.

Flora and Fauna

Though deer and small game can be observed in the forest today, early explorers and settlers contended with different animals. Black bears, timber wolves, elk, buffalo, prairie chickens, wild turkeys, bobcats and passenger pigeons all faded from the area with the influx of people and the subsequent changes in the habitat.

Facilities

The Kettle Moraine has 283 campsites split among four separate campgrounds: La Grange, Whitewater Lake, the Pine Woods Area and Ottawa Lake (with 48 electrical outlets). Showers are available, but not in

KETTLE MORAINE—SOUTHERN UNIT

all campgrounds. The forest also has a 100-person outdoor group camp. Reservations are accepted for the group camp and for some of the individual sites. Most of the picnic areas are located in the north and south portions of the forest near the campgrounds. Overhead shelters and swimming beaches are located at Whitewater Lake and Ottawa Lake recreation areas. Ottawa Lake also has a baseball field and volleyball courts.

Surrounding Area

An exciting sidelight to a Kettle Moraine visit is Old World Wisconsin, a large pioneer park near Eagle. Managed by the State Historical Society of Wisconsin, this is the only multinational, multicultural outdoor museum in the world. Barns, houses, outbuildings and other structures built by early Wisconsin immigrants have been moved to the site from every other part of the state. They are then reconstructed on land similar to that which the settlers first cleared, as in Europe's outdoor museums. Old World Wisconsin includes scattered farmsteads and a rural village that reflect the mixture of ethnic lifestyles and traditions that these people brought to Wisconsin. Because the site is still being expanded to eventually include some 100 buildings and as many as 20 ethnic groups, you will be able to see the restoration process.

The passing of the seasons at Old World Wisconsin is highlighted by a series of special weekend events that bring 19th-century rural Wisconsin vividly to life. For further information, write to Old World Wisconsin, Route 2, Box 18, Eagle, WI 53319; or phone 414-594-2116. You can also cross-country ski at the historic site on weekends during the winter (a fee is charged).

LAKE KEGONSA STATE PARK

Dane County. Three miles south of I-90 on County N, or five miles north of Stoughton on County N. Highway map index: 10-G.

Main Attraction

Lake Kegonsa, or "lake of many fishes" in the Winnebago language, is still one of southern Wisconsin's most productive fishing lakes. But bring your hiking shoes, too, because Lake Kegonsa State Park has a pleasing mixture of woods, prairie, and marshland to explore.

Winding through the prairie, the Yahara River connects Lake Kegonsa with three other Madison-area lakes: Waubesa, Monona and Mendota. Lake Kegonsa was called First Lake by the settlers because it was the first of these lakes they came to as they followed the river north.

Things To Do

Fishing is the favorite topic of conversation around the campfire. Experienced anglers like to try for the walleye and smallmouth bass near the lake's rocky bars. Lake Kegonsa is also well known for northern pike and panfish, including crappie, perch, yellow bass, bluegill and white bass.

Crappies are probably the most common fish in the lake and have a daily bag limit of 50. It's a good fish for the family—fun to catch and good eating. Night anglers try for catfish and bullheads, especially in mid-summer. If you want to rent a boat, there are several outboard motor and boat rental businesses around the lake.

If you want to take the whole family fishing, try Lake Kegonsa. Panfish are plentiful, and walleye, smallmouth bass and northern pike await the more experienced angler.

For hikers, the 342-acre park offers a varied landscape of oak woods, prairie and wetland marsh. The 1.3-mile White Oak Nature Trail loops through the stately oak woods at the park's north end. Signs de-

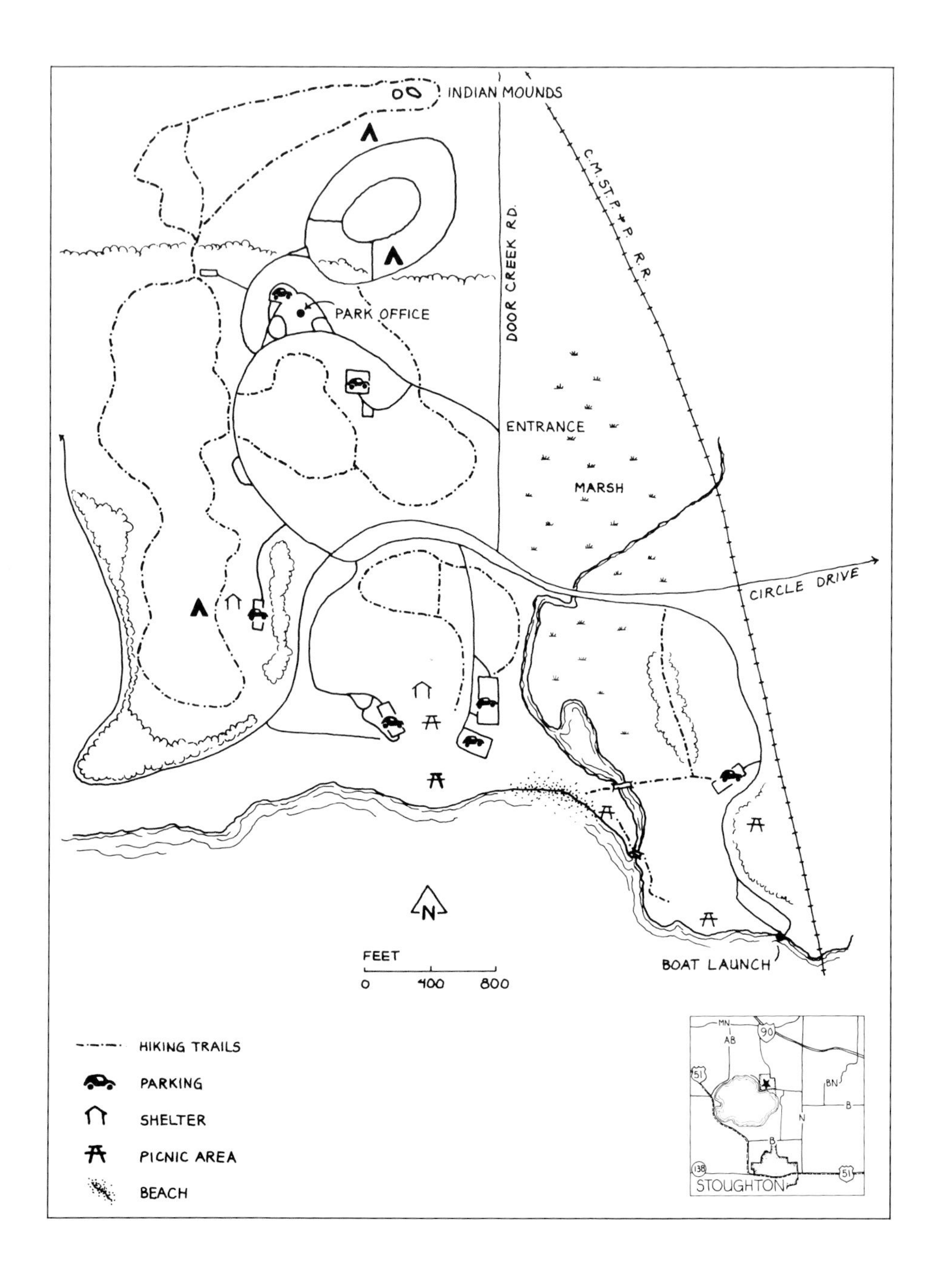
INDIAN MOUNDS
C.M. ST. P. & P. R.R.
DOOR CREEK RD.
PARK OFFICE
ENTRANCE
MARSH
CIRCLE DRIVE
BOAT LAUNCH
N
FEET
0
400
800
HIKING TRAILS
PARKING
SHELTER
PICNIC AREA
BEACH
MN
AB
90
51
BN
B
N
B
138
STOUGHTON
51

scribe the hardwood trees, forest wildflowers and bird habitats you'll see along the way.

In the woods along the nature trail are a series of peculiar earthen structures. Some Stoughton natives claim that settlers used the mounds as military embankments during the Blackhawk Indian Wars. The State Historical Society of Wisconsin, however, believes that they were constructed by a nomadic tribe of Woodland Indians called the Effigy Mound Builders. Though the burial mounds at Lake Kegonsa are linear, other mounds in southern Wisconsin are shaped like the deer, bears, birds, panthers and turtles that the Indians knew. You can see other effigy mounds at Wyalusing, Nelson Dewey, Devil's Lake, High Cliff and Governor Nelson state parks, and at Lizard Mound County Park (Washington County). Leaving the nature trail, you can hike to open fields and along the marsh border north of the beach. A new woodland trail, two footbridges and a lakeside path along the marsh are located between the beach and boat landing.

The fields have mowed paths that are easy to follow, and many types of prairie plants have been reintroduced here. When the early settlers came to this area, they found a vast land of rolling prairie with small oak groves. Now, over 60 acres of the park have been restored to native prairie grasses. By fall, some of these grasses reach a height of over eight feet.

Come to the park in winter for ice fishing and a peaceful change of pace. Panfish provide most of the action, but some northern and walleye are taken. Cross-country skiers can explore the park on over nine miles of groomed trails. Some skiers also tour on the park's unplowed roads. Snowmobiling is not allowed at Lake Kegonsa, but there are local and county trails in the area. Kids enjoy tobogganing and sledding on a small slope in the picnic area.

Flora and Fauna

The marsh is a natural spot to observe the wildlife that uses the area for nesting and feeding, and, in spring and fall, flocks of migrating geese. Early morn-

Southern Wisconsin parks offer more open areas which is fine if you want to enjoy the variety of wildflowers the fields produce.

ing and dusk are good times to hear warblers, see a great blue heron or perhaps watch some deer grazing. By the lake, you might hear the screams of gulls as they scout for food.

Facilities

Along the park's lake frontage is a good swimming beach and boat landing. The 3,209-acre lake is large enough for boating, fishing, waterskiing and sailing. Nearby picnic and playgrounds have good views of the lake, and are inviting spots for a relaxing afternoon in the shade. Two shelter buildings overlook the lake in separate picnic areas.

The 80-site campground is in a stand of mature white oak trees. Showers and electrical hookups are not available in the park. The outdoor group camp can accommodate up to 100 campers from organized groups. Advance registration for individual sites is not accepted, but it's a good idea to write ahead for the group sites. Supplies and laundry facilities are available in Stoughton.

Surrounding Area

Lake Kegonsa is close to a number of area attractions. Three state biking/hiking trails (Glacial Drumlin, Military Ridge and Sugar River) and the new Governor Nelson State Park are within easy driving distance of the park. Madison, just 12 miles from the park, is home to the State Capitol, the Vilas Park Zoo, the University Arboretum, and four metro area lakes. Stoughton hosts the largest Norwegian Independence Day celebration (called Syttende Mai) in the United States. Ask at the park office for further details of what there is to see and do in the area.

PIKE LAKE STATE PARK

Washington County. Between Slinger and Hartford on Highway 60; turn south into the park on Kettle Moraine Drive. Highway map index: 9-H.

Main Attraction

Pike Lake is one of the many glacial lakes that speckle southeastern Wisconsin. Lying between the two units of the Kettle Moraine State Forest, Pike Lake State Park has many of the same landforms found in the Kettle Moraine: conical heaps of soil and stone, winding ridges and bowl-shaped depressions. A segment of the 1,000-mile statewide Ice Age National Scenic Trail passes diagonally through the park. The trail, on its sweeping arc across the state, follows roughly the terminal moraines or farthest advance of the most recent glacier. The park ranger will tell you where you can hike and what glacial evidence to look for on the Ice Age Trail.

Things To Do

Other hiking trails make short loops in the park. Wander the trails a little to explore the woods, ponds, ridges, and valleys. Walk softly and stop often to observe woodchucks, pheasants or muskrats. Some hikers carry guidebooks to identify songbirds and wildflowers they spot. Signs along the self-guided nature trail are also a help in identifying some of Pike Lake's flora and fauna.

Pike Lake was named for its fine walleye fishing. You have a good chance of catching some perch or panfish, too, and maybe even a monstrous northern pike like the 42-inch, 30-pounder that was caught during a recent winter.

The lake is the park's highlight. On warm days, the beach and the picnic grounds are full of visitors who come for the sun and cool lake breezes. Watching the little kids, and the not so little ones, making elaborate sand creations, it seems that playing in the sand is almost as much fun as swimming in the lake.

The park does not have a boat landing, though there are public launches elsewhere on the lake. Boat landing maps with information about boat rentals and bait shops are available at the contact station and at the post office. Canoeing and waterskiing are other popular lake sports here.

Once you've visited Pike Lake during the summer, it's hard to picture ice fishing on the same lake that you jumped into for a refreshing swim. Come back in January to see for yourself, and bring your cross-country skis or snowmobile. The snowmobile trail is relatively short, but it connects with other trails that

This is another park filled with landforms sculpted by the last glacier, and as the name suggests, the walleye fishing is fine.

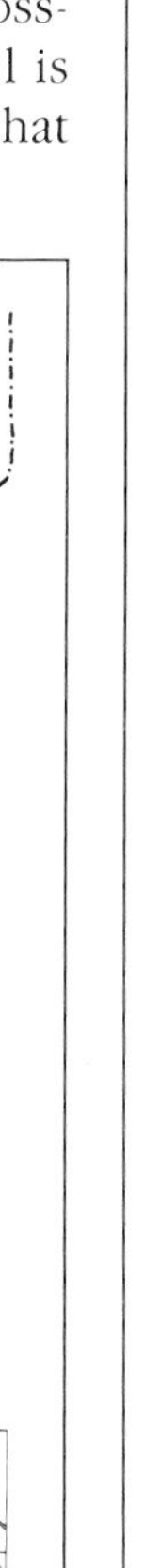

branch toward Hartford, Slinger and Ackerville. Cross-country skiers have a choice of several trail loops of varying degrees of difficulty that wind through the hills, fields and stands of hardwood in the park. The trails, one-way tracks from one to five miles long, all start at the shelter building next to the beach parking lot. You can also toboggan or sled down some of the hills at Pike Lake.

Facilities

Pike Lake currently has a 32-site family campground with showers. It fills up on peak summer weekends, so arrive early to get a site. Future park development plans include enlarging the campground, beach area and trail system, and building an observation tower on Powder Hill.

Surrounding Area

Take off your skis for a while and climb up to the top of Powder Hill. The broad view of the glacier country is impressive in any season. You can see Washington County's highest point, Holy Hill, from the top of Powder Hill. Historically, Holy Hill was the site of a legendary side trip by Marquette and Joliet when they passed through this region, but now it's a Carmelite monastery and a popular religious shrine.

Pike Lake State Park is a short drive from the Milwaukee metro area. The park is a handy stop for a picnic or a hike while exploring the Kettle Moraine Scenic Drive. Fall colors can be striking in the mixed hardwood forest here, and lure many visitors out from the city.

(opposite page)

For some, a visit to a state park is just the beginning of a life-long appreciation of the natural world.

For an interesting side trip, drive northeast of West Bend to Lizard Mound County Park. This peaceful, small park features a unique series of 31 Indian effigy mounds constructed over 1,000 years ago. You'll see burial mounds of various shapes, including lizards, panthers and birds, throughout the maple and beech woods. This is a quiet park, which seems fitting for the idea of the mounds as a final resting place. Pack along a picnic lunch and take the time to hike the nature trail that twists among the mounds.

GREATER MILWAUKEE

1. Havenwoods State Forest

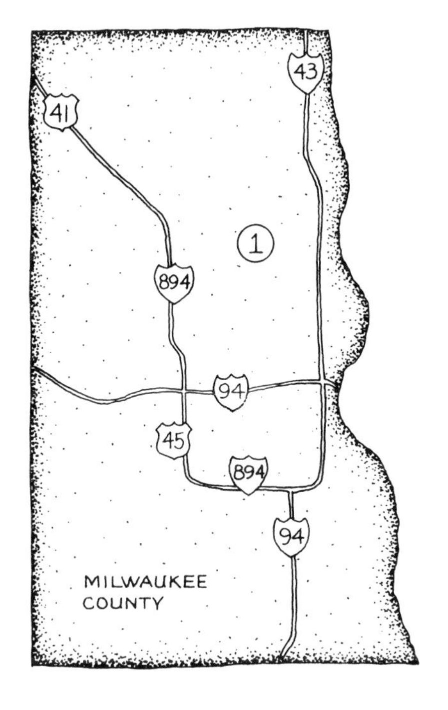

(opposite page)

Much of the natural world found in Wisconsin parks deserves close inspection, like these puff balls.

HAVENWOODS STATE FOREST PRESERVE (ENVIRONMENTAL AWARENESS CENTER)

Milwaukee County. 6141 North Hopkins Street (on Milwaukee's north side). Take W. Silver Springs Drive to N. 43rd St. Drive north on 43rd to Douglas Ave. Turn left on Douglas to stop sign. The entrance sign to Havenwoods will be in front of you.

Main Attraction

Although surrounded by the city of Milwaukee, Havenwoods is classified as a state forest preserve to emphasize its role as an environmental awareness center. Established in 1979, the preserve has evolved from a correctional facility, Nike missile site, military base and landfill to a 237-acre haven for outdoor enthusiasts. Visitors of all ages feel more in tune with the environment here, and have fun while learning.

Things To Do

Restoration is a key word at Havenwoods. You'll be able to see this process in action as natural plant communities and open grasslands take over. Several development projects have been completed. Over three miles of limestone-surfaced trails, accessible to disabled visitors, wind through fields and woods, and a four-acre pond attracts a variety of wildlife. The Children's Discovery Area gives kids a chance to build, climb, dig or roll in a natural place. The North Milwaukee Lions Club supports this project with annual donations.

The attractive new Environmental Awareness Center is the focal point for the forest preserve's interpretive activities. The 10,000-square-foot, passive solar building features a 70-seat auditorium, classroom space, display area and resource center. The educational programs, designed to inspire awareness and excitement about the natural world, have mushroomed in recent years.

Milwaukee-area children explore nature at Havenwoods while in an urban environment. Seasonal activities are geared to capture the curiosity of kids from kindergarten through high school. Naturalists lead explorations of the wetland, fields and woods, and help the students to identify signs of animals. Special preschool programs try to spark an interest in the outdoors by encouraging the children to touch, hear, smell and see.

The two key words here are restoration and education. As more projects are completed, this park is better able to teach visitors of all ages about the natural world.

Havenwoods appeals to grown-ups, too. Senior cit-

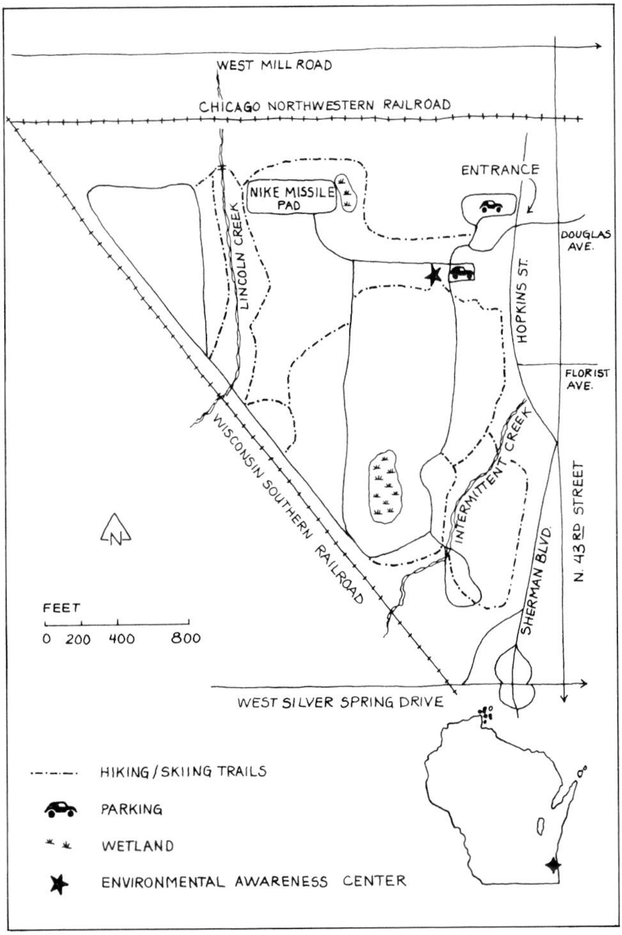

izens can get involved by participating in programs about nature crafts, wildflowers, insects, etc. Workshops for educators and youth leaders are held year-round to provide background, teaching methods and materials on Wisconsin's natural resources. Families enjoy the special activities like kite flying, festivals, nature movies and outdoor sports lessons. Field trips, guest speakers and panel discussions round out the diversity of events that are offered at Havenwoods.

Volunteers are a vital part of Havenwoods's success. Families, adults, teens and civic groups have pitched in to give the landscape a hand. Projects have included prairie seed collection, prairie wildflower planting and trail improvements. Some volunteers are trained as teacher/naturalists to assist in children's programs. Students have left their mark on the land by planting more than 30,000 trees and shrubs at Havenwoods.

Havenwoods State Forest Preserve is open all year as a day-use facility. The hiking and nature trails are used by cross-country skiers in the winter. Check at the Environmental Awareness Center for schedules of seasonal events and interpretive programs.

(opposite page)

There is little of the vast prairie left in Wisconsin, but restoration projects will teach coming generations what it was like.

ADDRESSES

All Regions

Department of Natural Resources Information Center, Box 7921, Madison, WI 53707, 608-266-2621

Wisconsin Division of Tourism, Box 7606, Madison, WI 53707, 800-372-2737

Central Wisconsin River Country

Buckhorn State Park, Necedah, 54646, 608-565-2789

Devil's Lake State Park, Baraboo, 53913, 608-356-8301

MacKenzie Environmental Education Center and State Game Farm, Poynette, 53955, 608-635-4498

Meadow Valley Wildlife Area, Babcock, 54413, 715-884-2437

Mirror Lake State Park, Baraboo, 53913, 608-254-2333

Natural Bridge State Park, Baraboo, 53913, 608-356-8301

Necedah National Wildlife Refuge, Necedah, 54646, 608-565-2551

Rib Mountain State Park, Wausau, 54401, 715-359-4522

Roche-a-Cri State Park, Friendship, 53934, 608-339-3385

Rocky Arbor State Park, Baraboo, 53913, 608-254-8001

East Wisconsin Waters

Ahnapee State Trail, Sturgeon Bay, 54235, 414-743-5123

Hartman Creek State Park, Waupaca, 54981, 715-258-2372

Heritage Hills State Park, Green Bay, 54301, 414-497-4368

High Cliff State Park, Menasha, 54952, 414-989-1106

Kettle Moraine State Forest (North), Campbellsport, 53010, 414-626-2116

(opposite page)

Sailing the Great Lakes has long been a challenging way to get from place to place in Wisconsin.

Kohler-Andrae State Park, Sheboygan, 53081, 414-452-3457
Newport State Park, Ellison Bay, 54210, 414-854-2500
Old Wade House State Park, Greenbush, 53026, 414-526-3271
Peninsula State Park, Fish Creek, 54212, 414-868-3258
Point Beach State Forest, Two Rivers, 54241, 414-794-7480
Potawatomi State Park, Sturgeon Bay, 54235, 414-743-8869
Rock Island State Park, Washington Island, 54246, 414-847-2235
Whitefish Dunes State Park, Sturgeon Bay, 54235, 414-823-2400

Hidden Valleys

Blackhawk Lake Recreation Area, Highland, 53543, 608-623-2707
Blue Mound State Park, Blue Mounds, 53517, 608-437-5711
Browntown–Cadiz Springs State Recreation Area, Monroe, 53566, 608-325-4844
Elroy-Sparta State Trail, Ontario, 54651, 608-337-4775
First Capitol State Park, Blanchardville, 53516, 608-523-4427
Governor Dodge State Park, Dodgeville, 53533, 608-935-2315
La Crosse River State Trail, Ontario, 54651, 608-337-4775
Lower Wisconsin State Riverway, DNR Box 7921, Madison, 53707, 608-266-3568 or 800-232-7367
Military Ridge State Trail, Dodgeville, 53533, 608-935-2315
Mill Bluff State Park, Ontario, 54651, 608-427-6692
Nelson Dewey State Park, Cassville, 53806, 608-725-5374
New Glarus Woods State Park, Monroe, 53566, 608-325-4844
Pecatonica State Trail, Blanchardville, 53516, 608-523-4427

Sugar River State Trail, Monroe, 53566, 608-325-4844
Tower Hill State Park, Spring Green, 53588, 608-588-2116
Wildcat Mountain State Park, Ontario, 54651, 608-337-4775
Wyalusing State Park, Bagley, 53801, 608-996-2261
Yellowstone Lake State Park, Blanchardville, 53516, 608-523-4427

Indian Head Country

Amnicon Falls State Park, Superior, 54880, 715-399-8073
Apostle Islands National Lakeshore, Rte 1 Box 4, Bayfield, 54814, 715-779-3397
Big Bay State Park, Washburn, 54891, 715-373-2015
Black River State Forest, Black River Falls, 54615, 715-284-5301
Brule River State Forest, Brule, 54820, 715-372-4866
Brunet Island State Park, Cornell, 54732, 715-239-6888
Buffalo River State Trail, Trempealeau, 54661, 608-534-6409
Chequamegon National Forest, Park Falls, 54552, 715-762-2461
Chippewa River State Trail, Menomonie, 54751, 715-232-2631
Copper Falls State Park, Mellen, 54546, 715-274-5123
Flambeau River State Forest, Winter, 54896, 715-332-5271
Governor Knowles State Forest, Grantsburg, 54840, 715-463-2898
Great River State Trail, Trempealeau, 54661, 715-534-6409
Hoffman Hills State Recreation Area, Menomonie, 54751, 715-232-2631
Interstate State Park, St. Croix Falls, 54024, 715-483-3747
Kinnickinnic State Park, River Falls, 54022, 715-425-1129
Lake Wissota State Park, Chippewa Falls, 54729, 715-382-4574

Lucius Woods State Park, Solon Springs, 54873, 715-378-2219
Merrick State Park, Fountain City, 54629, 715-687-4936
North Country National Scenic Trail, National Park Service, 1709 Jackson St., Omaha, NE 68102
North Country Trail Association, Box 311, White Cloud, MI 49349, 616-689-6876
Ojibwa State Park, Winter, 54896, 715-266-3511
Pattison State Park, Superior, 54880, 715-399-8073
Perrot State Park, Trempealeau, 54661, 608-534-6409
Red Cedar State Trail, Menomonie, 54751, 715-232-2631
St. Croix National Scenic Riverway, Box 708, St. Croix Falls, 54024, 715-483-3284
Trempealeau National Wildlife Refuge, Trempealeau, 54661, 608-539-2311
Tri-County Recreational Corridor, Box 648, Iron River, 54847, 715-372-8200
Tuscobia State Trail, Winter, 54896, 715-266-3511
Upper Mississippi River National Wildlife and Fish Refuge, Box 415, La Crosse, 54601, 608-783-6451
Willow River State Park, Hudson, 54016, 715-386-5931

Northwoods

Bearskin State Trail, Boulder Junction, 54512, 715-385-2727
Chequamegon National Forest, Park Falls, 54552, 715-762-2461
Copper Culture State Park, Marinette, 54143, 715-732-0101
Council Grounds State Park, Merrill, 54452, 715-536-8773
Nicolet National Forest, Rhinelander, 54501, 715-362-3415
Northern Highland–American Legion State Forest, Boulder Junction, 54512, 715-385-2727

Southern Gateway

Aztalan State Park, Stoughton, 53589, 608-873-9695
Big Foot Beach State Park, Lake Geneva, 53147, 414-248-2528
Bong State Recreation Area, Kansasville, 53139, 414-878-4416
Glacial Drumlin State Trail, Stoughton, 53589, 608-873-9695
Governor Nelson State Park, Waunakee, 53597, 608-831-3005
Harrington Beach State Park, Belgium, 53004, 414-285-3015
Horicon Marsh Wildlife Area, Horicon, 53032, 414-485-4434
Kettle Moraine State Forest.(Lapham Peak Unit), Delafield, 53018, 414-646-3025
Kettle Moraine State Forest (Southern Unit), Eagle, 53119, 414-594-2135
Lake Kegonsa State Park, Stoughton, 53589, 608-873-9695
Pike Lake State Park, Hartford, 53027, 414-644-5248

Greater Milwaukee

Havenwoods State Forest, Milwaukee, 53209, 414-527-0232

Further Reading

The following resources, listed by title, are just a sample of the publications written about outdoor recreation in Wisconsin:

Best Canoe Trails (Northern Wisconsin). Madison: Wisconsin Tales & Trails, Inc.

Guide to the Apostle Islands and the Bayfield Peninsula, by Michael E. Duncanson. Eau Claire: The Cartographic Institute.

Whitewater, Quietwater: A Guide to the Wild Rivers of Wisconsin, Upper Michigan, and NE Minnesota (includes technique and maps for canoes, kayaks and rafts), by Bob and Jody Palzer. Two Rivers (WI): Evergreen Paddleways (revised 1985).

Wisconsin Natural Resources Magazine. Published bimonthly by the Wisconsin Department of Natural Resources. For subscription information, contact the magazine at P.O. Box 7191, Madison, WI 53707.

A Traveler's Guide to Wisconsin State Parks & Forests. A book published by the Wisconsin DNR about the state's parks and forests.

Exploring Door County, by Craig Charles. Published by NorthWord Press Inc., Minocqua, WI. A comprehensive guide book to Door County.

Index

I

J

K

L

M

S

T

U

V

W

Photo Credits

Tony Casper/Third Coast, 23
George R. Cassidy, 95, 362
Ken Dequaine, cover, 140, 164–65, 187
Ken Dequaine/Third Coast, 117
Michael Douglas/Third Coast, 63
T. **Edwards**/Third Coast, X
Bruce Fritz, 231
Chuck Golueke, 84, 84
Scott Housum/Third Coast, 386, 409
Christine Linder, 41, 260, 331, 382, 423
William Meyer/Third Coast, 72
Brent Nicastro, 39
Lisbeth Quade, 149
Robert Queen/WI DNR, 45
Willard Romantini, 93, 191, 254, 312, 350, 434, 438
E.J. **Saur**/Third Coast, 28
Jim Umhoefer, 3, 14, 16, 32, 48, 52, 67, 71, 79, 89, 100, 106, 115, 116, 122, 132, 136, 152, 156, 160, 173, 178, 183, 197, 206–07, 212, 218, 222, 228, 229, 236, 241, 242, 268, 282, 286, 290, 300, 304, 321, 326, 336, 343, 361, 366, 372, 377, 390, 394, 399, 405, 428, 440
Mark Wallner, 58–59, 274, 433
Wisconsin Department of Natural Resources, 88, 343, 399
Wisconsin Department of Tourism Development, 110, 127, 249, 307, 354, 413

Author Biography

Jim Umhoefer is a freelance writer-photographer based in Sauk Centre, Minnesota. Originally from Colby, Wisconsin, Jim moved to Sauk Centre from Madison, Wisconsin, with his wife Margy, to manage a family resort.

Before settling in Sauk Centre, Jim and Margy took a year off to travel and develop Candid Perceptions, their writing and photography business. Jim's outdoor and travel articles and photographs have appeared in numerous national and regional publications. This is his third guidebook. His first two books focused on Wisconsin's and Minnesota's state park systems. The Wisconsin guide won a nonfiction award from the Council of Wisconsin Writers, Inc. in 1983.

The Umhoefers, including their daughter Nikki, love to camp, bicycle, canoe and ski.

ABOUT COWS
Sara Rath
About Cows is an affectionately humorous tribute to the domestic animal which produces 20% of the agricultural wealth of this country. Anyone with any connections with cows will love this illustrated collection of cow history, trivia and nostalgia. Sprinkled with anecdotes from farmers, cheesemakers, veterinarians and others who have crossed paths with cows.

About Cows features 32 color photographs of cows in their natural habitat and dozens of fascinating black-and-white illustrations.
$14.95 • 9¼ × 7⅜, 256 pages, paper • ISBN 0-942802-75-6

PRAIRIE VISIONS
Robert Gard
Author of thirty-eight books, Robert Gard is the premier storyteller of The Heartlands. *Prairie Visions* is his autobiographical journey into the heart of America. The book distills the stories and legends of mid-America and masterfully captures the mystique of the Heartland and its people.

Prairie Visions traces the steps of this award-winning author from his boyhood home in depression-racked Kansas to New York where he developed a regional theater program and to Wisconsin where his literary talents took firm root. Besides providing an intriguing record of the places he has been and the people he has met, *Prairie Visions* presents a spiritual profile of the Heartland itself.
$14.95 • 6½ × 9½, 320 pages, cloth • ISBN 0-942802-54-3

EXPLORING DOOR COUNTY
Craig Charles
The first comprehensive guide to enjoying the natural beauty of Door County, one of the most popular vacation areas of the Midwest. This guide focuses on the many parks, preserves and beaches that protect the area's natural beauty while offering unique recreational possibilities. All of the areas outlined, mapped and described in the guide are open to the public. Campers, city slickers and hard core hikers will all find something to their liking within the pages and on the trails of the Door Peninsula. Detailed maps and color photography.
$16.95 • 6 × 9, 224 pages, paper • ISBN 1-55971-011-X

OLD PENINSULA DAYS
The definitive history of Door County, a vacation paradise which attracts over 2 million visitors annually. More than local history, Holand, in his beautifully written narrative, details the step-by-step creation of a unique American community. The region is rich with cultural heritage, starting with the first missionary exploration only 14 years after the Pilgrims landed at Plymouth Rock.
$9.95 • 6 × 9, 256 pages, paper • ISBN 1-55971-057-8

FIRE & ICE
Don Davenport and Robert W. Wells
Combines two deadly disaster epics under one cover. "These are shocking tales of nature's fury: the 1958 killer storm that sent the big ore carrier *Carl D. Bradley* bubbling to the bottom of Lake Michigan, and the 1871 holocaust that charred bodies and blackened the landscape in Peshtigo, Wisconsin, the most disastrous fire in American history.

"*Shipwreck on Lake Michigan*, by Don Davenport, a Great Lakes scholar, is the kind of story a reader can't put down. Robert Wells tells the searing story of *Fire at Peshtigo* with the sure hand of a veteran newspaperman."—*The Milwaukee Journal*
$13.95 • 5½ × 8½, 450 pages, paper • ISBN 0-942802-04-7

OLD WORLD WISCONSIN
First published in 1944, this delightful book explores haunts, hilltops and byways and the ethnic traditions of Old World homes and families. Even more valuable today in the light of cultural assimilation, these vanishing epochs remain alive and vibrant through the author's deft touch. Told in a style that makes this new edition valuable, both as reliable history and as vivid literature.
$9.95 • 6 × 9, 256 pages, paper • ISBN 1-55971-056-X

To receive our free color catalog or order any of these books call toll free 1-800-336-5666. NorthWord Press Inc., Box 1360, Minocqua, WI 54548.